T0201269

Canon® EOS Rebel T8i/850D

by Julie Adair King

for
dummies®
A Wiley Brand

Canon® EOS® Rebel T8i/850D For Dummies®

Published by: **John Wiley & Sons, Inc.**, 111 River Street, Hoboken, NJ 07030-5774, www.wiley.com

Copyright © 2021 by John Wiley & Sons, Inc., Hoboken, New Jersey

Published simultaneously in Canada

For general information on our other products and services, please contact our Customer Care Department within the U.S. at 877-762-2974, outside the U.S. at 317-572-3993, or fax 317-572-4002. For technical support, please visit https://hub.wiley.com/community/support/dummies.

Wiley publishes in a variety of print and electronic formats and by print-on-demand. Some material included with standard print versions of this book may not be included in e-books or in print-on-demand. If this book refers to media such as a CD or DVD that is not included in the version you purchased, you may download this material at http://booksupport.wiley.com. For more information about Wiley products, visit www.wiley.com.

Library of Congress Control Number: 2020949814

ISBN 978-1-119-71621-1 (pbk); ISBN 978-1-119-71623-5 (ebk); ISBN 978-1-119-71622-8

Manufactured in the United States of America

SKY10022405_111120

Contents at a Glance

Table of Contents

Introduction

n 2003, Canon revolutionized the photography world by introducing the first digital SLR camera (dSLR) to sell for less than $1,000, the EOS Digital Rebel/300D. The camera delivered exceptional performance and picture quality, earning it rave reviews and multiple industry awards. No wonder it quickly became a best seller.

That tradition of excellence and value lives on in the EOS Rebel T8i/850D. Like its ancestors, this baby offers advanced controls for experienced photographers as well as features to help beginners be successful from the get-go. Adding to the fun, the camera also offers high-definition video recording and built-in Wi-Fi and Bluetooth that enable wireless connection to your computer, smartphone, or tablet.

In fact, the T8i/850D is so feature-packed that sorting out everything can be a challenge. For starters, you may not even know what SLR means, let alone have a clue about all the other terms you encounter in your camera manual — resolution, aperture, and ISO, for example. If you're like many people, you may be so over-whelmed by all the camera controls that you haven't yet ventured beyond fully automatic picture-taking mode. That's a shame because it's sort of like buying a Porsche Turbo and never pushing it past 35 miles per hour.

Therein lies the point of *Canon EOS Rebel T8i/850D For Dummies*. In this book, you can discover not only what each bell and whistle on your camera does but also when, where, why, and how to put it to best use. Unlike many photography books, this one doesn't require any previous knowledge of photography or digital imaging, either. Everything is explained in easy-to-understand language, with lots of illustrations to help clear up any confusion.

In short, what you have in your hands is the paperback version of a photography workshop tailored specifically to your camera. Whether your interests lie in taking family photos, exploring nature and travel photography, or snapping product shots for your business, you'll get the help you need to capture the images you envision.

A Quick Look at What's Ahead

This book is organized into four parts, each devoted to a different aspect of using your camera. Although chapters flow in a sequence that takes you from absolute beginner to experienced user, each chapter is designed to be as self-standing as possible so that you can explore topics that interest you in any order.

Here's an overview of each part:

>> **Part 1: Fast Track to Super Snaps:** This part contains three chapters that help you get up and running. Chapter 1 offers a brief overview of camera controls and walks you through initial setup and customization steps. Chapter 2 explains basic picture-taking settings, such as image-quality and flash options, and Chapter 3 shows you how to use the camera's simplest exposure modes, Scene Intelligent Auto and SCN (Scene).

>> **Part 2: Taking Creative Control:** Chapters in this part help you unleash the full creative power of your camera by moving into advanced shooting modes. Chapter 4 covers the all-important topic of exposure; Chapter 5 offers tips for manipulating focus; Chapter 6 explains color features; and Chapter 7 provides a summary of shooting strategies for specific types of pictures: portraits, action shots, landscape scenes, and close-ups. Wrapping up this part, Chapter 8 covers movie recording and playback.

>> **Part 3: Working with Picture Files:** As its title implies, this part discusses after-the-shot topics. Chapter 9 explains picture playback features, and Chapter 10 covers topics including rating, deleting, and protecting files; transferring pictures from your camera to your computer; processing Raw files; and preparing pictures for online sharing.

>> **Part 4: The Part of Tens:** In famous *For Dummies* tradition, the book concludes with two top-ten lists containing additional bits of information. Chapter 11 takes a look at ten camera-customization options not covered elsewhere. Chapter 12 introduces features that may not be on the top of your "Why I bought this camera" list, but are nonetheless interesting, useful on occasion, or a bit of both.

>> **Appendix: Exploring Wireless Connections:** Head here for information about establishing a wireless connection between your camera and a computer, smartphone, or tablet. You can then transfer files wirelessly and use your computer or smart device as a camera remote control, among other things.

>> **Cheat sheet:** When you have a minute or two, visit www.dummies.com and enter the name of this book in the search box. You'll find a link to a cheat sheet, which provides a handy reference to your camera's buttons, controls, and exposure modes.

Icons and Other Stuff to Note

If this isn't your first *For Dummies* book, you may be familiar with the large round icons that decorate its margins. If not, here's your very own icon-decoder ring:

TIP

A Tip icon flags information that saves you time, effort, money, or another valuable resource, including your sanity.

WARNING

When you see this icon, look alive. It indicates a potential danger zone that can result in much wailing and teeth-gnashing if it's ignored.

TECHNICAL STUFF

Lots of information in this book is of a technical nature — digital photography is a technical animal, after all. But if we present a detail that's useful mainly for impressing your geeky friends, we mark it with this icon.

REMEMBER

This icon highlights information that's especially worth storing in your brain's long-term memory or to remind you of a fact that may have been displaced from that memory by another pressing fact.

Additionally, replicas of some of your camera's buttons and onscreen graphics appear throughout the book to help you locate the button or setting being discussed.

Practice, Be Patient, and Have Fun!

To wrap up this preamble, I want to stress that if you initially think that digital photography is too confusing or too technical for you, you're in good company. *Everyone* finds this stuff mind-boggling at first. Take it slowly, trying just one or two new camera settings or techniques each time you pick up your camera. With time, patience, and practice, you'll soon wield your camera like a pro, dialing in the necessary settings to capture your creative vision almost instinctively.

So without further ado, I invite you to grab your camera and a cup of whatever you prefer to sip while you read and then start exploring the rest of this book. Your T8i/850D is the perfect partner for your photographic journey, and I thank you for allowing me, through this book, to serve as your tour guide.

1

Fast Track to Super Snaps

Familiarize yourself with the basics of using your camera, from attaching lenses to navigating menus.

Select the right exposure mode, shutter-release mode, picture aspect ratio, and image quality.

Discover options available for flash photography.

Take your first pictures in the easy-to-use Scene Intelligent Auto and SCN (scene) modes.

Chapter **1**

Getting Up and Running

S hooting for the first time with an SLR (single-lens reflex) camera can produce a blend of excitement and anxiety. On one hand, you can't wait to start using your new equipment, but on the other, you're a little intimidated by all its buttons, dials, and menu options.

Well, fear not: This chapter provides the information you need to start getting comfortable with your Rebel T8i/850D. The first section walks you through initial camera setup; following that, you can get an overview of camera controls, discover how to view and adjust camera settings, work with lenses and memory cards, and get advice on some basic setup options.

Preparing the Camera for Initial Use

After unpacking your camera, you have to assemble a few parts. In addition to the camera body and the supplied battery (charge it before the first use), you need two other items:

» **Lens:** Your camera accepts Canon EF and EF-S model lenses; the 18–55mm kit lens sold as a bundle with the camera body falls into the EF-S category. If you want to buy a non-Canon lens, check the lens manufacturer's website to find out which lenses work with your camera. Flip to the later section "Familiarizing Yourself with the Lens" for details on this critical component of your camera.

>> **SD (Secure Digital) memory card:** Like all digital cameras, the T8i/850D stores picture and movie files on a memory card. The camera accepts SD cards only. For information about buying SD cards, skip to the section "Working with Memory Cards."

With camera, lens, battery, and card within reach, take these steps:

1. **Make sure the camera is turned off.**

2. **Attach a lens.**

First, remove the caps that cover the front of the camera and the back of the lens. Then locate the proper *mounting index,* which is a mark on the camera's lens mount that indicates how to align the lens with the camera body. Your camera has two of these markers, one red and one white, as shown in Figure 1-1. Which marker you use depends on the lens type:

- *Canon EF-S lens:* The white square is the mounting index.

- *Canon EF lens:* The red dot is the mounting index.

Your lens also has a mounting index; align that mark with the matching one on the camera body, as shown in Figure 1-1. Place the lens on the camera mount and rotate the lens toward the side of the camera that sports the red *Rebel* logo. You should feel a solid click as the lens locks into place.

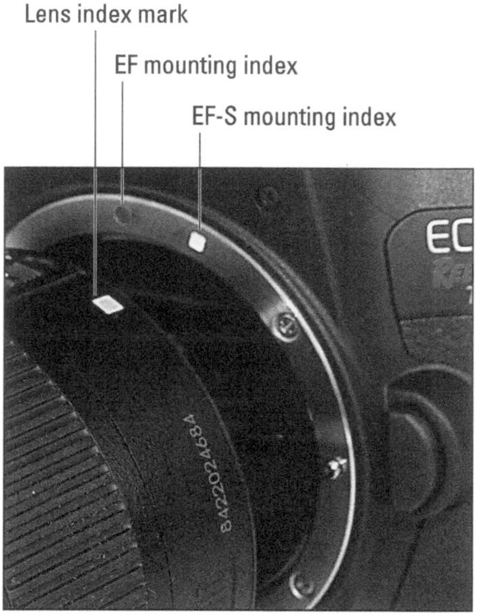

Lens index mark

EF mounting index

EF-S mounting index

FIGURE 1-1:
Align the mounting index on the lens with the one on the camera body.

3. **Install the battery.**

The battery compartment is on the bottom of the camera. When inserting the battery, hold it with the contacts down and the Canon imprint facing the right side of the camera grip (where the memory-card cover, shown in Figure 1-2, is located). Gently push the battery in until the gray lock clicks into place and then close the battery-cover door.

4. **Insert a memory card.**

   Open the memory-card door and orient the card so that the label faces the back of the camera, as shown in Figure 1-2. (If you look closely at the silver panel on the inside of the card door, you see a diagram that indicates the proper card orientation.) Push the card gently into the slot and close the card door.

REMEMBER

   The memory-card access lamp, labeled in Figure 1-2, blinks for few seconds to let you know that the camera recognizes the card. (The light appears even when the camera is turned off.)

5. **Rotate the monitor to the desired viewing position.**

   When you first take the camera out of its box, the monitor is positioned with the screen facing inward, protecting the screen from scratches and smudges. Gently lift the right side of the monitor up and away from the camera back. You can then rotate the monitor to move it into the traditional position on the camera back, as shown on the left in Figure 1-3, or swing the monitor out to get a different viewing angle, as shown on the right.

Memory-card access lamp

Card slot

FIGURE 1-2:
Insert the memory card with the label facing the back of the camera.

FIGURE 1-3:
Here are two possible monitor positions.

6. **Move the On/Off switch to the On position.**

Okay, that's an odd way to say "turn on the camera," right? Agreed, but there's good reason for it: This particular On/Off switch, shown in Figure 1-4, has three positions. When you rotate the switch to On, the camera comes to life and is ready to take still photos. If you move the switch one step further, to the movie-camera symbol, the camera turns on and sets itself to Movie mode. You can't take a still photograph in Movie mode; it's good for recording video only.

7. **Set the language, time zone, and date.**

FIGURE 1-4:
Rotate the switch to On to shoot photographs; move the switch one step further to set the camera to movie-recording mode.

When you power up the camera for the first time, the monitor displays a screen asking you to set the date, time, and time zone. The easiest way to adjust these settings is to use the touchscreen, which is enabled by default. Just tap an option to select it. Small triangles appear above and below the option to let you know that it's active, but you don't tap those triangles the change the value. Instead, look for the up and down triangles in the lower-left corner of the screen, and tap those arrows to set the value. Lather, rinse, and repeat until you complete all the adjustments you want to make. Finally, tap OK to exit the screen.

If you prefer not to use the touchscreen, you can adjust settings by using the Quick Control dial, which is the combination dial/toggle switch that surrounds the Set button. Rotate the dial or press the left or right edges of the dial to highlight the option you want to adjust; press the Set button to activate it. Again, triangles appear above and below the active option. Rotate the dial or press up or down on the top or bottom of the dial to change the value. Press Set again to lock in the new value. (I provide more information about using the Quick Control dial later in the chapter.)

TIP

The date/time information is included as *metadata* (hidden data) in the picture file. You can view metadata in some playback display modes (see Chapter 9) and in certain photo programs, including Canon Digital Photo Professional 4. (Refer to Chapter 10.) Also note the sun symbol to the left of the Time Zone option. That symbol represents the option that automatically adjusts the camera's clock when Daylight Saving Time begins and ends, if that's a thing in your part of the globe. The option is turned on by default.

8. **Select an exposure mode by rotating the Mode dial, labeled in Figure 1-4.**

   The exposure mode determines how much control you have over camera settings as well as whether any special effects are applied. Chapter 2 explains the various exposure modes. For easiest operation, set the dial to Scene Intelligent Auto, represented by the green A+, as shown in Figure 1-4. Be aware, though, that some features are available only in the advanced modes: P, Tv, Av, and M.

9. **Adjust the viewfinder to your eyesight.**

   This step is critical; if you don't set the viewfinder to your eyesight, subjects that appear out of focus in the viewfinder might actually be in focus, and vice versa. If you wear glasses while shooting, adjust the viewfinder with your glasses on.

WARNING

You control viewfinder focus through the dial labeled in Figure 1-5. (In official lingo, it's called the *diopter adjustment dial.*) After taking off the lens cap, follow these steps:

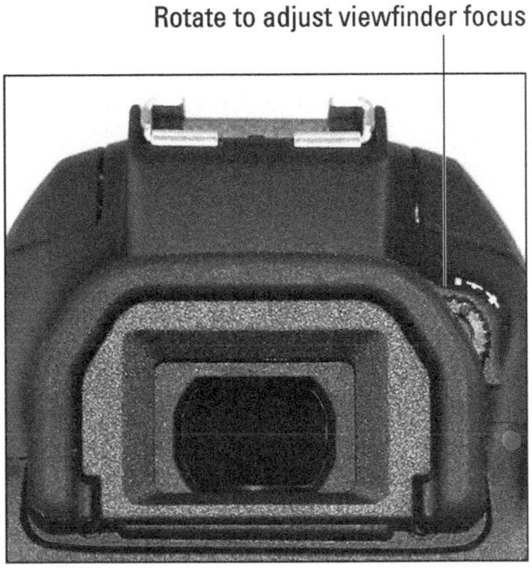

1. *Look through the viewfinder, press the shutter button halfway and then release it.*

2. *Concentrate on the lines that appear in the center of the frame and the row of data displayed at the bottom of the frame.*

3. *Rotate the adjustment dial until the viewfinder markings and data appear sharpest.*

Rotate to adjust viewfinder focus

FIGURE 1-5:
Use this dial to adjust the viewfinder focus to your eyesight.

Ignore the scene you see through the lens; that won't change because you're not actually focusing the camera. If the markings turn off before you finish making your adjustment, give the shutter button another quick half-press and release to redisplay them.

Can't get the display sharp enough? You may need an adapter that enables further adjustment of the viewfinder. Look for an E-series dioptric adjustment lens adapter.

That's all there is to it — the camera is now ready to go. The rest of this chapter familiarizes you with other major camera features and explains such basics as how to navigate menus, use the touchscreen, and view and adjust camera settings.

Exploring External Camera Features

Scattered across your camera's exterior are features that you use to change picture-taking settings, review your photos, and perform other operations. Later chapters explain how and when to use these tools; the following sections provide a basic "what's this thing do?" introduction to them. (Don't worry about memorizing the button names; throughout the book, figures and margin symbols tell you exactly which button or switch to use.)

TIP

If you're moving to the T8i/850D from an earlier version of this camera (such as the T7i/800D) or even other Rebel dSLR models, you probably noticed that certain buttons found on those models are nowhere to be found on this one — such as the button that's been used for years to raise the built-in flash and the one that accessed the setting known as Exposure Compensation. The good news is that the *functions* that the now-gone buttons accessed are still there; you just get to them in a different way.

Topside controls

Your virtual tour begins on the top of the camera, shown in Figure 1-6. Here are the items of note:

>> **On/Off/Movie mode switch:** As outlined in the preceding section, setting the switch to the movie-camera icon turns on the camera and sets it to movie-recording mode. Move the switch to On for still photography.

Even when the switch is in the On position, the camera automatically goes to sleep after a period of inactivity to save battery power. To wake the camera up, press the shutter button halfway and release it. See the information related to the Auto Power Off setting, found in the section "Setup Menu 2," later in this chapter, for help adjusting the timing of the automatic shutoff.

>> **Mode dial:** Rotate this dial to select an *exposure mode,* which determines whether the camera operates in fully automatic, semi-automatic, or manual exposure mode when you take still pictures. Chapter 2 introduces you to the various exposure modes.

>> **Viewfinder adjustment dial:** Use this dial to adjust the viewfinder focus to your eyesight, as outlined in the preceding section.

>> **Main dial:** As its name implies, this dial is central to many camera functions, from scrolling through menus to changing certain shooting and playback settings.

AF Method/AF Area Selection button   Shutter button

Speaker   Microphone   Main dial

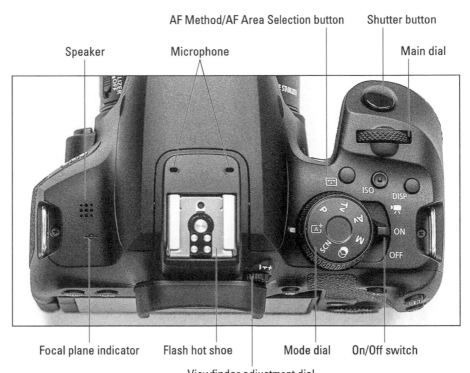

FIGURE 1-6:
Here's a guide to
controls found on
top of the
camera.

Focal plane indicator   Flash hot shoe   Mode dial   On/Off switch

Viewfinder adjustment dial

TIP

On some menu screens, you see a
symbol that resembles the top half
of a dial with notches around the
edge, as shown in Figure 1-7. That
symbol indicates that you use the
Main dial to adjust the setting. On
some screens curved arrows appear
near the Main dial symbol. In
Figure 1-7, you see one arrow under
the Main dial symbol and another
on the left side of the screen. When
using the touchscreen, you can tap
those arrows to adjust the setting
instead of using the Main dial.

Main dial symbol

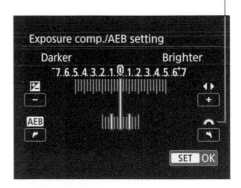

FIGURE 1-7:
The notched half-circle symbol tells you to use
the Main dial to adjust the setting.

>> **AF Method/AF Area Selection
button:** Press this button to access
the AF Method and AF Area Selection settings, both related to autofocusing.
Chapter 5 explains.

>> **ISO button:** True to its name, this button displays a screen where you can adjust the ISO setting, which determines how sensitive the camera is to light. Chapter 4 details this critical setting.

>> **DISP button:** This button affects the Quick Control screen, which displays shooting information when you're taking still pictures. (Check out "Displaying the Quick Control screen," later in this chapter, for a look.) Normally, the screen appears automatically when you turn the camera on or press the shutter button halfway and release it; the screen then turns off after a period of inactivity. But you can press the DISP button at any time to toggle the screen on and off.

>> **Shutter button:** You no doubt already understand the function of this button, but you may not realize that when you use autofocus and autoexposure, you need to use a two-stage process when taking a picture: Press the shutter button halfway, pause to let the camera set focus and exposure, and then press down the rest of the way to capture the image. You'd be surprised how many people mess up their pictures because they press that button with one quick jab, denying the camera the time it needs to set focus and exposure.

>> **Flash hot shoe:** Labeled in Figure 1-6, this is the connection for attaching an external flash and other accessories such as flash adapters and the Canon GP-E2 GPS Receiver.

TECHNICAL STUFF

>> **Focal plane indicator:** Should you need to know the exact distance between your subject and the camera, the *focal plane indicator,* labeled in Figure 1-6, is key. This mark indicates the plane at which light coming through the lens is focused onto the camera's image sensor. Basing your measurement on this mark produces a more accurate camera-to-subject distance than using the end of the lens or some other point on the camera body as your reference point. You might take advantage of this feature when taking pictures for a legal or scientific purpose that requires you to submit the camera-to-subject distance along with the photos.

>> **Speaker:** When you play a movie that contains audio, the sound comes wafting through these holes.

>> **Microphone:** You can record movie audio via the built-in microphone, which picks up sound from the two holes labeled "Microphone" in Figure 1-6.

Back-of-the-body controls

Traveling over the top of the camera to its back, you encounter the smorgasbord of controls shown in Figure 1-8.

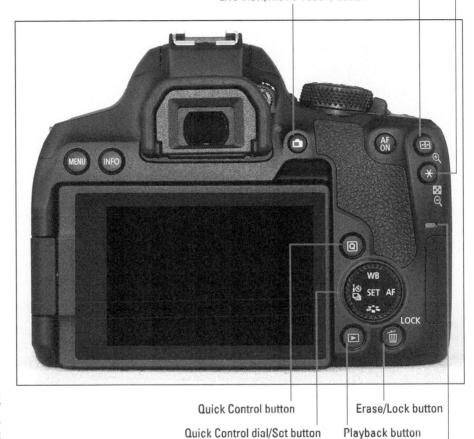

AE Lock/FE Lock/Index/Reduce button

AF Point Selection/Magnify button

Live View/Movie-record button

FIGURE 1-8:
Having lots of external buttons makes accessing the camera's functions easier.

Quick Control button

Quick Control dial/Set button

Erase/Lock button

Playback button

Memory-card access lamp

REMEMBER

Some buttons have multiple "official" names because they serve multiple purposes depending on whether you're taking pictures, reviewing images, recording a movie, or performing some other function. In most cases, this book refers to these buttons by the first label you see in the following list (and in Figure 1-8) to simplify things. Again, though, the margin icons and figures show you exactly which button to press to accomplish the task being discussed.

Here's an introduction to the controls on this side of the camera:

>> **AF Point Selection/Magnify button:** In certain shooting modes, you press this button to specify which autofocus points or zones you want the camera to use when establishing focus. You can also press and hold the button during Live View or Movie shooting to magnify the display to check focus. (Chapter 5 tells you about focusing features.) In Playback mode, covered in Chapter 9, you press the button to magnify the image display (thus the plus sign in the button's magnifying glass icon).

>> **AE Lock/FE Lock/Index/Reduce button:** During shooting, you can press this button to lock autoexposure (AE) settings, as covered in Chapter 4, or to lock flash exposure (FE), a feature detailed in Chapter 2.

This button also serves two playback functions: It switches the display to Index mode, enabling you to see multiple image thumbnails at once. And if you magnify a photo, pressing the button reduces the magnification level.

>> **AF ON button:** In the camera instruction manual, Canon uses the name *AF Start button* for this control, which no doubt will stymie many users' efforts to search the manual for information on the AF ON button. But *AF Start* actually is applicable in that pressing the button initiates autofocusing, giving you an alternative to pressing the shutter button halfway to get that job done. Experienced photographers refer to this as *back-button autofocus* because the button usually is located on the back of the camera, as it is on the T8i/850D. There are several situations in which using the AF ON button makes good sense; the autofocus sections of Chapter 5 provide more insight.

Two additional points about the AF ON button:

- *The AF ON function works only when the Mode dial is set to P, Tv, Av, or M.* In Canon lingo, those four shooting modes are called Creative Zone modes.

- You can assign a different function to the button if you don't want to use it for autofocusing. Chapter 11 explains how to modify the function of this and other buttons on your camera.

>> **Live View/Movie-record button:** Press this button to shift to Live View mode, which enables you to compose your pictures using the monitor instead of the viewfinder. When shooting movies, press the button to start and stop recording. (You must first set the On/Off/Movie switch to the Movie position.)

>> **Q (Quick Control) button:** Press this button to shift to Quick Control mode, which enables you to adjust major shooting settings quickly. See "Using Quick Control Mode," later in this chapter, for help.

>> **Memory-card access lamp:** Labeled in Figure 1-8, this lamp blinks while the camera is accessing the memory card. Don't power off the camera while the lamp is blinking, or you may damage the card or camera as well as corrupt files on the card.

>> **Quick Control dial/Set button:** Figure 1-8 points out this multifaceted control, shown in close-up view in Figure 1-9. Here are a few basics to know about using it:

- You can rotate the outer ring of the Quick Control dial to select and adjust some settings. If nothing happens when you rotate the ring or the word *Locked* appears on the screen, you may have inadvertently locked the dial, preventing it from having any effect. See the upcoming bullet point "Erase/Lock button" to find out more.

- Pressing the top, right, bottom, or left edge of the dial provides quick access to the four settings labeled in Figure 1-9. White Balance and Picture Style settings are discussed in Chapter 6; AF Operation, in Chapter 5; and Drive mode, in Chapter 2. You also may need to press the dial right/left or up/down when adjusting certain other settings. If I tell you to "press the right edge of the Quick Control dial," for example, press near where the AF label appears. (On previous editions of this camera, there were four arrow keys, called *cross keys,* surrounding the Set button. No more; now you just have to deduce that you can press the edges of the dial to get something done. Farewell, cross keys, we'll miss your easily understood nomenclature.) The camera's instruction manual, however, still refers to these edges as *arrow keys,* even though there aren't any arrow markings on the dial.

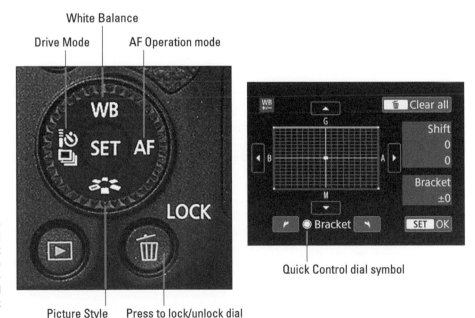

FIGURE 1-9: The Quick Control dial and Set button are key to making picture-taking and playback operations.

- The Set button is key to activating an option when you're scrolling through menus or settings screens. For example, you might need to rotate the Quick Control dial or press one of its sides to highlight an option and then press the Set button to unlock the option. Once the option is unlocked, you use the Quick Control dial to adjust the setting and then lock in your choice by pressing the Set button again.

- The symbol labeled in the menu screen on the right in Figure 1-9 represents the Quick Control dial and is your reminder that you can use the dial to adjust the setting marked by the symbol. This particular screen is related to an advanced White Balance function that I cover in Chapter 6.

 ❯❯ **Playback button:** Press this button to switch the camera into picture-review mode.

 ❯❯ **Erase/Lock button:** Sporting a trash can icon, the universal symbol for delete, this button lets you erase pictures from your memory card during playback. Chapter 9 has specifics.

But wait, what's with the word *Lock* above the button? (Refer to Figure 1-8.) Well, it's related to something Canon calls *Multi-Function Lock.* By default, pressing the Erase/Lock button once locks the outer edge of the Quick Control dial. The outer edge still rotates; it just doesn't adjust any settings that it normally would affect. The idea is to prevent you from accidentally adjusting a setting with an errant spin of the dial. You can still press up/down/right/left on the dial and use the Set button to adjust settings, though. To unlock the dial, press the Erase/Lock button again.

Two other critical bits of information about the Lock feature:

- *Customizing the lock feature*: You can disable the Quick Control dial lock feature as well as add the lock capability to the Main dial and to all touchscreen functions. (Ah, now you get why it's called *Multi Function Lock.*) Open Setup Menu 4 and choose Multi Function Lock, as shown on the left in Figure 1-10, to display the screen shown on the right in the figure. Place a check mark in the boxes of the functions you want the Erase/Lock button to control. (If you need help understanding how to work the menus, see "Ordering from Camera Menus," later in this chapter.)

- *When selected controls are locked, a reminder appears on the shooting display, as shown on the left in Figure 1-11.* Immediately after you initiate the lock, the message includes the symbol that represents the locked controls. In Figure 1-11, the message indicates that the Quick Control dial is locked, for example. The word *Lock* also appears near the bottom of the screen, as labeled in the figure. After a few seconds, the banner at the top of the screen disappears but the word *Lock* remains. When you press the Erase/Unlock button again, the camera briefly displays the message "Controls unlocked."

FIGURE 1-10:

Via the Multi Function Lock option, you can tell the camera what controls to disable when you press the Erase/ Lock button.

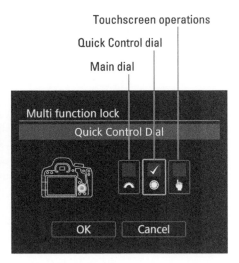

>> **Info button:** Flip back to Figure 1-8 for a look at this button, found on the upper-left corner of the camera back. In Live View, Movie, and Playback modes, pressing this button changes the picture-display style.

During viewfinder photography, you can press the Info button to cycle through three display options: Off (the screen goes to sleep), the Quick Control screen, and the electronic level. (The latter two displays are explained later in this chapter.) You have the option of setting the button so that it only toggles from Off to one of the two other displays. Check out the option named Info Button Display Options in the section that covers Setup Menu 4, toward the end of the chapter.

FIGURE 1-11:
Immediately after you engage the lock function, the camera tells you which items are locked and displays the word *Lock* until you unlock the control(s).

>> **Menu button:** Just to the left of the Info button, the Menu button does exactly what you would expect: Press it once to display camera menus; press it a second time to exit the menus. See the upcoming section "Ordering from Camera Menus" for help navigating menus.

And the rest . . .

The remaining external features are shown in Figures 1-12 and 1-13 and described in the following list:

>> **Lens-release button:** Press this button, labeled in Figure 1-12, to disengage the lens from the lens mount so that you can remove it from the camera. While pressing the button, rotate the lens toward the shutter-button side of the camera to dismount the lens.

>> **Built-in flash "handles":** On previous editions of this camera, you raised the built-in flash by pressing a Flash button on the side of the camera. If you owned any of those cameras, as I did, you may have searched a good while looking for a similar button on the T8i/850D — an expedition, it turns out, which is all for naught. On this camera, there is no Flash button. The only way to raise the built-in flash is to put your thumb and forefinger on the notches found toward the front of the flash — I labeled one "Built-in flash handle" in Figure 1-12 — and lift the flash up. To close the flash, just press down on the top of the flash unit.

Built-in flash "handle"

Lens-release button

Connection-terminal covers

FIGURE 1-12:
To remove a lens, first press the lens-release button to disengage the lens from the camera's lens mount.

>> **Connection ports:** Hidden under two rubber doors labeled "connection-terminal covers" in Figure 1-12 are inputs for connecting the camera to various devices. Open the smaller cover to access the connections for a wired remote control or external microphone. Under the larger door, you find a digital terminal for connecting the camera to your computer via USB and an HDMI-out port that sends the signal from your camera to an HDMI-equipped TV. To use either feature, you need to purchase a cable to make the connection. For USB downloading, check the Canon website for the cables that will do the trick. For HDMI output, you can use any HD cable that has a Type-C connection on one end (the end that goes into the camera).

See Chapter 12 for help with displaying images on an HD television. I don't cover USB-to-computer connections, most often used to transfer photos to a computer, in this book. Chapter 9 explains why and offers you a better alternative. See the appendix for information about connecting to your computer via the camera's wireless-connection features.

>> **Depth-of-Field Preview button:** Figure 1-13 shows you where to find this button, which you can press to see offers an approximation of the depth of field that will result from your selected aperture setting, or f-stop. *Depth of field* refers to the distance over which the scene appears to be in focus; Chapter 5 provides details. The button isn't labeled on the camera and is fairly well hidden; Figure 1-13 shows the camera body without a lens attached so you can see the button a little more clearly.

>> **Red-Eye Reduction/Self-timer Lamp:** Figure 1-13 also offers a look at this lamp. When you set your flash to Red-Eye Reduction mode, the lamp emits a brief burst of light prior to the real flash — the idea being that your subjects' pupils will constrict in response to the light, thus lessening the chances of red-eye. If you use the camera's self-timer feature, the lamp lights during the countdown period before the shutter is released. See Chapter 2 for more details about Red-Eye Reduction flash mode and the self-timer function.

Red-Eye Reduction/Self-timer Lamp

Depth-of-Field Preview button

FIGURE 1-13:
I removed the lens from the camera to make it easier to see the Depth-of-Field Preview button.

If you turn the camera over, you find a socket that enables you to mount the camera on a tripod that uses a ¼-inch screw; the chamber that holds the battery; and a port for attaching a Canon power adapter. (The port is inside the battery chamber.) See the camera manual for specifics on running the camera on AC power.

Changing from Guided to Standard Display Mode

By default, your camera is set to *Guided Display Mode.* In this mode, designed for novices, camera screens are simplified and offer explanations and feedback when you adjust certain settings.

For example, when you press the Menu button, you get a description of the contents of the current menu, as shown on the left in Figure 1-14. And when you rotate the Mode dial to choose an exposure mode, the display describes what that mode is designed to do. The right side of Figure 1-14 shows the screen that appears if you select the Tv (shutter-priority autoexposure) mode, for example.

FIGURE 1-14: In Guided Display mode, the camera offers simplified menus and brief details about the feature you're currently using.

Additionally, after you exit the screen that describes the exposure mode, the camera displays available picture-taking settings along with input on certain options. If you choose OK from the screen shown on the right in Figure 1-14, for example, you see the screen shown on the left in Figure 1-15, explaining that the main setting associated with the Tv mode is the shutter speed, which determines whether moving objects appear blurry or sharp. As you change that setting, the screen updates to offer input on how your picture will be affected, as shown on the right in Figure 1-15.

Guided mode is fine for users who don't aspire to master their camera or the ins and outs of photography. But assuming that you bought this book because you don't fall into that category, Standard mode is a better choice, for several reasons:

>> Although the Guided screens make understanding some options easier, in many cases, they can be just as baffling as the Standard screens. Take a look at the left screen in Figure 1-15, for example. The illustration indicates that you choose a number at the left end of the scale to blur motion (flowing) and

at the other end to freeze motion. But nowhere does it tell you *how* to change the setting (you can drag your finger along the scale or rotate the Main dial). Nor is there any indication that the setting involved is named *shutter speed*.

>> The Guided screens often focus on one particular aspect of a camera setting without explaining how that setting affects other characteristics of your picture. When you change the shutter speed, for example, the camera has to make adjustments to one or two other critical settings, aperture and ISO, in order to properly expose the picture. Those settings, detailed along with shutter speed in Chapter 4, have their own impact on the look of your picture.

>> Standard mode also saves you some steps as you make certain camera adjustments. For example, you don't have to bother dismissing the initial menu screen (left side of Figure 1-14) to get to the menu items.

>> In Guided mode, you can't use the Quick Control screen (explained later in this chapter) to adjust all the functions that you normally can when shooting in the P, Tv, Av, and M modes.

>> When you use the Guided mode, you can't access the My Menu feature, which enables you to create a custom menu that contains the menu options you use most.

FIGURE 1-15: Here are two guided screens that appear when you use the Tv exposure mode (shutter-priority autoexposure).

For these reasons, figures and instructions in this book relate to using the camera in Standard mode instead of Guided mode. Here's how to swap out the default guided screens with the standard versions:

1. **Press the Menu button to display the menu screen.**

2. **Open the Display Level Settings menu, as shown on the left in Figure 1-16.**

   Display the menu by tapping its icon, labeled in Figure 1-16, or by rotating the Main dial until the icon becomes highlighted and the menu appears.

Tap to open Display Level Settings menu

 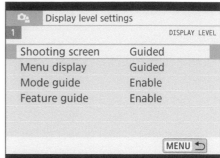

FIGURE 1-16:
Choose the
Display Level
Settings tab to
turn the Guided
mode features on
or off.

3. **Tap OK or press the Set button.**

You see the screen shown on the right in Figure 1-16. Each option turns a separate function of the Guided mode system on or off. By default, all four are turned on, as shown in the figure.

4. **Set the Shooting Screen and Menu Display options to Standard.**

To change a setting, tap it. Or press the top or bottom edge of the Quick Control dial to highlight the setting and then press the Set button. Either way, you're presented with the two options available for each setting: Standard and Guided. Tap Standard or highlight that option by pressing the bottom edge of the Quick Control dial. Finally, tap Set or press the Set button. Depending on the order in which you change the settings, you next see either the standard menu screen, shown on the left in Figure 1-17, or a screen displaying current shooting settings, as shown on the right.

The right screen in the figure is referred to as the Shooting Screen in the menu (refer to the top item in the menu screen on the left). But its official name is the Quick Control screen. This screen is the central station for viewfinder photography; see the section "Displaying the Quick Control screen," later in this chapter, for more information.

5. **(Optional) Disable the Mode Guide and Feature Guide options on the Display Level Settings menu (left screen in Figure 1-17).**

The Mode Guide, when enabled, displays a brief description of your chosen exposure mode for a few seconds after you rotate the Mode dial to select that setting. Similarly, the Feature Guide provides text hints for some options as you select them.

I leave it up to you whether to disable these features. After you're familiar with the various exposure modes and camera settings, the hints simply slow you down, so I turn them off. But if you find them helpful, by all means leave them set to Enable. Just remember that instructions from here on out won't mention them.

6. **To exit the menu system, tap Menu or press the Menu button.**

You can return to the Display Level menu at any time to turn the various features on or off as you see fit.

 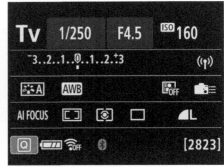

FIGURE 1-17: Here's how the menu and Quick Control screens appear in Standard mode.

Ordering from Camera Menus

Although you can adjust some settings by using external controls, you access the majority of options via camera menus. The next section provides the basics you need to know to navigate menus and select menu options. Following that, you can find out how to deal with a special category of menu screens, the Custom Functions.

Again, figures from this point forward show menus as they appear in Standard mode. See the preceding section if you need help switching from Guided to Standard menu display.

Mastering menu basics

Here's how to display menus and adjust the options on those menus:

>> **Opening and closing menus:** Press the Menu button (upper-left corner on the back of the camera) to display menus; press it again to exit the menu system and return to shooting. You also can just press the shutter button halfway and release it to exit to shooting mode.

» **Understanding menu screens:** Which menus and menu screens appear depends on the exposure mode, which you set by rotating the Mode dial on top of the camera. Things also change when you switch from still photography to Movie mode, which you accomplish by moving the On/Off switch to the movie-camera symbol. Figure 1-18 shows a menu screen as it appears for normal photography in the advanced exposure modes (P, Tv, Av, and M).

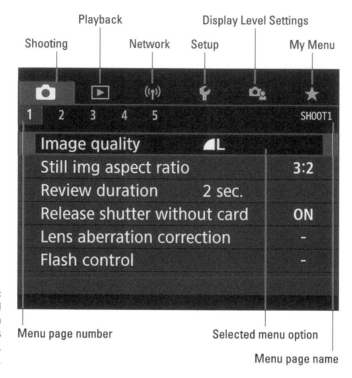

FIGURE 1-18:
You can access all menus only when the Mode dial is set to P, Tv, Av, or M.

However, the following menu elements are common to all exposure modes:

- *Menu icons:* Icons along the top of the screen represent individual menus. In the advanced exposure modes, you get the six menus labeled in Figure 1-18: Shooting, Playback, Network, Setup, Display Level Settings, and My Menu. The My Menu feature, which enables you to build a custom menu, isn't available in other exposure modes.

- *Menu page numbers:* Some menus are multi-page affairs. The numbers under the menu icons represent the various pages of the current menu. The Shooting menu offers five pages, as shown in the figure.

This book takes the same approach to menu-page references as the Canon instruction manual: *Shooting Menu 1* refers to page one of the Shooting menu, *Shooting Menu 2* to page two, and so on. How many pages appear for each menu depends, again, on the exposure mode and whether the camera is set to still photography or Movie mode.

The highlighted menu icon marks the active menu; options on that menu appear automatically on the main part of the screen. In Figure 1-18, Shooting Menu 1 is active.

>> **Selecting a menu or menu page:** You have these options:

- *Touchscreen:* Tap the menu icon to select that menu; tap a page number to display that page.

- *Quick Control dial or Main dial:* Press the right or left edge of the Quick Control dial or rotate the Main dial to scroll through the menu icons. With either technique, you have to scroll through all pages of a menu to get to the neighboring menu.

As you scroll through the menus, notice the color coding: red for the Shooting menu, blue for the Playback menu, purple for the Network menu, orangey-yellow (ochre?) for the Setup menu, teal for Display Level Settings, and green for My Menu.

>> **Select and adjust a menu setting:** Again, you have a choice of techniques:

- *Touchscreen:* Tap the menu item to display options for that setting. The current setting is highlighted; tap another setting to select it. On some screens, you see a Set icon; if it appears, tap that icon to lock in your selection and exit the settings screen.

- *Quick Control dial and Set button:* Press the top or bottom edge of the Quick Control dial to highlight the menu option and then press the Set button to display the available options for that setting. Press the edges of the Quick Control dial up, down, right, or left as needed to scroll to the setting you want to select. Then press the Set button to lock in your choice.

You can mix and match techniques, by the way. For example, even if you access a menu option via the Quick Control dial, you can use the touchscreen to select a setting.

Instructions from this point forward assume you don't need to be told the specifics of how to select menus and menu options at every turn. So instead of stepping you through each button press or touchscreen tap required to adjust a setting, instructions simply say something like "Choose Image Quality from Shooting Menu 1." If choosing a menu option involves any special steps, however, I provide guidance.

Navigating Custom Functions

Custom Functions are a group of advanced settings available only in the P, Tv, Av, and M exposure modes. (*Remember:* You set the exposure mode via the Mode dial on top of the camera.)

To explore Custom Functions, choose that item from Setup Menu 5, as shown on the left in Figure 1-19. You then see the options screen for a specific Custom Function, as shown on the right in the figure. Here's a guide to using the Custom Function screens:

>> **Interpreting the screens:** The Custom Functions screens are a little intimidating until you know what's what:

- *Custom Functions are grouped into three categories: Exposure, Autofocus/Drive, and Operation/Others.* The category number and name appear in the upper-left corner of the screen. In the right screen in Figure 1-19, for example, the label indicates that you're looking at a screen from the Autofocus/Drive category. (C.Fn II refers to Custom Functions group two.)

- The number of the selected function appears in the upper-right corner. Custom Function 9 is shown on the right in Figure 1-19.

- *Settings for the function appear in the middle of the screen.* Blue text indicates the current setting. The default setting is represented by the number 0. So in Figure 1-19, Auto is selected and is the default setting.

- *Numbers at the bottom of the screen show you the current setting for all Custom Functions.* The top row of numbers represents the Custom Functions, with the currently selected function indicated with a tiny horizontal bar over the number (9, in the figure). The lower row shows the number of the current setting for each Custom Function; again, 0 represents the default.

  For Custom Functions 11 and 13, you instead see a dash, which is Canon's way of letting you know that this menu option controls more than one camera setting (thus there isn't a single default setting).

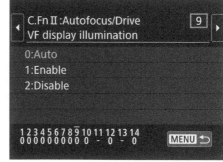

FIGURE 1-19: Choose Custom Functions from Setup Menu 5 to access additional customization options.

>> **Scrolling from one Custom Function to the next:** Press the left or right edge of the Quick Control dial or tap the left or right scroll arrows at the top of the screen. You can see the arrows in the right screen in Figure 1-19.

>> **Changing the setting:** Activate the menu item by pressing the Set button or tapping one of the available setting options. The screen changes to look similar to the one shown on the left in Figure 1-20. To select an option, tap it or press the top or bottom edge of the Quick Control dial to move the yellow selection box over it.

If you see up/down arrows on the right side of the screen, you need to scroll the menu screen to view all the available setting options. To do so, tap those arrows or press the top/bottom edge of the Quick Control dial.

To lock in your setting and deactivate the settings screen, tap the Set icon or press the Set button. The screen returns to its inactive state, as shown on the right in Figure 1-20. The setting you selected appears in blue, and the row of digits at the bottom of the screen reflects the number for that setting. A blue number indicates that you chose a setting other than the default.

>> **Exiting the Custom Functions submenu:** Tap the Menu icon in the lower-right corner of the screen or press the Menu button. Press Menu again to exit the menu system entirely and return to shooting.

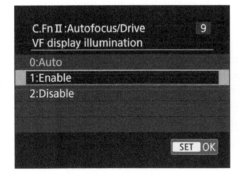 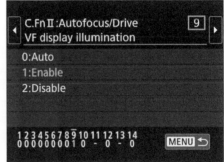

FIGURE 1-20: After you select a setting (left), the initial menu screen updates to reflect your choice (right).

Customizing the Touchscreen

When the camera's touchscreen is enabled, as it is by default, you can simply touch the monitor to choose menu commands, change picture settings, scroll through your pictures, and more.

How you touch the screen depends on the task at hand. Here's a rundown of the names assigned to various touchscreen moves, or *gestures:*

>> **Tap:** Tap a finger on the monitor. (Figures and instructions throughout the book indicate where to tap.)

>> **Drag:** Using light pressure, drag your finger across the screen. On some menu screens, for example, you can drag up or down to scroll through a list of options.

>> **Swipe:** Drag one or two fingers quickly across the screen. You use this gesture, known in some circles as a *flick,* to scroll through your pictures in playback mode, just as you do when showing off your photos on a smartphone.

>> **Pinch in/pinch out:** To pinch in, place your thumb at one edge of the screen and your pointer finger at the other. Then drag both toward the center of the screen. To pinch out, start in the center of the screen and swipe both fingers outward. Pinching is how you zoom in and out of pictures during playback.

TIP

You can customize the following aspects of the touchscreen's behavior:

>> **Adjust (or disable) touchscreen response:** You can choose from three settings, accessed via the Touch Control option, found on Setup Menu 3. Standard is the default, setting the screen to respond to a "normal" amount of pressure. Don't ask how the Powers That Be decided what that pressure level is — just know that if your normal pressure doesn't evoke a response, you can change the setting from Standard to Sensitive. Choose Disable to make the touchscreen totally inactive.

>> **Silence the touchscreen:** By default, the touchscreen emits a tiny "boop" with every tap. If you find that annoying, choose the Beep option, found just beneath the Touch Control option on Setup Menu 3. The option that hushes the boop is Touch to Silence — silence indicated by a little speaker with a slash through it. The Disable setting turns off touchscreen sounds and the beep the camera emits when focus is achieved.

>> **Enable/disable the touchscreen via the Multi Function Lock option on Setup Menu 4.** I discuss this menu option in the section "Back-of-the-body controls," earlier in this chapter. After choosing the menu option, put a checkmark in the Touch Control box and press Set or tap OK. You can then press the Erase/Lock button (lower-right corner of the camera back) to toggle touchscreen operation on and off.

CARING FOR THE CAMERA MONITOR

To keep the monitor in good working order, follow these precautions:

- *Don't use force when adjusting the monitor position.* Although the monitor assembly is sturdy, treat it with respect as you adjust the screen position. The monitor twists only in certain directions, and it's easy to forget which way it's supposed to move. So if you feel resistance, don't force things — you could break the monitor. Instead, rely on that feeling of resistance to remind you to turn the screen the other way.

- *Use only your finger to perform touchscreen functions.* Use the fleshy part of your fingertip (not the nail or any other sharp object), and be sure your fingers are dry because the screen may not respond if it gets wet.

- *Don't apply a screen protector.* Canon also advises against putting a protective cover over the monitor, such as the kind people adhere to their smartphones. Doing so can reduce the monitor's responsiveness to your touch.

- *Watch the crunch factor.* Before positioning the monitor back into the camera (whether face in or face out), use a lens brush or soft cloth to clean the monitor housing so there's nothing on it that could damage the monitor.

- *Clean smart.* To clean the screen, use only the special cloths and cleaning solutions made for this purpose. (You can find them in any camera store.) Do not use paper products such as paper towels because they can contain wood fibers that can scratch the monitor. And never use a can of compressed air to blow dust off the camera — the air is cold and can crack the monitor.

Viewing Camera Settings

Your camera offers several displays that show current picture-taking settings. The next sections explain the displays that are available during viewfinder photography. See the later section "Switching to Live View Mode" for information about displaying similar data when you take advantage of Live View, the feature that enables you to compose photos on the monitor instead of using the viewfinder.

REMEMBER

For still photography, you can use either the viewfinder or Live View screen to compose your shots. But when you set the camera to Movie mode, you're limited to Live View.

Displaying the Quick Control screen

The Quick Control screen appears on the monitor when the camera is in shooting mode — that is, you're not viewing menus, checking out your pictures in playback mode, and so on. The screen displays different data depending on your exposure mode and whether features such as flash are enabled. The left side of Figure 1-21 shows the screen as it appears in Scene Intelligent Auto exposure mode; the right side, Tv mode (shutter-priority autoexposure).

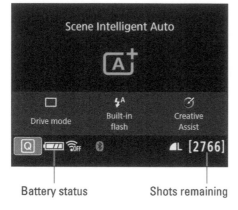
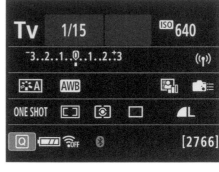

FIGURE 1-21: The data displayed on the Quick Control screen depends on your exposure mode.

Battery status   Shots remaining

Here are the keys to taking advantage of this screen:

>> **Displaying and hiding the Quick Control screen:** By default, the screen appears automatically when you turn on the camera and goes to sleep if no camera operations are performed for 30 seconds. You can wake up the display by pressing the shutter button halfway and then releasing it. If you want to turn off the display before the automatic shutoff occurs, press the DISP button (top of the camera, just behind the Main dial).

TIP

You can adjust the timing of the automatic shutdown of this screen and others by selecting the Auto Power Off option from Setup Menu 2. I provide the details near the end of this chapter, in the section devoted to that menu.

>> **Keep an eye on the battery symbol and the shots remaining value, both labeled in Figure 1-21.** A full battery like the one in the figure means that the battery is charged; as it runs out of power, bars disappear from the symbol. The shots remaining value indicates how many more pictures will fit in the free space available on your memory card. This value depends in large part on the Image Quality setting, which determines the resolution (pixel count) and file type (Raw or JPEG). If those terms are new to you, the next chapter explains them.

» **You can replace the Quick Control screen with an electronic level, shown in Figure 1-22.** This feature is helpful when you use a tripod and want to ensure the camera is level to the horizon. When the horizontal line appears green, as shown in Figure 1-22, you're good to go. By default, you need to press the Info button twice to shift from the Quick Control screen to the level. Your first press turns off the screen, and the second press brings up the level. Press Info again to return to the Quick Control screen. Again, which

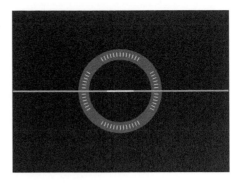

FIGURE 1-22:
You can swap out the Quick Control screen with an electronic level.

screens appear when you press the Info button depends on the Info Button Display Options setting, found on Setup Menu 4. You can find details on this option in the section "Setup Menu 4," found near the end of this chapter.

Decoding viewfinder data

A limited assortment of shooting data, such as the shutter speed and f-stop, appears at the bottom of the viewfinder, as shown in Figure 1-23. How much data appears depends on your exposure mode and what picture settings are currently in force; the figure shows the basics. Upcoming chapters explain the entire cadre of data.

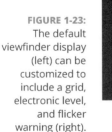

FIGURE 1-23:
The default viewfinder display (left) can be customized to include a grid, electronic level, and flicker warning (right).

 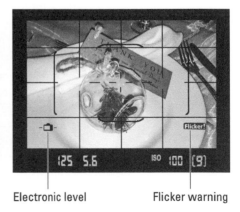

Electronic level   Flicker warning

In the framing area of the viewfinder, you may see marks that indicate the portion of the screen that contains autofocusing points. (The appearance of the autofocus markings depend on your autofocus settings, which you can explore in Chapter 5.) In the left screen in the figure, the four black brackets represent the autofocusing area.

Here's how to display and customize the viewfinder:

>> **Displaying viewfinder data:** The markings in the framing area of the viewfinder appear automatically when you first turn on the camera; to display the shooting data, press the shutter button halfway. The display remains active for a few seconds after you release the button, and then the viewfinder display shuts off to save battery power. To wake up the display, press the shutter button halfway and release it.

>> **Adding a level and gridlines to the display:** You can display gridlines in the viewfinder, as shown on the right in Figure 1-23, as well as a symbol that represents the electronic level. (When the lines at the sides of the symbol are horizontal, as in the figure, the camera is level.)

To hide or display these features, open Setup Menu 4 and choose Viewfinder Display. On the next screen, change the settings from Hide to Show. As you select each option, a preview appears at the bottom of the screen to remind you how enabling each feature affects the display.

>> **Display a flicker-detection warning:** When the Mode dial is set to an advanced exposure mode (P, Tv, Av, or M), the Viewfinder Display option on Setup Menu 4 offers a third setting, Flicker Detection. When the camera detects light sources that are blinking, which can mess up exposure and color, the word *Flicker!* appears in the area labeled in Figure 1-23. The biggest offenders are tubular fluorescent bulbs, which blink on and off so quickly that it's difficult for the human eye to detect them. When you see this warning, you may want to enable the Anti-flicker Shoot option found on Shooting Menu 4. This feature is covered in Chapter 4.

The number in brackets at the right end of the viewfinder does not represent the shots-remaining value, as it does in the Quick Control screen. Instead, that number — 9, in Figure 1-23 — represents the number of *maximum burst frames*. This number relates to shooting in the Continuous capture modes, where the camera fires off multiple shots in rapid succession as long as you hold down the shutter button. (Chapter 2 has details.) Although the highest number that the viewfinder can display is 9, the actual number of maximum burst frames may be higher. At any rate, you don't really need to pay attention to the number until it starts dropping toward 0, which indicates the camera's *memory buffer* (its tempo-rary internal data-storage tank) is filling up. If that happens, just give the camera a moment to catch up by lifting your shutter-button finger.

Switching to Live View Mode

Like most dSLRs sold today, your camera offers *Live View*, which disables the viewfinder and instead displays a live preview of your subject on the camera mon-itor. The following list explains the basics of using Live View:

>> **Switching to Live View for photography:** Press the Live View button, labeled in Figure 1-24, to shift from viewfinder shooting to Live View mode. You hear a clicking noise and then the viewfinder goes dark, and the monitor displays the live scene. By default, some shooting data appears as well, with the amount and type of information varying depending on your exposure mode and a few other settings. The figure shows the display as it appears in the Scene Intelligent Auto exposure mode when the default picture-taking settings are in force.

Press to change display style   Live View/Movie-record button

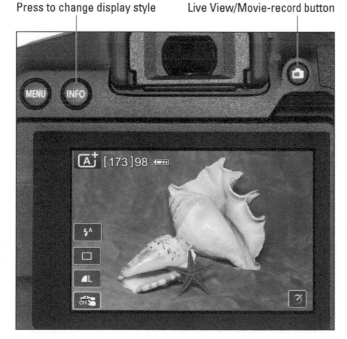

FIGURE 1-24: In Live View mode, a live preview of your subject appears on the monitor, and the view-finder is disabled.

If nothing happens after you press the Live View button, you may need to reset the Live View Shoot menu option to Enable. This is the default setting, but it's possible you or another user changed the setting to Disable at some point. Where you find the Live View Shoot option depends on your exposure mode; in the Auto, SCN, and Creative Filters modes, go to Shooting Menu 2, as shown on the left in Figure 1-25. In the advanced shooting modes (P, Tv, Av, and M), the option lives on Shooting Menu 4, as shown on the right.

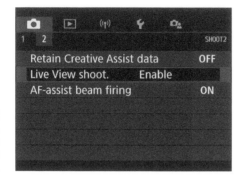
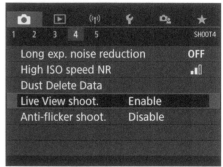

FIGURE 1-25:
To use Live View, make sure this menu option is set to Enable.

Why would Canon give you the option to disable Live View functionality? Because it's easy to accidentally press the Live View button and switch to that mode when you don't really want to go there.

>> **Engaging Live View for movie recording:** For movie recording, simply moving the On/Off switch to the Movie mode setting (represented by the movie-camera symbol) engages Live View. You can't use the viewfinder in Movie mode, so the setting of the Live View Shoot menu option has no impact.

In Movie mode, pressing the Live View button starts and stops recording. To exit Movie mode, move the On/Off switch to On if you want to begin shooting stills. Move the switch to Off if you're done shooting.

In many ways, shooting photos in Live View mode is the same as for viewfinder photography, but some important aspects, such as autofocusing, work very differently. Chapter 3 shows you how to take a picture in Scene Intelligent Auto exposure mode using Live View; Chapter 8 covers movie recording. Other chapters mention Live View variations related to specific picture-taking options.

Customizing the Live View display

By default, the Live View display offers the data shown on the left in Figure 1-26 when you're taking photographs in the Scene Intelligent Auto exposure mode. When you record movies in that exposure mode, the default display appears as shown on the right. In any exposure mode, the black bars at the top and bottom of the display indicate the boundaries of the 16:9 movie frame.

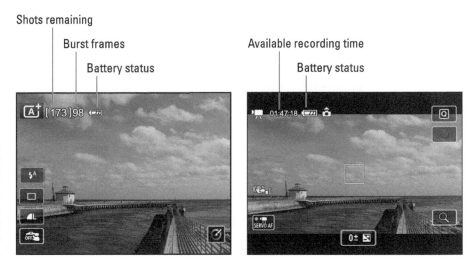

As is the case with other information displays, the type of data that appears changes when you shift from Scene Intelligent Auto mode to another exposure mode. As an example, the first screen in Figure 1-27 shows the default display when the Mode dial is set to Av (aperture-priority autoexposure). Regardless of your exposure mode, you can vary the data display by pressing the Info button. The other screens in Figure 1-27 show alternative displays available for photography in Av mode (or any advanced exposure mode). The display labeled Histogram/ Level in the figure isn't available for movie recording.

Additionally, you can add one of three grids to your screen, which can be helpful when checking alignment of objects in the frame. To enable or hide the grid, open Shooting Menu 4 and look for the Grid When Shooting option, featured in Figure 1-28. This menu option appears *only* when Live View is being used.

Default view

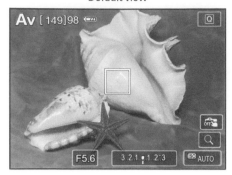

Detailed view

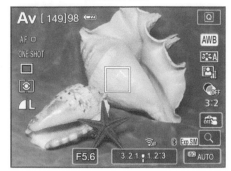

Histogram/Level view

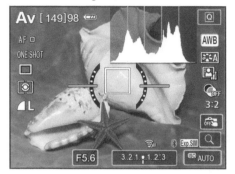

Focus frame only

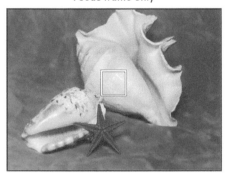

FIGURE 1-27:
Press the Info button to change the type of data that appears during Live View photography.

FIGURE 1-28:
Through this option, you can add one of three alignment grids to the Live View screen.

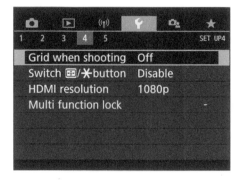

Although the various symbols and numbers on the displays shown in Figures 1-26 and 1-27 won't make much sense until you explore the rest of the book, here are details that may give you a basic understanding of some symbols:

>> **Check the areas labeled in Figure 1-26 to view the battery status.** The symbol shown in the figure represents a full battery.

>> **The number of shots remaining or the available movie recording time appears next to the battery symbol.** Again, Figure 1-26 shows you where to look.

>> **The number just to the right of the shots-remaining value is the burst value.** I explain this value in the earlier section, "Decoding viewfinder data," but here's a refresher: When you're using the camera's continuous-shooting mode, the burst value shows how many consecutive frames you can click off before the camera needs to take a breather. Just to make things confusing, the highest value that can appear in the viewfinder is 9 because only one digit was accommodated in that display. The Live View display, on the other hand, has room for additional digits, which is why the burst value in Figure 1-26 is 98. It's not because you can capture a larger burst in Live View mode; it's simply a matter of screen space available for the data to be displayed. See Chapter 2 for more information about shooting continuous bursts of photos and don't give the burst value in either display no more never-mind.

>> **You can't display the electronic level when the camera is set to the default AF Method setting (Face+Tracking).** To display the level, you must switch to another AF Method setting. (Chapter 5 has details.) Unfortunately, you can't make the shift when the Mode dial is set to Scene Intelligent Auto. No AF Method choices or electronic level for you!

TIP

If you like having a level available at all times and don't want to fiddle with the electronic version, you can buy tiny bubble levels that slide into the camera's flash hot shoe. A basic model costs about $15; make sure to buy one that is sized to fit a Canon flash mount. Vello is one popular brand (www.vellogear.com).

>> **The chart that appears in the histogram display (lower-left screen in Figure 1-27) is a tool you can use to gauge exposure.** See the Chapter 9 discussion on interpreting a histogram to find out how to make sense of what you see. But note that when you use flash, the histogram is dimmed. The histogram can't display accurate information because the final exposure will include light from the flash and not just the ambient lighting. In addition, the histogram dims when you use M (Manual) exposure mode and set the shutter speed to Bulb, which keeps the shutter open for as long as you hold down the shutter button. The camera can't predict how long you're going to hold that button down, so it can't create a histogram that will reflect your final exposure.

>> **Also note the Exposure Simulation symbol (Exp. SIM) that appears in the second and third displays in Figure 1-27.** (Look in the lower-right corner of the frame.) This symbol indicates whether the monitor is simulating the actual exposure that you'll record. If the symbol blinks or is dimmed, the camera can't provide an accurate exposure preview, which can occur if the ambient light is either very bright or very dim. Exposure Simulation is also disabled when you use flash.

Live View safety tips

Take the following precautions when you use Live View and Movie modes:

>> **Light that enters the viewfinder can affect exposure.** For this reason, it's a good idea to cover the viewfinder while you're shooting. Canon used to supply a viewfinder cover that was stored on the camera strap, but no more. I trust you can figure out a suitable alternative, although my guess is that you won't experience any issues unless you're shooting really long exposures.

>> **Using Live View or Movie mode for an extended period can harm your pictures and the camera.** Using the monitor full-time causes the camera's innards to heat up more than usual, and that extra heat can create the right conditions for *noise,* a defect that looks like speckles of sand. More critically, the increased temperatures can damage the camera.

>> **A white thermometer symbol appears on the monitor to warn you when the camera is getting too hot**. If you keep shooting and the temperature continues to increase, the symbol turns red and blinks, alerting you that the camera soon will shut off automatically.

>> **Aiming the lens at the sun or other bright lights also can damage the camera.** Of course, you can cause problems doing this even during normal viewfinder shooting, but the possibilities increase when you use Live View and Movie modes.

>> **Live View and Movie mode put additional strain on the camera battery.** Extra juice is needed to power the monitor for extended periods of time. If you do a lot of Live View or movie shooting, you may want to invest in a second battery so you have a spare on hand when the first one runs out of gas.

Using Quick Control Mode

Earlier in this chapter, the section "Viewing Camera Settings" introduces the Quick Control screen, which displays current picture settings when you use the viewfinder to compose pictures. Because digital photography isn't confusing enough, the T8i/850D also offers Quick Control *mode*, which enables you to change certain settings from the Quick Control screen, saving you the trouble of using menus or function buttons such as the ISO button.

REMEMBER

You can take advantage of this feature for viewfinder photography as well as for Live View and movie shooting. To try it out, first set the Mode dial to Tv so that your screens will look like the ones in the upcoming figures. (More about how things work in other modes in a bit.)

1. **Press the Q button or tap the Q icon on the touchscreen.**

   Figure 1-29 shows you where to find the icon during viewfinder shooting (left screen) and during Live View shooting (right screen).

   During viewfinder shooting, the monitor display changes to look similar to the one shown on the left in Figure 1-30. In Live View mode, the display appears as shown on the left in Figure 1-31.

Tap to enter Quick Control mode

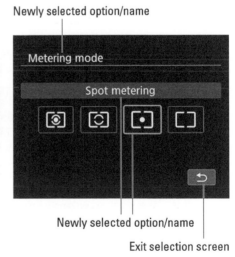

FIGURE 1-29: To activate Quick Control mode, tap the Q symbol or press the Q button.

Tap to enter Quick Control mode

Active setting

Newly selected option/name

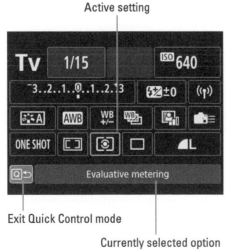

FIGURE 1-30: After selecting the setting you want to change, rotate the Main dial to cycle through available options for that setting (left) or press the Set button to view all options on a separate screen (right).

Exit Quick Control mode

Currently selected option

Newly selected option/name

Exit selection screen

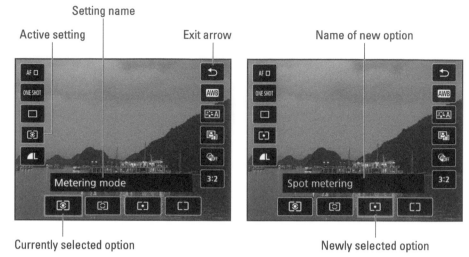

Setting name

Active setting

Exit arrow

Name of new option

FIGURE 1-31:
In Live View mode, the name of the setting you're adjusting initially appears at the bottom of the screen (left) but as you explore the available options, the name of the current one appears instead (right).

Currently selected option

Newly selected option

2. **Select the setting you want to adjust.**

The currently selected setting is highlighted; in the figures, the Metering Mode setting is active, for example. To choose a different setting, tap it or press the edges of the Quick Control dial to move the highlight box over the setting.

During viewfinder shooting, the name of the option that's currently in force appears at the bottom of the screen. For example, in the left screen in Figure 1-30, Evaluative Metering is the selected Metering Mode option.

During Live View shooting, the text banner initially shows the name of the setting you're changing, as shown on the left in Figure 1-31 — again, Metering Mode, in the figure. The icons at the bottom of the screen represent the available options. The one surrounded by the orange box is currently selected.

3. **Rotate the Main dial to cycle through available options for the setting.**

As soon as you rotate the dial, the text label in the Live View display shows the name of the selected option. In the right screen in Figure 1-31, for example, the label indicates that the newly selected Metering Mode option is Spot metering. (Chapter 4 explains these and other Metering Mode options.)

TIP

During viewfinder photography, you can also display all the available options on a single screen, as shown on the right in Figure 1-30. To do so, press the Set button or tap the setting that you're adjusting (Metering Mode, in the figure). On the selection screen, select an option by tapping it. Depending on the setting, you also may be able to rotate the Main dial or Quick Control dial to highlight the option you want to use. After selecting the option, tap the exit arrow, labeled in Figure 1-30, or press the Set button to exit the settings screen.

4. **Repeat Steps 2 and 3 as needed to adjust other settings.**

5. **To exit Quick Control mode, press the Q button.**

    During viewfinder photography, you also can tap the Q symbol in the lower-left corner of the screen. During Live View shooting, tap the exit arrow in the top-right corner of the screen. (Refer to Figure 1-31.)

A couple of important tips about Quick Control mode:

>> When the Mode dial is set to Scene Intelligent Auto, no Quick Control icon appears on the Live View screen. If you press the Quick Control button, you access the Creative Assist features available in Scene Intelligent Auto mode. (Chapter 3 explains these tool.) You can get to the same features by tapping the Creative Assist symbol in the lower-right corner of the Live View screen. The symbol looks like a paintbrush inside a colored circle; refer to the left screen in Figure 1-26 for a.

>> You also can use the Quick Control method to adjust movie-recording settings. However, when the camera is set to Movie mode, the screen serves up a different assortment of settings. When the camera is in Playback mode, the Quick Control screen offers features related to after-the-shot functions. See Chapter 8 for help using the movie-related Quick Control screen; refer to Chapter 9 for playback Quick Control features.

>> For some settings, the Live View preview updates to show the result of your choice. If you adjust the White Balance setting, which affects how colors are rendered, you see colors shift in the preview, for example.

>> After you choose some settings or select specific options available for those settings, additional touch-control icons appear. For example, you may see an an Info label. By tapping that label or pressing the Info button, you gain access to an additional layer of options. Instructions throughout the book alert you when these extra options are available.

REMEMBER

As with instructions for choosing menu items, the rest of this book assumes that you're now cool with the basics of using Quick Control mode. So instead of repeat-ing all the preceding steps for each feature that you can modify by using Quick Control mode, instructions merely say something like "Shift to Quick Control mode to adjust this setting." Just for good measure, though, the Q button symbol appears in the margin of paragraphs that discuss using Quick Control mode.

Familiarizing Yourself with the Lens

If you're never used a dSLR before, you may be unfamiliar with how to operate the lens. The following basics are specific to the 18–55mm kit lens sold with the T8i/850D, but they apply to many other lenses that support autofocusing with the camera. (You should explore the lens manual for specifics, of course.)

>> **Focusing:** Set the lens to automatic or manual focusing by moving the AF/MF switch, labeled in Figure 1-32. Move the switch to the AF position for autofocusing and to MF for manual focusing. Then proceed as follows:

- *Autofocusing:* Press and hold the shutter button halfway or press the AF ON button. In Live View mode, you also have the option of tapping the touchscreen to focus. (You must enable this feature; Chapter 5 has details.)

- *Manual focusing:* After setting the AF/MF switch to MF, rotate the focusing ring on the lens until your subject appears sharp in the viewfinder or on the Live View screen. The position of the focusing ring varies depending on the lens; again, Figure 1-32 shows the ring as it appears on the 18–55mm kit lens.

WARNING

To save battery power, the focus motor in STM (stepping motor) lenses, such as the 18–55mm kit lens, automatically goes to sleep after a period of inactivity. While the lens is napping, manual focusing isn't possible (the focusing ring is free to turn, but the lens does not focus). The same is true if the camera itself goes into sleep mode, which is determined by the Auto Power Off feature on Setup Menu 2. Either way, wake up the camera and lens by pressing the shutter button halfway.

See Chapter 5 for more help with both automatic and manual focusing.

>> **Zooming:** If you bought a zoom lens, it has a movable *zoom ring*. The location of the zoom ring on the kit lens is shown in Figure 1-32. To zoom in or out, rotate the ring.

TIP

Zooming changes the lens *focal length*. (If you're new to that term, the sidebar "Focal length and the crop factor," later in this chapter, explains the subject.) On the kit lens, you can determine the focal length of the lens by looking at the number aligned with the bar that I labeled *focal-length indicator* in Figure 1-32.

>> **Enabling image stabilization:** Many Canon lenses, including the kit lens, offer this feature, which compensates for small amounts of camera shake that can occur when you handhold the camera. Camera movement during the exposure can produce blurry images, so turning on image stabilization can help you get sharper handheld shots.

AF/MF switch

Focal-length indicator

Image Stabilizer switch

Manual focusing ring   Zoom ring   Lens-release button

FIGURE 1-32:
Here are a few features that may be found on your lens.

WARNING

However, when you use a tripod, image stabilization can have detrimental effects because the system may try to adjust for movement that isn't actually occurring. Although this problem shouldn't be an issue with most Canon IS lenses, if you do see blurry images while using a tripod, try turning the feature off. (You also save battery power by turning off image stabilization.) If you use a monopod, leave image stabilization turned on so it can help compensate for any accidental movement of the monopod.

On non-Canon lenses, image stabilization may go by another name: *anti-shake, vibration compensation,* and so on. In some cases, the manufacturers recommend that you leave the system turned on or select a special setting when you use a tripod, so check the lens manual for information.

Whatever lens you use, image stabilization isn't meant to eliminate the blur that can occur when your subject moves during the exposure. That problem is related to shutter speed, a topic you can explore in Chapter 4.

>> **Removing a lens:** After turning the camera off, press and hold the lens-release button on the camera (refer to Figure 1-32), and turn the lens toward the shutter button side of the camera until the lens detaches from the lens mount. Put the rear protective cap onto the back of the lens and, if you aren't putting another lens on the camera, cover the lens mount with its cap, too.

WARNING

Always switch lenses in a clean environment to reduce the risk of getting dust, dirt, and other contaminants inside the camera or lens. Changing lenses on a sandy beach, for example, isn't a good idea. For added safety, point the camera body slightly down when performing this maneuver; doing so helps prevent any flotsam in the air from being drawn into the camera by gravity.

>> **Decoding Canon lens terminology:** When you shop for Canon lenses, you encounter these lens specifications:

- *EF and EF-S:* EF stands for *electro focus;* the S stands for *short back focus.* And that simply means the rear element of the lens is closer to the sensor than with an EF lens. The good news is that your T8i/850D works with both of these Canon lens types.

- *IS:* Indicates that the lens offers image stabilization.

- *STM:* Refers to *stepping motor technology,* an autofocusing system that is designed to provide smoother, quieter autofocusing.

The 18–55mm kit lens is an EF-S lens with both image stabilization and stepping motor technology. You can find complete lens info on the ring surrounding the front element of the lens.

FOCAL LENGTH AND THE CROP FACTOR

The angle of view that a lens can capture is determined by its *focal length,* or in the case of a zoom lens, the range of focal lengths it offers. Focal length is measured in millimeters. The shorter the focal length, the wider the angle of view. As focal length increases, the angle of view narrows, and the subject occupies more of the frame.

Generally speaking, lenses with focal lengths shorter than 35mm are considered *wide angle lenses* and lenses with focal lengths greater than 80mm are considered *telephoto* lenses. Anything in the middle is a "normal" lens, suitable for shooting scenes that don't require either a wide or narrow angle of view.

Note, however, that the focal lengths stated in this book and elsewhere are *35mm-equivalent focal lengths.* Here's the deal: When you put a standard lens on most dSLR cameras, including the T8i/850D, the available frame area is reduced, as if you took a picture on a camera that uses 35mm film negatives and cropped it. This *crop factor* varies depending on the camera, which is why the photo industry adopted the 35mm-equivalent measuring stick as a standard. With the T8i/850D, the crop factor is roughly 1.6x. In the figure here, the red frame indicates the portion of a 35mm frame that is captured at that crop factor.

When shopping for a lens, it's important to remember this crop factor to make sure you get the focal length designed for the type of pictures you want to take. Just multiply the lens focal length by 1.6 to determine the actual angle of view.

Working with Memory Cards

As the medium that stores your picture files, the memory card is a critical component of your camera. See the steps at the start of this chapter for help installing a card; follow these tips for buying and maintaining cards:

>> **Buying SD cards:** SD (Secure Digital) cards carry slightly different names depending on their storage capacity: SD cards offer less than 4GB of storage space; SDHC cards can hold 4GB–32GB of data; and SDXC cards can store more than 32GB.

Aside from card capacity, the other specification to note is card speed, which indicates how quickly data can be moved to and from the card. Card speed is indicated in several ways. The most common spec is SD Speed Class, which rates cards with a number between 2 and 10, with 10 being the fastest. Most cards also carry another designation, UHS-1, -2, or -3; UHS (Ultra High Speed) refers to a new technology designed to boost data transmission speeds above the normal Speed Class 10 rate. The number 1, 2, or 3 inside a little U symbol tells you the UHS rating.

TIP

Your camera can use UHS-2 and -3 cards, but you won't get any extra speed benefit; the speed advantage with the T8i/850D tops out at UHS-1.

Some SD cards also are rated in terms of how they perform when used to record video — specifically, how many frames per second the card can handle. As with the other ratings, a higher video-speed number indicates a faster card.

>> **Formatting a card:** The first time you use a new memory card, format it by choosing the Format Card option on Setup Menu 1. This step ensures the card is properly prepared to record your pictures. See the upcoming section "Setup Menu 1" for more information.

>> **Removing a card:** First, check the status of the memory-card access lamp, found just above the card door on the back-right side of the camera. After making sure that the lamp is off, indicating that the camera has finished recording your most recent photo, turn off the camera. Open the memory card door, depress the memory card slightly and then lift your finger. The card should pop halfway out of the slot, enabling you to grab it by the tail and remove it.

>> **Handling cards:** Don't touch the gold contacts on the back of the card. (See the right card in Figure 1-33.) When cards aren't in use, store them in the protective cases they came in or in a memory card wallet. Keep cards away from extreme heat and cold as well.

>> **Locking cards:** The tiny switch on the side of the card, labeled "Lock switch" in Figure 1-33, enables you to lock your card, which prevents any data from being erased or recorded to the card. If you insert a locked card into the camera, a message on the monitor alerts you to that fact.

TIP

You can safeguard individual images from accidental erasure by using the Protect Images option on Playback Menu 1; Chapter 10 tells you how. Note, though, that formatting the card *does* erase even protected pictures; the safety feature prevents erasure only when you use the camera's Erase function, also covered in Chapter 10.

Lock switch   Contacts (don't touch!)

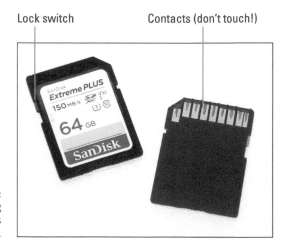

FIGURE 1-33:
Avoid touching the gold contacts on the card.

Reviewing Basic Setup Options

Your camera offers scads of options for customizing its performance. Later chapters explain settings related to picture-taking, such as those that affect flash behavior and autofocusing. The rest of this chapter offers a quick rundown of options on the Setup menu, which are mainly (but not all) related to general camera operations. Some of these features deserve only a brief glance; others may require your attention on a regular basis. I've also included advice on a few additional pre-use options you may want to consider that aren't found on the Setup menu.

REMEMBER

If you haven't yet done so, also follow the instructions provided in the earlier section "Changing from Guided to Standard Display Mode" to turn off Guided mode for the four options found on the Shooting Display Settings menu. Otherwise, screens you see on your camera won't match the figures in this book, and some instructions won't work as spelled out, either.

Also note that menu offerings change depending on your exposure mode — Scene Intelligent Auto, P, SCN, and so on — and whether the camera is set to Movie mode, Live View photography mode, or viewfinder photography mode. For now, put the camera in still photo mode (the On/Off switch should be set to On) and exit Live View mode if it's active. (The Live View button is just to the right of the viewfinder and is marked with a camera symbol.) Then rotate the Mode dial on top of the camera to the P, Tv, Av, or M position. You can adjust all the camera's options only in these advanced exposure modes.

Note that when you shoot in Live View or Movie mode, some menus offer additional or different options than when you use the viewfinder. I mention these options in the following lists even though they don't appear in the accompanying figures, which feature the menus as they appear during viewfinder shooting. Yeah, I know, this is all getting fairly dense; don't panic, the goal here is just to give you a menu overview that you can access quickly. I detail many settings further when discussing the relevant shooting topics later in the book.

Setup Menu 1

Display Setup Menu 1, shown in Figure 1-34, to access the following options:

>> **Select Folder:** By default, your camera creates an initial file-storage folder named 100Canon and puts as many as 9,999 images in that folder. When you reach image 9999, the camera creates a new folder, named 101Canon, for your next 9,999 images. The camera also creates a new folder if you perform a manual file-numbering reset (details are provided later in this section).

Choose Select Folder to see the list of folders on your memory card. If the card contains multiple folders, the currently selected one is highlighted. The number to the right of the folder name shows you how many pictures are in the folder. You also see a thumbnail view of the first and last pictures in the folder, along with the file numbers of those two photos. To choose a different folder, tap it or press the top or bottom edge of the Quick Control dial to select it and then press the Set button. You also can create a new folder by choosing the Create Folder setting on the menu screen; Chapter 11 provides details on this feature.

FIGURE 1-34:
Setup Menu 1 contains the Format Card option with a handful of others.

>> **File Numbering:** This option controls how the camera names your picture files. After selecting File Numbering from the menu, choose the Numbering option to select one of these choices:

- *Continuous:* This is the default; the camera numbers your files sequentially, from 0001 to 9999, and places all images in the same folder (100Canon, by default) unless you specify otherwise using the Select Folder option. The numbering sequence is retained even if you change memory cards.

  When you reach picture 9999, the camera automatically creates a new folder (101Canon, by default) and restarts the file numbering at 0001 — again, the folder issue is dependent on the status of the Select Folder option.

- *Auto Reset:* File numbering restarts at 0001 each time you put in a different memory card or create a new folder. It's easy to wind up with multiple photos that have the same file number if you're not careful about storing them in separate folders. So think twice — or maybe three times — about using this option.

WARNING

You also find a separate option, Manual Reset. Select this setting to begin a new numbering sequence starting at 0001. A new folder is automatically created to store your new files. The camera then returns to whichever Numbering mode is selected (Continuous or Auto Reset).

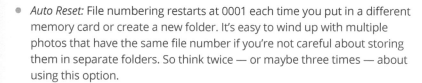

WARNING

Beware of one gotcha that applies to both the Continuous and Auto Reset options: If you swap memory cards and the new card already contains images, the camera may pick up numbering from the last image on the new card, which throws a monkey wrench into things. To avoid this problem, transfer the images to your computer or hard drive and format the new card before putting it into the camera, as explained later in this list.

>> **Auto Rotate:** This option determines whether vertically oriented pictures are rotated to appear upright during picture playback or when you view them in a photo editor. Stick with the default "On" setting, represented by the icon shown in Figure 1-34, until you explore Chapter 9, which discusses this and other playback issues.

This setting doesn't affect movies. See the next bullet point for a similar item that does come into play for movie recording.

REMEMBER

>> **Add Movie Rotate Info:** If you set the camera to Movie mode (rotate the On/Off switch to the movie-camera position), the menu displays this option. When enabled, this feature inserts into the movie data information about whether you held the camera vertically or horizontally when shooting the movie. Movies that you shot in the vertical orientation then play back in the same orientation as recorded when you display them on a smartphone or other smart device. You can read more about this movie-recording feature in Chapter 8.

>> **Format Card:** Choose this option to wipe the installed memory card clean of all contents and ensure that it's properly prepared for use in the camera. For extra-deep cleaning, select the Low-Level formatting box after you select the menu option. However, the standard formatting (Low-Level box unchecked) is usually adequate.

Setup Menu 2

Setup Menu 2, posing in Figure 1-35, contains these options:

>> **Auto Power Off:** To save battery power, the camera automatically goes to sleep after a certain period of inactivity. At the default setting, the camera nods off after only 10 seconds unless the camera is in Playback mode, Live View mode, or Movie mode, in which case it waits until 30 seconds have passed.

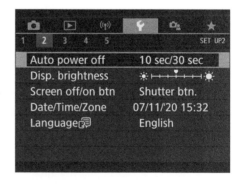

FIGURE 1-35:
Through the first option on this menu, you can adjust the delay time of the camera's automatic shutdown feature.

You can adjust this timing so that 30 seconds is the minimum delay time (the 10-second variation is disabled at the 30-second setting). Or you can extend the delay up to as long as 15 minutes. To disable auto shutdown altogether, select Off — but be aware that even at that setting, the monitor still turns off if you ignore the camera for 30 minutes.

Regardless of the shutoff time you select, you can bring the camera out of hibernation mode by giving the shutter button a quick half-press and release or by pressing the DISP button.

>> **Disp. Brightness:** This option enables you to make the monitor display brighter or darker. But if you take this step, what you see on the display may not be an accurate rendition of exposure. The default setting is 4, which is the position at the midpoint of the brightness scale.

>> **Screen Off/On Btn:** Through this option, available only for viewfinder photography, you tell the camera what to do with regards to the Quick Control display when you press the shutter button halfway. At the default setting, Shutter Btn, your half-press of the button then turns the monitor off, and releasing the button turns the monitor back on.

Option 2, Shutter/DISP, still results in the monitor shutting itself off when you half-press the shutter button, but to bring the monitor back to life, you have to press the DISP button. And Option 3, Remains On, lives up to its name: The screen stays on even after you press the shutter button halfway. If you want to shut the monitor off, you have to press the INFO button.

I suggest keeping this one set to the default (Shutter Btn.). Whatever you choose, remember that the setting has no effect during Live View or movie shooting. In fact, if the camera is in Movie mode or Live View is turned on, the option disappears from the menu.

>> **Date/Time/Zone:** If you didn't do so when following the initial camera setup steps at the start of this chapter, enter the time, date, and time zone now. Keeping the date/time accurate is important because that information is recorded as part of the image file. In your photo browser, you can then see when you shot an image and, equally handy, search for images by the date they were taken. Chapter 9 shows you where to locate the date/time data when browsing your picture files.

TIP

When the Time Zone setting is active, the Time Difference value that's displayed in the upper-right corner of the display is the difference between the Time Zone you select and Coordinated Universal Time, or UTC, which is the standard by which the world sets its clocks. For example, New York City is 5 hours behind UTC. This information is provided so that if your time zone isn't in the list of available options, you can select one that shares the same relationship to the UTC.

>> **Language:** This option determines the language of any text displayed on the camera monitor.

Setup Menu 3

Setup Menu 3, shown in Figure 1-36, contains the following offerings:

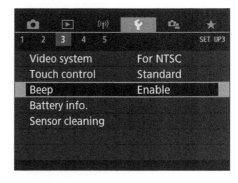

>> **Video System:** This option relates to viewing your images and movies on a television. Select NTSC if you live in North America or other countries that adhere to the NTSC video standard; select PAL for playback in areas that follow that code of video conduct. Your selection also determines what frame rate settings you can select when recording movies (refer to Chapter 8).

FIGURE 1-36:
Still more customization features await on Setup Menu 3.

>> **Touch Control:** Choose this setting to adjust the sensitivity of the touchscreen or disable the touchscreen altogether. (I often do this when wearing my camera on a neck strap so that I can't accidentally adjust a touchscreen-enabled setting if the monitor bumps against my chest as I walk.)

Remember that you can also use the Multi Function Lock feature to toggle the touchscreen operation on and off by pressing the Erase/Lock button. See the earlier section "Back-of-the-body controls" — specifically, the details about the Erase/Lock button — for information.

>> **Beep:** Choose Enable if you want the camera to emit an audio cue when you select an option by tapping the touchscreen and when the autofocusing system has found its focus point. The second option, Touch, disables touch-screen sounds only; choose Disable to turn off both sound effects.

>> **Battery Info.:** Select this option to see battery information, such as the type of battery in the camera, how much battery juice is left, and the battery's recharge performance. For this last feature, three green bars mean that the battery is working fine; two bars means that recharging is slightly below par; and one red bar means that you should invest in a new battery as soon as possible.

>> **Sensor Cleaning:** Choose this option to access features related to the camera's internal sensor-cleaning mechanism. These work like so:

- *Auto Cleaning:* By default, the camera's sensor-cleaning mechanism activates each time you turn the camera on and off. This process helps keep the image sensor — which is the part of the camera that captures the image — free of dust and other particles that can mar your photos. You can disable this option, but it's hard to imagine why you would choose to do so.

- *Clean Now:* Select this option and press Set to initiate a cleaning cycle. For best results, set the camera on a flat surface during cleaning.

- *Clean Manually:* When the Mode dial is set to P, Tv, Av, or M, you can access this third option, which prepares the camera for manual cleaning of the sensor. Because you can easily damage the image sensor, rendering your camera a paperweight, use extreme caution if you decide to try cleaning the sensor yourself. You're really better off taking the camera to a good service center for cleaning.

Setup Menu 4

Figure 1-37 shows Setup Menu 4, which you can access only in the advanced exposure modes: P, Tv, Av, and M.

FIGURE 1-37:
To display Setup Menu 4, you must set the Mode dial to P, Tv, Av, or M.

>> **Viewfinder Display:** Here's where you find the options that add a grid, electronic level, and/or a flicker detection warning to the viewfinder display. See the earlier section "Decoding viewfinder data" for details. You don't see this option on the menu when using Live View or Movie mode, both of which disable the viewfinder.

>> **Info Button Display Options:** Select this menu item to tell the camera what information you want to see on the monitor when you press the Info button when the camera is in shooting mode. By default, pressing the button cycles the display through three views: Off, the Quick Control display, and the electronic level. You can reduce the possible displays to just two by disabling either the electronic level or the Quick Control display through this option.

>> **Grid When Shooting:** This option doesn't appear in Figure 1-37 because it shows up only when the camera is set in Live View or Movie mode. In those modes, select Grid When Shooting to add a grid to the screen. Refer to the earlier section "Customizing the Live View display" for more information about this and other Live View screen features.

>> **Shutter Btn Function for Movies:** Another movie-related feature (and also not shown in Figure 1-37), this menu item lets you tell the camera what you want it to do when you press the shutter button halfway or completely. Chapter 8 offers details.

>> **Switch AF Point Selection and AE Lock Button:** In the menu itself, this item appears as shown on the third line in Figure 1-37, with symbols replacing the words AF Point Selection and AE Lock. Through this menu option, you can customize the functions of the two buttons; Chapter 11 has details. (But don't swap them now, or later instructions that involve the buttons won't work.)

>> **HDMI Resolution:** If you decide to connect your camera to an HDTV in order to view your photos and movies, you may experience smoother playback if you change this menu option from the default setting, Auto, to 1080p. Chapter 12 explains more about this setting and other steps involved in connecting your camera to an HDMI display. (You don't need to worry about this menu option until you're ready to screen your work; it doesn't affect how your pictures and movies are recorded.)

>> **Multi Function Lock:** I detail this option earlier in this chapter, in the section "Back-of-the-body controls." Look for the specifics in the bullet point devoted to the Erase/Lock button.

Setup Menu 5

Bring up Setup Menu 5, shown in Figure 1-38, to access the following items:

>> **Custom Functions:** Selecting this option opens the door to *Custom Functions,* which are a set of advanced features. See "Navigating Custom Functions," earlier in this chapter, for tips on making your way through these screens.

REMEMBER

>> **Clear Settings:** Via this option, you can restore the default menu settings. You also can reset all the Custom Functions settings to their defaults.

FIGURE 1-38:
Setup Menu 5 is home to the Custom Functions options, among other items.

>> **Copyright Information:** Using this option, explained in Chapter 11, you can embed copyright information in your files.

>> **Manual/software URL:** Canon provides a printed camera manual in the T8i/850D shipping box. But the print version doesn't tell you the whole story about the camera. If you want the full manual, you can download it in an electronic format (PDF, to be specific) and then read it on your smartphone, tablet, or computer.

To make finding the download site easy, choosing this menu option displays a QR code (Quick Response code). If your smartphone or tablet has an app that can read these codes, you simply aim the device's camera at the code to display the download site's web address (URL, or *Universal Resource Locator*). The site also provides access to the Canon software that's available for free download to purchasers of the camera.

>> **Certification Logo Display:** You have permission to ignore this screen, which simply displays logos for a couple electronics-industry certifications claimed by the camera. You can find additional logos on the bottom of the camera.

>> **Firmware:** This item tells you the version number of the camera firmware (internal operating software). At the time of publication, the current firmware version was 1.0.0.

WARNING

Keeping your camera firmware up-to-date is important, so visit the Canon website (www.canon.com) regularly to find out whether your camera sports the latest version. Follow the instructions given on the website to download and install updated firmware if needed.

A few other critical menu options before you go

Before moving on to other parts of the book, I suggest that you also consider a few final options not found on the Setup menus:

TIP

>> **Network menu 1, Airplane mode:** By default, all of the camera's wireless connection functions are enabled. My theory is that Canon wanted the wireless functions on from the get-go to make it easier for new users to share photos online. Problem is, all that connectivity stuff eats battery power. So I suggest that you turn it off until you need it. The easiest method is to enable Airplane mode, as shown on the left in Figure 1-39. It works just like the Airplane mode on your smartphone or tablet, disabling all wireless signals. When it's enabled, you see an airplane symbol on the Quick Control screen, as shown on the right in the figure.

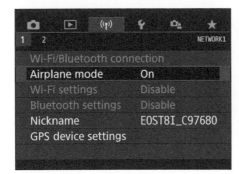

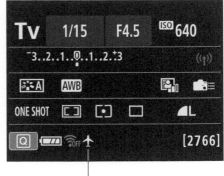

Airplane mode enabled

FIGURE 1-39:
Enabling Airplane mode saves battery power by shutting down wireless signals.

>> **Network menu 1, GPS Device Settings:** If your work or hobby requires you to tag your images or movies with GPS coordinates, investigate this Network Menu 1 option before you start shooting. You can add geotagging data by attaching the optional Canon GPS Receiver GP-E2 or by connecting the camera to a smartphone via the Canon Camera Connect app, which I cover in the appendix to this book. Unfortunately, for the latter connection to work, you have to enable Bluetooth, which means you have to disable Airplane mode. You can still save a little battery power by manually disabling the camera's Wi-Fi signal via the Wi-Fi Settings option on Network Menu 1.

>> **Shooting menu 1, Release Shutter without Card:** By default, this option is turned on, allowing you to take pictures even when there's no memory card in the camera. Well, actually, you can *take* a picture; you just can't view it or download it because it isn't stored anywhere. It's a dangerous setting to leave on, and I can't for the life of me understand why Canon would make it the default setting. You do you, as the kids say, but when I do me, I turn that sucker off and never look back. Figure 1-40 shows the option turned off.

FIGURE 1-40:
Turn this feature off so that you can't accidentally take pictures without a memory card installed.

IN THIS CHAPTER

» **Picking an exposure mode**

» **Changing the shutter-release (Drive) mode**

» **Understanding the Image Quality settings (resolution and file type)**

» **Choosing the image aspect ratio**

» **Using flash**

Chapter **2**

Choosing Basic Picture Settings

E very camera manufacturer strives to ensure that your initial encounter with the camera is a happy one. To that end, the default camera settings are designed to make it as easy as possible to take a decent picture the first time you press the shutter button. However, the default settings don't produce optimal results in every situation. You may be able to shoot an acceptable portrait, for example, but adjusting a few options can greatly improve that picture.

So that you can start fine-tuning settings to match your subject, this chapter introduces you to four basic options: exposure mode, Drive mode, Image Quality, and Aspect Ratio. Additionally, the last part of the chapter discusses how to take advantage of the built-in flash as well as some options available when you add an auxiliary flash unit to the camera.

Note: This chapter relates to still photography; for information about choosing settings for movies, see Chapter 8.

Choosing an Exposure Mode

The first picture-taking setting to consider is the exposure mode, sometimes referred to as *shooting mode.* Whatever you call it (this book uses *exposure mode*), your choice determines how much control you have over certain picture settings, including those that determine exposure and focus.

Choose an exposure mode via the Mode dial, found on top of the camera and shown in Figure 2-1. As labeled in the figure, Canon groups exposure modes into two categories: Basic Zone and Creative Zone. The next sections provide an introduction to the exposure modes in each zone.

Creative Zone modes

Basic Zone modes

FIGURE 2-1:
The exposure mode you choose determines how much control you have over picture settings.

Basic Zone exposure modes

These exposure modes provide almost fully automatic photography. Here's the scoop on each mode:

>> **Scene Intelligent Auto:** The most basic mode, Scene Intelligent Auto is the closest you get to fully automatic shooting with the T8i/850D. The name stems from the fact that the camera is smart enough to analyze the scene and select the settings it thinks would best capture that subject.

>> **SCN (Scene):** Rotate the Mode dial to this setting to select from a list of common scenes, such as portraits, landscapes, group photos, food shots, and more. After you select a scene, the camera selects settings geared to deliver results that are traditionally considered appropriate for that type of shot, such as a blurred background for a portrait.

>> **Creative Filters:** Choose this mode to add special effects as you shoot.

Chapter 3 provides specifics on using Scene Intelligent Auto and SCN modes; Chapter 12 explains Creative Filters mode. But be forewarned: To remain easy to use, all these modes prevent you from taking advantage of advanced exposure, color, and autofocusing features. In fact, you can't even access the full complement of camera menus in these modes. That's not to say you can't take good pictures in the automated modes — just that stepping up to a Creative Zone mode, outlined next, gives you a much stronger hand in the look of your photos.

Creative Zone modes (P, Tv, Av, and M)

To take more control over the camera, choose a Creative Zone exposure mode: P (programmed autoexposure), Tv (shutter-priority autoexposure), Av (aperture-priority autoexposure), or M (manual exposure). All four modes enable you to take advantage of the camera's complete cadre of exposure, color, autofocusing, and other settings.

Which mode is better? Well, the main difference between them is the level of input you have over two critical exposure settings: aperture and shutter speed. Chapter 4 explains in detail, but here's the short story (well, *short* being a relative term for this storyteller, I suppose):

>> **For moving subjects, I recommend Tv mode.** In that mode, you specify shutter speed, which affects whether moving objects appear blurry or frozen in time. The camera then selects the aperture setting for you.

>> **For portraits, landscapes, and other still subjects, I suggest Av mode.** That mode enables you to choose the f-stop, or aperture setting, which affects depth of field (the distance over which focus appears acceptably sharp). Again, the camera takes care of the other half of the equation, selecting the shutter speed.

>> **Turn to M mode when you want to control both aperture and shutter speed rather than let the camera handle one or the other.** I also use this mode when I'm after an exposure result that the camera might consider "abnormal" — maybe I want to produce a very dark exposure to create a moody image, for example. This mode also enables you to access a special long-exposure shutter speed, Bulb, which keeps the shutter open as long as you hold down the shutter button.

REMEMBER

One often-misunderstood aspect about the M exposure mode: This M has nothing to do with manual focusing. You can choose from manual focusing or autofocusing in any exposure mode, assuming your lens offers autofocusing. However, access to some options that modify how the autofocus system works is limited to P, Tv, Av, and M modes.

P mode (which does *not* stand for *professional mode,* by the way), gets pulled out of the closet about as rarely as the winter coat I thought I'd bring "just in case" when I moved to from Indianapolis to south Florida. Which is to say, uh, never. In P mode, the camera chooses both aperture and shutter speed for you, which is convenient but almost defeats the purpose of moving out of Scene Intelligent Auto. I say *almost* because one advantage P mode does give you is that you gain access to all camera settings, so you can fiddle with autofocus and color options that aren't available in the Basic Zone modes. So if you don't want to worry about aperture or shutter speed but you do want to play with advanced features that are off-limits in Basic Zone modes, P might serve your needs.

Changing the Drive Mode

Known generically as the *shutter-release mode*, the Drive mode determines how and when the camera records a picture when you press the shutter button. Here are your options:

 » **Single:** Records a single image each time you press the shutter button.

» **Continuous:** Sometimes known as *burst mode*, this mode records a continuous series of images as long as you hold down the shutter button.

You can choose from two continuous modes:

 • *High-speed continuous:* Captures a maximum of about 7 frames per second (fps) during viewfinder photography and about 7.5 fps during Live View shooting.

 • *Low-speed continuous:* Captures about 3 fps for both viewfinder and Live View shooting.

Why would you ever choose the low-speed setting? Well, frankly, unless you're shooting something that's moving at an extremely fast pace, not too much is going to change between frames when you shoot at 7 fps. So you wind up with a ton of images that are exactly the same, wasting space on your memory card.

However, be aware that whether you use High-speed or Low-speed Continuous mode, you may not be able to achieve the maximum frame rates I just stated. A number of picture settings can hamper the camera's frame rate, including shutter speed and autofocusing options, all covered in Part 2 of the book.

» **10-Second Self-Timer/Remote Control:** Want to put yourself in the picture? Select this mode, depress the shutter button, and run into the frame. You have 10 seconds to pose before the image is recorded.

As an alternative to the press-and-run technique, you can trigger the shutter release remotely via a Bluetooth wireless connection. This option involves either purchasing the Canon BR-E1 remote unit or installing the Canon Camera Connect app on a smartphone or tablet and then using the app to trigger the shutter release. See the appendix for more about this and other features provided by the Canon Camera Connect app.

 » **Self-Timer: 2 Second/remote control:** This mode works just like the mode just described, but the capture happens 2 seconds after you press the shutter button.

Consider using this setting when you're shooting long exposures and using a tripod. In that scenario, the mere motion of pressing the shutter button can cause slight camera movement, which can blur an image. The ideal solution is to use a remote control to trigger the shutter release, but if you don't have that option, set the Drive mode to the 2-second self-timer mode, press the shutter button, and then take your hands off the camera until the picture is recorded.

>> **Self-Timer: Continuous:** With this option, the camera waits 10 seconds after you press the shutter button and then captures a continuous series of images. You can set the camera to record two to ten images per each shutter release. Wireless remote-control shooting isn't possible at this setting.

If you use a wired remote control such as the Canon RS-60E3 unit, you can select any Drive mode — you're not limited to the two Remote Control settings, which are available for wireless remotes. Wired remotes attach to the camera via the port under the small cover on the left side of the camera, as shown in Figure 2-2. After making the connection, you press the shutter button on the remote control unit just as you would the shutter button on the camera. With most units, a half-press initiates autofocusing, and when you fully depress the button, the shutter is released according to the selected Drive mode.

Wired remote-control terminal

FIGURE 2-2:
Wired remote-control units connect to the camera via this port.

Now that you understand what each Drive mode does, here's how you figure out which one is currently in force:

>> **Checking the Drive mode during viewfinder photography:** A symbol representing the current mode appears on the Quick Control screen, but exactly where that symbol appears depends on your exposure mode. Figure 2-3 shows you where to find the symbol in Scene Intelligent Auto (left screen) and in the Tv and other advanced modes (right screen). Don't see the Quick Control screen? Press the Info button (you may have to press twice)or press the shutter button halfway and release it.

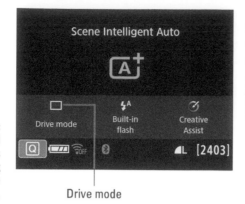
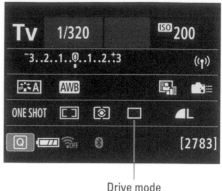

FIGURE 2-3:
The Quick Control
screen displays
an icon indicating
the current Drive
mode.

Drive mode   Drive mode

>> **Checking the Drive mode during Live View photography:** The Drive mode symbol doesn't appear in the default Live View display. To see that symbol and other shooting data, press Info until you see the more detailed screens like the ones shown in Figure 2-4. Again, the left screen shows the display as it appears in Scene Intelligent Auto mode; the right screen shows the display as it looks in advanced exposure modes such as Tv.

FIGURE 2-4:
In Live View
mode, press Info
to display settings
including the
Drive mode.

Drive mode   Drive mode

To change the Drive mode, take one of these paths:

>> **Select a Drive mode by using the Quick Control method.** Press the Q button or, in exposure modes that display an onscreen Q symbol, tap that symbol. After the camera shifts to Quick Control mode, select the Drive mode icon, as shown in Figures 2-5 and 2-6. (Figure 2-5 shows the screens as they appear during viewfinder photography; Figure 2-6 offers a look at the Live View versions.) Rotate the Quick Control dial or Main dial to change the setting.

In Live View mode, remember that an orange border appears around the icon that represents the setting you're about to change as well as around the option that's currently chosen. So on left screen in Figure 2-6, for example, you see the orange frame around the Drive mode icon on the vertical strip to the left of the screen. And at the bottom of the screen, the orange frame appears around the option I chose for the Drive mode, Self-Timer Continuous. (The text label above the option icons help you remember what each one means.)

Available options   Current option   Set number of shots

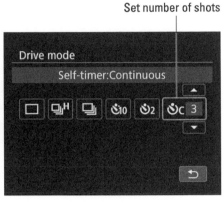

Name of current option

FIGURE 2-5:
For viewfinder photography, rotate the Quick Control or Main dial to cycle through Drive mode options (left) or press Set to display all options on a single screen (right).

FIGURE 2-6:
In Live View mode, rotate the Quick Control or Main dial to change the Drive mode (left); press the Info button to choose the number of shots you want the camera to take in Self-Timer Continuous mode (right).

For Self-Timer Continuous mode, the default (and minimum) number of frames that will be captured is two. To change that value, you have to take one more step:

- *Viewfinder photography:* Press Set to display all available settings on a separate screen, as shown on the right in Figure 2-5. Then press the top or bottom edge of the Quick Control dial or tap the arrows that appear above and below the current frame number. Tap the exit arrow in the lower-right corner of the screen to jump out of the settings screen.

- *Live View shooting:* Press the Info button to display the screen shown on the right in Figure 2-6. Then adjust the number of continuous frames you want the camera to capture by pressing the left or right edge of the Quick Control dial or by tapping the arrow symbols that sit next to the frame number (2, in the figure).

>> **During viewfinder photography, get fast access to the Drive mode by pressing the left edge of the Quick Control dial.** The left edge of the dial is marked with a couple of Drive mode symbols, as shown in Figure 2-7. Pressing that edge of the dial whisks you directly to the screen shown on the monitor in the figure. Here, you can change the Drive mode and set the number of continuous frames without changing screens. Tap Set or press the Set button to confirm your choice and exit the screen. Sorry, this technique doesn't work when Live View is engaged.

Press to access Drive mode settings

FIGURE 2-7: For viewfinder photography, a faster way to get to the Drive mode setting is to press the left edge of the Quick Control dial.

Understanding the Image Quality Setting

Another critical camera option, the Image Quality setting determines two important aspects of your pictures: *resolution*, or pixel count; and *file type*, which refers to the kind of file used to store picture data (JPEG or Raw). The next section explains how these factors affect your pictures so that you can choose the right combination of resolution and file type for your needs. If you already have that knowledge and just want to know how to change the setting on your T8i/850D, move ahead to the section "Adjusting the Image Quality setting."

Considering resolution: L, M, S1, or S2?

To choose an Image Quality setting, the first decision you need to make is how many pixels you want your image to contain. *Pixels* are the little square tiles from which all digital images are made; *pixel* is short for *picture element*. You can see some pixels close up in the right image in Figure 2-8, which shows a greatly magnified view of the eye area in the left image.

FIGURE 2-8:
Pixels are the building blocks of digital photos.

When describing a digital image, photographers use the term *resolution* to refer to the number of pixels it contains. Every image starts with a specific number of pixels, which you select via the Image Quality setting. You have four choices: Large, Medium, Small 1, and Small 2; Table 2-1 shows you the pixel count that results from each. The table assumes your camera is set to record pictures using the default aspect ratio of 3:2. If you change that setting, the resolution of the photo changes. See the upcoming section "Setting the Photo Aspect Ratio" for details.

TABLE 2-1

The Resolution Side of the Image Quality Setting

Symbol	Setting	Pixel Count
L	Large	6000 x 4000 (24MP)
M	Medium	3984 x 2656 (11MP)
S1	Small 1	2976 x 1984 (5.9MP)
S2	Small 2	2400 x 1600 (3.8MP)

TECHNICAL
STUFF

In the table, the first pair of numbers in the Pixel Count column represents the *pixel dimensions* — the number of horizontal pixels and vertical pixels. The values in parentheses indicate the total resolution, which you get by multiplying the horizontal and vertical pixel values. This number is usually stated in *megapixels*, or MP for short. The camera displays the resolution value using only one letter *M*, however. Either way, 1 MP equals 1 million pixels.

Resolution affects your pictures in three ways:

>> **Print size:** Pixel count determines the size at which you can produce a high-quality print. When an image contains too few pixels, details appear muddy, and curved and diagonal lines appear jagged. Such pictures are said to exhibit *pixelation*.

To ensure good print quality, aim for approximately 300 pixels per linear inch, or *ppi*. To produce an 8 x 10-inch print at 300 ppi, for example, you need a pixel count of 2400 x 3000, or about 7.2 megapixels. Depending on the printer and the photo, you may be happy with a lower resolution, however, so don't consider 300 ppi a hard and fast rule.

WARNING

Even though many photo-editing programs enable you to add pixels to an existing image — known as *upsampling* — doing so doesn't enable you to successfully enlarge your photo. In fact, upsampling typically makes matters worse.

To give you a better idea of the impact of resolution on print quality, Figures 2-9 through 2-11 show you the same image at 300 ppi, at 50 ppi, and then resampled from 50 ppi to 300 ppi. As you can see, there's no way around the rule: If you want quality prints, you need the right pixel count from the get-go.

>> **Screen display size:** Resolution doesn't affect the quality of images viewed on a monitor or television, or another screen device, the way it does for printed photos. Instead, resolution determines the *size* at which the image appears. Chapter 10 explains this issue in the section related to preparing photos for onscreen use. For now, just know that you need *way* fewer pixels for onscreen photos than you do for prints. In fact, even the lowest resolution setting on your camera, Small 2, creates a picture that's more than large enough for most onscreen uses.

300 ppi

FIGURE 2-9:
A high-quality
print depends on
a high-resolution
original.

50 ppi

FIGURE 2-10:
At 50 ppi, the
image has a
jagged,
pixelated look.

50 ppi resampled to 300 ppi

FIGURE 2-11:
Adding pixels in a
photo editor
doesn't rescue a
low-resolution
original.

>> **File size:** Every additional pixel increases the amount of data required to create a digital picture file. So a higher-resolution image has a larger file size than a low-resolution image.

Large files present several problems:

- You can store fewer images on a memory card, computer hard drive, online storage site, and removable storage media such as a DVD.

- The camera needs more time to process and store the image data, which can hamper fast-action shooting.

- When you share photos online, larger files take longer to upload and download.

- When you edit photos in your photo software, your computer needs more resources to process large files.

As you can see, resolution is a bit of a sticky wicket. What if you aren't sure how large you want to print your images? What if you want to print your photos *and* share them online? Well, if you want to take the better–safe–than–sorry route, follow these recommendations:

>> **Shoot at a resolution suitable for print.** You then can create a low-resolution copy of the image for use online. In fact, your camera has a built-in Resize tool that can do the job; look for the tool on Playback Menu 3. Chapter 10 shows you how to use that feature.

>> **For everyday images, Medium is a good choice.** Even at the Medium setting, your pixel count (3984 x 2656) is a bit over what you need for an 8 x 10-inch print at 300 ppi.

>> **Choose Large for an image that you plan to crop, print very large, or both.** The benefit of maxing out resolution is that you have the flexibility to crop your photo and still generate a decent-sized print of the remaining image.

Consider Figure 2-12 as an example. When I took the original shot, shown on the left in the figure, I couldn't get close enough to fill the frame with my main subject of interest, the two juvenile herons at the center of that first frame. But because I took the picture using the Large resolution setting, I could crop the photo to eliminate everything but those birds and still have enough pixels left to produce a great print, as you see in the right image. In fact, the cropped version has enough pixels to print much larger than fits on this page.

FIGURE 2-12:
When you can't get close enough to fill the frame with the subject, capture the image at the Large resolution setting (left) and crop later (right).

Understanding file type (JPEG or Raw)

In addition to establishing the resolution of your photos, the Image Quality setting determines the *file type,* which refers to the kind of data file that the camera produces. Your camera offers two file types — JPEG (*jay-pegg*) and Raw (as in uncooked) — with a few variations of each. The next sections explain the pros and cons of JPEG and Raw.

JPEG: The imaging (and web) standard

This format is the default setting on your camera, as it is for most digital cameras. JPEG is popular for two main reasons:

» **Immediate usability:** JPEG is a longtime standard format for digital photos. All web browsers and email programs can display JPEG files, and you also can get JPEG photos printed at any retail outlet, whether it's an online or local printer. Additionally, any program that has photo capabilities, from photo-editing programs to word-processing programs, can handle JPEG files.

» **Small files:** JPEG files are smaller than Raw files. And smaller files mean that your pictures consume less room on your camera memory card and on your computer's hard drive.

The downside (you knew there had to be one) is that JPEG creates smaller files by applying *lossy compression.* This process actually throws away some image data. Too much compression produces a defect called *JPEG artifacting.* Figure 2-13 compares a high-quality original (left photo) with a heavily compressed version that exhibits artifacting (right photo).

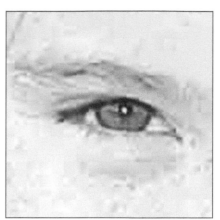

FIGURE 2-13:
The reduced quality of the right image is caused by excessive JPEG compression.

The amount of compression applied to your photos depends on whether you choose an Image Quality setting that carries the label Fine or Normal:

>> **Fine:** At this setting, very little compression is applied, so you shouldn't see many compression artifacts, if any. Canon uses the symbol that appears in the margin here to indicate the Fine compression level; however, the S2 setting also uses the Fine level even it doesn't sport the symbol.

>> **Normal:** Switch to Normal, and the compression amount rises, as does the chance of seeing some artifacting. Notice the jagged edge of the Normal icon, shown in the margin? That's your reminder that all may not be "smooth" sailing when you choose a Normal setting.

Note, though, that the Normal setting doesn't result in anywhere near the level of artifacting that you see in the example in Figure 2-13. Again, that example is exaggerated to help you recognize artifacting defects and understand how they differ from other image-quality issues. In fact, if you keep your image print or display size small, you aren't likely to notice a great deal of quality difference between the Fine and Normal compression levels. The differences become apparent only when you greatly enlarge a photo.

Given that the differences between Fine and Normal aren't all that easy to spot until you really enlarge the photo, is it okay to shift to Normal and enjoy the benefits of smaller files? Well, only you can decide what level of quality your pictures demand. For most photographers, the added file sizes produced by the Fine setting aren't a huge concern, given that the prices of memory cards fall all the time. Long-term storage is more of an issue; the larger your files, the faster you fill your computer's hard drive and the more space you need for archiving purposes.

But in the end, I believe that the best practice is to take the storage hit in exchange for the lower compression level of the Fine setting. You never know when a casual snapshot is going to be so great that you want to print or display it large enough that even minor quality loss becomes a concern. And of all the defects that you can correct in a photo editor, artifacting is one of the hardest to remove. So stick with Fine when shooting in the JPEG format.

If you don't want *any* risk of artifacting, bypass JPEG and change the file type to Raw. The next section offers details.

Raw: The purist's choice

The other picture-file type that you can create is *Camera Raw*, or just *Raw* for short. Raw is popular with advanced photographers for these reasons:

>> **Greater creative control:** With JPEG, internal camera software tweaks your images, adjusting color, exposure, and sharpness as needed to produce the results that Canon believes its customers prefer (or according to certain camera settings you chose, such as the Picture Style). With Raw, the camera simply records the original, unprocessed image data. The photographer then copies the image file to the computer and uses software known as a *raw converter* to produce the actual image, making decisions about color, exposure, and so on, at that point. The upshot is that "shooting Raw" enables you, not the camera, to have the final say on the visual characteristics of your image.

>> **More flexibility:** Having access to the Raw photo data means that you can reprocess the same photo with different settings over and over again without losing any quality.

>> **Higher bit depth:** *Bit depth* is a measure of how many color values an image file can contain. JPEG files restrict you to 8 bits each for the red, blue, and green color components, or *channels,* that make up a digital image, for a total of 24 bits. That translates to roughly 16.7 million possible colors. On your camera, a Raw file delivers a higher bit count, collecting 14 bits per channel.

Although jumping from 8 to 14 bits sounds like a huge difference, you may not ever notice any difference in your photos — that 8-bit palette of 16.7 million color values is more than enough for superb images. Where having the extra bits can come in handy is if you really need to adjust exposure, contrast, or color after the shot in your photo-editing program. In cases where you apply extreme adjustments, having the extra original bits sometimes helps avoid a problem known as *banding* or *posterization,* which creates abrupt color breaks where you should see smooth, seamless transitions. (A higher bit depth doesn't always prevent the problem, however, so don't expect miracles.)

>> **Best picture quality:** Because Raw doesn't apply the destructive compression associated with JPEG, you don't run the risk of the artifacting that can occur with JPEG.

But just like JPEG, Raw isn't without its disadvantages:

>> **You can't do much with your pictures until you process them in a Raw converter.** You can't share them online, for example, or have them printed at a retail photo-printing kiosk or other common printing site. So when you shoot Raw, you have to do some post-capture work, taking away time that you might prefer to spend shooting. Your camera has a built-in Raw conversion tool, which I detail in Chapter 10, but it's fairly limited. For more control, you should do your Raw processing on a computer, using a capable image-editing program. One such program is the free Canon offering, Digital Photo Professional 4, which I introduce in the image-download section of Chapter 10.

>> **Raw files are larger than JPEG files.** Unlike JPEG, Raw doesn't apply lossy compression to shrink files, so Raw files consume more storage space.

Whether the upside of Raw outweighs the downside is a decision for you to ponder based on your photographic needs, schedule, and computer comfort level. If you opt for Raw, you can select from these variations:

>> **RAW:** This is the regular, old-timey flavor of Canon's Raw format. No file compression is applied, so this setting produces much larger file sizes than even the JPEG/Fine option — about 27.2MB (megabytes) for the Raw file versus 8.4MB for JPEG/Fine. (*Note:* Don't confuse MB, megabytes, which refers to the size of the data container needed to hold the picture data, with MP, which refers to the number of megapixels in an image, also known as the image resolution.)

>> **cRAW:** Pronounced *see-Raw,* this is a relatively new format developed by Canon. The *c* stands for *compact* and refers to the fact that this file type produces a smaller image by applying some file compression, just like JPEG. But this compression is *lossless* — meaning that it doesn't result in the degradation of image quality that's associated with JPEG's lossy compression. A cRaw file on the T8i/850D has a file size of roughly 15.8MB.

The jury is still debating (and probably will continue to do so ad infinitum) whether the difference in image quality between cRaw and Raw is actually detectable and, if so, just how *much* so. My guess is that few people will be able to spot any flaws created by cRaw compression and then, only if they're doing serious "pixel peeping" (inspecting each pixel in an image for hints of image defects). For me, there's a larger issue: Because this is a relatively new format, some older photo-editing programs can't open or process cRaw files. If you plan to rely on Canon's software to process your Raw files, you'll probably be perfectly happy with cRaw. But do your own tests and make your own judgments. You may decide that cRaw offers all the benefits of Raw at file sizes that are significantly smaller than Raw files.

Whichever Raw option you choose, your files will carry the file extension *.CR3*, which simply translates to Canon Raw, version 3.

Final JPEG versus Raw recommendations

At this point, you may be finding all this technical goop a bit much, so here's a simplified summary of which option to choose:

» If you require the absolute best image quality and have the time and interest to do the Raw conversion process, shoot Raw. Choose standard Raw if file size is no issue; opt for cRaw if you want slightly smaller files and are willing to accept the possibility of a slightly lower image quality, albeit a difference that will probably (I said *probably*) be undetectable to most eyes at standard print and display sizes.

» If great photo quality is good enough for you, you don't have wads of spare time, or you aren't that comfortable with the computer, stick with JPEG Fine (the setting that sports the smooth arc symbol).

» To enjoy the best of both worlds, consider Raw+JPEG, which produces two files: the Raw file plus a JPEG file. The advantage is that you can share the JPEG version online or get prints made immediately and then process the Raw when you have time.

TIP

If you know that you only want to use the JPEG version for the web or email, choose the Small 2 Image Quality setting for that file to save space on your memory card. Raw files are always captured at maximum resolution, so you can use that version when you need a large file (if you want to print the photo, for example). If you need top quality for both files, choose Raw+JPEG Large/Fine.

Of course, creating two files for every image eats up substantially more space on your memory card and your computer's hard drive. The total file size hit is 48MB — 24MB for each file if you go the Raw+JPEG Large/Fine route. Drop down to cRaw+Large/Fine, and the combined file size is about 24.2MB.

» Avoid JPEG Normal (jagged-edge arc symbol) unless you're shooting Raw+JPEG and know that you'll only ever use the JPEG for the web or email or you're running critically low on memory-card space during a shoot. The smaller file size of the Normal option enables you to squeeze more frames into the remaining space. A better practice, however, is to carry a couple of spare cards so you don't have to make the trade-off between file size and image quality.

Adjusting the Image Quality setting

By default, the T8i/850D selects the Large/Fine JPEG Image Quality setting — a perfectly safe and reasonable option if you don't care to dig into all the whys and wherefores of the other choices. If you want to see whether that default is still in force or to change the setting, here's what you need to know:

>> **Viewing the current Image Quality setting:** An icon representing the current setting appears on the Quick Control and Live View displays. Figure 2-14 shows you where to find the symbols when shooting in the P, Tv, Av, and M modes. In other modes, the symbols appear elsewhere on the screen. The symbol in the figures represents the default setting, JPEG Large/Fine.

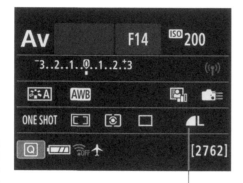 

FIGURE 2-14: This symbol represents the Image Quality setting.

Image Quality setting (Large/Fine)

>> **Changing the setting via Shooting Menu 1.** After opening the menu, tap Image Quality or highlight the option, as shown on the left in Figure 2-15, and press the Set button. You see the screen shown on the right in the figure, with all the available options listed.

As labeled in the figure, the text banner near the top of the screen indicates the total resolution and the pixel dimensions produced by the selected setting — 24 megapixels (MP) and 6000 x 4000 pixels, in the case of the Large/Fine JPEG option. At the end of the banner, the value in brackets tells you how many shots can fit in the available space on your memory card given the file size produced by the selected setting.

Below the banner, you see a row of options for the Raw format and a row for the JPEG format. To spin through the Raw settings, rotate the Main dial. (Remember, the little jagged half wheel at the end of the row represents the Main dial.) If you don't want to capture files in the Raw format, select the minus sign, as in the figure.

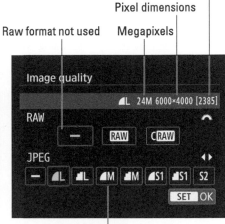

Shots remaining

Pixel dimensions

Raw format not used   Megapixels

FIGURE 2-15:
Here's a guide to
the hieroglyphics
you encounter
when changing
the Image Quality
setting via
Shooting Menu 1.

JPEG quality/size settings

To select a JPEG option, press the left or right edge of the Quick Control dial — this time, the left and right triangles near the right side of the screen, atop the row of JPEG symbols, are your reminder of how to cycle through the settings. To use Raw instead of JPEG, select the minus sign at the left end of the JPEG row.

TIP

Remember that for JPEG, the smooth arc represents the Fine quality setting, and the jagged arc represents the Normal quality option. You can read more about how the two options affect the look of your pictures in the preceding section. For the S2 (Small 2) option, the Fine quality setting is always applied, so there's no arc accompanying that option.

When you're happy with your choice, tap Set or press the Set button.

» **Changing the setting via the Quick Control method (P, Tv, Av, and M modes only):** You also can adjust the Image Quality setting by shifting to Quick Control mode, but things work a little differently depending on whether you're composing photos using the viewfinder or Live View mode.

- *Viewfinder photography:* After pressing the Q button or tapping the Q icon to shift to Quick Control mode, highlight the Image Quality icon, as shown on the left screen in Figure 2-16. A label describing the current setting appears at the bottom of the screen. Rotate the Quick Control dial or Main dial to display a strip of icons that represent the various Image Quality settings, as shown on the right in Figure 2-16. Not all the icons are visible at one time; to get to all the options, you need to scroll the display right or left. As you land upon a setting, the information strip updates to reflect the resulting pixel dimensions and shots remaining value.

 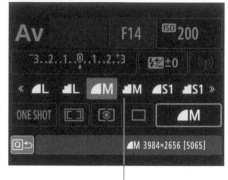

FIGURE 2-16:
In P, Tv, Av, and M exposure modes, you also can shift to Quick Control mode to change the Image Quality setting.

Current Image Quality setting   Rotate main dial to display other options

When you change the Image Quality setting this way, you don't see the minus signs that enable you to deselect one of the two formats. Instead, the scrolling list offers you every possibility of JPEG only, Raw only, and JPEG+Raw options. If you prefer to see everything in one place, highlight the Image Quality setting and then press the Set button (or just tap the Image Quality setting icon) to display all the settings on the same screen shown on the right in Figure 2-15.

To exit the Quick Control screen, press the Q button or tap the Q icon displayed in the lower-left corner of the screen.

- *Live View photography:* After shifting to Quick Control mode, highlight the Image Quality symbol, labeled on the left screen in Figure 2-17. Initially, you see the text banner shown on the left in the figure, letting you know what setting you're about to adjust, along with a strip of icons representing *some* of the available options at the bottom of the screen. The icons shown relate to just one file type, JPEG. (Hang with me, it will get a little less confusing shortly!) Rotate the Main dial or Quick Control dial to scroll through the available JPEG settings. As you do, the text banner updates to show you the total resolution, pixel dimensions, and shots remaining value for the currently selected option.

Image Quality setting   Available options   Setting details

If you want to choose the Raw format instead of — or in addition to — the JPEG format, press the Info button, as indicated on the text banner you see on the screens in Figure 2-17. Now you see a screen like the one shown in Figure 2-18, showing the available Raw settings. Rotate the Quick Control dial or Main dial to cycle through the three settings — Off (the minus sign), standard Raw, and cRaw. In the figure, I selected the standard Raw format. The text banner in the figure indicates that between the two selection screens, I've ordered the camera to record my next shots using both the JPEG Large/ Fine and Raw formats. Again, the resolution, pixel dimensions, and resulting available shot capacity of the memory card appear on the banner.

Select to turn off Raw capture

FIGURE 2-18:
To access Raw options from the Live View Quick Control screen, press the Info button.

To exit the screen after making your selection, tape the Exit arrow in the upper-right corner of the screen or press the Q button.

Setting the Photo Aspect Ratio

Normally, photos have a 3:2 *aspect ratio* (the relationship of a photo's width to its height). But you can choose a different aspect ratio if you shoot in the P, Tv, Av, or M exposure mode.

Adjust this picture property via the Still Img Aspect Ratio setting on Shooting Menu 1, as shown on the left in Figure 2-19, or, in Live View mode, press the Q button to activate the Quick Control settings screen, as shown on the right in the figure. Highlight the Aspect Ratio option, as shown in the figure, and rotate the Quick Control dial or Main dial to select from one of the four choices, shown at the bottom of the screen.

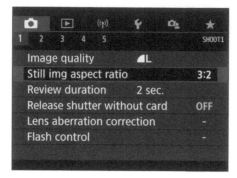

FIGURE 2-19: Change the Aspect Ratio setting from Shooting Menu 1 (left) or, in Live View mode, via the Quick Control settings screen (right).

Possible aspect ratios are 3:2, 4:3, 16:9, and 1:1. At any setting except 3:2, the viewfinder and Live View displays provide guides to indicate the framing area for the selected aspect ratio. In the Live View screen shown in Figure 2-20, for example, I selected the 1:1 setting; thus the square framing boundaries.

REMEMBER

How many pixels your image contains depends on the aspect ratio; at the 3:2 setting, you get the full complement of pixels delivered by your chosen Image Quality setting. After you change the setting using the Live View Quick Control method, a text banner shows the resulting resolution (in megapixels) and pixel dimensions, as shown in Figure 2-20.

Resolution

Pixel dimensions

FIGURE 2-20: When you change the Aspect Ratio setting using the Live View Quick Control method, the camera displays the resulting framing area and pixel dimensions.

TIP

Note, too, that if you set the Image Quality option to record JPEG pictures, the camera creates the different aspect ratios by cropping a 3:2 original, and the cropped data can't be recovered. Raw photos, although they appear cropped on the camera monitor, actually retain all the original data, which means you can change your mind about the aspect ratio later, when you process your Raw files. (Read about that subject in Chapter 10.)

Adding Flash

When the ambient light in a scene is insufficient to expose a photo, the built-in flash on your camera offers an easy, convenient solution. Upcoming sections provide details on various flash-related settings found on the T8i/850D. First, here are a few general bits of flash knowledge:

REMEMBER

>> **You must manually raise and lower the built-in flash.** Unlike previous models of this camera, the T8i/850D has no Flash button that you press to raise the built-in flash. Nor does the flash pop up on its own if you select Auto Flash mode and the camera thinks flash is needed — also a change from previous editions of the camera. Instead, a lightning bolt icon appears in the viewfinder or on the screen to indicate that flash is suggested.

For reasons that are a mystery to me, Canon decided that on this camera, the user has to physically lift the flash out of its hidey hole. To do so, look for the notches on the front sides of the flash. I labeled them "handles" in Figure 2-21 for lack of a better term. Grasp the flash cover by those handles and gently lift upwards to raise the flash. To close the flash, press down on the top of the flash cover.

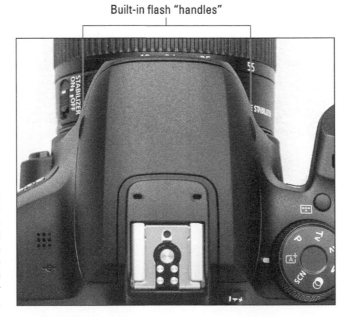

Built-in flash "handles"

FIGURE 2-21:
The secret to raising the built-in flash lies in these "handles;" use them to get a grip on the flash cover and then lift it up.

» **The built-in flash won't fire in certain SCN (Scene) Modes and Creative Filters modes, even if the flash is raised.** The affected SCN modes are Landscape, Candlelight, and HDR Backlight Control; the no-flash Creative Filters modes are the four HDR effects modes.

» **In dim lighting, you may want to raise the flash even when you don't actually want to use flash or you're shooting in an exposure mode that prohibits flash.** I know: "Wait, what?" Here's the deal: When there's not much ambient light and you press the shutter button halfway to initiate autofocusing, the camera emits a small beam of light from the flash to help the autofocus system find a target. That light is called the AF-assist beam, and it's only available when the flash unit is up. If you want the AF-assist beam but not the flash, some exposure modes enable you to disable the flash by setting the Flash Firing setting to Off, as discussed in the next section.

» **The effective range of the built-in flash depends on the ISO setting.** The ISO setting affects the camera's sensitivity to light; Chapter 4 has details. At the lowest ISO setting, ISO 100, the maximum reach of the flash ranges from about 3 to 10 feet, depending on whether you're using a telephoto or wide angle lens, respectively. To illuminate a subject that's farther away, use a higher ISO speed or an auxiliary flash that offers greater power than the built-in flash.

» **Watch for shadows cast by the lens or a lens hood.** When you shoot with a long lens, you can wind up with unwanted shadows caused by the flash light hitting the lens. Ditto for a lens hood.

» **While the flash is recycling, a "Busy" signal appears in the viewfinder and Live View display.** Figure 2-22 shows you how the signal appears in the viewfinder (look in the lower-left corner of the data display). The lightning bolt shown in the screen on the right side of the figure indicates that flash is ready to fire. In the Live View display, the lightning bolt appears near the lower-left corner of the screen, but only in display modes that show detailed shooting data. (Press the Info button to change the display mode.)

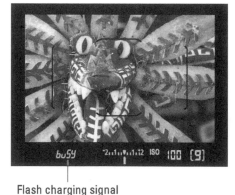 

FIGURE 2-22: The "busy" signal means that the flash is recharging; the lightning bolt means the flash is good to go.

Flash charging signal   Flash ready symbol

REMEMBER

» **Shutter speed affects flash results.** Detailed in Chapter 4, *shutter speed* determines how long the camera's shutter remains open, allowing light to hit the image sensor and expose the photo. In other words, shutter speed determines *exposure time,* which is measured in seconds.

Shutter speed has an impact on the overall image brightness and also determines whether action appears frozen (fast shutter speed) or blurry (slow shutter speed). But it also plays a role in how much flash power the camera uses to light your subject, which in turn affects the look of your flash pictures, as follows:

- *Slow shutter speeds produce softer flash lighting and brighter backgrounds.* The longer the shutter remains open, the more time the camera has to soak up the ambient light. And the more ambient light, the less flash light is needed to expose the image. Because light from the built-in flash is narrow and fairly harsh, reducing flash power typically results in softer, more flattering lighting. Additionally, objects beyond the reach of the flash are brighter than when you use a fast shutter speed.

  Figure 2-23 offers an example: The left image was taken at a shutter speed of 1/60 second; the right, at 1/8 second. How slow a shutter speed you need to get the background brightness you want depends on the amount of ambient light, so some experimentation is needed.

Shutter speed, 1/60 second   Shutter speed, 1/8 second

FIGURE 2-23: When you use a slow shutter speed with flash, backgrounds are brighter, and the flash light is softer.

WARNING

A slow shutter speed can produce blurring if the camera or subject moves during the exposure. So use a tripod and tell your subject to remain as still as possible.

For more about combining flash with a long exposure time, check out the information detailing the Slow Synchro option, which I cover in the last section of this chapter. This picture-taking setup is usually referred to as *slow-sync flash.*

- *With a fast shutter speed, flash is the primary light source, leaving objects beyond the flash range dark.* That result can be helpful when you want to diminish the impact of distracting background objects. Notice how the sand pit in the background of the first photo in Figure 2-23 nearly fades from view, for example. The downside is that because more flash power is needed, the light can appear harsh.

TIP

Unfortunately, you have control over shutter speed only in the Creative Zone modes (P, Tv, Av, and M). However, if you want the slow-shutter flash look and aren't ready for the advanced exposure modes, set the Mode dial to SCN and try Night Portrait mode. The camera automatically selects a slower shutter speed in that exposure mode.

» **The range of available shutter speeds for flash photography is more limited than when you go flash-free.** This restriction is due to the way the camera has to synchronize the flash firing with the opening of the shutter. Here are the numbers you need to know:

- *The fastest shutter speed available for flash photography is 1/200 second.* Because a quickly moving subject may appear blurry even at 1/200 second, flash isn't a good tool for fast-action photography. Again, see Chapter 4 for help understanding the role of shutter speed in action photography.

- *The slowest shutter speed depends on the exposure mode.* In Basic Zone modes, the slowest setting is 1/60 second. The exception is Night Portrait SCN mode, which automatically uses a slow shutter to produce results similar to what you see on the right in Figure 2-23. You can't control the shutter speed in that mode or any Basic Zone mode, though, so don't think too much about it.

  In P, Tv, and Av modes, which do enable you to adjust shutter speed, you can set the exposure time (shutter speed) to as long as 30 seconds when using flash. In M mode, you can also use a special shutter speed, *Bulb,* which keeps the shutter open as long as the shutter button is depressed. Chapter 4 explains how to adjust shutter speed.

These guidelines as well as other information presented in the rest of the chapter apply to using the built-in flash. If you attach an external flash, things work differently, so consult the flash unit's instruction manual. The camera's instruction manual also contains extensive flash information that may be of interest to advanced flash photographers; unfortunately, this book doesn't not have enough pages to cover all those features. If you do attach an external flash, you may be able to add flash to pictures taken in exposure modes that put the built-in flash off-limits, such as Landscape SCN mode.

Setting the flash to fire (or not)

I know that I should appreciate it when camera companies make basic options complex, because if they didn't, you might not need my help sorting things out. But even I think that Canon's gone a bit overboard when it comes to the basic flash setting, Flash Firing. The options aren't hard to understand, but which ones are available, how you determine the current setting, and how to change the setting varies depending on the current exposure mode.

Let's start with the easy stuff. There are three possible settings, represented by the icons in the following list:

>> **Auto:** This setting gives the camera control over whether the flash fires (although you still have to manually raise the flash unit, as outlined in the preceding section). When you press the shutter button halfway to initiate autofocusing and exposure metering, the camera measures the ambient light. If the camera thinks more light is needed, the flash fires. Otherwise, the flash doesn't go off, even when the flash unit is raised.

>> **On:** If the flash is raised, it fires when you fully depress the shutter button, regardless of the ambient light. To find out why you might want to use this setting even in bright light, such as for an outdoor portrait on a sunny day, see the sidebar "Using flash outdoors," later in this chapter.

>> **Off:** The flash does not fire, no way, no how, even if the flash is raised. This option is useful when you're shooting in dim lighting and need the AF-assist beam for autofocusing, but you don't want to add flash light to the scene, as discussed in the preceding section.

Now for the breakdown of which exposure modes offer which (if any) of the three Flash Firing settings:

>> **Auto, On, and Off:** Scene Intelligent Auto and P (programmed autoexposure).

>> **Auto and On:** You can choose either of these options in the following SCN modes: Portrait, Smooth Skin, Group Photo, Close-Up, and Kids. The Auto and On flash settings are also available in all Creative Filters modes except the HDR modes.

>> **On and Off:** Tv (shutter-priority autoexposure), Av (aperture-priority autoexposure), and M (Manual exposure).

>> **Auto only:** Night Portrait mode (available when the Mode dial is set to SCN).

>> **On only:** This is your only Flash Firing choice for two SCN modes, Handheld Night Scene and Food.

Remember, no matter what the Flash Firing setting, if you keep the flash unit closed, the flash can't fire. By the same token, even if the flash is raised, it won't fire if you set the Mode dial to SCN and select the Landscape, Sports, Candlelight, and HDR Backlight Control scene type. Nor will it fire when you shoot in Creative Filters mode and select one of the HDR filters available in that mode. When the flash *is* raised and you're using a no-flash exposure mode or set the Flash Firing setting to Off, the AF-assist beam will be emitted from the flash unit in dim lighting.

How you view and adjust the Flash Firing setting also depends on your exposure mode and whether the camera is in Live View mode or using the viewfinder. Here's the drill:

>> **Checking the Flash Firing setting in Basic Zone exposure modes:** If the exposure mode offers a choice of Flash Firing settings, a symbol representing the setting appears in the Quick Control and Live View displays. For example, Figure 2-24 shows how the screens look in Scene Intelligent Auto mode. You also see a lightning bolt symbol in the viewfinder, as shown on the second screen in Figure 2-24.

>> **Checking the Flash Firing Settings in Creative Zone modes (P, Tv, Av, and M):** During viewfinder photography, the Quick Control display shows a lightning bolt symbol when the flash is set to On, but you have to be quick to spot it: Press the shutter button halfway, and the symbol appears for a second or two at the bottom of the screen, to the left of the shots remaining value. If the Flash Firing option is set to Off, no symbol appears to remind you.

FIGURE 2-24:
These symbols
indicate the Auto
Flash Firing
mode.

Flash Firing setting

The Live View display also shows a lightning bolt to represent the Flash On setting; look in the area labeled in Figure 2-25. (You may need to press the Info button a couple of times to get to a Live View display that shows the setting.) However, the Flash Off symbol appears only when you use that setting in P mode. I know, I don't get it either. I guess the thinking is that in the M, Tv, and Av modes, you have only two Flash Firing options — On and Off — so you can just assume that if you don't see the lightning bolt, the function is set to Off.

Flash Firing On symbol

FIGURE 2-25:
In the P, Tv, Av, and M modes, a symbol representing the Flash Firing setting appears in the Live View display.

In the viewfinder, the lightning bolt appears as shown on the right in Figure 2-24 if the Flash Firing option is set to On or, in P mode, if you selected Auto and the camera plans to use flash.

» **Changing the Flash Firing setting:** You have a couple of options, but as usual, which ones you can use depends on the exposure mode:

- *Select the setting by choosing Flash Control from Shooting Menu 1.* Although you can go the menu route in any exposure mode, Shooting Menu 1 appears different depending on whether you're shooting in a Basic or Creative Zone mode. The left screen in Figure 2-26 shows the Basic Zone version; the right screen shows the Creative Zone version, which offers lots more flash-related settings. (I cover these later in the chapter.)

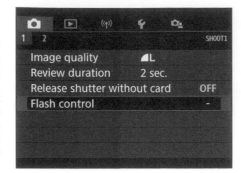
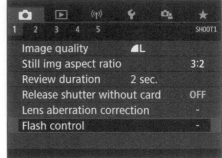

FIGURE 2-26:
Select Flash Control from Shooting Menu 1, shown here as it appears in a Basic Zone exposure mode (left) and Creative Zone mode (right).

On the screen that appears after you choose Flash Control from either menu, select Flash Firing. You then get a screen offering the available flash options for your current exposure mode. Figure 2-27 shows this part of the process as it looks when you shoot in the P exposure mode. (The screen on the left in Figure 2-27 is much less complex when you shoot in a Basic Zone exposure mode.)

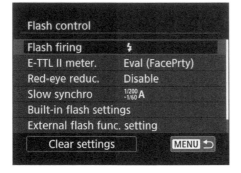

FIGURE 2-27:
Select Flash Firing (left) to display the options available for the current exposure mode (right).

- *Set the Flash Firing option by using the Quick Control method.* This method isn't available in the P, Tv, Av, and M exposure modes, unfortunately. But if you're shooting in Scene Intelligent Auto mode and using the viewfinder to compose your photos, press the Q button to shift to Quick Control mode and then tap the Built-in Flash option to activate it. Figure 2-28 shows you where to find the option; when selected, it's surrounded by an orange border. After you select the Built-in Flash icon, rotate the Main dial or the Quick Control dial to choose the flash option you prefer. You also can press Set to see all your Flash Firing options on a single screen.

When you shoot in Scene Intelligent Auto and use Live View, *don't* press the Q button. Instead, just tap the Flash Firing option to activate and adjust the setting. Pressing Q in this scenario opens the door to the Creative Assist features, explained in Chapter 3.

In SCN and Creative Filters exposure modes that offer flash, press the Q button to shift to Quick Control mode for both viewfinder and Live View photography. You can then tap or select the Flash Firing setting to adjust it.

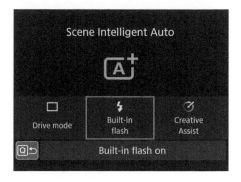

FIGURE 2-28:
In Scene Intelligent Auto mode, you can change the setting via the Quick Control screen.

TIP

USING FLASH OUTDOORS

Although most people think of flash as a tool for nighttime and low-light photography, adding light from the built-in flash can improve many photos that you shoot outdoors during bright daylight. If the main light source — the sun or bright sky — is above or behind your subject, there may not be enough light hitting the front of the subject to expose it properly. In outdoor portraits, the problem is exacerbated when your subject's face is partially shaded by a hood or cap. The no-flash and with-flash examples illustrate how adding flash can fix the problem.

Be aware of a couple issues that arise when you supplement the sun with flash, however:

- **You may need to make a white balance adjustment.** Adding flash may result in colors that are slightly warmer (more yellow/red) or cooler (bluish) because the camera's white balancing system can get tripped up by mixed light sources. If you don't appreciate the shift in colors, see Chapter 6 to find out how to make a white balance adjustment to solve the problem.

(continued)

(continued)

- **You may need to stop down the aperture or lower ISO to avoid overexposing the photo.** When you use flash, the fastest shutter speed you can use is 1/200 second, which may not be fast enough to prevent overexposure if you use a wide aperture or high ISO setting. If you use some external Canon flash units, you may be able to access shutter speeds faster than 1/200 second, solving the problem. Chapter 4 explains all these exposure settings and also offers other ways to solve exposure problems.

- **You must shoot in an exposure mode that lets you set the Flash Firing option to On.** In Auto Flash Firing mode, the camera is unlikely to see the need for flash because of the bright ambient light. Scene Intelligent Auto mode and P, Tv, Av, and M exposure modes all offer the On setting; see the section "Setting the flash to fire (or not)" for other exposure modes that provide the setting.

Flash off   Flash on

Adding Red-Eye Reduction

Red-eye, the phenomenon that turns eyes red in flash portraits, is caused when flash light bounces off a subject's retinas and is reflected back to the camera lens. If you notice red-eye in your portraits, try enabling Red-Eye Reduction. When you turn on this flash feature, the Red-Eye Reduction Lamp on the front of the camera lights up when you press the shutter button halfway and focus is achieved. The light from the lamp shrinks the subject's pupils, reducing the amount of flash light that enters the eye and, thus, the chances of red-eye. The flash itself fires when you press the shutter button the rest of the way. (Warn your subjects to wait for the flash, or they may stop posing after they see the light from the Red-Eye Reduction Lamp.)

You can enable Red-Eye Reduction in any exposure mode that permits flash. Choose Flash Control from Shooting Menu 1, as outlined in the preceding section (the exact steps depend on your shooting mode and whether Live View is engaged). When the Flash Control options screen appears, choose Red Eye Reduc. to enable the red-eye reduction feature, as shown in Figure 2-29. (The screen shown in the figure appears in the P, Tv, Av, and M exposure modes; in Basic Zone modes, the screen offers only two options, Flash Firing and Red-Eye Reduction.)

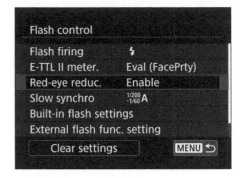

FIGURE 2-29:
Open Shooting Menu 1 and choose Flash Control to access the Red-Eye Reduction feature.

A few tips on the Red-Eye Reduction feature:

>> The camera doesn't include any symbols in the viewfinder or other displays to remind you that Red-Eye Reduction mode is in force.

>> Changing the setting affects all exposure modes, regardless of which mode you were using when you turned the feature on or off.

>> After you press the shutter button halfway, a row of vertical bars appears at the bottom of the viewfinder display. The bars quickly turn off, starting from the outside and working toward the center. For best results, wait until all the bars are off to take the picture. The delay gives the subject's pupils time to constrict in response to the Red-Eye Reduction Lamp. This countdown display isn't available during Live View shooting.

Remember that this feature is named Red-Eye Reduction, not Red-Eye Elimination. Even with the option turned on, you may wind up with red-eye in some portraits. Fortunately, the problem can usually be fixed by using the red-eye correction tool built into your camera (see Playback Menu 2) or in the photo software that comes with your camera. I explain how to use the camera's red-eye removal tool in Chapter 10.

Reviewing Advanced Flash Options

In the P, Tv, Av, and M exposure modes, you have access to flash options beyond those already discussed (Flash Firing and Red-Eye Reduction). The rest of this chapter fills you in on these additional flash options.

Adjusting flash output with Flash Exposure Compensation

On some occasions, you may want a little more or less flash power than the camera thinks is appropriate. If so, take advantage of *Flash Exposure Compensation*.

Flash Exposure Compensation settings are stated in terms of *exposure value (EV)* numbers. A setting of EV 0.0 indicates no flash adjustment; you can increase the flash power to EV +2.0 or decrease it to EV −2.0.

Figure 2-30 shows an example of how changing the flash power can affect your results. The left image shows you a flash-free shot. Clearly, a little more light was needed, but at normal flash power, the flash was too strong, blowing out the highlights in some areas, as shown in the middle image. Reducing the flash power to EV −1.3 resulted in a softer light output that straddled the line perfectly between no flash and too much flash, as shown in the third photo.

No flash	Flash EV 0.0	Flash EV -1.3

FIGURE 2-30: When normal flash output is too strong, lower the Flash Exposure Compensation value.

As for boosting the flash output, well, you may find it necessary on some occasions, but don't expect the built-in flash to work miracles even at a Flash Exposure Compensation of +2.0. Any built-in flash has a limited range, so the light simply can't reach faraway objects.

Here are ways to enable Flash Exposure Compensation:

>> **Quick Control method (available only for viewfinder photography):** After shifting to Quick Control mode, highlight the Flash Exposure Compensation value, as shown on the left in Figure 2-31. This value does not appear on the Quick Control display when the setting is EV 0.0 (no adjustment) until you shift to Quick Control mode.

FIGURE 2-31:
For viewfinder
photography, you
can change the
Flash Exposure
Compensation
from the Quick
Control screen.

After highlighting the Flash Exposure Compensation value, rotate the Quick Control dial or the Main dial to set the amount of flash adjustment. Or, if you prefer, tap the Flash Exposure Compensation icon or highlight it and press the Set button. The screen shown in Figure 2-32 appears. Adjust the setting by tapping the arrows at the end of the settings scale, by dragging your finger along the scale, or by pressing the right or left edge of the Quick Control dial. Tap the return arrow (bottom-right corner of the screen) or press the Set button to exit the screen.

FIGURE 2-32:
To see just the Flash Exposure Compensation settings, as here, tap the setting's symbol after switching to Quick Control mode.

>> **Shooting Menu 1:** You also can get to the Flash Exposure Compensation setting through Shooting Menu 1, but it's a long slog: Start by choosing Flash Control from the menu. Next, choose Built-in Flash Settings, as shown on the left in Figure 2-33, and then select Exp. Comp. from the next screen, as shown on the right in the figure.

When Flash Exposure Compensation is set to any value except EV 0.0, the value remains visible in the Quick Control display after you exit Quick Control mode. In the Live View display, the setting appears in the area indicated on the left screen in Figure 2-34. In the viewfinder, you see a +/- flash symbol without the actual Flash Exposure Compensation value, as shown on the right in Figure 2-34.

FIGURE 2-33:
After selecting
Flash Control
from Shooting
Menu 1, follow
this path to get to
the Flash
Exposure
Compensation
setting.

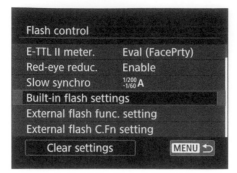
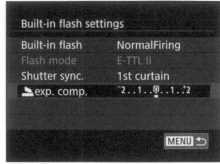

FIGURE 2-34:
When flash
compensation is
enabled, the
value appears in
the detailed Live
View display (left);
the viewfinder
just shows that
the feature is
enabled (right).

Flash Exposure Compensation amount   Flash Exposure Compensation enabled symbol

WARNING

Any Flash Exposure Compensation adjustment you make remains in force until you reset the value to EV 0.0, even if you turn off the camera. So be sure to check the setting before using your flash. Additionally, the Auto Lighting Optimizer feature, available in the P, Tv, Av, and M exposure modes, can interfere with the effect produced by Flash Exposure Compensation, so you might want to disable it. The setting is accessible via Shooting Menu 2; Chapter 4 has details.

Locking the flash exposure

You might never notice it, but when you press the shutter button to take a picture with flash enabled, the camera emits a brief *preflash* before the actual flash. This preflash is used to determine the proper flash power needed to expose the image.

TIP

Occasionally, the information that the camera collects from the preflash can be off-target because of the assumptions the system makes about what area of the frame is likely to contain your subject. To address this problem, your camera has a feature called *Flash Exposure Lock*, or FE Lock. This tool enables you to set the flash power based on only the center of the frame. It's especially helpful when your subject is much brighter or darker than the background, a situation that can cause the flash to either use too little or too much light to properly illuminate the subject.

Unfortunately, FE Lock isn't available in Live View mode. If you want to use this feature, you must use the viewfinder to frame and shoot your images. Additionally, you must shoot in one of the Creative Zone exposure modes (P, Tv, Av, or M).

Follow these steps to use FE Lock:

1. **With the flash raised and the Flash Firing option set to On, frame your photo so that your subject falls under the center autofocus point.**

   You want your subject smack in the middle of the frame. You can reframe the shot after locking the flash exposure, if you want. Remember: You get to the Flash Firing option by choosing Flash Control from Shooting Menu 1.

2. **Press the shutter button halfway.**

   The camera meters the light in the scene. If you're using autofocusing, focus is set on your subject. (If focus is set on another spot in the frame, see Chapter 5 to find out how to select the center autofocus point.) You can now lift your finger off the shutter button, if you want.

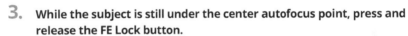

3. **While the subject is still under the center autofocus point, press and release the FE Lock button.**

   You can see the button in the margin here. The camera emits the preflash, and the letters FEL display for a second in the viewfinder. (FEL stands for *flash exposure lock.*) Don't worry if you don't see the brief FEL label; after it disappears, the camera lets you know that flash exposure lock is in force by displaying an asterisk symbol — the one that appears on the FE Lock button on the camera body — next to the flash icon at the left end of the viewfinder data display.

4. **If needed, reestablish focus on your subject.**

   In autofocus mode, press and hold the shutter button halfway. (Take this step only if you released the shutter button after Step 2.) In manual focus mode, rotate the focusing ring on the lens to establish focus.

5. **Reframe the image to the composition you want.**

   While you do, keep the shutter button pressed halfway to maintain focus if you're using autofocusing.

6. **Press the shutter button the rest of the way to take the picture.**

   The image is captured using the flash output setting you established in Step 3.

TIP

Flash exposure lock is also helpful when you're shooting portraits. The preflash sometimes causes people to blink, which means that with normal flash shooting — in which the actual flash and exposure occur immediately after the preflash — their eyes are closed at the exact moment of the exposure. With flash exposure lock, you can fire the preflash and then wait a second or two for the subject's eyes to recover before you take the actual picture.

Better yet, the flash exposure setting remains in force for about 16 seconds, meaning that you can shoot a series of images using the same flash setting without firing another preflash at all.

Investigating other flash options

In the P, Tv, Av, and M modes, you can access additional flash options by select Flash Control on Shooting Menu 1, as shown on the left in Figure 2-35. The Flash Control screen, shown on the right in the figure, offers the following settings in addition to the Flash Firing, Red-Eye Reduction, and Flash Exposure Compensation features already discussed:

>> **E-TTL II Meter:** The option name refers to the Canon flash metering system. The *E* stands for *evaluative, TTL* stands for *through the lens,* and *II* refers to the fact that this system is an update to the first version of the system.

At any rate, this menu option enables you to choose from three flash-metering setups. You probably don't need me to tell you to choose Eval (FacePrty) — which sounds like it should be used for face parties but actually stands for face priority. It's supposed to set the flash power based on the ambient light falling on people's faces, and even though the camera manual warns that it may not always give the right results, it's worth a try.

FIGURE 2-35: When you shoot in the P, Tv, Av, or M exposure modes, choose Flash Control from Shooting Menu 1 (left) to uncover advanced flash settings (right).

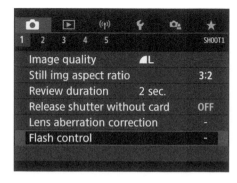
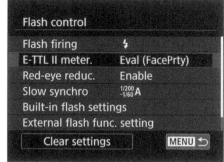

In regular Evaluative mode, the camera exposes the background using ambient light when possible and then sets the flash power to serve as fill light on the subject. If you instead select the Average option, the flash is used as the primary light source, meaning the flash power is set to expose the entire scene without relying on ambient light. Typically, this results in a more powerful (and possibly harsh) flash lighting and dark backgrounds.

» **Slow Synchro:** Earlier in this chapter, Figure 2-23 illustrates how shutter speed affects the look of a flash photo. A slow shutter speed produces brighter backgrounds and softer lighting, as illustrated in the figure. At the same time, using a slow shutter speed requires a very steady hand or use of a tripod to avoid camera shake that can blur the photo.

Because combining a slow shutter speed with flash is known as *slow-sync flash,* you might assume that the Slow Synchro menu option sets up your camera to take photos that have the slow-sync look. That would be a reasonable assumption, but it's not what this option actually does.

The Slow Synchro menu option actually sets the range of shutter speeds the camera can select when you use flash in the Av and P exposure modes. In both modes, the camera sets the shutter speed for you.

By default, the camera can select shutter speeds ranging from 1/200 second to 1/60 second when you use flash in the P and Av exposure modes. That range should work well for most photos, and I suggest sticking with it. But if you're after a slow-sync flash look, you can try changing to the 1/200 to 1/30 second setting. There's no guarantee that the camera will set the shutter speed at the low end of that range, though; this setting just gives it the option to do so. The third option fixes the shutter speed at 1/200 second for every flash shot. You might want to use that setting when you're trying to use flash with a moving subject — the faster shutter speed can help freeze the action. Just keep in mind that with a fast shutter, the object nearest the flash will be bright while the background may be very dark.

REMEMBER

My advice, however, is that if you want to control shutter speed in your flash photos, you're better off shooting in the Tv or M exposure modes, both of which let you control the shutter speed. The top shutter speed with flash remains 1/200 second, but you can drop as low as 1/30 second in Tv mode when you're after the slow-sync flash look. In M mode, you can use a shutter speed as slow as 30 seconds or even set the shutter to Bulb mode, which keeps the shutter open for as long as you keep the shutter button depressed. The flash fires at the beginning of a bulb-mode exposure, assuming that you set the Flash Firing mode to On. (Chapter 4 makes all this shutter-speed stuff clear, if the term is new to you.)

» **Built-in Flash Settings:** Choose this option, as shown on the left in Figure 2-36, to access the following settings, shown on the right in the figure:

- *Built-in Flash:* This function enables you to configure the built-in flash for normal use (NormalFiring) or choose between two wireless flash methods, Easy Wireless or Custom Wireless. In both modes, the built-in flash is used to wirelessly trigger compatible off-camera flash units.

   The Canon wireless flash system is a great way to gain added lighting flexibility without having to carry around a lot of bulky studio lights. Although working with that system is beyond the scope (or page count!) of this book, the camera instruction manual has technical details, and you can find many tutorials and other useful information about multiple-flash photography online.

FIGURE 2-36:
Select Built-in
Flash Settings to
set even more
options, such as
the flash sync
mode (first- or
second-curtain
sync).

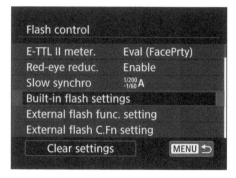 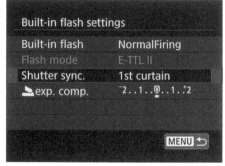

- *Flash Mode:* Ignore this option. It's related to using an external flash and isn't adjustable when you use the built-in flash.

- *Shutter Sync:* By default, the flash fires at the beginning of the exposure. This flash timing, known as *first-curtain sync,* is the best choice for most subjects. The other option, known as *second-curtain sync* (or rear-curtain sync) is designed for creating motion-trail effects and requires you to also use a shutter speed slower than 1/30 second. I used this flash setting and a shutter speed of 3 seconds when shooting the clock shown in Figures 2-37 and 2-38. Yes, I'm the kind of person who has a dog-face clock on my living room wall. At the bottom of the clock, there's a tongue that wags back and forth as the seconds tick off. I regret that you can't see in this photo how dang adorable it is.

Shutter speed, 3 seconds

Flash Shutter Sync mode, 2nd curtain

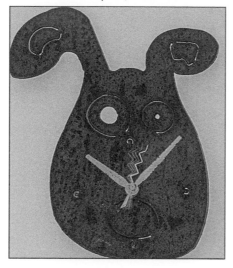

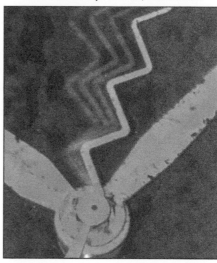

FIGURE 2-37:
With rear-curtain sync, motion trails appear to follow the moving object, as here.

Shutter speed, 3 seconds

Flash Shutter Sync mode, 1st-curtain sync

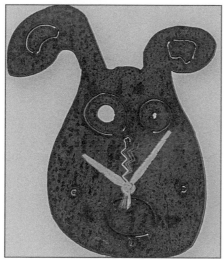

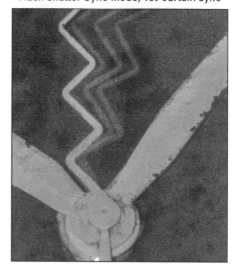

FIGURE 2-38:
With front-curtain sync (the default setting) and a long exposure, motion trails appear forward of the moving object, as shown here.

Okay, with my decorating choice now adequately covered, back to the subject at hand, which is how the timing of the flash affects the way moving objects appear in a photo. In my clock example, the second hand is the moving object, so take a moment to notice the difference between the way the second hand was rendered in Figure 2-37, which used 2nd curtain sync, and in Figure 2-38, which was taken using 1st curtain sync.

To understand why the flash timing altered the outcome, you need to know that when you use a slow shutter speed, the moving object is recorded as a faint, blurred version of itself, appearing several times throughout the frame. When the flash fires, the object is recorded as solid, with its action frozen at that moment. If the flash fires at the beginning of the exposure, the motion trails created by the object blur appear in *front* of the moving object, as shown in Figure 2-38. I suppose you could use such an image to illustrate a disruption of the time-space continuum, which science-fiction lovers know is a dangerous move. But if you want the image to make visual sense in the real world, you want the motion trails to follow the moving object, as they do in Figure 2-37. On the T8i/850D, the flash fires twice in this mode: once when you press the shutter button and again at the end of the exposure.

Don't forget that you must set the shutter speed slower than 1/30 second; otherwise, the camera switches to first-curtain sync automatically. And in order to use that slow of a shutter speed, you must shoot in the Tv or M exposure mode.

>> **External Flash controls:** The last two options on the Flash Control list relate to external flash heads; they don't affect the performance of the built-in flash. However, they apply only to Canon EX-series Speedlites that enable you to control the flash through the camera. If you own such a flash, refer to the flash manual for details.

>> **Clear Settings:** Choose this option to access three settings that restore flash defaults. The first one, Clear Built-in Flash Set, restores the settings for the built-in flash. Sorry, you could have figured that out for yourself. The second option restores defaults for external flash settings, and the third restores the external flash head's Custom Function menu settings.

Chapter **3**

Taking Great Pictures, Automatically

When you set your camera to a Creative Zone exposure mode (P, Tv, Av, or M), you can access a slew of features that enable you to precisely control exposure, color, focus, and more. But if you're not yet acquainted with those advanced options — or you're just not interested in "going there" right now — take advantage of Basic Zone exposure modes. In these modes, the camera selects most picture-taking settings for you, providing almost fully automatic photography.

Even in these modes, however, you can get better results by following the techniques outlined in this chapter. In addition to walking you through the steps of taking your first pictures in Scene Intelligent Auto mode, the pages to come contain tips for using SCN modes (Portrait, Landscape, and so on). The one Basic Zone mode not covered in this chapter is Creative Filter mode; see Chapter 12 for help with that special-effects shooting mode.

REMEMBER

If what you see on your monitor looks vastly different from what you see in figures here and elsewhere, your camera is likely set to the Guided display level, as it is by default. For reasons explained in Chapter 1, this book provides instructions based on the Standard display level. To set your camera to match, open the Display Level menu. Set the first two menu options to Standard and the other two to Disable.

Using Scene Intelligent Auto Mode

For the simplest camera operation, set the Mode dial to Scene Intelligent Auto, as shown in Figure 3-1. Most people refer to this setting as simply *Auto,* but this book sticks with the official Canon name so that when you search the Canon website or the instruction manual, you're sure to land at the right spot.

Scene Intelligent Auto mode

REMEMBER

The only tricky part about using Scene Intelligent Auto is that how you focus the camera varies depending on whether you use the viewfinder to compose your images or opt for Live View mode, which displays a live preview of your subject on the monitor. The next two sections provide the basics for each shooting option. After you get familiar

FIGURE 3-1:
Set the Mode dial to Scene Intelligent Auto for point-and-shoot simplicity.

with those basics, check out the upcoming section "Exploring Creative Assist adjustments," which explains how you can tweak picture characteristics such as color saturation and the amount of background blur.

Viewfinder shooting

The following steps show you how to take a picture the "old fashioned" way, looking through the viewfinder to frame your subject:

1. **Set the Mode dial to Scene Intelligent Auto (refer to Figure 3-1).**

   The Quick Control display appears, as shown in Figure 3-2.

2. **Set the lens focusing method (auto or manual).**

   On the 18–55mm kit lens, set the switch to AF, as shown in Figure 3-3, to take advantage of autofocusing. For manual focusing, set the switch to MF (and ignore upcoming instructions related to autofocusing).

FIGURE 3-2:
Even in Scene Intelligent Auto mode, you have control over the Drive mode and Flash mode.

If you use a different Canon lens or a third-party lens, check its instruction manual to find out how to set the lens to your preferred focusing method.

3. **If you're handholding the camera, set the Image Stabilizer switch to the On setting, as shown in Figure 3-3.**

Image stabilization helps produce sharper images by compensating for camera movement that can occur when you handhold the camera. If you're using a tripod, you can save battery power by turning stabilization off. Again, if you use a lens other than one of the two kit lenses, check your lens manual for details about its stabilization feature, if provided.

Image Stabilizer switch

Manual focusing ring   Auto/Manual focus switch

FIGURE 3-3:
Set the lens switch to AF to use autofocusing; enable Image Stabilization for handheld shooting.

4. **If you want to use flash or are uncertain about whether you need the extra light it provides, raise the flash unit and specify the Flash Firing mode (Auto or On).**

To bring the flash out of hiding, grip the flash cover by the small tabs that extend from the front sides of the flash cover and gently lift upward. To let the camera decide whether flash lighting is needed, set the Flash Firing mode to Auto (the default setting, shown in Figure 3-2). To force the flash to fire, set the mode to On.

The fastest way to adjust the Flash Firing setting is via the Quick Control method. Press the Q button or tap the Q symbol in the lower-left corner of the display. Highlight the Flash Firing setting and then rotate the Main dial or Quick Control dial to adjust the setting. Press or tap Q again to return to shooting mode.

Don't want to use flash? Just leave the flash unit closed. Even in dim lighting, the camera won't raise and fire the flash automatically, as it did when you used previous editions of this camera (and most other EOS Rebel models).

Don't want to use flash? Just leave the flash unit closed. Even in dim lighting, the camera won't raise and fire the flash automatically, as it did when you used previous editions of this camera (and most other EOS Rebel models).

5. **Set the Drive mode to Single.**

   At this setting, which is the default, the camera takes a single picture each time you press the shutter button. The Single Drive mode is represented by the rectangle you see in Figure 3-2. The fastest way to access the setting is to press the left edge of the Quick Control dial. You also can use the Quick Control method as just described for changing the Flash Firing setting. Chapter 2 offers more details about the Drive mode setting.

6. **Looking through the viewfinder, frame the image so that your subject appears within the autofocus brackets.**

   The brackets, labeled in Figure 3-4, represent the area of the frame that the camera analyzes to set the focusing distance when you use autofocusing.

7. **Press and hold the shutter button halfway down.**

   The camera's autofocus and autoexposure meters begin to do their thing. If the flash is raised, the flash may emit an AF-assist beam, a

Autofocus bracket

FIGURE 3-4:
Frame your subject so that it falls within the autofocus brackets.

few rapid pulses of light designed to help the autofocusing mechanism find its target in dim lighting. (The AF stands for autofocus.)

TIP

If you didn't raise the flash in Step 4 and you see a blinking lightning bolt at the left end of the viewfinder data display, the camera's sending you a message that you may want to reconsider the decision to go flash-free. You're not bound by that suggestion, though.

When the camera establishes focus, one or more of the camera's autofocus points appear in the viewfinder to indicate which areas of the frame are in focus. For example, in Figure 3-5, which documents the year that pork products were celebrated at the Indiana State Fair, the camera focused on the front of the pig and other surfaces that were the same distance from the lens. In dim lighting, the autofocus points may blink red in the viewfinder for a second to help you see them.

In most cases, you also hear a tiny beep, and the focus indicator in the lower-right corner of the viewfinder lights, as shown in Figure 3-5. Focus is locked as long as you keep the shutter button halfway down.

If the camera senses motion in the scene, you may instead hear a series of small beeps, and the focus lamp may not light. Both signals mean that the camera switched to continuous autofocusing, which enables it to track a moving object, adjusting focus as necessary up to the time you take the picture. For this feature to work, you need to keep the subject within the autofocus brackets and keep the shutter button pressed halfway.

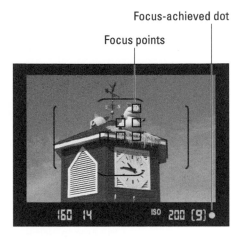

Focus-achieved dot

Focus points

FIGURE 3-5:
When focus is achieved, you see the focus points the camera used to set the focusing distance.

8. **Press the shutter button the rest of the way down to take the picture.**

When the flash is raised and the Flash Firing setting is On, the flash fires after you fully depress the shutter button. In Auto Flash Firing mode, the flash goes off if the camera thinks that the ambient light is insufficient to produce a good exposure.

After the camera records the picture data to the memory card, the image appears briefly on the camera monitor. If the picture doesn't appear or you want to take a longer look at the image, see Chapter 9, which covers picture playback.

A few additional points to help you understand Scene Intelligent Auto mode:

» **Exposure:** After the camera meters exposure, it displays its chosen exposure settings at the bottom of the viewfinder, as shown in Figure 3-5. (The 160 indicates a shutter speed of 1/160 second; the 14 indicates an aperture setting of f/14.) You can ignore all this data except for the shutter speed value. If that value blinks, the camera needs to use a slow shutter speed (long exposure time) to expose the picture. Because any movement of the camera or subject can blur the picture at a slow shutter speed, use a tripod and tell your subject to remain as still as possible.

Additionally, dim lighting may force the camera to use a high ISO setting, which increases the camera's sensitivity to light. Unfortunately, a high ISO can create noise, a defect that makes your picture look grainy. See Chapter 4 for tips on dealing with this and other exposure problems.

>> **Flash:** The built-in flash has a relatively short reach, so if the flash fires but your picture is still too dark, move closer to the subject.

When shooting portraits that require flash, you may want to enable Red-Eye Reduction to lessen the chances of the flash causing red-eye. To get to the Red-Eye Reduction setting, open Shooting Menu 1 and choose Flash Control. Chapter 2 has details about how to get the best performance when using this flash feature.

If you enable flash, a lightning bolt symbol appears at the left end of the viewfinder data strip. The symbol doesn't appear in Figure 3-5 because I didn't enable the flash. Although I often use flash outdoors, especially for portraits, in this case the subject was well lit by the sun and was beyond the limited reach of the flash anyway.

>> **Autofocusing tips:** Note these autofocusing pitfalls:

- *If the camera can't establish focus, you may be too close to your subject.* Check your lens instruction manual to find out its minimum close-focusing distance.

- *At the autofocus settings used by Scene Intelligent Auto, the camera focuses on the closest object.* So if you're shooting a portrait of someone standing behind a sign, the sign may appear in sharp focus, but your subject may not.

- *Some subjects confuse autofocusing systems.* Water, highly reflective objects, and subjects behind fences are some problematic subjects. One trick is to find an object that's about the same distance from the camera as your subject, set focus on that object, and then reframe the scene — keeping the shutter button pressed halfway as you do. When you depress the shutter button fully, the camera will use the focusing distance you set on the stand-in object.

Chapter 5 discusses methods to modify the autofocusing system in ways that may solve some of these issues. But often, a better option is to switch to manual focusing and set focus by rotating the focusing ring on the lens. (The close-focus distance of the lens still applies.) The focusing ring on the 18–55mm kit lens is highlighted in Figure 3-3.

Live View photography in Scene Intelligent Auto mode

The initial steps for taking a picture in Live View mode are the same as for view-finder photography: Rotate the Mode dial to the Scene Intelligent Auto setting (refer to Figure 3-1) and then set the focusing method (auto or manual) via the switch on the lens (refer to Figure 3-3). If handholding the camera, also enable image stabilization if your lens offers it. On the kit lens and many other Canon models, you enable this feature by moving the IS switch to the On position.

From there, take this path:

1. **Press the Live View button to engage Live View.**

   The viewfinder pulls the blanket over its head and goes to sleep, and the scene in front of the lens appears on the monitor. What data you see superimposed on top of the scene depends on your display mode; both screens in Figure 3-6 show the default display mode. Press Info to cycle through the available display options.

   If the camera doesn't engage Live View when you press the Live View button, open Shooting Menu 2 and set the Live View Shoot option to Enable. To change the menu setting to Disable, you first need to exit Live View mode; the setting doesn't appear on the menu when Live View is active.

Flash Firing mode

Portrait icon   Face Detection frame

FIGURE 3-6:
In Live View mode, tap the Drive mode or Flash Firing symbol to change that setting.

Drive mode

Touch Shutter on/off

Image Quality

2. **To adjust the Drive mode or Flash Firing setting, tap the setting's symbol on the screen.**

   I labeled the icons in Figure 3-6. *Remember:* In Scene Intelligent Auto mode, you don't have to tap the Q button to enter Quick Control mode in order to access picture settings. In fact, if you do tap the Q button, you bring up the Creative Assist options, as explained in the next section.

3. **If you want to use flash or think flash may be needed, raise the built-in flash unit.**

Again, just use the tabs that extend out from the front sides of the flash cover to get a grip on the cover. Then lift the cover up to expose the flash. Set the Flash Firing mode to On if you know you want the flash to fire; choose Auto flash if you want the camera to decide whether flash is needed.

4. **Compose your shot and then press and and hold the shutter button halfway down.**

The camera's autofocusing and autoexposure systems start doing their jobs.

By default, the camera uses a Live View autofocusing method called Face+Tracking. The idea behind this setting is that the camera assumes that if any people are in the scene, they are your subject of interest. So if it detects a face, a white frame appears over the face, as shown on the right in Figure 3-6. That face will be used to set the focusing distance. To choose a different face, move the frame over it by pressing the right or left edge of the Quick Control dial or just tap the face.

If the camera doesn't detect a face, it sets its focusing sights on the object closest to the lens or, sometimes, the largest object near the lens.

5. **Wait for a green autofocus frame or for one or more green focus points to appear on the screen.**

In a scene that doesn't contain faces, one or more green focus points appear, as shown on the left in Figure 3-7, to let you know where the focusing distance will be set. You also hear a beep to signal that focus has been set. In a portrait shot, the face frame turns green when focus is achieved, as shown on the right in the figure.

Focus-achieved boxes

Focus-achieved face frame

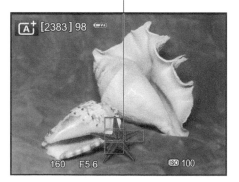

FIGURE 3-7: Green focus points (left) or a green face-detection frame (right) indicate that focus is established.

If you see orange focus points or face frames or the camera displays corner-boundary markers like the ones in Figure 3-8, the camera is telling you that it can't lock on to a focus target. Sometimes, you may simply be too close to your subject; try backing away a little to see if that helps. Other times, your subject may simply not be conducive to autofocusing; most cameras can't autofocus through water, for example. You can always shift to manual focusing if needed. Regardless, the camera won't let you take the picture until the focus issue is solved.

Focus boundary marks   Flash advice

FIGURE 3-8:
The red boundary lines are an indication that the autofocusing system can't lock onto anything in the frame.

6. **Press the shutter button fully to take the shot.**

    If you raised the flash, it may fire, depending on your Flash Firing setting. After the camera finishes recording the picture data to the memory card, you see your just-captured image on the monitor for a few seconds before the Live View preview returns.

7. **To exit Live View, press the Live View button again.**

    You can then return to framing your images through the viewfinder.

The tips on exposure, flash, and autofocusing at the end of the preceding section apply to Live View shooting as well. Also keep in mind these additional notes related only to Live View mode:

>> **Automatic scene selection:** See the little A+ symbol in the upper-left corner of the left screen in Figure 3-7? That symbol appears when you first set the exposure mode to Scene Intelligent Auto mode. But after you compose your shot, you may notice that the symbol has changed. For example, in the right screen in Figure 3-7, the symbol looks like a human figure (okay, use your imagination). This icon shape-shifting happens because in Scene Intelligent Auto mode, the camera analyzes the frame and tries to determine the type of scene you're trying to shoot. When it finishes its calculation, it displays the symbol representing the scene it sees. In Figure 3-7, it accurately detected a portrait and so displayed the symbol for that scene type.

There are dozens of possible scenes: portrait, portrait of a moving subject, portrait with blue sky included — and that's just for shots where people are detected. You can find a chart listing all the possible symbols in the Live View section of the camera manual, but it's pretty pointless to memorize them because you can't do anything to change the camera's mind about the scene type. In fact, the only reason this bullet point exists is so that when you see the icon changing, you don't worry that something is wrong. Also, know that after the camera decides on a scene type, it adjusts some camera settings in ways it thinks will produce the best photograph of that scene.

>> **Tap to focus:** In Live View mode, you can tap your subject on the monitor to let the camera know where to set focus. However, if the touch shutter feature is turned on, your tap not only establishes a focus point but also triggers the shutter release, and the picture is recorded at that moment. If you want your tap to focus only, make sure the Touch Shutter icon, labeled on the left in Figure 3-6, is set to off. (The word *Off* indicates the feature's status.) Tapping the icon toggles the Touch Shutter on and off. You also can turn the feature on and off via the Touch Shutter option on Shooting Menu 2. This menu option disappears when you exit Live View mode.

>> **Additional Live View autofocusing features:** You have access to several other helpful autofocusing options during Live View photography, such as Eye Detection AF, which tells the camera to hunt for and focus specifically on an eye in a portrait. Because these features apply to all exposure modes and are a bit complex, I save them for the larger discussion of Live View autofocusing in Chapter 5.

>> **Live View selfie mode:** When Live View mode is engaged and you rotate the monitor to face the front of the camera, you get access to a hidden mode called Self Portrait mode. You can read more about it in the upcoming section "Discovering Selfie Mode." First, though, check out the next section, which explains Creative Assist features, some of which are available in Self Portrait mode as well as in the normal Scene Intelligent Auto mode.

Exploring Creative Assist Adjustments

In Scene Intelligent Auto mode, you can manipulate certain aspects of your pictures through the Creative Assist feature. The best way to understand this feature is to put the camera in Live View mode because when Live View is engaged, the camera updates the monitor preview to show the impact of the currently selected Creative Assist option.

The following steps walk you through the basic process of using Creative Assist in Live View mode. Here, as always, I assume that you changed the default Display Level menu options to Standard and Disable, as suggested in Chapter 1. If you opted not to take that step, you may see some on-screen help screens that tell you to tap a certain area of the screen at various points in the process. Most of these screens also offer a box you can select that tells the camera not to show you that screen again in the future.

Back to the subject at hand: Step this way to try out the Live View version of Creative Assist shooting:

1. **Set the Mode dial to Scene Intelligent Auto and press the Live View button to enable the live preview.**

2. **Tap the Creative Assist icon, labeled on the left in Figure 3-9, or press the Q button.**

    In Scene Intelligent Auto mode, the Q button doesn't access the Quick Control screen during Live View shooting as it does in other exposure modes. Instead, it displays the Creative Assist options screen shown on the right in Figure 3-9. At the bottom of the screen, a strip of icons appears, with each icon representing one of the Creative Assist options.

FIGURE 3-9: In Live View mode, press the Q button or tap the Creative Assist icon (left) to display the available options (right).

 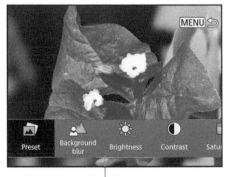

Creative Assist icon   Creative Assist options icons

3. **Rotate the Main dial or Quick Control dial to scroll through the available adjustments.**

4. **To apply the currently selected adjustment, press the Set button or tap the adjustment's icon.**

    You then see options related to that setting. For example, Figure 3-10 shows options related to the Color Tone 2 adjustment. This adjustment enables you to make colors more magenta and less green or vice versa

Name of active adjustment

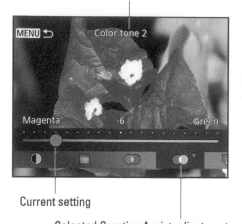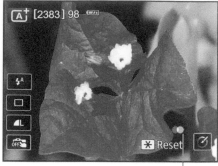

FIGURE 3-10:
After you adjust a
setting (left), an
icon representing
that setting
appears on the
Live View
shooting screen
as a reminder
(right).

Current setting

Selected Creative Assist adjustment

Current adjustment reminder icon

5. **Set the specific level or type of adjustment you want to.**

For most adjustments, you're presented with a scale like the one in Figure 3-10. You set the strength or type of adjustment by moving a little dot along the scale, which you can do by either tapping the scale or rotating the Main dial or Quick Control dial. In the figure, I moved the orange dot (labeled "Current setting") toward the magenta side of the scale.

6. **After choosing the settings for the selected option, tap OK or press the Set button.**

You're returned to the initial Creative Assist screen (left screen in Figure 3-9), with an icon representing the adjustment that's now in force.

7. **To apply additional adjustments, repeat Steps 3 through 6.**

8. **When you're done adding Creative Assist adjustments, tap the Menu symbol in the upper-left corner of the screen or press the Menu button.**

You're returned to the Live View shooting screen. Next to the Creative Assist symbol in the lower-right corner of the screen, icons appear that represent the effects you applied. For example, in the right screen in Figure 3-10, the Color Tone 2 icon appears.

As for the asterisk symbol and the Reset label, they're there to tell you that if you change your mind about the effects you selected, you can press the AE Lock button (the one marked with an asterisk) to reset all the effects to their default positions, which is to say, no effect. You can read more about the reset function in the upcoming section "Placing the final pieces of the Creative Assist puzzle."

9. **Take the picture.**

For viewfinder shooting, you can access the Creative Assist options via the normal Quick Control route: Press the Q button and then tap the Creative Assist symbol, shown highlighted in Figure 3-11. Or for an even quicker result, press the ISO button — no Q button required. Either way, you then see the strip of adjustment icons, as shown on the left in Figure 3-12. As you scroll through the icon strip, graphics appear that show you what to expect from the adjustment. For example, in the left screen in Figure 3-12, you learn that Color Tone 2 enables you to shift colors along the green-to-magenta axis. From there, everything works as just described except that you can't see a live preview of the effect you're applying.

FIGURE 3-11:
During viewfinder shooting, shift to Quick Control mode and select Creative Assist, as shown here, or just press the ISO button.

Don't forget that you after you scroll to the icon representing the adjustment you want to make, you have to press Set to access the options for that adjustment. For example, the right screen in Figure 3-12 shows the options that appear after you select Color Tone 2 and press Set.

FIGURE 3-12:
Scroll to the effect you want to apply (left) and press Set to access its options (right).

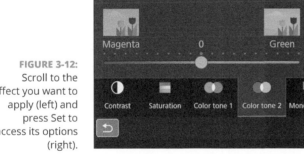
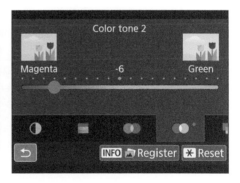

Now that you understand how to open the Creative Assist vault, the next section gives you a quick rundown of the available adjustments. Well, some of the run-downs are quick; a couple of the adjustments are a little complicated. Following that, discover some additional Creative Assist tricks that may come in handy.

Exploring the Creative Assist lineup

Some of the Creative Assist adjustments are pretty self-explanatory; others, not so much. And a few of the adjustments— I'm looking at you, Background Blur — *should* be self-explanatory but come with a long list of ifs, thens, and maybes. Here's a quick-as-possible guide to the available Creative Assist options:

>> **Presets:** Presets are like digital recipes that give your image a specific look. For example, one preset produces vivid colors, while another results in soft focus. You can even create and save your own preset to use at any time. (See the next section for details.)

>> **Background Blur:** When you select this option, you're presented with a slider that you use to specify whether you want the background to be soft or sharp — a picture characteristic known as *depth of field* and explained fully in Chapter 5.

REMEMBER

Although Background Blur sounds like a cool feature and seems easy enough to implement, it comes with a number of gotchas:

- *You can't use flash.* Background Blur is disabled when the Flash Firing mode is set to Auto or On. Chapter 2 tells you more about this flash setting.

- *Depending on the lighting and your lens, you may not be able to access the entire range of blurry-to-sharp settings.* To create background blur (or sharpness), the camera adjusts an exposure setting called the f-stop (aperture), which you can explore in Chapter 4. For now, the critical point is that the range of f-stop settings the camera can use and still properly expose the photo depends on the lighting in the scene. Additionally, the range of available f-stops depends on your lens.

  If you discover that the camera won't let you set the Background Blur amount at either end of the adjustment scale, don't waste time trying to force things. It's not happening; move along.

- *Disregard the Auto setting.* The Background Blur option also has an Auto setting, which the camera manual says "adjusts the background blurring to match the scene brightness." That's helpful, eh? After all, if you wanted the camera to determine depth of field for you, you wouldn't choose the Background Blur setting, right? The good news is that there are other ways to affect depth of field, so you're not reliant on the Background Blur option to control this aspect of your pictures. See the end of Chapter 5 to discover all your depth-of-field options (it's not that difficult, I promise).

- The camera can't achieve much background blurring unless your subject is at least a few feet away from the background. And if your subject is a long distance from the background, the background will likely appear softly focused even if you select the Background Blur setting that results in least amount of blurring.

>> **Brightness:** Use this option to alter image exposure on your next shot.

>> **Contrast:** This tool enables you to make the lightest parts of your image even brighter while at the same time making the shadows darker — *increasing contrast,* in photo terms. You can also go the other direction if you want a low-contrast look.

>> **Saturation:** Adjust this setting to make all colors more or less intense. Note: I said *all* colors. You can't make skies bluer, for example, without also making the hot pink hat of the woman who photobombed your shot even more noticeable.

>> **Color Tone 1:** Select this option to shift colors along the blue-to-amber color axis. In other words, you can take all areas of the scene that are blue and make them appear more amber. Or you can go the other direction, making amber areas more blue.

In photo speak, blues are referred to as *cool tones,* while amber tones are *warm.*

>> **Color Tone 2:** This setting is based on another color pair, green and magenta. You can reduce the amount of green while adding magenta or, again, go in the opposite direction. And to answer your question, no, you can't add one color without reducing the other — the same is also true for the blue/amber color adjustment just described.

>> **Monochrome:** If you select this option, you can shoot a standard black-and-white image or one that has one of four tints applied (sepia, blue, purple, or green).

I don't recommend shooting with this option enabled. Instead, shoot the image in full color and then use photo-editing tools to create a monochrome or tinted image. Assuming that you have a capable photo-editing program, you get more control over how your final image looks if you go that route. At the least, shoot one version of your subject in full color and another with the Monochrome setting applied. You can always go from full color to mono-chrome, but the opposite isn't true.

If you don't have a photo-editing program or app that does a good job at this type of color conversion, you can create a monochrome or tinted copy of any image that you shoot in the Raw file format by applying the Monochrome Creative Assist filter during picture playback. Chapter 2 explains how to set the camera to capture a Raw/cRaw photo (look for information related to the Image Quality setting); check out Chapter 10 to find out how to use Creative Assist features with Raw photos. Also check out the end of Chapter 6, where I discuss the Monochrome option available via the Picture Style setting. (Spoiler alert: My advice regarding shooting with the Monochrome Picture Style in force is the same as for using capturing images using the Monochrome Creative Assist setting.)

Placing the final pieces of the Creative Assist puzzle

If you're thinking, "Gee, this Creative Assist thing seems way too involved to be part of a shooting mode that's supposed to be the easiest to use," I'm right there with you. So just remember, you're free to completely ignore this feature — your Scene Intelligent Auto photos will likely be just fine without any Creative Assist adjustments. If you do want to play around with the feature, though, here are a few more critical pieces of information to help you use it to its best advantage.

>> **Creating your own presets:** You can create a custom preset that contains all of the current adjustments so that in the future, you can simply select that preset instead of applying all the adjustments one by one. After you enable all the adjustments you want to include in the preset, access the Creative Assist settings screen, as shown on the left in Figure 3-13. Tap Info, as indicated in the figure, or press the Info button. A message appears asking if you want to register the settings in a preset; tap OK or press the Set button to do so. Your new preset shows up as User 1, as shown on the right in Figure 3-13.

You can create up to three custom presets. When you try to create a fourth preset, the camera asks you which of the three existing presets you want to overwrite in order to create the new one.

FIGURE 3-13: Create up to three custom presets so that you can apply a batch of adjustments at once.

Tap to create custom preset   User Preset 1

Tap to reset options to default settings

>> **Retaining Creative Assist settings without adding a preset.** When you turn off the camera or switch out of Scene Intelligent Auto mode, all Creative Assist settings are returned to their default settings automatically. If you instead want the camera to keep those settings in effect, open Shooting Menu 2, select Retain Creative Assist Data, and change the setting to Enable. This

feature comes in handy if you're full up on presets and need another way to apply the same adjustments to a batch of pictures that you shoot throughout the day, some with Creative Assist adjustments and some without. Or, you know, when you power the camera off so you can take a lunch break but then need to get right back to shooting. After a little nap, of course.

>> **Don't forget to check which Creative Assist adjustments are in force before you shoot a new subject.** The camera always presents icons telling you which adjustments it will apply, although you have to dig into the Creative Assist screen to figure out exactly what settings you requested for each adjustment. During viewfinder photography, the icons appear in the area labeled in Figure 3-14; in Live View photography, the icon(s) appear in the area labeled on the right screen in Figure 3-10.

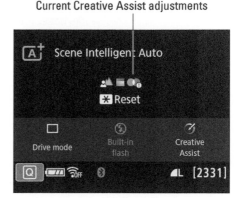

Current Creative Assist adjustments

FIGURE 3-14:
The icons represent Creative Assist adjustments that will be applied on your next shot.

>> **Resetting adjustments:** To reset all the Creative Assist adjustments to their default settings, press the AE Lock button, often referred to as the asterisk button. A confirmation screen appears; tap OK or press Set to go forward. If you take this step either from the main Quick Control or Live View screen, all Creative Assist options are set back to their defaults. If you want to reset just a single adjustment, bring that adjustment up while in the Creative Assist selection screen and press the AE Lock button. (You can also just manually restore the original setting for that option. For example, on the Color Tone 1 slider, move the selection dot back to the center of the scale.)

>> **You can apply the effects either as you shoot or, if you capture images in the Raw format, *after* you take the picture.** In Chapter 2, I explain your camera's two basic file types, JPEG and Raw. For JPEG pictures, you need to select the Creative Assist filters you want to use before you shoot. The camera applies the filters as it takes the picture.

If you instead select Raw (or its companion format, cRaw), you also have the option of applying *some* of the filters through the Creative Assist option found on Playback Menu 2. The camera applies the effects and then saves a copy of your original Raw file as a JPEG image. The one effect you can't apply after the fact is Background Blur; that effect depends on certain settings the camera selects in order to keep the background sharp or soft as it takes the picture. (The main setting involved is the f-stop, which is introduced in Chapter 4.)

>> **Additional creative effects are available if you shoot in the Creative Filters mode, represented by the interlocking circles on the Mode dial.** These effects are more of the special-effects variety, so I cover them in Chapter 12.

>> **Creative Assist is available only in Scene Intelligent Auto exposure mode.** However, if you're after a specific look, check out the SCN mode settings explained in the next section. You may find that one of those exposure modes works better for the photo you have in mind than the Creative Assist features.

Discovering Selfie Mode

Here's a camera feature that I'm willing to bet most people won't discover without reading this book or (heaven forbid) the camera manual: Your T8i/850D actually has a special shooting mode called Self Portrait, designed to make it easy to take selfies. But Self Portrait mode isn't found on the Mode dial or included in the SCN (scene) modes. Instead, Self Portrait mode is a hidden aspect of Scene Intelligent Auto mode.

Here's how to take advantage of this feature:

1. **Set the Mode dial to Scene Intelligent Auto and engage Live View.**

   Self Portrait mode isn't designed for viewfinder shooting.

2. **Rotate the camera monitor so that the screen faces the front of the camera.**

   You should then see the Self Portrait icon on the left side of the monitor, as shown in the first screen in Figure 3-15.

   If you don't see the icon, make sure that the screen is perfectly straight up and down. If you tilt the screen at all, maybe aiming it downward to achieve an angle that helps hide a double chin (come on, we all do it), and Self Portrait mode won't come out to play.

3. **Tap the Self Portrait icon to display the new batch of icons and settings shown on the right screen in Figure 3-15.**

   Notice a couple of things about this screen:

   - The Self Portrait icon appears in the upper-left corner, indicating that you're now using that shooting mode.

   - Check out the buffer mode value, set between the shots remaining value and the battery symbol at the top of the screen. Notice that it dropped all the way to 1 when you activated Self Portrait mode. That's because you can't shoot a continuous burst of frames in this mode; you're limited to just one frame at a time.

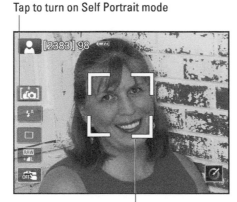

Tap to turn on Self Portrait mode

Tap to access additional settings

Background Blur

Brightness

Face-detection focus frame

Exit screen

Soften Skin

Touch Shutter

FIGURE 3-15:
After putting the camera in Live View mode, rotate the monitor to face the front of the camera and tap the Self Portrait icon.

4. **On the right side of the screen, tap the Q icon to display the settings screen shown in Figure 3-16.**

You see more icons, each representing a different setting, as follows:

- *AF Method (eye-detection AF on/off):* In Self Portrait mode, the camera always uses Face+Tracking autofocus, but you can enable or disable the eye-detection feature associated with that autofocus mode. Tap the AF Method icon and then press the Info button, as prompted by the onscreen label, to turn eye detection on or off. (When the label reads *Enable* and you see the eyeball icon just to the left, as in the figure, eye detection is on.) Chapter 5 provides the full story on this and other Live View autofocusing options.

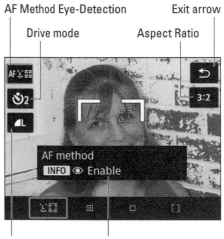

AF Method Eye-Detection

Drive mode

Exit arrow

Aspect Ratio

Image Quality

Eye-detection AF status

FIGURE 3-16:
When the camera is in Self Portrait mode, tap the Q icon or press the Q button to get to this Quick Control settings screen.

- *Drive mode:* By default, the Drive mode is set to the 2-second Self-Timer mode. But you can also choose Single or 10-second Self-Timer.

- *Image Quality:* You can choose only JPEG options; Raw and cRaw aren't available.

- *Aspect Ratio:* You get the full complement of Aspect Ratio choices: 3:2 (the default); 4:3; 16:9; and 1:1.

Chapter 2 explains the Drive mode, Image Quality, and Aspect Ratio settings.

5. **After selecting options from the screen shown in Figure 3-16, tap the exit arrow in the upper-right corner to return to the main settings screen (second screen in Figure 3-15).**

6. **Adjust remaining settings by tapping the other four icons on the right side of the screen.**

    Again, refer to Figure 3-15 for a hint as to what you can tweak with each setting: Background Blur, Brightness, and Skin Softening (yes please).

    The bottom icon toggles the camera's touch shutter on and off. When this feature is enabled, tapping the screen sets focus and then immediately takes the picture. Turn it off if you prefer to use the shutter button or a remote control to release the shutter. (You can still tap the screen to set focus even if the touch shutter is disabled.)

7. **To return to the main Self Portrait screen, tap the box labeled "Exit screen" in Figure 3-15.**

8. **Take the picture.**

Although you'd think a shooting mode designed for taking selfies would be really easy to figure out, there actually are a lot of fine details that can muck up the works. Allow me to save you a little time and frustration by imparting a few more bits of Self Portrait knowledge:

» **The Flash Firing, Image Quality, and other settings in force before you shift to Self Portrait mode don't mean diddly squat.** (Can I say that in polite company? I think I can, but apologies if not.) Here's what I mean: Take a look at the settings icons on the left side of the first screen in Figure 3-15. It shows the Flash Firing mode set to Auto, the Drive mode set to Single Frame, and the Image Quality option set to Raw. You would rightly expect those settings to stick for your selfie. But you would be wrong. As soon as you tap that Self Portrait mode icon, those settings become irrelevant. As stated in the preceding steps, you can only use JPEG as the Image Quality format, and the default Drive mode is 2-second Self-Timer. If you want to use the Single Drive mode, you have to change it in the Q settings screen (see Figure 3-16).

As for Flash Firing, well, that becomes completely irrelevant because you can't use flash in Self Portrait mode. Part of this is because of the Blur Background option, which is incompatible with flash. But flash is also likely disabled for safety reasons: Many people may position themselves very near the camera to take their selfies, and having the flash fire into your eyes at close distance isn't really safe. Suffice it to say, you're going to have to find another way to illuminate your shot than using flash.

>> **The camera remains in Self Portrait mode until you tap the exit screen symbol labeled in Figure 3-15.** You also can exit Live View mode or move the camera monitor out of the face-forward position to return to regular Scene Intelligent Auto mode.

>> **For easiest self-portraiture, put the camera on a tripod and, if possible, use a remote control (or a smart device with Canon's Camera Connect app, covered in the appendix) to trigger the shutter release.** That way, you can refer to the monitor while perfecting your pose and then take the picture without having to get up to press the shutter button. You also can position yourself a little farther from the lens than you may be able to do if you're handholding the camera.

>> **To prevent the monitor from shutting off just as you're perfecting your smile, adjust the Auto Power Off setting on Setup Menu 2.** While you're shooting selfies, you may even want to choose the Disable setting so that the monitor never turns off. Just be aware that the longer the monitor remains on, the more battery juice the camera consumes. Also, Live View mode heats up the camera more than viewfinder shooting, and if the camera gets too warm, it will power down regardless of this setting.

Taking Advantage of SCN (Scene) Modes

In Scene Intelligent Auto mode, the camera tries to figure out what type of picture you want to take. If you don't want to rely on the camera to make that judgment, you can instead take advantage of *scene modes,* each of which is tailored to a specific type of photo. After you select a scene mode, the camera automatically selects picture settings that render the subject according to the photography style traditionally considered "best."

The next sections describe each scene mode and explain how to set your camera to use them. Before you dig into that information, though, you need to know that none of the scene modes can deliver their intended results all the time. How close the camera can hit the mark depends on the lighting conditions. Specifically, the amount of available light determines which shutter speed and aperture settings the camera needs to use to expose the picture. And those two settings, in turn, affect motion blur and whether the background appears sharp or blurry. Your lens also has an impact: First, the range of available aperture settings varies depending on the lens. Second, lens focal length (18mm, 55mm, 200mm, and so on) also affects *depth of field,* or the distance over which focus remains sharp.

To fully understand these issues, check out Chapter 4, which explains exposure, and Chapter 5, which covers ways to manipulate depth of field. In the meantime, just don't expect miracles from the scene modes.

As for actually taking a picture, the process for most scene modes is the same as spelled out for Scene Intelligent Auto mode, earlier in this chapter. If you need to do anything differently, the description of the scene mode provides details.

Accessing Scene modes

If you've worked with other Canon digital cameras, you may be used to seeing symbols representing a couple of popular scene modes, such as Portrait and Sports modes, on the Mode dial. On the T8i/850D, the Mode dial sports a less cluttered look, and those icons are gone. Instead, you access the Scene modes by setting the dial to SCN, as shown in Figure 3-17.

The next section describes the available SCN modes. How you choose the one you want to use depends on whether you're composing shots using the viewfinder or have Live View engaged:

FIGURE 3-17:
Set the Mode dial to SCN to access the scene modes.

>> **Viewfinder photography:** After you set the mode dial to SCN, the Quick Control screen displays the name of the currently selected Scene mode, as shown in Figure 3-18. To choose a different scene, press the Q button or tap the Q icon in the lower-left corner of the screen to enter Quick Control mode. Then highlight Choose Scene, as shown on the left in Figure 3-19, and press Set to display the selection screen shown on the right in the figure. You also can get to the selection screen by simply tapping the Choose Scene after you're in Quick Control mode.

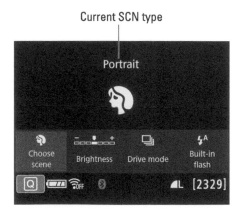

FIGURE 3-18:
The current SCN mode setting appears as soon as you set the dial to SCN.

Select to display available SCN types

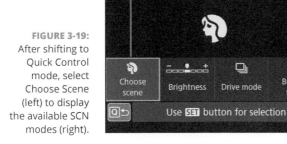

>> **Live View mode:** An icon representing the currently selected SCN type appears in the upper-left corner of the screen, as shown in Figure 3-20. Tap that icon to display the same scrolling list of SCN options shown on the right in Figure 3-19.

After opening the scene-selection screen, scroll through the list by rotating the Quick Control dial or Main dial. Or just press the top or bottom edge of the Quick Control dial. Tap OK or press the Set button to use the currently displayed scene type. You're returned to the shooting display.

Both the Quick Control and Live View displays show the major picture options available in your selected scene mode, such as Flash Firing and Drive mode. For example, Figures 3-18 and 3-20 show the options available for Portrait mode. (If your Live View screen doesn't show the same data as in the figure, press the Info button as needed to display the available settings.) You can use the Quick Control mode to adjust the options visible on the screen.

A few scene types offer some of the same adjustments available through the Creative Assist feature; check out the earlier section "Exploring the Creative Assist lineup" for details about those settings. See Chapter 2 for help understanding the Drive mode, Image Quality, Aspect Ratio, and Flash Firing settings. Remember that the Flash Firing option doesn't appear on the screen unless you manually raise the flash.

Current SCN mode icon (Portrait)

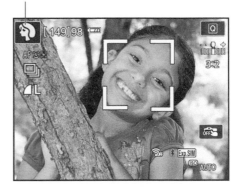

Reviewing the available scene modes

I don't have room in this book to completely detail each of the modes you can access when you set the Mode dial to SCN, but the following list provides a quick introduction. Some of the modes are pretty useful, while others rate a "meh" (from me, anyway; feel free to assign your own ratings).

REMEMBER

Which picture settings you can adjust depends on the selected scene mode. In most cases, you can press the Q button or tap the onscreen Q icon to shift to Quick Control mode to adjust the available settings. And you may or may not be able to use flash; some SCN modes prohibit it. If you're unsure, raise the flash unit. If flash is an option, the Flash Firing setting should be one of those you can change via the Quick Control screen. When the flash is closed, the camera may display a blinking lightning bolt symbol, which is your cue to raise the flash so that the camera can add more light to the scene.

>> **Portrait:** This mode produces the classic portraiture look featured in the Live View screen shown in Figure 3-20: a sharply focused subject, blurry background, with skin enhanced to appear slightly softer and warmer (less blue, more amber).

One setting that may seem odd for this mode: By default, the camera uses the Continuous Low Drive mode. As covered in Chapter 2, that Drive mode captures a burst of images as long as you hold down the shutter button. Capturing a burst of frames is actually helpful for portrait subjects who are "blinkers," upping the odds that their eyes will be open in at least one frame. If you raise the built-in flash, you can use flash to illuminate the subject — a good idea if your subject is backlit like the one in Figure 3-20. Remember that in a scene like the one in the figure, you should set the Flash Firing mode to On because in Auto mode, the camera probably will see all the bright background and not see the need for additional lighting.

>> **Smooth Skin:** Ah, the easy way to younger, more flawless skin. In this mode, the camera applies slight blurring to the skin, diffusing fine lines and wrinkles. The areas selected for the smoothing effect are chosen automatically based on color, so be aware that if an object in the background is similar in color to your subject's skin, that object, too, gets the softening effect.

>> **Group Photo:** This setting selects camera options that extend the distance over which focus remains sharp (depth of field) so that if your photo includes people who are standing at varying distances from the lens, all will be in focus.

» **Landscape:** Taking the traditional approach to landscape photography, this mode chooses settings with both foreground and background appearing sharp and with blues and greens strengthened. Figure 3-21 shows an example.

» **Close-up:** Like Portrait mode, Close-up mode blurs the background to draw the eye directly to the subject, as shown in Figure 3-22. Colors are not manipulated in Close-up mode as they are in Portrait mode.

How close you can get to your subject depends on your lens; choosing Close-up mode has nothing to do with that limitation as it does on some compact cameras you may have used. Check your lens manual to find out its minimum focusing distance.

FIGURE 3-21:
Landscape mode keeps both the background and foreground as sharply focused as possible and boosts blue and green hues.

» **Sports:** Sports mode freezes motion, as shown in Figure 3-23, whether you're actually photographing sports or some other moving subject. Flash is not available in this mode.

» **Kids:** This mode attempts to accommodate fidgety younger subjects by choosing a shutter speed that prevents motion blur and using the High Speed Continuous Drive mode (the camera captures a burst of frames as long as you keep the shutter button fully pressed). According to Canon, skin tones will appear "healthy" if you use this mode, although it's probably not the best idea to force a kid with the flu to pose for pictures anyway. You can use flash, but the frames-per-second the camera can capture slows if you do.

» **Food:** This setting is designed to make your dessert look especially appealing by brightening exposure a tad. It also removes any red tint that would otherwise affect image colors when your plate is lit by candlelight or tungsten lights. If the ambient lighting isn't sufficient, raise the built-in flash and change the Flash Firing mode from Off to On.

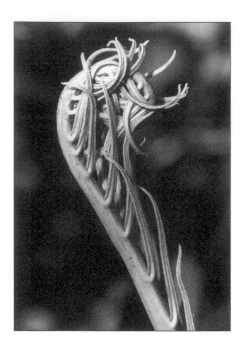

FIGURE 3-22:
Close-up mode also produces short depth of field.

FIGURE 3-23:
To freeze the action of moving subjects, try Sports mode.

>> **Candlelight:** This mode disables flash so that your subject is lit only by the warm glow of the candlelight and, unlike Food mode, leaves the reddish tint added by that light source intact. A slow shutter speed (long exposure time) is necessary, so use a tripod and ask your subjects to remain as still as possible. Otherwise, camera shake and subject motion can blur the image.

>> **Night Portrait:** This setting also uses a slow shutter and less flash power than normal, producing more flattering light on your subject. Again, you need a tripod and a subject that can remain still to avoid blurring.

>> **Handheld Night Scene:** This mode is designed to produce a sharper picture when you handhold the camera in dim lighting, which requires a slow shutter speed and thus increases the risk of picture-blurring camera shake.

REMEMBER

To produce this result, the camera records four shots in quick succession when you press the shutter button. Then it blends the images in a way that reduces blurring.

You don't have to reserve this setting for nighttime shots, despite the mode name. For example, I used it to capture the shot in Figure 3-24, taken from the top flight of stairs inside a lighthouse. No way was I going to lug a tripod up 200-some steps to that vantage point, so I set the camera to Handheld Night

Scene Mode, pointed the camera downward, held my breath, and pressed the shutter button. At a shutter speed of 1/40 second, that would normally be a recipe for a blurry image, but with the help of the Handheld Night Scene mode, the shot is acceptably sharp. (Enabling image stabilization, if available for your lens, also helps.)

FIGURE 3-24: Handheld Night Scene captured this handheld shot from a vantage point at the top of a lighthouse.

WARNING

The angle of view of the final image may be smaller than what you see through the viewfinder. This occurs if the camera needs to crop the image to get the four shots to align properly in the merged image. Frame your subject a little loosely so that important parts of the scene aren't lost in the cropping process.

>> **HDR Backlight Control:** Try this mode when your subject is *backlit* — the light is behind the subject — which normally either leaves the subject too dark or the background too bright. This mode uses some digital voodoo to brighten the darkest parts of the image while holding onto more highlight detail than is otherwise possible. Figure 3-25 offers an example of the difference this mode can make. Both the highlight and shadow areas in the HDR version contain more detail than the one shot in Scene Intelligent Auto. To achieve this result, the camera records three consecutive images each time you press the shutter button, adjusting exposure between each frame. Then the three frames are merged into one final HDR image.

TECHNICAL STUFF

HDR stands for *high dynamic range. Dynamic range* refers to the range of brightness values that a device can record. HDR refers to an image that contains a greater spectrum of brightness values than can normally be captured by a camera.

As with the Handheld Night Scene mode, the camera needs to crop the image a little to properly align the multiple frames into one. So frame your subject a little loosely so that important areas of the scene don't get cropped out of the final HDR image. Also use a tripod; this ensures that each frame records the same image area, helping the camera properly align frames when merging them. Finally, keep in mind that anything that's moving in the scene usually appears at partial opacity in different parts of the frame in the merged image. (On the other hand, you may be able to claim that you captured a ghost in your picture. . . .)

Scene Intelligent Auto

HDR Backlight Control

FIGURE 3-25: Try shooting high-contrast scenes in HDR Backlight Control mode to retain more detail in both shadows and highlights.

Adjusting camera settings in SCN mode

In addition to changing the scene type, a process explained in the earlier section "Accessing Scene modes," you may be able to adjust a few other picture-taking settings. In most cases, the fastest way to access the options is via Quick Control mode. Remember, press the Q button or tap the onscreen Q icon to make the jump to Quick Control mode.

Here's a look at the most common settings you may be able to control — again, depending on the scene type:

REMEMBER

>> **Image Quality:** Covered in Chapter 2, this option determines the file type (Raw or JPEG) and the image resolution (Large, Medium, Small 1, or Small 2). In Live View mode, you can select the setting via the Quick Control screen, but during viewfinder shooting, you need to change it through Shooting Menu 1.

In the HDR Backlight Control and Handheld Night Scene modes, you're limited to JPEG as your file type (that is, any setting but Raw or cRaw).

>> **Drive mode:** Also detailed in Chapter 2, this setting determines whether the camera captures a single frame at a time or records a burst of images as long as you hold down the shutter button. You also may be able to access the two Self-Timer options (2-second delay and 10-second delay.)

When Live View isn't engaged, you can whoosh to the Drive mode settings screen by pressing the left edge of the Quick Control dial.

>> **Flash Firing mode:** For modes that permit flash, you may be able to choose from these flash modes: Auto flash (the camera decides when it's needed), On (the flash always fires), and Off. When flash is enabled, you can also enable or disable Red-Eye Reduction flash. Access both options by opening Shooting Menu 1 and then choosing Flash Control.

REMEMBER

If you want to use flash, you must raise it manually. (Grab the little notches found near the front of the cover and lift up.) See Chapter 2 for details on using the built-in flash.

>> **Brightness:** True to its name, this option enables you to request a brighter or darker exposure on your next shot. After selecting the option, rotate the Quick Control or Main dial to move the marker along the brightness scale. In Live View mode, the option is represented by the little exposure meter graphic, labeled in Figure 3-26. As you change the Brightness setting in Live View mode, the preview updates to provide an approximation of how the scene will look at the new setting.

>> **Color Tone:** This setting enables you to request a warmer (more amber) or cooler (more blue) rendition of

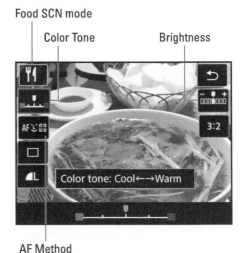

Food SCN mode

Color Tone

Brightness

AF Method

FIGURE 3-26:
Here's a look at the settings you can adjust when you set the SCN type to Food and use Live View.

your subject on the next shot. Again, rotate the Quick Control or Main dial to move the marker toward the red or blue end of the scale. If you're using Live View, the onscreen colors change to reflect the new setting.

>> **Autofocusing:** For viewfinder photography, you can't deviate from the default autofocusing settings, which work as outlined in the earlier section "Viewfinder shooting." In Live View mode, you can vary the autofocusing behavior by shifting to Quick Control mode and then adjusting the AF Method, labeled in Figure 3-26. But until you have time to read the section of Chapter 5 that explains how those options work, stick with the default settings and set focus as detailed in the section "Live View photography in Scene Intelligent Auto mode," also found earlier in this chapter.

2
Taking Creative Control

IN THIS PART . . .

Find out how to control exposure when you step up to Creative Zone (advanced) exposure modes: P, Tv, Av, and M.

Master the focusing system and discover how to manipulate depth of field.

Tweak color by using White Balance and other color options.

Get pro tips for shooting portraits, action shots, landscapes, and close-ups.

Take advantage of your camera's HD movie-recording features.

IN THIS CHAPTER

» **Understanding the three main exposure settings: aperture, shutter speed, and ISO**

» **Choosing the right advanced exposure modes: P, Tv, Av, or M?**

» **Picking a metering mode**

» **Tweaking autoexposure results**

» **Taking advantage of Automatic Exposure Bracketing (AEB)**

Chapter **4**

Taking Charge of Exposure

U nderstanding exposure is one of the most intimidating challenges for a new photographer. Discussions of the topic are loaded with technical terms — *aperture, metering, shutter speed, ISO,* and the like. Add the fact that your camera offers many exposure controls, all sporting equally foreign names, and it's no wonder that many people decide to stick with Scene Intelligent Auto mode and let the camera take care of exposure automatically.

I fully relate to the confusion you may be feeling — I've been there. But I can also promise that when you take things nice and slow, digesting a piece of the exposure pie at a time, the topic is *not* as complicated as it seems on the surface. The payoff will be worth your time, too. You'll not only gain the know-how to solve most exposure problems but also discover ways to use exposure to put your creative stamp on a scene.

To that end, this chapter provides everything you need to know about controlling exposure, from a primer in exposure terminology (it's not as bad as it sounds) to tips on using the P, Tv, Av, and M exposure modes, which are the only ones that offer access to all exposure features. (There's good reason why Canon calls these four modes the *Creative Zone* modes.)

Note: The one exposure-related topic not covered in this chapter is flash, which I cover in Chapter 2 because it's among options you can access even in Scene Intelligent Auto mode. Also, this chapter deals with still photography; Chapter 8 covers movie exposure.

Introducing the Exposure Trio: Aperture, Shutter Speed, and ISO

Any photograph, whether taken with a film or digital camera, is created by focusing light through a lens onto a light-sensitive recording medium. In a film camera, the film negative serves as the medium; in a digital camera, it's the image sensor, which is an array of light-responsive computer chips.

Between the lens and the sensor are two barriers, the aperture and shutter, which together control how much light makes its way to the sensor. The actual design and arrangement of the aperture, shutter, and sensor vary depending on the camera, but Figure 4-1 offers an illustration of the basic concept.

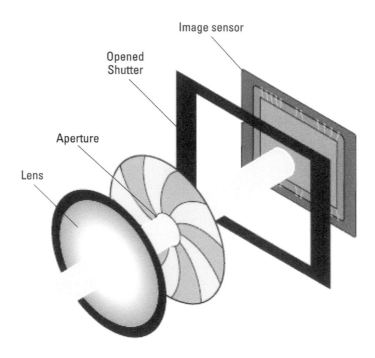

FIGURE 4-1: The aperture size and shutter speed determine how much light strikes the image sensor.

The aperture and shutter, along with a third feature, ISO, determine *exposure* — what most people would describe as picture brightness. This three–part exposure formula works as follows:

>> **Aperture (controls amount of light):** The aperture is an adjustable hole in a diaphragm set inside the lens. By changing the size of the aperture, you control the size of the light beam that can enter the camera. Aperture settings are stated as f-stop numbers, or simply f-stops, and are expressed with the letter *f* followed by a number: f/2, f/5.6, f/16, and so on. The lower the f-stop number, the larger the aperture, as illustrated in Figure 4-2. The range of available aperture settings varies from lens to lens.

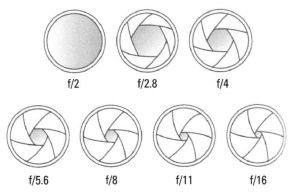

f/2   f/2.8   f/4

FIGURE 4-2: The smaller the f-stop number, the larger the aperture.

f/5.6   f/8   f/11   f/16

>> **Shutter speed (controls duration of light):** Set behind the aperture, the shutter works something like shutters on a window. When you aren't taking pictures, the camera's shutter stays closed, preventing light from striking the image sensor. When you press the shutter button, the shutter opens briefly to allow light that passes through the aperture to hit the image sensor. The exception to this scenario is when you compose in Live View mode — the shutter remains open so that your image can form on the sensor and be displayed on the monitor. When you press the shutter release in Live View mode, the shutter first closes and then reopens for the actual exposure.

The length of time that the shutter is open is the *shutter speed* and is measured in seconds: 1/60 second, 1/250 second, 2 seconds, and so on.

>> **ISO (controls light sensitivity):** ISO, which is a digital function rather than a mechanical structure on the camera, enables you to adjust how responsive the image sensor is to light. The term *ISO* is a holdover from film days, when an international standards organization rated each film stock according to light sensitivity: ISO 100, ISO 200, ISO 400, ISO 800, and so on. A higher ISO rating means greater light sensitivity.

On a digital camera, the sensor doesn't actually get more or less sensitive when you change the ISO — rather, the light "signal" that hits the sensor is either amplified or dampened through electronics wizardry, sort of like how raising the volume on a radio boosts the audio signal. But the upshot is the same as changing to a more light-reactive film stock: A higher ISO means that less light is needed to produce the image, enabling you to use a smaller aperture, faster shutter speed, or both.

Distilled to its essence, the image-exposure formula is this simple:

>> Aperture and shutter speed together determine the quantity of light that strikes the image sensor.

>> ISO determines how much the sensor reacts to that light.

The tricky part of the equation is that aperture, shutter speed, and ISO settings affect your pictures in ways that go *beyond* exposure:

>> Aperture affects depth of field, or the distance over which focus appears acceptably sharp.

>> Shutter speed determines whether moving objects appear blurry or sharply focused.

>> ISO affects the amount of image *noise,* a defect that looks like grains of sand.

You need to be aware of these side effects, explained in the next sections, to determine which combination of the three exposure settings will work best for your picture. If you're already familiar with this stuff and just want to know how to adjust exposure settings, skip ahead to the section "Setting ISO, Aperture, and Shutter Speed."

Aperture affects depth of field

The aperture setting, or f-stop, affects *depth of field,* or the distance over which focus appears sharp. With a shallow depth of field, your subject appears more sharply focused than faraway objects; with a large depth of field, the sharp-focus zone spreads over a greater distance.

When you reduce the aperture size — "stop down the aperture," in photo lingo — by choosing a higher f-stop number, you increase depth of field. As an example, see Figure 4-3. For both shots, I set focus on the fountain statue. Notice that in the first image, taken at f/13, the background is sharper than in the right example, taken at f/5.6. Aperture is just one contributor to depth of field, however; the focal length of the lens and the distance between that lens and your subject also affect how much of the scene stays in focus. See Chapter 5 for the complete story. Also be aware that depth of field affects not only objects behind your subject, but also those in front of it.

f/13, 1/25 second, ISO 200   f/5.6, 1/125 second, ISO 200

FIGURE 4-3:
Widening the aperture (choosing a lower f-stop number) decreases depth of field.

TIP

One way to remember the relationship between f-stop and depth of field, or the distance over which focus remains sharp, is to think of the *f* as *focus:* The higher the *f*-stop number, the greater the zone of sharp *focus.* (Please *don't* share this tip with photography elites, who will roll their eyes and inform you that the *f* in *f-stop* most certainly does *not* stand for focus but, rather, for the ratio between aperture size and lens focal length — as if *that's* helpful to know if you aren't an optical engineer. Chapter 1 explains focal length, which *is* helpful to know.)

Shutter speed affects motion blur

At a slow shutter speed, moving objects appear blurry, whereas a fast shutter speed captures motion cleanly. This phenomenon has nothing to do with the actual focus point of the camera but rather on the movement occurring — and being recorded by the camera — while the shutter is open.

Compare the photos in Figure 4-3, for example. The static elements are perfectly focused in both images, although the background in the left photo appears sharper because that image was shot using a higher f-stop, increasing the depth of field. But how the camera rendered the moving portion of the scene — the fountain water — was determined by shutter speed. At 1/25 second (left photo), the water blurs, giving it a misty look. At 1/125 second (right photo), the droplets appear more sharply focused, almost frozen in mid-air. How fast a shutter speed you need to freeze action depends on the speed of your subject.

If your picture suffers from overall image blur, like the picture shown in Figure 4-4, where even stationary objects appear out of focus, the camera moved during the exposure. This movement, or *camera shake,* is always a danger when you hand-hold the camera at slow shutter speeds. The longer the exposure time, the longer you have to hold the camera still to avoid the blur caused by camera shake.

How slow a shutter speed can you use before camera shake becomes a problem? The answer depends on a couple factors, including your physical abilities and your lens — the heavier the lens, the harder it is to hold steady. Camera shake also affects your picture more when you shoot with a lens that has a long focal length. You may be able to use a slower shutter speed with a 55mm lens than with a 200mm lens, for example. Finally, it's easier to detect slight blurring in an image that shows a close-up view of a subject

FIGURE 4-4:
If both stationary and moving objects are blurry, camera shake is the usual cause.

than in one that captures a wider area. Moral of the story: Take test shots to determine the slowest shutter speed you can use with each of your lenses.

Of course, to avoid the possibility of camera shake altogether, mount your camera on a tripod. If you must handhold the camera, investigate whether your lens offers *image stabilization,* a feature that helps compensate for small amounts of camera shake. The 18–55mm kit lens does provide that feature; enable it by moving the Stabilizer switch on the lens to the On position.

Freezing action isn't the only way to use shutter speed to creative effect. When shooting waterfalls, for example, many photographers use a slow shutter speed to give the water even more of a blurry, romantic look than you see in the fountain example. With colorful subjects, a slow shutter can produce some cool abstract effects and create a heightened sense of motion. Chapter 7 offers examples of both effects.

ISO affects image noise

As ISO increases, making the image sensor more reactive to light, you increase the risk of *noise.* Noise is similar in appearance to film *grain,* a defect that often mars pictures taken with high ISO film. Figure 4-5 offers an example of digital noise.

FIGURE 4-5: Noise is caused by a very high ISO or long exposure time, and it becomes more visible as you enlarge the image.

Ideally, then, you should always use the lowest ISO setting on your camera to ensure top image quality. But sometimes the lighting conditions don't permit you to do so. Take the rose photos in Figure 4-6 as an example. When I shot these pictures, I didn't have a tripod, so I needed a shutter speed fast enough to allow a sharp handheld image. I opened the aperture to f/5.6, which was the widest setting on the lens I was using, to allow as much light as possible into the camera. At ISO 100, the camera needed a shutter speed of 1/40 second to expose the picture, and that shutter speed wasn't fast enough for a successful handheld shot. You see the blurred result on the left in Figure 4-6. Raising the ISO to 200 allowed a shutter speed of 1/80 second, which was fast enough to capture the flower cleanly, as shown on the right in the figure.

Fortunately, you don't encounter serious noise on the T8i/850D until you really crank up the ISO, which is why the one-step bump from ISO 100 to ISO 200 produces no noticeable change in the amount of noise in my example photos. In fact, some people wouldn't even notice the noise in the left image in Figure 4-5 unless they were looking for it. But as with other image defects, noise becomes more apparent as you enlarge the photo, as shown on the right in that same figure. Noise is also easier to spot in shadow areas of your picture and in large areas of solid color.

ISO 100, f/5.6, 1/40 second

ISO 200, f/5.6, 1/80 second

FIGURE 4-6:
Raising the ISO allowed a faster shutter speed, which produced a sharper handheld shot without introducing any objectionable noise.

How much noise is acceptable — and, therefore, how high of an ISO is safe — is your choice. Even a little noise isn't acceptable for pictures that require the highest quality, such as images for a product catalog or a travel shot that you want to blow up to poster size.

WARNING

A high ISO isn't the only cause of noise: A long exposure time and a very slow shutter speed — say, 1 second or longer — can also produce the defect. So if you use both a high ISO and slow shutter speed, expect a double-whammy in the noise department. Your camera offers tools that combat both types of noise; check out the section "Looking at a few other exposure solutions," later in this chapter, for information.

Doing the exposure balancing act

Aperture, shutter speed, and ISO combine to determine image brightness. So changing any one setting means that one or both of the others must also shift to maintain the same image brightness.

Suppose that you're shooting a soccer game and you notice that although the overall exposure looks great, the players appear slightly blurry at the current shutter speed. If you raise the shutter speed, you have to compensate with either a larger aperture, to allow in more light during the shorter exposure, or a higher ISO setting, to make the camera more sensitive to the light. Which way should you go? Well, it depends on whether you prefer the shallower depth of field that comes with a larger aperture or the increased risk of noise that accompanies a higher

ISO. Of course, you can also adjust both settings to get the exposure results you need, perhaps upping ISO slightly and opening the aperture just a bit as well.

All photographers have their own approaches to finding the right combination of aperture, shutter speed, and ISO, and you'll no doubt develop your own system when you become more practiced at using the advanced exposure modes. In the meantime, here are some handy recommendations:

>> Use the lowest possible ISO setting unless the lighting conditions are so poor that you can't use the aperture and shutter speed you want without raising the ISO.

>> If your subject is moving, give shutter speed the next highest priority in your exposure decision. Choose a fast shutter speed to ensure a blur-free photo or, on the flip side, select a slow shutter speed to intentionally blur that moving object, an effect that can create a heightened sense of motion.

>> For nonmoving subjects, make aperture a priority over shutter speed, setting the aperture according to the depth of field you have in mind. For portraits, for example, try using a wide-open aperture (a low f-stop number) to create a shallow depth of field and a nice, soft background for your subject.

WARNING

Be careful not to go too shallow with depth of field when shooting a group portrait. Unless all the subjects are the same distance from the camera, some may be outside the zone of sharp focus. A shallow depth of field also makes action shots more difficult because you have to be absolutely spot on with focus. With a larger depth of field, the subject can move a greater distance toward or away from you before leaving the sharp-focus area, giving you a bit of a focusing safety net.

Keeping all this information straight is a little overwhelming at first, but the more you work with your camera, the more the whole exposure equation will make sense to you. You can find tips in Chapter 7 for choosing exposure settings for specific types of pictures; keep moving through this chapter for details on how to monitor and adjust aperture, shutter speed, and ISO settings.

Stepping Up to Advance Exposure Modes (P, Tv, Av, and M)

Through the Background Blur, Brightness, and Contrast adjustments available through the Creative Assist option, you may be able to affect exposure and depth of field to some extent in Scene Intelligent Auto mode as well as in certain SCN modes. I say "may be" because how much of an adjustment you can make depends on the current lighting as well as a few other factors you can explore in Chapter 3. Point is, your creative control in Scene Intelligent Auto and the SCN modes is limited.

If you're really concerned with exposure and depth of field — and you should be — set the Mode dial to one of the four Creative Zone exposure modes highlighted in Figure 4-7. In these modes, you get precise control over aperture, shutter speed, and other features that affect exposure and contribute to depth of field.

Creative Zone modes

Each of the four modes offers a different level of control over aperture and shutter speed. Chapter 2 provides a basic definition of each mode; here's a recap plus a few additional details:

FIGURE 4-7:
To fully control exposure and other picture properties, choose one of these exposure modes.

>> **P (programmed autoexposure):** The camera selects both the aperture and shutter speed to deliver a good exposure at the current ISO setting. But you can choose from different combinations of the two for creative flexibility (which is why this mode is sometimes referred to as *flexible programmed autoexposure*).

>> **Tv (shutter-priority autoexposure):** You select a shutter speed, and the camera chooses the aperture setting that produces a good exposure at that shutter speed and the current ISO setting.

Why *Tv?* Well, shutter speed controls exposure time; *Tv* stands for time value.

>> **Av (aperture-priority autoexposure):** The opposite of shutter-priority autoexposure, this mode gives you control over the aperture setting — thus *Av,* for aperture value. The camera then selects the appropriate shutter speed to properly expose the picture — again, based on the selected ISO setting.

>> **M (manual exposure):** In this mode, you specify both shutter speed and aperture.

To sum up, the first three modes are semiautomatic modes that offer exposure assistance while still providing some creative control. Note one important point, however: In extreme lighting conditions, the camera may not be able to select settings that will produce a good exposure, and it doesn't stop you from taking a poorly exposed photo. You may be able to solve the problem by using features designed to modify autoexposure results, such as Exposure Compensation (explained later in this chapter), or by adding flash, but you get no guarantees.

Manual mode puts all exposure control in your hands. If you're a longtime photographer who comes from the days when manual exposure was the only game in town, you may prefer to stick with this mode. In fact, in some ways, manual mode is simpler than the semiautomatic modes — if you're not happy with the exposure, you just change the aperture, shutter speed, or ISO setting and shoot again. You don't have to fiddle with features that modify the results delivered by the autoexposure system as you do in the P, Tv, and Av modes.

Whichever Creative Zone mode you choose, check out the next several sections to find out how to view and adjust exposure settings.

Monitoring Exposure Settings

When you press the shutter button halfway, the current f-stop, shutter speed, and ISO speed appear in the viewfinder display, as shown in Figure 4-8.

REMEMBER

Don't confuse the number in brackets — 9, in the figure — for the shots-remaining value, which appears in brackets in the other displays. In the viewfinder, the bracketed number reflects the buffer value, which is relevant only when you shoot in one of the Continuous Drive modes. Introduced in Chapter 1, the *buffer* is internal memory the camera uses to temporarily store image data until it has time to record the data to the memory card. The buffer actually can hold more than 9 shots, but there's only room in the viewfinder readout for a single-digit value, so that display always shows 9 even when more storage is available. At any rate, when the buffer value drops to 0, the buffer is full, and the camera won't take any more pictures until it catches up with its data-recording work.

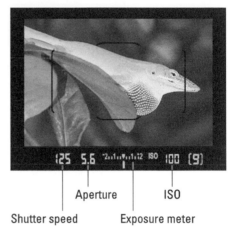

Shutter speed   Aperture   ISO   Exposure meter

FIGURE 4-8:
The shutter speed, f-stop, and ISO speed appear at the bottom of the viewfinder.

You also can view exposure settings in the Quick Control and Live View displays, as shown in Figure 4-9. In the Quick Control display, shown on the left in the figure, the buffer value appears only when the buffer value drops to 9 or below; that's why it isn't present in the figure. In the Live View display, however, the buffer value is given two digits' worth of screen space and appears just to the left of the battery-status icon, in the upper-right corner of the screen. In the Live View screen shown in Figure 4-9, for example, the buffer value is 98. Again, though, you don't really need to pay attention to this number until it drops near zero.

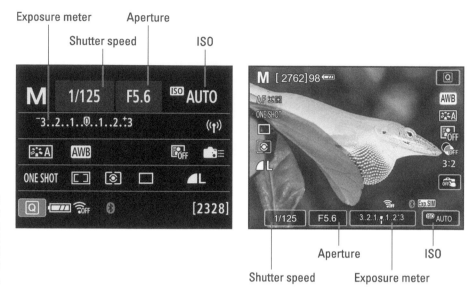

FIGURE 4-9:
You also can view the settings in the Quick Control display (left) and Live View display (right).

REMEMBER

In the viewfinder, shutter speeds are presented as whole numbers, even if the shutter speed is set to a fraction of a second. For example, for a shutter speed of 1/125 second, you see just the number 125, as shown in the Figure 4-8. In the other displays, the speed appears as a fraction (1/125 in Figure 4-9). In all displays, a shutter speed of 1 second or longer is indicated by quotation marks after the number — 1" indicates a shutter speed of 1 second, 4" means 4 seconds, and so on.

The viewfinder, Quick Control display, and Live View display also offer an *exposure meter,* labeled in Figures 4-8 and 4-9. This graphic serves two different purposes, depending on the exposure mode:

>> **In M mode, the meter indicates whether your settings will properly expose the image.** Figure 4-10 gives you three examples. When the *exposure indicator* (the bar under the meter) aligns with the center point of the meter, as shown in the middle example, the current settings will produce a proper exposure. If the indicator moves to the left of center (toward the minus side of the scale), as in the left example in the figure, the camera is alerting you that the image will be underexposed. If the indicator moves to the right of center, as in the right example, the image will be overexposed. The farther the indicator moves toward the + or – sign, the greater the potential exposure problem.

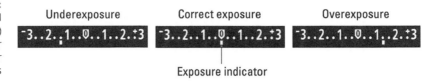

Underexposure   Correct exposure   Overexposure

Exposure indicator

REMEMBER

Keep in mind that the information reported by the meter is dependent on the *metering mode,* which determines what part of the frame the camera uses to calculate exposure. You can choose from four metering modes, as covered in the next section. Also, consider the meter a guide, not a dictator — the beauty of manual exposure is that *you* decide how dark or bright an exposure you want, not the camera.

» **In the P, Tv, and Av exposure modes, the meter displays the current Exposure Compensation setting.** Remember that in these modes, the camera sets either the shutter speed or aperture, or both, to produce a good exposure — again, depending on the current metering mode. Because the camera is tasked with choosing the right settings to produce a good exposure, you don't need to refer to the meter for guidance. Instead, in these semi-automatic exposure modes, the meter instead indicates whether you enabled *Exposure Compensation,* a feature that forces a brighter or darker exposure than the camera thinks is appropriate. (Look for details later in this chapter.) When the exposure indicator is at 0, no compensation is being applied. If the indicator is to the right of 0, you applied compensation to produce a brighter image; when the indicator is to the left, you asked for a darker photo.

WARNING

In some lighting situations, the camera *can't* select settings that produce an optimal exposure in the P, Tv, or Av modes. Because the meter indicates the exposure compensation amount in those modes, it needs another way to warn you of the potential problem. How it goes about sending that alert depends on your exposure mode:

- *Av mode (aperture-priority autoexposure):* The shutter speed value blinks to let you know the camera can't select a shutter speed that will produce a good exposure at the aperture you selected. Choose a different f-stop or adjust the ISO.

- *Tv mode (shutter-priority autoexposure):* The aperture value blinks to tell you the camera can't open or stop down the aperture enough to expose the image at your selected shutter speed. Your options are to change the shutter speed or ISO.

- *P mode (programmed autoexposure):* In P mode, both the aperture and shutter speed values blink if the camera can't select a combination that will properly expose the image. Your only recourse is to adjust the lighting or change the ISO setting.

ARGH, STOP TURNING OFF THE METER BEFORE I CAN READ IT!

When you shoot in Live View mode, the camera is set by default to turn off the meter after 8 seconds to conserve battery power. That means that after you press the shutter button halfway to kickstart the metering system, you have a meager 8 seconds to see what the meter display has to report.

If you find that time limit frustrating, head for Shooting Menu 2, choose Metering Timer, and select a longer shutoff duration. You can specify a time as long as 30 minutes, but that's *too* long, in my opinion, unless you really want to burn through camera batteries at a rapid pace. Maybe something more moderate, such as 16 seconds or 30 seconds, will serve your needs better.

Note that this menu option *only* appears when the camera is in Live View mode. Additionally, you can reduce or extend the time the camera waits before it puts itself into sleep mode, shutting down the meter and all displays. To customize this feature, go to Setup Menu 2 and select Auto Power Off. This setting applies for viewfinder shooting as well as Live View shooting.

Choosing an Exposure Metering Mode

The *metering mode* determines which part of the frame the camera analyzes to calculate the proper exposure. Your camera offers four metering modes, described in the following list and represented in the Quick Control and Live View displays by the icons you see in the margin.

REMEMBER

You can access all four metering modes only in the Creative Zone modes (P, Tv, Av, and M). In Basic Zone modes, the camera selects the metering mode, with the Evaluative mode used in most cases.

>> **Evaluative metering:** The camera analyzes the entire frame and then selects exposure settings designed to produce a balanced exposure.

>> **Partial metering:** The camera bases exposure only on the light that falls in the center 6 percent of the frame. In the Live View display, a circle appears to indicate the size of the metering area, as shown on the left in Figure 4-11.

Partial metering circle   Spot metering circle

Partial metering symbol   Spot metering symbol

FIGURE 4-11:
The Live View screen displays circles representing the area measured in Partial metering mode (left) and Spot metering mode (right).

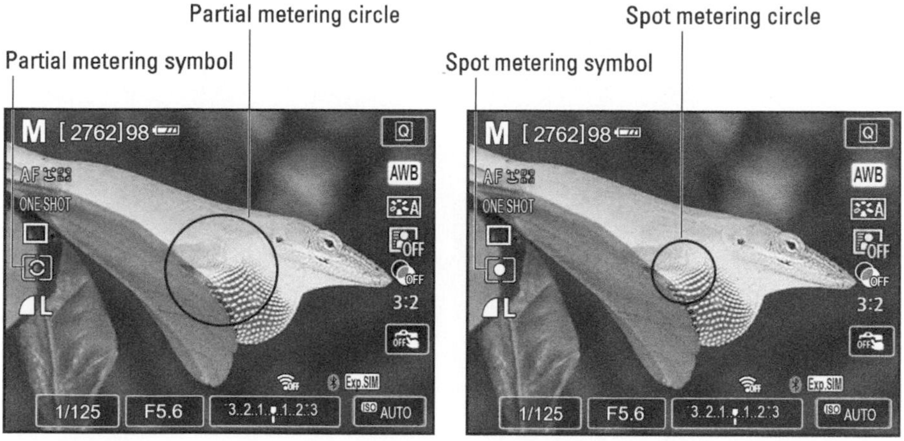

>> **Spot metering:** This mode works like Partial metering but uses a smaller region of the frame to calculate exposure. Again, a circle marking the metering area appears in the Live View display. You also see the circle in the viewfinder when you use Spot metering.

>> **Center-Weighted Average metering:** The camera bases exposure on the entire frame but puts extra emphasis — or *weight* — on the center.

In most cases, Evaluative metering does a good job of calculating exposure. But it can get thrown off when a dark subject is set against a bright background, or vice versa. For example, in the left image in Figure 4-12, the amount of bright background caused the camera to select exposure settings that underexposed the statue, which was the point of interest for the photo. Switching to Partial metering properly exposed the statue. (Spot metering would produce a similar result for this subject.)

TIP

Of course, if the background is very bright and the subject is very dark, the exposure that does the best job on the subject typically overexposes the background. You may be able to reclaim some lost highlights by turning on Highlight Tone Priority, a feature explored later in this chapter. Also, if you want to use Spot or Partial metering but you don't want your subject to appear in the center of the frame, see the later section "Locking Autoexposure Settings" to find out how to accomplish that goal. (Spoiler alert: The section shows you how to frame the scene initially with your subject in the metering area, lock the exposure settings, and then reframe to your desired composition.)

Evaluative

Partial

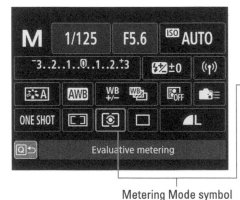

FIGURE 4-12:
In Evaluative mode, the camera underexposed the statue; switching to Partial metering produced a better result.

To change the metering mode, use either of these two options:

>> **Quick Control method:** After shifting to Quick Control mode, choose the icon labeled in Figure 4-13 and rotate the Quick Control dial or Main dial to cycle through the four modes. In Live View mode, the text label that appears after you select the Metering Mode icon initially identifies the setting you're adjusting, as shown in the figure. But as soon as you choose a different setting, the text changes to show the name of that option.

FIGURE 4-13:
You can quickly adjust the metering mode in Quick Control mode.

Metering Mode symbol

When you're not using Live View, you also can display all four metering mode settings on a separate screen by pressing the Set button after you highlight the metering mode option on the Quick Control screen. If you go that route, tap your choice of metering mode and then tap the exit arrow or press the Set button to return to the initial Quick Control screen.

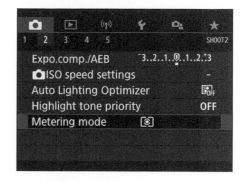

>> **Shooting Menu 2:** Look for the Metering mode option at the bottom of the menu, as shown in Figure 4-14. Select the option to display the screen where you can choose the metering mode you want to use.

FIGURE 4-14:
You also can access the Metering mode from Shooting Menu 2.

TIP

In theory, the best practice is to check the Metering mode before each shot and choose the mode that best matches your exposure goals (when in Live View, the monitor shows you the anticipated results of the current exposure settings). But in practice, it's a pain, not just in terms of having to adjust yet one more setting but also in terms of having to *remember* to adjust one more setting. So until you're comfortable with all the other controls on your camera, just stick with Evaluative metering. It produces good results in most situations, and after all, you can see in the Live View monitor whether you like your results and, if not, adjust exposure settings and reshoot. This option makes the whole Metering mode issue a lot less critical than it is when you shoot with film.

The exception might be when you're shooting a series of images in which a significant contrast in lighting exists between subject and background. Then, switching to Spot or Partial metering may save you the time spent having to adjust the exposure for each image. Many portrait photographers, for example, rely on Spot metering exclusively because they know their subject will usually be hovering near the center of the frame. Spot metering is also helpful when you need a very accurate metering of a specific element in the photo to keep it from being over- or underexposed.

Setting ISO, Aperture, and Shutter Speed

REMEMBER

To control ISO, aperture (f-stop), or shutter speed, set the camera to P, Tv, Av, or M exposure mode. Then check out the next several sections for the steps to follow to adjust these settings.

Controlling ISO

To refresh your memory about the ISO information presented at the start of this chapter: The ISO setting controls how sensitive the camera's image sensor is to light. At higher ISO values, you need less light to expose an image correctly. But the downside to raising ISO is a greater possibility of image noise. Refer to Figure 4-5 for a reminder of what that defect looks like.

You can control ISO only in P, Tv, Av, or M exposure mode for still photography and in M mode for movie recording. In all other modes, the camera adjusts ISO automatically.

If you're shooting in an exposure mode that offers ISO control, you have the following choices:

» **Select a specific ISO setting.**
Normally, you can choose ISO settings ranging from 100 to 25600. But if you really want to push things, you can amp ISO up to 51200. To take advantage of that option, navigate to Setup Menu 5 and choose Custom Functions. Scroll to Custom Function 2, ISO Expansion, shown in Figure 4-15. If you set the option to Enable, the list of possible ISO values for photography includes an H (High) setting, which delivers ISO 51200.

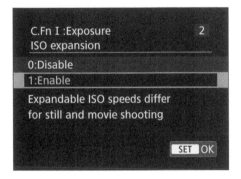

FIGURE 4-15:
By enabling Custom Function 2, you can push the available ISO range to 51200 for still photography.

As the Custom Function screen indicates, the expanded ISO range varies for movie shooting. In Movie mode, the ISO range tops out at 25600. (The highest ISO setting normally available for Movie mode is 12800.)

REMEMBER

One complication: If you enable Highlight Tone Priority, an exposure feature covered later in this chapter, you lose the option of using ISO 100 as well as the H setting.

» **Let the camera choose the ISO for you (Auto ISO).** Normally, I like to set the ISO value myself because I want to control how much noise might appear in the image. But even a control freak like me sometimes wants to hand off the ISO reins to the camera. Here's why: When the light is changing quickly or your subject is moving from light to dark areas at a rapid pace, taking even a few seconds to adjust the ISO between frames can cause you to miss a great shot. That's when Auto ISO can save the day.

But what about the noise potential, you ask? Well, here's the cool part about the using Auto ISO in the Creative Zone exposure modes: You can specify the highest ISO setting that you want the camera to use, starting with a value as low as ISO 400 and going up to ISO 25600. To set this limit, open Shooting Menu 2 and choose ISO Speed Settings, as shown on the left in Figure 4-16. On the second screen, shown on the right in the figure, select Max for Auto to set the top ISO setting the camera can choose. The default is ISO 6400.

FIGURE 4-16: Follow this menu path to limit the highest ISO setting the camera can choose when Auto ISO is enabled.

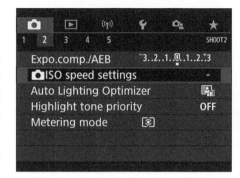
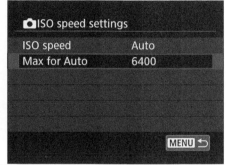

TIP

You can view the current ISO setting in Quick Control and Live View displays as well as in the viewfinder. Refer to Figures 4-8 and 4-9 if you need a reminder of where to look. In Figure 4-8, the ISO is set to 100; in Figure 4-9, Auto ISO is selected.

To adjust the ISO setting, you have these options:

TIP

>> **Press the ISO button (top of the camera, labeled in Figure 4-17).** You then see the screen shown on the right, where you can choose your desired setting by dragging your finger along the scale. Alternatively, choose the setting by rotating the Quick Control or Main dial, pressing the left or right edge of the Quick Control dial, or tapping the left/right arrows.

To quickly return to the Auto ISO setting, press the Info button or tap the Info symbol on the touchscreen.

>> **Choose ISO Speed Settings from Shooting Menu 2, as shown in Figure 4-16.** On the next screen, select ISO Speed. You're shown the same settings screen that you see on the right in Figure 4-17.

>> **During viewfinder shooting, press the Q button or tap the Q symbol and enter Quick Control mode.** After choosing the ISO option, you again see the settings screen shown in Figure 4-17.

Press to display ISO settings screen   Selected ISO value

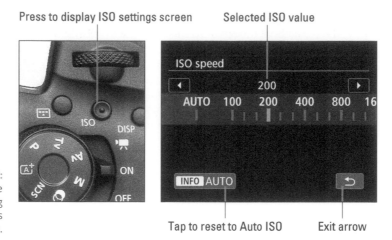

FIGURE 4-17:
The fastest route
to the ISO setting
screen is to press
the ISO button.

Tap to reset to Auto ISO   Exit arrow

>> **In Live View mode, tap the ISO setting, labeled on the left in Figure 4-18.**
Then adjust the ISO setting on the screen that appears, as shown on the right
in the figure. You can change the setting by rotating the Main or Quick Control
dial, tapping the triangles at the left and right ends of the number scale, or
just dragging your finger along the scale. Tap the exit arrow in the upper-right
corner of the screen to return to the Live View shooting display. Or exit the
settings screen by simply pressing the shutter button halfway and releasing it.

TIP

When the camera is set to Auto ISO, the ISO value in Quick Control and Live View
displays initially shows Auto, as you would expect. But when you press the shutter
button halfway, which initiates exposure metering, the value changes to the specific ISO value the camera selected. In the viewfinder, the specific ISO value always
appears, whether you dialed in that setting yourself or the camera selected it in
Auto ISO mode.

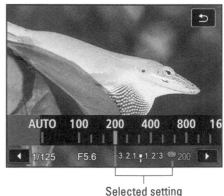

FIGURE 4-18:
During Live View
shooting, tap the
ISO setting (left)
to display the
settings screen
(right).

Tap to access ISO setting   Selected setting

EXPOSURE STOPS: HOW MANY DO YOU WANT TO SEE?

In photo terminology, the word *stop* refers to an increment of exposure. To increase exposure by one stop means to adjust the aperture or shutter speed to allow twice as much light into the camera as the current settings permit. To reduce exposure a stop, you use settings that allow half as much light. Doubling or halving the ISO value also adjusts exposure by one stop.

By default, most exposure-related settings on your camera are based on 1/3 stop adjustments. If you prefer, you can tell the camera to present certain exposure adjustments in 1/2 stop increments so that you don't have to cycle through as many settings each time you want to make a change.

To make this change, display Setup Menu 5 and choose Custom Functions. Through Custom Function 1, Exposure Level Increments (left figure here), you can affect the increments that are displayed on the exposure meter and that are available when you change the shutter speed and f-stop settings. Custom Function 3, ISO Speed Setting Increments, (right figure) enables you to limit the ISO setting to one-stop changes.

In both cases, the default setting, 1/3 stop, provides the greatest degree of exposure fine-tuning, so I stick with that option. In this book, all instructions assume that you're using the defaults as well.

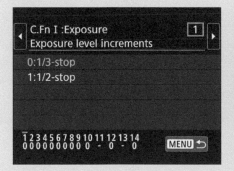 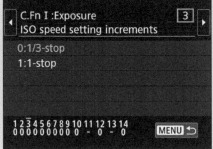

Also, because of some rules set by the camera's designers, the value that appears in the displays when you use Auto ISO may not be exactly the value that the camera uses. For display purposes, the camera uses whole-step increments of ISO adjustment — ISO 100, 200, 400, and so on. But when actually setting the ISO, it can select from finer increments — ISO 125 or 160, for example. You can see the actual value used when you view shooting data during playback; see Chapter 9 to find out how to view that data. And if you need to use a specific ISO value for some reason, jump out of Auto ISO mode and dial in that number yourself.

Adjusting aperture and shutter speed

Which Creative Zone exposure mode you use determines your level of control over aperture and shutter speed and also determines the method you use to adjust those settings:

>> **P:** You can choose from different combinations of aperture and shutter speed, but have no direct control over either. To view the camera's recommended combination, compose your shot and then press the shutter button halfway. To select a different combination of the two settings, rotate the Main dial.

>> **Tv:** You control shutter speed; adjust that setting by rotating the Main dial. After selecting the shutter speed, frame your shot and press the shutter button halfway to initiate autoexposure metering. The displays then show the aperture setting that the camera selected to expose the picture at your chosen shutter speed and the current ISO.

>> **Av:** The opposite of Tv mode, Av mode enables you to set the f-stop while the camera selects the shutter speed. Rotate the Main dial to set the aperture setting you want to use. Then frame your subject and press the shutter button halfway. The camera then displays the shutter speed it selected.

Even though you're in aperture-priority mode and so concentrating on the f-stop, always check the shutter speed that the camera selected for you. If the shutter speed drops so low that handholding the camera or capturing a moving subject won't be possible, you can either open the aperture (choose a lower f-stop number) or dial in a higher ISO setting, which will enable the camera to select a faster shutter speed at your preferred f-stop.

>> **M (manual exposure):** You set both aperture and shutter speed. Use these techniques:

- *Adjust shutter speed.* Rotate the Main dial.

  In M mode, you have access to *Bulb* mode, which keeps the shutter open as long as you keep the shutter button pressed fully down. To get to the Bulb setting, go one step past the slowest possible normal shutter speed (30 seconds).

- *Adjust aperture.* Rotate the Quick Control dial.

Be sure to use the Main dial to lock in your setting when working in the P, Tv, or Av modes. In those modes, rotating the Quick Control dial applies an exposure adjustment called Exposure Compensation, which you can read about a little later in the chapter.

In the Av, Tv, and M exposure modes, you also can adjust the exposure settings as follows:

>> **For viewfinder photography, use Quick Control mode.** After pressing the Q button or tapping the Q touchscreen symbol, highlight the setting you want to change and then rotate the Main dial. The Quick Control method doesn't work in Live View mode, unfortunately.

>> **In Live View mode, use the touchscreen.** Just tap the setting on the touch-screen to display a screen that offers the available values for that setting.

A few more words of wisdom related to aperture and shutter speed:

>> **Check the meter for guidance in M exposure mode.** Of course, you don't have to follow the camera's guidance — you can take the picture using any settings you like, even if the meter indicates that the image will be under- or overexposed.

>> **In Live View mode, keep an eye on the Exp Sim symbol.** The live monitor preview updates as you adjust exposure settings to show you the change in image brightness. But if the camera can't display an accurate preview, the Exp Sim symbol in the lower-right corner of the screen appears dimmed. (This happens, for example, when you use flash.)

>> **In P, Tv, and Av mode, the shutter speed or f-stop value blinks if the camera isn't able to select settings that produce a good exposure.** If the problem is too little light, try raising the ISO or adding flash to solve the problem. If there's too much light, lower the ISO value or attach an *ND (neutral density)* filter, which is sort of like sunglasses for your lens — it simply cuts the light entering the lens. (The *neutral* part just means that the filter doesn't affect image colors, just brightness.)

>> **Say "nay" to Safety Shift.** If you dig into the Custom Functions warehouse found on Setup Menu 5, you find Custom Function 4, Safety Shift. This feature, when enabled, gives the camera permission to fiddle with your chosen f-stop in Av mode or shutter speed in Tv mode if it thinks that you're headed for an exposure disaster. The option is disabled by default, and that's how I'd leave it if I were you. My recommendation is based on a couple of assumptions. First, if you're using Av or Tv mode, it's because *you* want to be the one controlling the f-stop or shutter speed. If you wanted the camera to stick its nose into your business, you'd shoot in Scene Intelligent Auto or P mode.

Second, the camera does alert you to impending doom by blinking the f-stop or shutter speed value in the displays, as mentioned earlier. If you pay attention to those signals, you can decide how you want to solve the problem. You — not the camera. Finally, if Auto ISO is enabled, the camera is already free to adjust ISO as an exposure assist — although, granted, it may not be able to choose an ISO low enough to avoid overexposure or high enough to prevent underexposure.

On some higher-end Canon models, you can give the camera a couple of options for how it responds when it senses exposure peril in Av or Tv modes. But on the T8i/850D, you either can say "yay" or "nay," which means that you don't really know how your settings will be adjusted. So for me, Safety Shift is a no-brainer: Keep it turned off.

>> **You can adjust the exposure results that you get in the P, Tv, and Av modes.** When you use these semi-automatic exposure modes, the settings that the camera selects are based on what it thinks is the proper exposure. If you don't agree with the camera, you have two options. Option one is to switch to manual exposure (M) mode and simply dial in the aperture and shutter speed that deliver the exposure you want. Or if you want to stay in P, Tv, or Av mode, your other option is to try using exposure compensation, one of the exposure-correction tools described in the next section.

Sorting Through Your Camera's Exposure-Correction Tools

In addition to the normal controls over aperture, shutter speed, and ISO, your camera offers a collection of tools that enable you to solve tricky exposure problems. The next sections give you the lowdown on these features.

Overriding autoexposure results with Exposure Compensation

REMEMBER

In the P, Tv, and Av exposure modes, you have some input over exposure: In P mode, you can rotate the Main dial to choose from different combinations of aperture and shutter speed; in Tv mode, you can dial in the shutter speed; and in Av mode, you can select the aperture setting. (See the first sections of this chapter if you don't yet understand how changing the shutter speed and aperture affect your picture.)

Because P, Tv, and Av are all semiautomatic modes, though, the camera ultimately controls the final exposure. If your picture turns out too bright or too dark in P mode, you can't simply choose a different f-stop/shutter speed combo because they all deliver the same exposure — which is to say, the exposure that the camera has in mind. And changing the shutter speed in Tv mode or adjusting the f-stop in Av mode won't help either because as soon as you change the setting that you're controlling, the camera automatically adjusts the other setting to produce the same exposure it initially delivered.

Not to worry: You actually do have final say over exposure in these exposure modes. The secret is Exposure Compensation, a feature that tells the camera to produce a brighter or darker exposure on your next shot, whether or not you change the aperture or shutter speed (or both, in P mode).

Best of all, this feature is probably one of the easiest on the camera to understand. Here's all there is to it:

>> **Exposure compensation is stated in EV (Exposure Value) numbers, as in EV +2.0.** Possible values range from EV +5.0 EV to EV –5.0 EV for viewfinder shooting and EV +3.0 EV to EV –3.0 for Live View photography. You're also limited to the 3-stop adjustment range for movie recording and if the Shooting Screen option on the Display Level menu is set to Guided. (Yeah, I don't get that either, but Chapter 1 discusses the Display Level menu settings.) A setting of EV 0.0 results in no exposure adjustment.

>> **Each full number on the EV scale represents an exposure shift of one stop.** Again, a stop refers to an increment of exposure adjustment. If you adjust the aperture or shutter speed to allow half as much light to hit the image sensor as the current settings, you're decreasing exposure by one stop. Allowing twice as much light increases exposure by one stop. So if you change the Exposure Compensation setting from EV 0.0 to EV –1.0, you're asking for a one-stop decrease in exposure, resulting in a darker image. If you instead raise the value to EV +1.0, the camera increases exposure by one stop, producing a brighter photo.

TIP

Exposure compensation is especially helpful when your subject is much lighter or darker than an average scene. For example, take a look at the image on the left in Figure 4-19. Because of the very bright sky, the camera chose an exposure that made the tree too dark. Setting the Exposure Compensation value to EV +1.0 resulted in a properly exposed image.

EV 0.0

EV +1.0

FIGURE 4-19:
For a brighter exposure than the autoexposure mechanism chooses, dial in a positive Exposure Compensation value.

Sometimes you can cope with situations like this one by changing the metering mode, as discussed earlier in this chapter. For the image in Figure 4-19, I used Evaluative mode, for example, which meters exposure over the entire frame. Switching to Partial or Spot metering probably wouldn't have helped because the area the camera meters in those modes — the center of the frame — is bright in this scene. In any case, it's usually easier to simply adjust exposure compensation than to experiment with metering modes.

REMEMBER

The following steps show the fastest—but potentially most dangerous—way to apply Exposure Compensation. You can use it both for viewfinder shooting and Live View shooting:

1. **Press the shutter button halfway to initiate exposure metering.**

   You can release the shutter button now if you want. (You just need to press it halfway to wake up the autoexposure metering system.)

2. **Rotate the Quick Control dial.**

   As you rotate the dial, the exposure indicator (the little bar under the exposure meter) moves to indicate the amount of adjustment. For example, in Figure 4-20, the bar shows that I requested an adjustment of EV +1.0. The left screen shows the Exposure Compensation symbol and setting as they appear in the Quick Control display; the right screen, in the viewfinder display. Figure 4-21 shows the same +1.0 adjustment as it appears in the Live View display.

Exposure Compensation symbol

Exposure Compensation setting

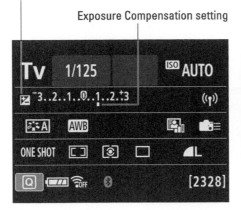

FIGURE 4-20:
The notch on the exposure meter indicates the amount of Exposure Compensation when you shoot in the P, Tv, and Av exposure modes.

Exposure Compensation symbol

Exposure Compensation setting

Notice the +/− symbol at the end of the meter in the displays. This symbol, which is universal for exposure compensation, provides an extra reminder that the adjustment is in force. If you reset the value to EV 0.0, the symbol disappears.

3. **Take the picture.**

"Okay," you're thinking, "what's so 'dangerous' about this technique?" The risk is that it's easy to inadvertently rotate the Quick Control dial and specify some amount of Exposure Compensation when you had no intention of doing so. And then you're likely to waste time trying to figure out why your exposure is off. One solution is to lock the dial so that it has no effect. By default, pressing the Erase/Lock button toggles the lock on and off. (The information on the Multi-Function Lock feature in Chapter 1 has more details.) Just remember that you have to then unlock the dial to use it to set the f-stop value in M exposure mode or to adjust any other settings normally responsive to the dial.

Exposure Compensation setting

Exposure Compensation symbol

FIGURE 4-21:
In Live View mode, the Exposure Compensation setting appears in the meter at the bottom of the display.

You don't have to use the Quick Control dial to change the Exposure Compensation setting, though. Here are other ways to get that job done:

» **Display Shooting Menu 2 and choose Expo Comp/AEB, as shown on the left in Figure 4-22.** You then see the screen shown on the right in the figure. The screen has a double purpose, as indicated by its name. You use it to enable automatic exposure bracketing (AEB) as well as exposure compensation.

Exposure Compensation controls

 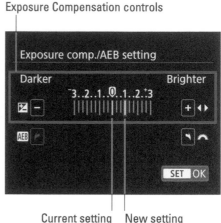

Current setting   New setting

FIGURE 4-22:
After reaching this screen, set the Exposure Compensation value by rotating the Quick Control dial or by tapping the + and – signs on either end of the meter.

WARNING

If you're not careful, you can wind up changing the wrong setting, so stop texting for a sec and pay attention:

● The labels on the second screen in Figure 4-22 show which of the controls affect the Exposure Compensation setting. When AEB isn't in force, you see only a single meter, as shown in the figure; that meter represents the exposure compensation setting.

● To apply exposure compensation, *don't rotate the Main dial* — that dial adjusts the AEB setting. Instead, press the left or right edges of the Quick Control dial, tap the + or – signs at the ends of the exposure compensation meter, or rotate the Quick Control dial. The blue marker indicates the default or most current setting (EV 0.0) in the figure; the marker labeled "New setting" in the figure shows the amount of adjustment you just dialed in.

- Even though the meters displayed on the monitor initially show a range of just +/– three stops (two in the case of the viewfinder), you can access the entire five-stop range available for Exposure Compensation shifts when you're not using Live View. Just keep rotating the Quick Control dial or using the other methods of adjusting the setting to display the far ends of the range.

After setting the amount of Exposure Compensation, tap the Set label in the lower-right corner of the screen or press the Set button to lock in the amount of exposure compensation and return to Shooting Menu 2. Press the Menu button to exit the menus altogether.

» **Use the Quick Control method (available during viewfinder shooting only).** Press the Q button or tap the Q symbol to shift to Quick Control mode. Highlight the exposure meter and then rotate the Quick Control dial to move the exposure indicator along the meter. If you tap the exposure meter or press Set while it's highlighted, you see the same screen featured in Figure 4-22 and discussed in the preceding encyclopedia of bullet points.

» **Change the setting via the touchscreen (Live View only):** Tap the exposure meter at the bottom of the Live View screen, labeled in Figure 4-21, to display a screen that contains a scale on which you specify the amount of Exposure Compensation you want to use. You can accomplish that job by rotating the Main dial or Quick Control dial, dragging your finger along the scale, pressing the right or left edge of the Quick Control dial, or tapping the + and – signs at the end of the scale. Tap the exit arrow in the upper-right corner of the screen to leave the settings screen.

» **Customize the Set button so that you can use it and the Main dial to set the amount of Exposure Compensation.** Chapter 12 shows you how to customize the Set button so that it's linked to the Exposure Compensation setting. After you make that change, you can adjust the amount of compensation by holding down the Set button while rotating the Main dial. But there's a hitch: When you press the Set button during normal photography, the monitor turns off temporarily, and you have to rely on the viewfinder to see the amount of adjustment you're applying. In Live View mode, the monitor remains on, so this setup works fine. Note that this is just one of several functions you can assign to the Set button; again, see Chapter 12 to explore the possibilities.

REMEMBER

When you dial in an Exposure Compensation adjustment of greater than three stops, the notch under the viewfinder meter disappears and is replaced by a triangle at one end of the meter — at the right end for a positive Exposure Compensation value and at the left for a negative value. However, the meter on the Quick Control screen and on Shooting Menu 2 adjusts to show the actual setting. (Remember, using Live View limits you to an adjustment range of three stops, so this issue doesn't come into play.)

Whatever EV setting you select, the way the camera arrives at the brighter or darker image you request depends on the exposure mode:

>> In Av (aperture-priority) mode, the camera adjusts the shutter speed but leaves your selected f-stop in force. Keep an eye on the shutter speed to make sure that it doesn't drop so low that camera shake or movement of your subject will blur the picture.

>> In Tv (shutter-priority) mode, the opposite occurs: The camera opens or stops down the aperture, leaving your selected shutter speed alone. Keep in mind that the camera can adjust the aperture only so much, according to the aperture range of your lens. If you reach the end of that range, you have to compromise on your selected shutter speed or ISO.

>> In P (programmed autoexposure) mode, the camera decides whether to adjust aperture, shutter speed, or both to accommodate the Exposure Compensation setting.

These three rules of the road assume that you have a specific ISO setting selected rather than Auto ISO. If you do use Auto ISO, the camera may adjust that value instead. Additionally, you can't use flash when Auto ISO and Exposure Compensation are both enabled.

Speaking of Auto ISO: If you use Auto ISO, you actually can apply Exposure Compensation even in M (manual exposure) mode. Remember, in manual exposure mode, you set the f-stop and shutter speed. But if you turn on Auto ISO and let the camera pick the ISO, you may occasionally be unhappy with the resulting exposure. You could dump out of Auto ISO mode and pick a higher ISO for a brighter image or a lower number for a darker result, but if you want to stick with Auto ISO, you can use Exposure Compensation to tell the camera to make that change for you. In M mode, the camera doesn't mess with your selected shutter speed or f-stop; instead, it adjusts exposure by changing the ISO setting.

REMEMBER

By default, the Exposure Compensation value is reset to EV 0.0 when you turn the camera off. If you don't want the reset to happen, head for Setup Menu 5, choose Custom Functions, and change the setting for Custom Function 5 (Exposure Compensation Auto Cancel) to Disable. Just don't forget that the compensation is still in force the next time you use the camera.

Improving high-contrast shots with Highlight Tone Priority

When a scene contains both very dark and very bright areas, achieving a good exposure can be difficult. If you choose exposure settings that render the shadows properly, the highlights are often overexposed, as in the left image in Figure 4-23. Although the dark lamppost in the foreground looks fine in the first shot, the white building behind it became so bright that all detail was lost. The same thing occurred in the highlight areas of the church steeple.

Highlight Tone Priority off

Highlight Tone Priority on

FIGURE 4-23: Highlight Tone Priority can help prevent overexposed highlights.

To produce a better image in this situation, try enabling Highlight Tone Priority, which helps keep highlight areas intact without darkening shadows. The feature did the trick for the scene in Figure 4-23; the results appear in the second image in the figure. The difference is subtle, but the windows in the building are at least visible, the steeple regained some of its color, and the sky, too, has a bit more blue.

REMEMBER

Highlight Tone Priority is available only in the P, Tv, Av, and M modes. It's turned off by default, which may seem like an odd choice after looking at the improvement it made to the scene in Figure 4-23. What gives? The answer is that in order to do its thing, Highlight Tone Priority needs to play with a few other camera settings, as follows:

>> **The ISO range is reduced to ISO 200–25600.** The camera needs the more limited range in order to favor the image highlights. (If you enable the feature for movie recording, the top end of the ISO range is 12800.)

>> **Auto Lighting Optimizer is disabled.** This feature, which attempts to improve image contrast, is incompatible with Highlight Tone Priority. So read the next section, which explains Auto Lighting Optimizer, to determine which of the two exposure tweaks you want to use.

>> **You can wind up with more noise in shadow areas of the image.** Again, noise is the defect that looks like grains of sand.

REMEMBER

The only way to enable Highlight Tone Priority is via Shooting Menu 2, shown in Figure 4-24. Choose D+ for the standard amount of adjustment (I used this setting in Figure 4-23) or select D+2 for a stronger effect. Canon says that whether the stronger effect actually produces any greater impact on the highlights depends on the lighting conditions, however. Also, D+2 isn't available for movie recording.

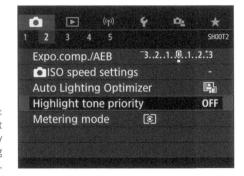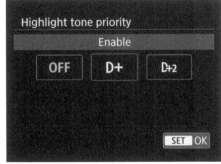

FIGURE 4-24:
Enable Highlight
Tone Priority
from Shooting
Menu 2.

As a reminder that Highlight Tone Priority is enabled, a D+ or D+2 symbol appears near the ISO value in the Quick Control and Live View displays, as shown in Figure 4-25. The same symbol appears with the ISO setting in the viewfinder and in the shooting data that appears in Playback mode. (See Chapter 9 to find out more about picture playback.) Notice that the symbol that represents Auto Lighting Optimizer, also labeled in the figure, is dimmed because that feature is disabled automatically as soon as you turn on Highlight Tone Priority.

TECHNICAL
STUFF

In case you're wondering why the letter D is assigned to this feature, it's related to the term *dynamic range*, or the range of brightness values, from black to white, that an imaging device can capture.

Highlight Tone Priority on

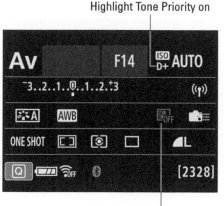

Auto Lighting Optimizer off

FIGURE 4-25: These symbols indicate that Highlight Tone Priority is enabled and Auto Lighting Optimizer is disabled.

Auto Lighting Optimizer off

Highlight Tone Priority on

Experimenting with Auto Lighting Optimizer

When you select an Image Quality setting that results in a JPEG image file — that is, any setting other than Raw — also experiment with the Auto Lighting Optimizer feature. Unlike Highlight Tone Priority, which concentrates on preserving highlight detail only, Auto Lighting Optimizer tries to improve underexposed, low-contrast, or high-contrast shots by adjusting both shadows and highlights. The adjustment is made as the image is captured.

In the Basic Zone exposure modes, you have no control over how much adjustment is made. But in P, Tv, Av, and M modes, you can decide whether to enable Auto Lighting Optimizer. You also can request a stronger or lighter application of the effect than the default setting, which is Standard. Figure 4-26 offers an example of the impact of each Auto Lighting Optimizer setting.

Given the level of improvement that the Auto Lighting Optimizer correction made to this photo, it may seem crazy to ever disable the feature. But it's important to note a few points:

>> **The level of shift that occurs between each Auto Lighting Optimizer setting varies depending on the subject.** This particular example shows a fairly noticeable difference between the High and Off settings. But you don't always see this much impact from the filter. Even in this example, it's difficult to detect much difference between Off and Low.

Off

Low

Standard

High

FIGURE 4-26:
For this image,
Auto Lighting
Optimizer
brought more life
to the shot.

>> **Although the filter improved this particular scene, at times you may not find it beneficial.** For example, maybe you're purposely trying to shoot a backlit subject in silhouette or produce a low-contrast image. Either way, you don't want the camera to insert its opinions on the exposure or contrast you're trying to achieve.

>> **Enabling Auto Lighting Optimizer may slow your shooting rate.** That slowdown occurs because the filter is applied after you capture the photo, while the camera is writing the data to the memory card.

WARNING

>> **In some lighting conditions, Auto Lighting Optimizer can produce an increase in image noise.** As shown near the start of this chapter, in Figure 4-5, noise becomes more apparent when you enlarge a photo. It also tends to be most visible in areas of flat color.

>> **The corrective action taken by Auto Lighting Optimizer can make some other exposure-adjustment features less effective.** So turn it off if you don't see the results you expect when you're using the following features:

- Exposure compensation, discussed earlier in this chapter

- Flash compensation, discussed in Chapter 2

- Automatic exposure bracketing, discussed later in this chapter

>> **You can't use this feature while Highlight Tone Priority is enabled.** In fact, as soon as you turn on that feature, explained in the preceding section, the camera automatically disables Auto Lighting Optimizer.

You can view the current Auto Lighting Optimizer setting in the Quick Control and Live View displays; look for the icon representing the setting in the areas labeled in Figure 4-27.

Auto Lighting Optimizer symbol (Standard setting)

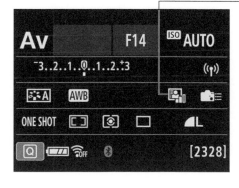

FIGURE 4-27: These symbols tell you the status of the Auto Lighting Optimizer setting.

TIP

Notice the vertical bars in the graphic — the number of bars tells you how much adjustment is being applied. Two bars, as in Figure 4-27, represent the Standard setting; three bars, High; and one bar, Low. The bars are replaced by the word *Off* when the feature is disabled.

By default, the Auto Lighting Optimizer level is set to Standard for the P, Tv, and Av modes. In M mode, the feature is disabled by default. You can adjust these settings in two ways:

>> **Shooting Menu 2:** Choose Auto Lighting Optimizer, as shown on the left in Figure **4-28**, to display the settings screen shown on the right in the figure. Here, you can select the level of adjustment you want to apply.

Just below the four adjustment-level symbols, notice the check box next to the Info label. This is the option that determines whether Auto Lighting Optimizer is applied in the M exposure mode. By default, the box is checked, as in the figure, telling the camera *not* to make the adjustment during manual exposure. If you do want to add the adjustment, tap the check box or press the Info button to toggle the check mark off.

Tap Set or press the Set button to return to Shooting Menu 2.

>> **Quick Control method:** You also can adjust the setting using the Quick Control method. After pressing Q or tapping the Q symbol to shift to Quick Control mode, highlight the Auto Lighting Optimizer icon and press Set (or just tap the symbol). You're presented with the same options screen you see in Figure 4-28.

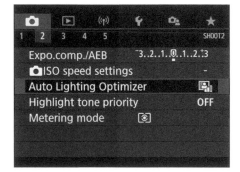
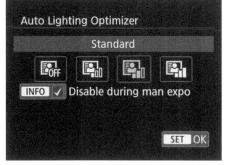

FIGURE 4-28:
You can also adjust Auto Lighting Optimizer settings through Shooting Menu 2.

TIP

If you're not sure what level of Auto Lighting Optimizer might work best or you're concerned about the other drawbacks of enabling the filter, consider shooting the picture in the Raw file format. For Raw pictures, the camera applies no post-capture tweaking, regardless of whether this filter or any other one is enabled. Then, by using Canon Digital Photo Professional, the software provided free with the camera, you can apply the Auto Lighting Optimizer effect when you convert your Raw images to a standard file format. (See Chapter 10 for details about processing Raw files.) You can even apply the adjustment from the camera's built-in Raw converter, also covered in Chapter 10.

Looking at a few other exposure solutions

In addition to the exposure correction tools covered in the preceding sections, you may find the following features helpful on occasion:

>> **Peripheral Illumination Correction:** Some lenses produce pictures that appear darker around the edges of the frame than in the center, even when the lighting is consistent throughout. This phenomenon is commonly known as *vignetting,* and your camera offers a tool that may help correct the problem. To check it out, open Shooting Menu 1, choose Lens Aberration Correction, and then select Peripheral Illumination Correction, as shown in Figure 4-29.

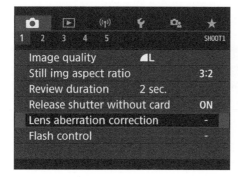 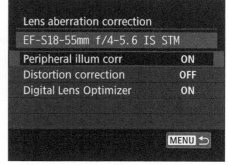

FIGURE 4-29: Peripheral Illumination Correction works to combat vignetting, which makes the corners of an image appear unnaturally dark.

REMEMBER

This adjustment is available in all your camera's exposure modes, but it has an impact only when the Image Quality option (also on Shooting Menu 1) is set to capture the photo in the JPEG file format. However, if you prefer to shoot in the Raw format, most Raw-processing tools offer a tool for correcting vignetting, often with more precision than the camera's automated version. Chapter 10 explains how to use Canon Digital Photo Professional software to process a Raw file. You also can apply the correction tool if you use the built-in Raw converter tool, also covered in Chapter 10.

A few other points about Peripheral Illumination Correction:

• *The feature is enabled by default if the camera's firmware (internal software) contains data about your lens.* The second screen in Figure 4-29 shows that the data is available for the 18–55mm kit lens, for example. (The lens model appears above the list of menu options.)

TECHNICAL STUFF

If you use a Canon lens and the screen indicates that the camera doesn't have data for that lens, you may be able to add its information to the camera. Canon calls this step *registering your lens,* a process you accomplish by connecting the camera to your computer and then using a registration tool included with Canon EOS Utility software. That software, along with others covered in Chapter 10, is available for free with your camera purchase. See the EOS Utility instruction manual, available for download from the Canon support pages, if you're interested in registering a lens.

WARNING

- *For non-Canon lenses, Canon recommends disabling Peripheral Illumination Correction even if correction data is available.* If you shoot in the Raw format, you can still apply the correction when you process the file.

- *The correction may produce increased noise at the corners of the photo.* This problem occurs because exposure adjustment can make noise more apparent.

>> **Long Exposure Noise Reduction:** A long exposure time can result in noise, the digital defect that gives your pictures a grainy look (refer to Figure 4-5). You may be able to reduce the appearance of noise created by a long exposure by enabling — surprise — a feature called Long Exposure Noise Reduction. In Basic Zone modes, the camera determines when to use this tool; in the P, Tv, Av, and M modes, you can make the call. Look for the setting on Shooting Menu 4. Long Exposure Noise Reduction offers three settings:

- *Off:* No noise reduction is applied. This setting is the default.

- *Auto:* Noise reduction is applied when you use a shutter speed of 1 second or longer, but only if the camera detects the type of noise that's caused by long exposures. (The other common cause of noise, a high ISO setting, creates a slightly different type of noise.)

- *On:* Noise reduction is always applied at exposures of 1 second or longer. (**Note:** Canon suggests that this setting may result in more noise than either Off or Auto when the ISO setting is 1600 or higher.)

WARNING

Although Long Exposure Noise Reduction can be fairly effective, it has a significant downside because of the way it works. Say that you make a 30-second exposure. After the shutter closes at the end of the exposure, the camera takes a *second* 30-second exposure to measure the noise by itself, and then subtracts that noise from your *real* exposure. So your shot-to-shot wait time is twice what it would normally be. For some scenes, that may not be a problem, but for shots that feature action, such as fireworks, you definitely don't want that long wait time between shutter clicks.

>> **High ISO Speed Noise Reduction:** Also found on Shooting Menu 4 and adjustable only in P, Tv, Av, and M modes, this tool attempts to conquer the second type of noise, a high ISO setting, just as its name implies. After choosing the option, as shown on the left in Figure 4-30, you can select from these settings, shown on the right in the figure:

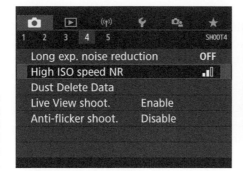 

FIGURE 4-30:
The Multi Shot
setting captures
four images and
merges them into
a single JPEG file.

- *Off:* Turns off the filter.

- *Low:* Applies a little noise removal.

- *Standard:* Applies a more pronounced amount of noise removal; this setting is the default.

- *High:* Goes after noise in a more dramatic way.

- *Multi Shot:* Tries to achieve a better result than High by capturing four frames in a quick burst and then merging them together into a single image. The final image is saved in the JPEG format. This option is unavailable when the Image Quality option is set to Raw or Raw+JPEG.

As with the Long Exposure Noise Reduction filter, this filter is applied after you take the shot. You may experience a slight delay in capture rate when you choose the Multi Shot setting.

A few other caveats apply:

- *High ISO noise-reduction filters work primarily by applying a slight blur to the image.* Don't expect this process to eliminate noise entirely, and expect some resulting image softness.

- *The Multi Shot setting has several limitations.* In addition to being off-limits for Raw (or Raw+JPEG) image captures, it's not available when any of the following are enabled: Long Exposure Noise Reduction, Auto Exposure Bracketing, or White Balance Bracketing. Additionally, you can't use flash or the Bulb shutter speed.

- *For best results, use a tripod to avoid camera shake and to ensure that each frame covers the same area.* Otherwise, your image may exhibit blur or ghosting. Moving objects may also appear blurry, so this feature works best with still-life and landscape shots.

Finally, remember that the High ISO Noise Reduction setting automatically reverts to Standard if you turn off the camera, switch to a fully automatic exposure mode or Movie mode, or set the shutter speed to Bulb.

>> **Anti-Flicker Shooting:** Some types of lights, by design, cycle on and off rapidly. It usually happens too quickly for the human eye to detect, but the camera's exposure system may be affected nonetheless. If the camera meters the light during an on cycle and takes the photo in an off cycle, the exposure will be too dark, and vice versa. The Anti-Flicker Shooting option, found on Shooting Menu 4 and shown in Figure 4-31, may help in this situation. By default, Anti-Flicker Shooting is disabled, as in the figure. When you enable Anti-Flicker Shooting, the camera tries to adjust the timing of the shutter release to capture the shot at a moment when the lights are less likely to cause a problem. Unfortunately, you don't have access to this option in Live View or Movie mode or when the exposure mode is set to any setting other than P, Tv, Av, or M.

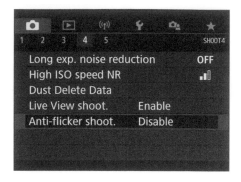

FIGURE 4-31: Anti-Flicker Shooting may produce more consistent exposures when you shoot under certain types of lights.

As mentioned in Chapter 1, you can tell the camera to display the word *flicker* in the viewfinder if it detects the type of lighting that can cause problems so that you can turn on Anti-Flicker Shooting. To enable this alert, open Setup Menu 4, choose Viewfinder Display, and then set Flicker Detection to Show.

Why not just leave Anti-Flicker Shooting enabled all the time? Because it has some drawbacks. If you shoot in the Av or P mode, the shutter speed may change automatically between frames, which can result in color shift from one frame to the next. Also, Anti-Flicker Shooting may create some lag between the time you press the shutter button and the time the picture is recorded because the camera has to wait to accommodate the on/off cycle of the lights. The continuous-capture frame rate may also slow down. For best anti-flicker results, shoot in the Tv or M exposure mode so that the shutter speed is fixed.

Locking Autoexposure Settings

To help ensure a proper exposure, your camera continually meters the light until the moment you press the shutter button fully to shoot the picture. In autoexposure modes — that is, any mode but M — the camera also keeps adjusting exposure settings as needed.

For most situations, this approach works great, resulting in the right settings for the light that's striking your subject when you capture the image. But on occasion, you may want to lock in a certain combination of exposure settings. For example, perhaps you want your subject to appear at the far edge of the frame. If you were to use the normal shooting technique, you would place the subject under a focus point, press the shutter button halfway to lock focus and set the initial exposure, and then reframe to your desired composition to take the shot. The problem is that exposure is then recalculated based on the new framing, which can leave your subject under- or overexposed.

The easiest way to get around this issue is to switch to M (manual exposure) mode and select the exposure settings that work best for your subject, regardless of composition. But if you prefer to use autoexposure, you can use AE Lock (autoexposure lock), which prevents the camera from adjusting exposure when you reframe your shot. To put it another way, you can interrupt the normal continuous exposure adjustment at any point before you take the picture. This option is available in the P, Tv, and Av exposure modes.

REMEMBER

To use AE Lock successfully, you need to know that the camera establishes and locks exposure differently depending on the metering mode, the focusing mode (automatic or manual), and an autofocusing setting called AF Point Selection. (Chapter 5 explains this option.) Here's the scoop:

>> **Evaluative metering and automatic AF Point Selection:** Exposure is based on the focusing point that achieved focus.

>> **Evaluative metering and manual AF Point Selection:** Exposure is locked on the autofocus point you select.

>> **All other metering modes:** Exposure is based on the center autofocus point, regardless of the AF Point Selection mode.

>> **Manual focusing:** Exposure is based on the center autofocus point.

This information is critical because you need to compose your shot initially so that your subject falls under the area of the frame the camera will use to meter exposure. For example, if you use Spot metering, place your subject at the center of the frame, set and lock exposure, and then reframe as desired.

If you can keep those details in mind, using AE Lock is easy. After framing your shot according to the guidelines just presented, press and hold the shutter button halfway to initiate exposure metering and autofocusing. Then, keeping the shutter button pressed halfway, press the AE Lock button. Exposure is now locked and remains locked for 4 seconds, even if you release the AE Lock button. Reframe to your desired composition and then press the shutter button the rest of the way to take the picture.

To remind you that AE Lock is in force, the camera displays an asterisk at the left end of the viewfinder or, in Live View mode, in the lower-left corner of the display.

Note: If your goal is to use the same exposure settings for multiple shots, you must keep the AE Lock button pressed during the entire series of pictures. Every time you let up on the button and press it again, you lock exposure anew based on the light that's in the frame. (Really, switching to manual exposure is much easier in this situation.)

Bracketing Exposures Automatically

Exposure bracketing simply means to capture several shots of your subject, using different exposure settings for each shot. The idea is to give yourself a safety net when you're shooting in tricky lighting or just aren't sure what exposure result will work best artistically.

Bracketing is also key to *HDR photography.* HDR stands for *high dynamic range,* which refers to an image that contains a greater range of brightness values than the camera can record in a single exposure. To produce an HDR image, the photographer records the same scene multiple times, again using different exposure settings for each image. The images are then combined using special computer software, often called HDR or *tone-mapping software,* to combine the exposures in a way that uses specific brightness values from each shot.

TIP

With the HDR Backlight Control SCN, covered in Chapter 3, you can create limited HDR effects; that mode captures three frames and merges the result into a single JPEG image. But capturing the bracketed frames yourself gives you control over how many frames are recorded and how great an exposure shift occurs between each frame. You also wind up having access to all the captured frames, whereas HDR Backlight Control only creates one composite image.

Whether you're interested in exposure bracketing for HDR or just want to cover your bases to make sure that at least one frame is exposed to your liking, your camera offers a tool that simplifies the process. This feature, called Automatic Exposure Bracketing (or AEB), captures three frames, shooting the first one at the current exposure settings and then automatically capturing two additional frames, one darker and one brighter.

Upcoming steps show you how to shoot a bracketed series; first, here are a few things you need to know about the AEB feature:

>> **AEB is available only in P, Tv, Av, and M exposure modes.** In M mode, you can't set the shutter speed to Bulb (the setting that keeps the shutter open as long as you hold down the shutter button).

>> **You can request an exposure change of up to two stops between frames.** Two stops doesn't sound like very much, but in fact, it's a fairly large jump between exposures. You may even wind up with one frame that's seriously overexposed and one that's just as underexposed, so experiment to find the magic number that gives you the exposure shift you're after.

>> **How the camera delivers the darker and brighter shots depends on your exposure mode and whether Auto ISO is enabled.** Here's how things work in each exposure mode:

- *P:* If the ISO setting is Auto, the camera adjusts ISO between frames. Otherwise, it adjusts both aperture and shutter speed to produce the different exposures.

- *Tv:* The camera respects your selected shutter speed and instead adjusts the ISO setting if Auto ISO is enabled. If not, the ISO remains the same between frames and the camera achieves the exposure shift by changing the aperture setting.

- *Av:* The camera uses your selected f-stop for all three frames. Again, if Auto ISO is enabled, the camera changes the ISO setting between frames. But if you dialed in a specific ISO setting, the shutter speed varies between shots instead.

- *M mode:* ISO is adjusted between frames if Auto ISO is enabled. Otherwise, the camera assumes that you want to maintain the same depth of field between shots and so adjusts shutter speed to produce the various exposures.

TIP

If you want to keep the depth of field constant between shots — especially important when you plan to combine bracketed frames into an HDR image — shoot in M or Av mode so that the camera uses the same f-stop for all frames. (Remember that aperture affects depth of field.) If anything in the scene is moving, though, you also want the shutter speed to remain consistent, so in that case, the best option is to use M exposure mode and enable Auto ISO adjustment.

REMEMBER

>> **Flash:** AEB isn't available when you use flash. In fact, if you set up the camera to record a bracketed series and then enable flash, all your bracketing settings are undone.

>> **Exposure Compensation:** You can combine AEB with exposure compensation if you want. The camera simply applies the compensation amount when

it calculates the exposure for the three bracketed images. For example, if Exposure Compensation is set to EV +1.0 and the bracketing amount is set to one stop, you get one frame exposed at EV +1.0, one at EV 0.0 (darkest shot), and a third at EV +2.0 (brightest shot).

>> **Auto Lighting Optimizer:** Because Auto Lighting Optimizer adjusts contrast after the shot, it can render AEB ineffective. So it's best to disable the feature when bracketing. You can turn it off in Quick Control mode or via the Auto Lighting Optimizer option on Shooting Menu 2.

>> **A couple other features put AEB off-limits.** Specifically, if you shoot in Live View mode and apply Creative Filters through the Quick Control screen, you can't use AEB. Additionally, automatic bracketing doesn't work if you set the High ISO Noise Reduction filter to the Multi Shot setting.

With those preliminaries out of the way, the following steps explain how to set up and shoot a bracketed series of photos:

1. **Display Shooting Menu 2 and choose Expo Comp/AEB, as shown on the left in Figure 4-32.**

   After you select the menu option, you see the screen shown on the right in Figure 4-32. Remember, this screen is used to set the amount of Exposure Compensation, explained earlier in this chapter, as well as to set up bracketing. The Exposure Compensation controls are near the top of the screen; I labeled them in Figure 4-32. The options relevant to bracketing, also labeled in the figure, are at the bottom of the screen. Note that you won't see the lower meter bars until after you take Step 2.

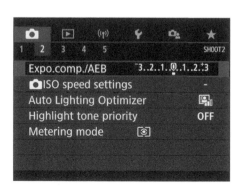

Exposure Compensation setting

Automatic Exposure Bracketing (AEB) settings

Main dial symbol

FIGURE 4-32: Automatic Exposure Bracketing records your image at three exposure settings.

When you're not using Live View, you can use the Quick Control feature to get to the settings screen instead of using the menus. Press Q or tap the Q touchscreen symbol, highlight the exposure meter, and press Set.

2. **Rotate the Main dial to enable Automatic Exposure Bracketing and establish the amount of exposure change you want between images.**

As soon as you rotate the dial (or tap the AEB touchscreen arrows), the AEB portion of the screen comes to life, displaying the meter shown in Figure 4-32. This meter represents the maximum two-stop exposure shift available through AEB. The meter is set up in one-third stop increments; the tall lines represent the full stop positions (+/– 1 or 2 stops). The smaller lines represent third-stop positions.

The three colored lines represent the three frames the camera will capture. The first shot, represented by the middle line, is always taken at the current exposure setting. The left line represents the second shot, which will be darker; the right line, the third shot, which will be brighter. In the figure, the meter shows bracketing set to produce a one-stop shift between the neutral, darker, and brighter exposure. Keep rotating the Main dial or tapping the AEB arrows until the bars indicate the amount of exposure shift you have in mind.

If you're familiar with the Exposure Compensation feature, you may notice something different about the top meter in the right screen in Figure 4-32: It indicates a maximum Exposure Compensation adjustment of plus or minus seven stops instead of the usual five. What gives? Well, if you set Exposure Compensation to +5.0 and set the bracketing amount to +2.0, your brightest shot is captured at EV +7.0; the neutral shot at EV +5.0; and the darkest shot at EV +3.0.

To adjust the Exposure Compensation setting, rotate the Quick Control dial, press the right/left edges of the dial, or tap the +/– signs at the end of the meter. The bracketing meter scoots left or right in tandem as you adjust the Exposure Compensation setting.

3. **Tap Set or press the Set button.**

AEB is now enabled. To remind you of that fact, the exposure meter on Shooting Menu 2 and on the Quick Control screen now includes three markers, representing the three bracketed frames, as shown in Figure 4-33. You see the same markers on the viewfinder meter as well as on the meter that appears at the bottom of the screen in Live View mode.

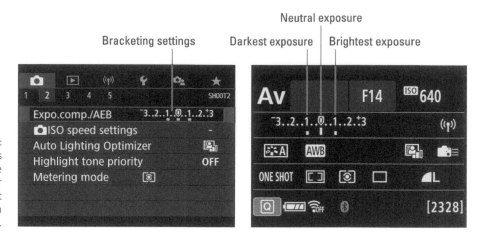

Neutral exposure

Bracketing settings   Darkest exposure   Brightest exposure

4. **Shoot the bracketed series.**

How you do this depends on which Drive mode you're using, as follows:

- *Single Drive mode:* You take each exposure separately, pressing the shutter button fully three times to record your trio of images. After you take the first shot, the indicators under the exposure meter in the displays blink to remind you that you're in the middle of a three-frame series. When the blinking stops, you've captured the last frame in the series.

- *Continuous Drive mode:* Press and hold the shutter button down to record a burst of three frames. (Be sure to wait for the camera to record all three frames before you release the shutter button.) To record another series, release and then press the shutter button again. When AEB is enabled, you can't capture more than three frames with each shutter button press as you normally can.

- *Self-Timer modes:* All three exposures are recorded with a single press of the shutter button. But you don't need to hold down the shutter button as you do in Continuous mode — just press and release.

Along with the blinking exposure meter indicators, an asterisk blinks in the viewfinder display between frames.

5. **To turn off Automatic Exposure Bracketing, change the AEB setting back to 0.**

Just repeat Steps 1 and 2, rotating the Main dial or tapping the AEB arrows until the AEB meter disappears. Be sure to also take Step 3, pressing the Set button or tapping Set on the touchscreen. Otherwise, the change won't stick.

AEB is also turned off when you power down the camera, enable the flash, replace the camera battery, replace the memory card, or shoot in M exposure mode and set the shutter speed to Bulb.

REMEMBER

IN THIS CHAPTER

» **Understanding autofocusing options**

» **Choosing a specific autofocusing point**

» **Using continuous autofocusing to track a moving subject**

» **Taking advantage of manual-focusing aids**

» **Manipulating depth of field**

Chapter **5**

Controlling Focus and Depth of Field

To many people, the word *focus* has just one interpretation when applied to a photograph: The subject is either in focus or blurry. But an artful photographer knows there's more to focus than simply getting a sharp image of a subject. You also need to consider *depth of field,* or the distance over which other objects in the scene appear sharply focused.

This chapter explains how to manipulate both aspects of an image. After a reminder of how to set your lens to auto- or manual focusing, the first part of the chapter details focusing options available for viewfinder photography; following that, you can get help with focusing during Live View photography and movie recording.

A word of warning: The two systems are different, and mastering them takes time. If you start feeling overwhelmed, simplify things by following the steps laid out at the beginning of Chapter 3, which show you how to take a picture using the default autofocus settings. Then return another day to study the focusing options discussed here.

Things get much easier (and more fun) at the end of the chapter, which covers ways to control depth of field. Thankfully, the concepts related to that subject apply whether you're using the viewfinder, taking advantage of Live View photography, or shooting movies.

Setting the Lens to Automatic or Manual Focusing Mode

REMEMBER

Regardless of whether you're using the viewfinder, Live View, or Movie mode, your first focus task is to set the lens to auto- or manual focusing (assuming that your lens supports autofocusing with the T8i/850D). On most lenses, including the 18–55mm kit lens, you find a switch with two settings: AF for autofocusing and MF for manual focusing, as shown in Figure 5-1. The position of the manual focusing ring varies from lens to lens; Figure 5-1 shows you where to find it on the kit lens.

Manual focusing ring   Auto/Manual focus switch

FIGURE 5-1:
On the kit lens, as on many Canon lenses, you set the switch to AF for autofocusing and to MF for manual focusing.

Depending on your lens, you may be able to adjust focus manually even when the lens switch is set to AF. This feature, called autofocusing with manual override, enables you to set focus initially using autofocusing and then fine-tune focus by turning the manual focusing ring. See your lens manual to find out if your lens offers this option. The kit lens does, but in a limited way; see the nearby sidebar devoted to the Lens Electronic MF feature for details.

WHAT'S LENS ELECTRONIC MF?

If your lens doesn't offer autofocusing with manual override, you may be able to take advantage of the camera's Lens Electronic MF feature. Simply put, this feature gives you the same autofocusing flexibility as a lens that has the manual-override option built in.

However, Lens Electronic MF is available only under the following conditions: One, your lens must be compatible with the feature as it's implemented on the T8i/850D. The 18–55mm kit lens qualifies; the camera's instruction manual lists other compatible lenses. Two, you must shoot in the P, Tv, Av, or M exposure mode. And third, you must set the AF Operation mode to One-Shot autofocusing. This setting, explained later in this chapter, tells the camera to lock focus when you press and hold the shutter button halfway. To put it another way, Lens Electronic MF isn't compatible with continuous autofocusing.

Assuming those conditions are met, set focus by pressing and holding the shutter button halfway down or by pressing and holding the AF ON button all the way down. Then rotate the manual focusing ring to fine-tune focus. Be careful not to lift your finger off the shutter button or AF ON button; if you do, autofocusing begins anew when you press the shutter button to take the picture.

By default, electronic manual focusing is disabled. To try it out, open Shooting Menu 5 and choose Lens Electronic MF, as shown in the left image here. On the next screen, choose Enable After One-Shot AF, as shown in the right image. Note that you see the menu option only when the Mode dial is set to P, Tv, Av, or M.

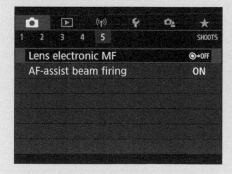
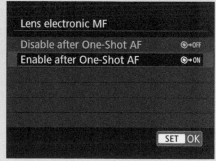

Discovering the AF ON button

In the upper-right corner of the camera back lives a button labeled AF ON, shown in Figure 5-2. If you've worked with other cameras that have this button, you may expect the one on the T8i/850D to serve the same purpose as it does on most dSLRs, which is to enable you to initiate autofocusing and lock the focusing distance without also kicking the camera's autoexposure metering system into gear. Being able to separate the two functions offers advantages in certain shooting scenarios, and a lot of pros use the AF ON button to autofocus all the time. (The option is referred to as *back-button autofocus* because the button is normally on the back of the camera.)

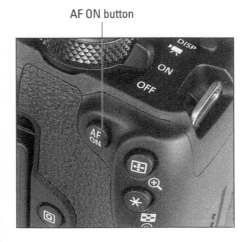

AF ON button

FIGURE 5-2:
In P, Tv, Av, and M modes, holding down the AF ON button achieves the same result as pressing and holding the shutter button halfway.

On the T8i/850D, however, the AF ON button simply gives you another way to accomplish the same thing as pressing the shutter button halfway. Pressing and holding the AF ON button launches both autofocusing and exposure metering.

That's not to say the AF ON button is entirely without merit, though. On occasion, you may want to set autofocus and autoexposure a few minutes (or more) in advance of when you take the shot. Imagine, for example, photographing a school graduation. You want exposure and focus to be set ahead of time so that when your grad reaches for the diploma, all you have to do is press the shutter button the rest of the way to take the picture — you don't have to wait for the autofocus and autoexposure systems to do their thing. In situations like this, I find it easier to hold down the AF ON button than to keep the shutter button pressed halfway. Nine times out of 10, my shutter-button finger will twitch and depress the button all the way, taking the picture before I'm ready. Keeping my thumb on the AF ON button is easier for me. Then it's just a matter of pressing the shutter button all the way down to take the picture when I'm ready.

If you don't care to use the AF ON button for its default purpose, you can assign it other tasks via the Custom Controls menu item, which is Custom Function 13. (Open Setup Menu 5 and choose Custom Functions to access all the Custom Functions item.) In fact, you can customize five different controls through this menu item. Chapter 12 explains your options.

Exploring Viewfinder Focusing Options

Chapters 1 and 3 offer brief primers on focusing, but in case you're not reading the book from front to back, here's a quick recap. Again, this information applies when you use the viewfinder to compose your image; details about focusing in Live View and Movie modes come later.

>> **To autofocus:** After setting the lens switch to the autofocusing mode (AF, on the kit lens), frame your subject in the viewfinder so that it appears within the autofocus brackets, highlighted in the left screen in Figure 5-3. Then press and hold the shutter button halfway.

Autofocus brackets   Selected focus points   Focus-achieved light

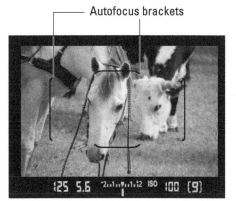 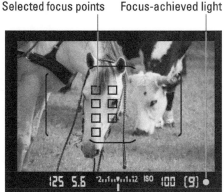

FIGURE 5-3: The viewfinder offers these focusing aids.

What happens next depends on your exposure mode:

- *Scene Intelligent Auto and all Creative Filter modes except the four HDR settings:* With stationary subjects, one or more focus points appear to indicate where the camera set the focusing distance, as shown on the right in Figure 5-3. (In dim lighting, the focus brackets and focus points first flash red to help you spot them.) You also see the focus-achieved light, also labeled in the figure, and hear a beep. Focus remains locked as long as you hold down the shutter button.

  If the camera detects subject motion, however, it tracks the movement and adjusts focus continuously until you take the picture. As this focus tracking happens, different focus points may flash on and off to show you what area of the frame the camera considers to be the current focusing target. You don't see the viewfinder's focus-indicator light, but the beep sounds each time the camera re-establishes focus.

For continuous autofocusing to work, you must adjust framing as necessary to keep the subject under the area covered by the autofocus area brackets.

- *Sports and Kids SCN modes:* The continuous-autofocusing setup is used.

- *All other SCN modes and P, Tv, Av, and M modes:* The camera assumes that you're shooting a stationary subject so it locks focus when you press the shutter button halfway. In the P, Tv, Av, and M exposure modes, however, you can switch to continuous autofocusing if you want; see the upcoming section "AF Operation mode: Focus lock or continuous autofocusing" for details.

In all cases, if the viewfinder focus light blinks rapidly, the camera can't find a focusing target. Try focusing manually instead. Also try backing away from your subject a little; you may be exceeding the close-focusing capabilities of your lens.

>> **To focus manually:** After setting the lens switch to the manual focusing (MF) position, rotate the focusing ring on the lens.

Even when focusing manually, you can confirm focus by pressing the shutter button halfway. The focus point or points over the area that's in focus flash for a second or two, the viewfinder's focus lamp lights, and you hear the focus-achieved beep.

By the way, if the focus-achieved beep becomes intrusive or just plain annoying, you can disable it via the Beep option on Setup Menu 3. However, if you disable the focusing beep, you also disable the sounds the camera makes when you tap the touchscreen.

Adjusting autofocus performance

By default, your camera's autofocusing system behaves as outlined in the preceding section. But depending on your exposure mode, you may be able to modify autofocus performance through one or both of the following settings:

>> **AF Area Selection mode:** This setting determines which of the 45 autofocus points the camera uses to establish focusing distance. You can leave all 45 in play, giving the camera wide latitude on finding a focus target, or you can require the autofocusing system to lock focus only within a particular portion, or *zone,* of the frame. You also can set focus based on just a single focus point that you select.

>> **AF Operation:** This option determines whether the camera locks focus when you press the shutter button halfway or continues to adjust focus until you press the button the rest of the way to take the shot.

The next few sections detail both autofocusing options. A few reminders before you dig in:

>> **You have control over both settings only in P, Tv, Av, and M exposure modes.** In most other exposure modes, you can adjust the AF Area Selection mode but not the AF Operation mode. A few exposure modes lock you out of both settings.

>> **In the P, Tv, Av, and M exposure modes, symbols representing both options appear in the Quick Control display, as shown in Figure 5-4.** In Basic Zone modes, this information isn't provided in the display.

>> **Information in this chapter assumes that you haven't changed the default settings for Custom Functions related to autofocusing.** Straying from the defaults will definitely confuse your journey as you familiarize yourself with the autofocusing system. But after you have the focusing system down cold, check out the upcoming section "Considering a few other autofocusing settings" to read about other ways to customize things.

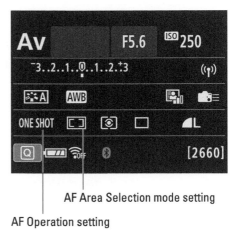

AF Area Selection mode setting

AF Operation setting

FIGURE 5-4:
In P, Tv, Av, and M exposure modes, the Quick Control display contains icons representing the two main autofocusing options.

AF Area Selection mode: One focus point or many?

One way you can control autofocusing behavior is to specify how you want the camera to select the autofocus point that it uses to set the focusing distance. The option that controls this autofocusing behavior is the AF Area Selection mode.

You have access to this setting in all exposure modes except Candlelight Scene mode and two Creative Filters modes, Fisheye and Miniature. Assuming that you're not shooting in those modes, you can choose from the following options.

I listed the options starting with the one that gives you the least control over which focus point is used to the setting that gives you complete control.

>> **Auto Selection AF:** The camera selects the autofocus point for you, considering all 45 focus points within the autofocus brackets when looking for a focusing target. If the camera detects faces in the scene, it assumes that you're trying to shoot a portrait and usually sets the nearest face as the focusing target. If the camera doesn't detect a face, it focuses on the closest object.

>> **Manual Selection: Large Zone AF:** The camera's 45 focus points are divided into three zones: left, right, and center, with each zone containing 15 points. For example, the left screen in Figure 5-5 shows the points contained in the center zone. You select which of the three zones you want to use, and the camera selects a point within that zone for you. Again, the camera gives focusing priority to skin tones and then the closest object that falls within the selected zone.

>> **Manual Selection: Zone AF:** This mode also uses the zone concept, but with smaller zones of nine points each. In the right screen in Figure 5-5, for example, the nine points at the center of the frame are highlighted. The camera will select one of those nine points when focusing.

>> **Manual Selection: 1-Point AF:** This mode is the only one that puts you in complete control over which focus point is used. You can choose any of the 45 focus points, and the camera bases focus only on that point.

Large Zone AF, center 15 points active   Zone AF, center nine points active

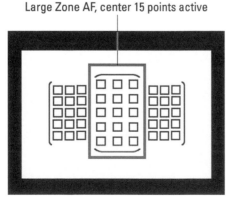

FIGURE 5-5:
Zone AF modes limit the camera to choosing a focus point within a specified portion of the frame.

Although the AF Area Selection options aren't that hard to understand, the way you lock in the setting you want to use is, shall we say, "less than intuitive." Here's how to get the job done:

>> **Accessing the AF Area Selection mode setting:** You can press either of the two buttons labeled in Figure 5-6 to display a screen where you choose the option you want to use. (If nothing happens when you press the buttons, the camera may be in sleep mode; to wake it up, press the shutter button halfway and release it. Then try again.)

However, because the AF Point Selection button has no other function when it comes to this setting than to toggle the selection screen off and on, make your life a little easier and forget about it for the purpose of setting the AF Area Selection mode. Instead, handle everything with the AF Area Selection Mode button.

In the P, Tv, Av, and M exposure modes, you also can adjust the setting via the Quick Control screen. See the last point in this list for specifics.

>> **Decoding the settings screen:** The appearance of the AF Area Selection mode settings screen changes depending on which option is active. Figure 5-7 shows you how things look in Auto Selection AF mode (left) and the Manual Selection: Large Zone AF mode (right).

Here's a guide to the various screen elements:

● *A text label at the top of the screen indicates the name of the current mode.* The label is a little confusing because the Large Zone, Zone, and Single-Point labels begin with the words "Manual select," which may lead you to believe you've switched to manual focusing somehow. You haven't — the

TIP

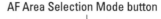
AF Area Selection Mode button

AF Point Selection button

FIGURE 5-6:
These curiously marked buttons both access the settings screen, but only the AF Area Selection mode button enables you to actually change the setting as well.

camera is just telling you that in the current mode, you manually select the zone or focus point you want to use instead of having the camera choose it automatically. So concentrate on the words after "Manual select"; that text tells you the name of the current mode.

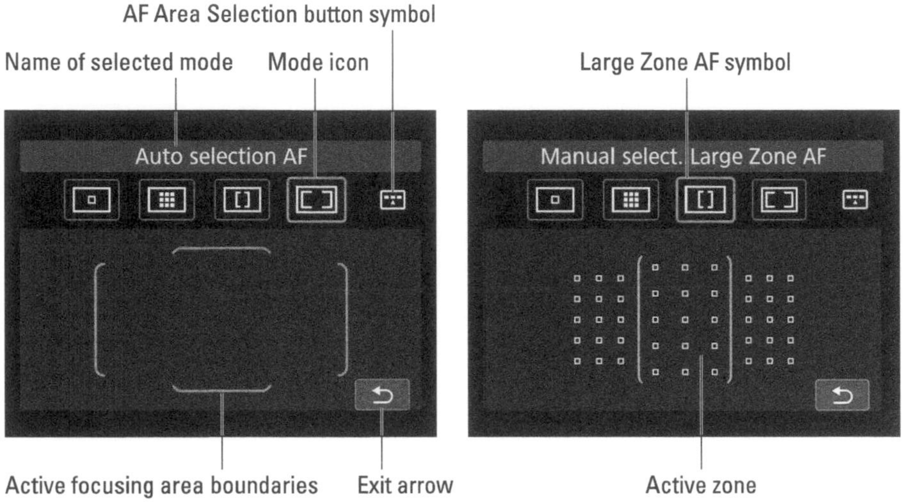

AF Area Selection button symbol

Name of selected mode   Mode icon   Large Zone AF symbol

Auto selection AF   Manual select. Large Zone AF

FIGURE 5-7: In Auto Area and Large Zone modes, the brackets indicate the current autofocusing area.

Active focusing area boundaries   Exit arrow   Active zone

- *The icons below the text label represent the four settings.* An orange highlight box surrounds the currently selected option.

- *The diagram below the icons shows you which focus points are active.* In Auto Selection AF mode, you see the same brackets that appear in the viewfinder, indicating that anything within that portion of the frame is a potential focusing target. Brackets also appear in the Manual Selection: Large Zone AF mode, this time indicating which of the three zones is active — left, center, or right. In the right screen in Figure 5-7, the center zone is active.

  Figure 5-8 shows you how the screen appears in Manual Selection: Zone mode (nine active points) and Manual Selection: 1-Point modes. On these screens, the selected focus points appear in color.

- *The appearance of the Automatic Selection screen varies depending on the AF Operation setting.* If that option is set to One-Shot, the screen appears as shown on the left in Figure 5-7, with just the focus brackets visible. But if you use continuous autofocusing — AI Servo is the official setting name — the frame shown in Figure 5-9 appears, showing all 45 focus points, with the center point in color. This altered diagram is designed to remind you that when you use continuous autofocusing, the camera sets focus initially on a

REMEMBER

single point — the center point, by default. (The next section explains more about the AF Operation setting.)

Making things even more confusing, you can't control the AF Operation setting in the Basic Zone shooting modes, and different modes use different settings. So which version of the screen you see depends on the Basic Zone exposure mode you use. The key thing to remember is that if you see the version shown in Figure 5-9, frame your subject so that it falls under the center focus point before setting focus.

Zone AF, center nine points selected

Single-point AF, center point selected

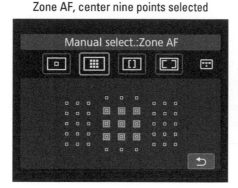
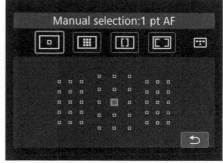

FIGURE 5-8: In Manual Selection: Zone AF mode (left) and Manual Selection: 1-Point AF mode (right), the orange points are active.

>> **Choosing a different AF Area Selection mode:** And now for the most perplexing part of adjusting this setting: Once you get to the settings screen shown in Figures 5-7 through 5-9, how the heck do you switch from one mode to the other? The usual techniques of rotating the Quick Control or Main dial or pressing the left or right edge of the Quick Control dial don't do the trick. The simplest solution is to use the touchscreen and tap the setting you want to use.

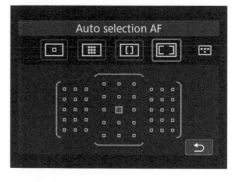

FIGURE 5-9: When the AF Operation is set to AI Servo (continuous autofocusing), the Auto Selection AF display changes to remind you to initiate focusing with your subject under the center focus point.

If you don't want to use the touchscreen, press the AF Area Selection mode button to cycle from one AF Area Selection mode to the next. See the symbol to the far right of the setting icons (refer to Figure 5-9)? It's the same one that appears on the button, and it's there to remind you that the button is the key to changing the mode. It's okay; *no one* figures this one out or remembers what it means the next time they change the setting. Thank you Canon, for the type of mystery markings that keep these books a viable product.

When you shoot in the P, TV, Av, and M exposure modes, you *can* use the Main dial to change the setting. However, you need to enable that option via Custom Function 7, named AF Area Selection Method. (Access Custom Functions via Setup Menu 5.) If you make this change, however, you can't use the Main dial for its normal purpose when you're selecting an autofocus area, which is to select the zone or single focus point you want to use, as explained next.

» **Selecting a zone or focus point:** Again, using the touchscreen to tap the zone or point you want to use is easiest, although selecting a single point can be dicey because the points are small. You do have other options:

- *Large Zone:* Rotate the Quick Control or Main dial to cycle through the available zones. You also can press the left/right edges of the Quick Control dial.

- *Zone:* Use the same techniques as for Large Zone, but note that you can also press the top and bottom edges of the Quick Control dial to travel up and down through the grid of zones.

- *1-Point AF:* Oh boy, here we go. Use the Quick Control dial to scroll up or down through the field of points; use the Main dial to scroll right or left. You also can scroll up/down/right/left by pressing the top/bottom/right/left edge of the Quick Control dial.

- *Automatic Selection AF:* You can choose an initial focusing point only when continuous autofocusing is used. To use a point other than the center one, use the same techniques just described for 1-Point AF.

Press the Set button to quickly select the center zone or focus point.

» **Looking at viewfinder symbols:** After you press either of the two buttons that bring the AF Area Selection mode screen to life, the viewfinder displays the same focus-point grids that you see on the monitor when you're choosing a focusing zone or point. In the readout at the bottom of the viewfinder, you see one of two graphics: AF with a dashed rectangle or SEL with a single rectangle. The AF graphic appears for Auto Selection, Large Zone, and Zone modes. SEL represents the 1-Point mode. However, you're on your own as far as remembering that you press the AF Area Selection button to cycle through the four modes; the icon reminder shown on the monitor screen doesn't appear.

» **Taking advantage of Quick Control mode:** In the P, Tv, Av, and M exposure modes, you also can adjust the AF Area Selection mode setting via the Quick Control screen. After selecting the setting, as shown on the left in Figure 5-10, rotate the Main dial to display icons representing each mode in the middle of the screen, as shown on the right in the figure. Keep rotating the dial to select the mode you want to use. To display the zone or point selection screen, press the Set button. After choosing the zone or point you want to use, tap the Menu icon or press the Menu button to exit to the Quick Control screen, which remains active. Press the Q button or tap the Q touchscreen symbol to exit to shooting mode.

AF Operation mode: Focus lock or continuous autofocusing?

In the P, Tv, Av, and M exposure modes, you also can adjust autofocus performance by changing the AF Operation mode, which determines how and when focus is set. The following list explains your three choices, but first, a little reminder: On your camera, you can initiate autofocusing either by pressing the shutter button halfway or by pressing the AF ON button all the way. Read the earlier section "Discovering the AF ON Button" to familiarize yourself with that button if you think you may prefer using it.

Back to the subject at hand: The three AF Operation modes work as follows:

>> **One-Shot:** This mode, geared to shooting stationary subjects, locks focus when you press and hold the shutter button halfway down or press the AF ON button.

WARNING

One important point to remember about One-Shot mode is that if the camera can't achieve focus, it won't let you take the picture, no matter how hard you press the shutter button or AF ON button. Also be aware that if you pair One-Shot autofocusing with one of the Continuous Drive modes, detailed in Chapter 2, focus for all frames in a burst is based on the focus point used for the first shot.

WARNING

>> **AI Servo:** In this mode (the *AI* stands for *artificial intelligence,* if you care), the camera adjusts focus continually as needed from the time you initiate autofocusing until the time you take the picture. This mode is designed to make focusing on moving subjects easier.

For AI Servo to work, you must reframe as needed to keep your subject under the active autofocus point or zone if you're using the 1-Point, Zone, or Large Zone AF Area Selection modes. If the camera is set to Automatic Selection AF, the camera bases focus initially on the center focus point, but you can select a different point if you like. (See the preceding section for how-tos.) If the subject moves away from the chosen point, focus should still be okay as long as you keep the subject within the area covered by one of the other autofocus points.

In either case, the green focus dot in the viewfinder blinks rapidly if the camera isn't tracking focus successfully. If all is going well, the focus dot doesn't light, and you don't hear the beep that normally sounds when focus is achieved. (You can hear the autofocus motor whirring a little when the camera adjusts focus.)

If you use AI Servo with the Continuous Drive mode, focus is adjusted as needed between frames, which may slow the maximum shots-per-second rate. However, it's still the best option for shooting a moving subject.

>> **AI Focus:** This mode automatically switches the camera from One-Shot to AI Servo as needed. When you first press the shutter button halfway or press the AF ON button, focus is locked on the active autofocus point (or points), as in One-Shot mode. But if the subject moves, the camera shifts into AI Servo mode and adjusts focus as it thinks is warranted.

TIP

Because AI Focus can sometimes misinterpret what it sees and choose the wrong autofocusing setup, it's best to ignore this option. Instead, stick with One–Shot for stationary subjects and AI Servo for moving subjects.

Here's one way to remember which mode is which: For still subjects, you need only *one shot* at setting focus. For moving subjects, think of a tennis or volleyball player *serving* the ball — so use *AI Servo* for action shots.

You can choose the AF Operation setting in two ways:

>> **AF button:** Your fastest move is to press this button, shown in Figure 5-11. The selection screen shown on the monitor in the figure appears. As always, if pressing the button produces no results, you may need to wake the camera out of sleep mode by pressing the shutter button halfway and releasing it.

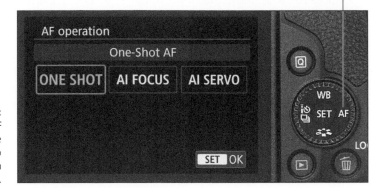

Press to display AF Operation screen

FIGURE 5-11:
Pressing the AF button is the fastest path to the AF Operation setting.

With the settings screen displayed, select the option you want to use by rotating the Quick Control or Main dial, pressing the right/left edges of the Quick Control dial, or just tapping the setting you want to use. To exit the screen, tap the Set icon or press the Set button.

>> **Quick Control method:** After pressing the Q button or tapping the Q touchscreen symbol, select the AF Operation icon, as shown in Figure 5-12. The name of the selected setting appears at the bottom of the screen. Rotate the Main dial to cycle through the three mode options.

If you prefer, you can tap the icon or press Set to display the same screen shown in Figure 5-12, where all three choices appear on a single screen.

AF Operation setting

FIGURE 5-12:
You also can adjust the setting via the Quick Control screen.

Choosing the right autofocus combo

You'll get the best autofocus results if you pair your chosen AF mode with the most appropriate AF Area Selection mode because the two settings work in tandem. Here are the combinations that I suggest:

>> **For still subjects: AF Area Selection mode, 1-Point AF; AF Operation mode, One-Shot.** You select a specific focus point, and the camera locks focus on that point at the time you press the shutter button halfway. Focus remains

locked on your subject even if you reframe the shot as long as you keep the shutter button half-pressed.

>> **For moving subjects: AF Area Selection mode, Automatic Selection AF; AF Operation mode, AI Servo.** Begin by selecting an initial focusing point. By default, the center point is selected, but you can select a different point if you prefer. Frame your subject initially so that it's under the selected point, and then press the shutter button halfway to set the initial focusing distance. The camera adjusts focus as needed if your subject moves within the frame before you take the shot. All you need to do is keep the shutter button pressed halfway and reframe the shot as needed to keep your subject within the boundaries of the autofocus brackets.

Keeping these two combos in mind should greatly improve your autofocusing accuracy. But in some situations, no combination will enable speedy or correct autofocusing. For example, if you try to focus on a very reflective subject, the camera may hunt for an autofocus point forever. And if you try to focus on a subject behind a fence, the autofocus system may continually insist on focusing on the fence instead of your subject. In such scenarios, don't waste time monkeying around with the autofocus settings — just switch to manual focusing.

Finally, remember that to have control over the AF Operation mode, you must use one of the advanced exposure modes (P, Tv, Av, or M).

Considering a few other autofocus settings

In the P, Tv, Av, or M exposure modes, you have access to the following additional Custom Functions (Setup Menu 5), all of which enable you to make additional tweaks to the autofocusing system. These features relate only to viewfinder shooting:

>> **Custom Function 6: Auto AF Point Selection: EOS iTR AF:** This setting revolves around the camera's ability to detect and automatically focus on people. By default, the AF system is programmed to give priority to facial skin tones. The name for this particular setting, assigned the number 0 like all Custom Function defaults, is EOS iTR AF (Face Priority). Option 1, Enable, also is designed to hunt for and focus on people, but it's not limited to faces. Option 2, Disable, is for times when you don't want the camera to prioritize people during autofocusing.

A few points to help you understand this setting: First, it applies only when the AF Area Selection mode is set to Large Zone, Zone, or Auto Selection. In 1-Point mode, the camera respects your focus-point decision and doesn't look for another area of the frame to use for focusing. Second, if you set Custom Function 6 to 0 (Face Priority) or 1 (Enable, which looks for people) and the camera doesn't find a human in the frame, it focuses on the object nearest the lens. Additionally, if the flash is raised and emits the AF-assist beam — always a possibility in dim lighting — the whole face/person recognition thing doesn't happen.

My take? I stick with the default, giving the camera permission to prioritize faces. If I want to ensure that a specific focus point is used, regardless of whether there are any people in the scene, I use Single-Point AF, which renders Custom Function 6 moot.

>> **Custom Function 8: AF Point Display During Focus:** By default, the selected AF points (or brackets) are displayed in the viewfinder any time the camera is ready to shoot. The markings also appear when you're choosing an AF point, during autofocusing, and when focus is achieved. Through this menu option, you can indicate when you want the focus points to appear or specify that you always want to see all points, all the time. (You're probably going to get tired of that option, named All, quickly.)

>> **Custom Function 9: VF Display Illumination:** This setting, too, affects the viewfinder display. At the default setting, Auto, AF points used to achieve focus appear black in normal light and turn bright red in dim light. If you want the points to appear red regardless of the ambient light, change the setting to Enable. To instead have the focus markings always appear black, choose Disable.

If you're new to Custom Functions, check out Chapter 1 for a primer in how to make your way through these menu screens.

WARNING

PREVENTING SLOW-SHUTTER BLUR

A poorly focused photo isn't always caused by incorrect focusing. A slow shutter speed can also be the culprit.

Chapter 4 explains shutter speed in detail, but here's the short story as it relates to focus: When you photograph moving subjects, a slow shutter speed can make them appear blurry because their motion is recorded the entire time the shutter is open. When you handhold the camera, a slow shutter speed increases the chances of camera movement — camera *shake* — during the exposure, which can blur the entire photo.

You can avoid camera shake by using a tripod, of course. But when you don't have a tripod or other way to steady the camera, some lenses offer a feature that can compensate for small amounts of camera shake. On Canon lenses, this feature is called image stabilization, but other manufacturers use different names, such as vibration reduction (VR) or optical image stabilization (OIS). The Canon lens featured in this book offers image stabilization; enable and disable it via the Stabilizer switch on the lens.

Focusing in Live View and Movie Modes

You can opt for autofocusing or manual focusing during Live View and movie shooting, assuming that your lens supports autofocusing with the T8i/850D. The actual focusing process is the same as for viewfinder photography: To autofocus, press and hold the shutter button halfway or, alternatively, if you're shooting in the P, Tv, Av, or M exposure mode, press and hold the AF ON button. To focus manually, rotate the focusing ring on the lens. (See the first section of the chapter for help setting the lens to automatic or manual focusing.) In Live View and Movie mode, however, you also have the option of using the monitor to set focus directly on the screen by tapping your chosen focus point.

When focus is achieved, the focus frame turns green, as shown in Figure 5-13. The focus frame appearance varies depending on the autofocusing settings you choose; later sections provide details.

Spot AF focus frame   Touch shutter status

FIGURE 5-13:
When the Touch Shutter feature is Off, tapping the touchscreen sets focus but doesn't trigger the shutter release.

WARNING

For still photography, remember that if the Touch Shutter feature is enabled, the camera takes the shot as soon as you lift your finger off the screen. Look for the touch shutter status in the lower-right corner of the display, as shown in Figure 5-13. (If you don't see the symbol, press the Info button to change the data that's displayed.) Toggle the touch shutter on and off by tapping the symbol. In the figure, the feature is turned off.

The next several sections offer more details about focusing in Live View and Movie modes.

AF Method: Setting the focusing area

As with viewfinder photography, the camera offers two settings that enable you to tweak autofocus performance. First up is the AF Method, which is the equivalent of the AF Area Selection mode option provided for viewfinder photography. It enables you to tell the camera which region of the frame to analyze when setting focus. You can control this setting in the same exposure modes that you can during viewfinder photography — that is, any mode but the Candlelight SCN mode and the Fisheye and Miniature Creative Filters modes.

The autofocus settings available for Live View and Movie mode are different than for viewfinder photography, however. You have the following choices, represented by the symbols labeled in the next few figures. (Don't worry if you can't see the symbols clearly in the figures; I just pointed them out so that you know where to look. You can get a closer look at each symbol on the select screens where you choose the mode you want to use.)

» **Face+Tracking AF:** This setting is designed to speed up focusing when you shoot portraits. If the camera detects a face, it automatically places a focus frame over that face, as shown on the left in Figure 5-14. If the person attached to the face moves before you initiate autofocusing, the camera tracks the movement (thus, *Face+Tracking*), automatically repositioning the focus frame. In a group portrait, you can move the frame over a different face than the one the camera initially selects by pressing the right or left edge of the Quick Control dial; the triangles on either side of the face focus frame are there to remind you of that option. To position the frame over the person at the center of the screen, press the Set button.

Face+Tracking AF symbol

Selected face focus frame

Eye-detection on symbol

Eye-detection frame

FIGURE 5-14:
In Face+Tracking mode, a focus frame appears over a detected face (left); if Eye Detection is enabled, a smaller frame appears over the eye and will be the focus target (right).

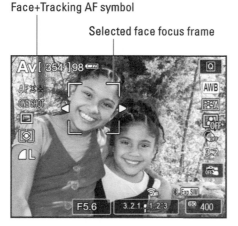
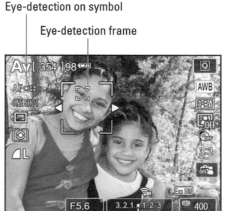

REMEMBER

Note that the face-selection process is only part of the game; you still have to press the shutter button halfway, press the AF ON button, or tap the touchscreen to initiate autofocusing. But with face tracking, autofocusing can happen a little faster because the camera knows exactly where to set focus.

If the camera doesn't detect a face, it looks for a focusing target elsewhere in the frame. Note that "elsewhere" has its limits — the camera can't set focus on anything that's very near the edges of the frame. Also, you don't see any indicators of where the camera plans to focus until you press the shutter button halfway or press the AF ON button to initiate autofocusing. You also can tap your subject on the screen to set focus on that area.

>> **Face+Tracking AF with Eye Detection AF:** First things first: This isn't an official AF Method setting. Rather, if you choose Face+Tracking AF, you can enable Eye Detection AF as an add-on. This feature, as its name implies, scans the frame for a forward-looking face and then, if possible, locks onto one of the person's eyes. You then see both the normal face-detection frame plus a smaller frame over one eye, as on the right in Figure 5-14. Having the eyes in focus is usually the main goal for a portrait, so this feature is well worth investigating.

>> **Zone AF:** With this setting, the camera displays a frame like the one you see on the left in Figure 5-15. You position the frame over the area that contains your subject, and then the camera is free to choose a focusing target within the "zone" covered by the focus frame. When focus is set, green boxes appear that indicate the object used to establish the focusing distance, as shown on the right in the figure. You can reposition the frame by pressing the edges of the Quick Control dial.

This focusing setup works pretty well for a scene like the one in Figure 5-15, where you expect your subject to remain fairly stationary or at least confine its movements to within a limited area. As long as the subject stays within the zone frame, the camera should be able to find the right focus target when you initiate autofocusing.

Tap to move focus frame to center

Zone AF symbol   Zone AF frame   Selected focus points

FIGURE 5-15: In Zone AF, move the frame over the area that contains your subject (left); when focus is set, one or more green focus points appear inside that frame (right).

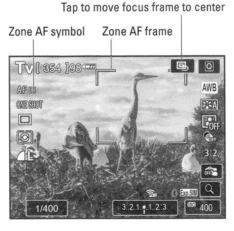
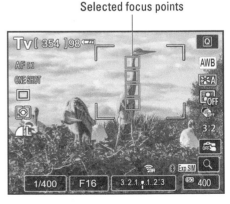

Notice the symbol labeled "Tap to move focus frame to center" on the left in Figure 5-15. This symbol appears when you set the AF Method to any option but Face+Tracking and the focus frame is not already in the center of the screen. You can tap it to quickly center the focus frame. Or, if you find it easier, just press the Set button to accomplish the same thing. The icon disappears after you set focus.

>> **1-Point AF:** This mode works just like Zone AF except that the focusing frame is smaller, enabling you to more precisely indicate the intended focusing target. The left screen in Figure 5-16 offers a look at the 1-point focus frame. Again, note the symbol just to the left of the Q symbol, in the upper-right corner of the screen. As with Zone AF, you can tap that symbol to whoosh the focus frame to the exact center of the screen. (I labeled the symbol in Figure 5-15, if you need clarification.)

>> **Spot AF:** Want an even tinier focus frame than 1-Point AF? Choose Spot AF. The second screen in Figure 5-16 shows you this diminutive frame, which is designed to enable you to precisely lock on a specific area in the scene.

1-point AF symbol

1-point AF frame

Spot AF symbol

Spot AF frame

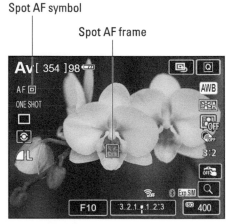

FIGURE 5-16: To limit focus to a smaller area, choose 1-Point AF frame (left) or, for pinpoint focusing, Spot AF (right).

In any mode, if you see an orange focus frame instead of a green one after you initiate autofocusing, the camera's autofocusing system can't lock on to a target. In Face+Tracking mode, which looks for targets throughout the frame, the orange "not happening" frame appears around the perimeter of the Live View display.

To adjust the AF Method setting, you have a couple of choices:

» **Use the Quick Control method.** Press the Q button or tap the Q touchscreen symbol to put the camera in Quick Control mode. Figure 5-17 shows the still photography Live View screen with the AF Method setting selected. When the camera is in Movie mode, the AF Method setting appears in the same spot, but several other options on the screen relate to movie recording instead of still photography.

AF Method option

Name of selected method

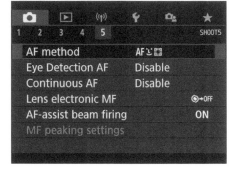

FIGURE 5-17: Change the AF Method via the Quick Control screen (left) or Shooting Menu 5 (right).

Eye-detection on symbol

Tap to turn eye-detection on/off

Selected method

Rotate the Quick Control dial to cycle through the four AF Method options. You also can rotate the Main dial or press the right/left edges of the Quick Control dial or simply tap the icon representing the mode you want to use.

When the Face+Tracking mode is selected, as in the figure, you can toggle Eye Detection autofocus on and off by tapping the Info label or pressing the Info button. If you want the feature turned on, make sure that the word Enable appears next to the Info label, as in the left screen in Figure 5-17. (That seems counterintuitive to me — I assumed that when the accompanying text label says "Enable," I should press or tap Info to turn on the feature, and when the label says Disable, I should press or tap Info to turn Eye Detection off. But the opposite is true.)

If you get confused as I did on this one, check the AF Method icon after you exit the Quick Control screen. If you see an eyeball to the right of the letters *AF,* as in the right screen of Figure 5-14, Eye Detection is turned on. Additionally, if the camera detects an eye, a tiny frame appears over that eye — again, refer to Figure 5-14.

>> **Change the setting via Shooting Menu 5, as shown on the right in Figure 5-17.** When Face+Tracking is selected, as it is in the figure, you can enable and disable Eye Detection AF via the menu option located one line below the AF Method option. Choose Enable if you want to use Eye Detection AF.

>> **Press the AF Area Selection mode button to display the simplified selection screen shown in Figure 5-18.** The button is just in front of the Mode dial, next to the ISO button. It's the same button you use to access the AF Area Selection option during viewfinder shooting. (Refer to Figure 5-6 for a look at the button.) After the selection screen appears, press the AF Area Selection mode button as needed to cycle through the four settings. The icon at the right end of the settings strip, visible in Figure 5-18, has the same markings as the button to help you remember which button to use to make your selection.

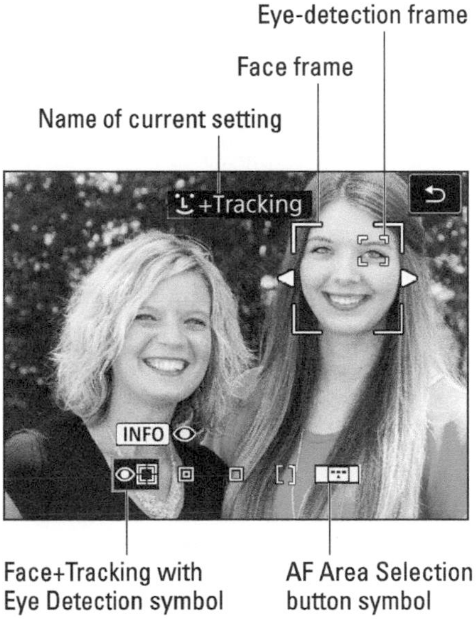

Eye-detection frame

Face frame

Name of current setting

Face+Tracking with Eye Detection symbol

AF Area Selection button symbol

FIGURE 5-18:
To quickly access just the AF Method settings, press the AF Area Selection button.

As you scroll to each setting, the focus frame associated with that setting appears on the screen. In the figure, the face-detection frame appears because the Face+Tracking option is selected. And you also see the smaller eye-detection frame because the Eye Detection option is set to Enable. (You can tell by looking at the symbol labeled Face+Tracking with Eye Detection in the figure; if the eyeball appears to the left of the little square, eye detection is in force.) After you choose the setting you want to use, tap the exit arrow in the upper-right corner to lock in your choice and return to shooting.

This is my least-favorite way to change the AF Method setting because I never remember that it's even possible. Come on, this is all convoluted enough, and now I'm supposed to remember that a button that sports a tiny grid-like marking is related to autofocusing? A button that's hidden from view until I peer at the top of the camera? Yeah, not gonna happen, sorry. Maybe your brain is better (gad, I hope so), but I just rely on the Quick Control button or the Menu button to get this job done. If you *do* develop an affinity for the AF Area Selection Mode button, though, it certainly offers a quicker way to change this particular setting than to use the Quick Control or Menu methods.

AF Operation: One-Shot or Servo?

The second Live View autofocusing control, AF Operation, works just like its viewfinder-photography counterpart, determining when the final focusing distance is set. For Live View photography, though, you have only two options:

>> **One-Shot AF:** Focus locks when you press the shutter button halfway or press and hold the AF ON button.

>> **Servo AF:** Like the AI Servo option available for viewfinder photography, Live View Servo AF enables continuous autofocusing. When you press the shutter button halfway or press and hold the AF ON button, the camera chooses initial focus points and displays them in blue. But focus is continuously adjusted to track a moving subject up to the time you take the picture, as long as you keep the shutter button pressed halfway or the AF ON button pressed all the way. The blue focus points move through the focus frame or area as the camera adjusts the focusing distance.

There is no AI Focus setting, which is the viewfinder-photography setting that lets the camera decide which of the two options to use.

How you choose the AF Operation setting depends on whether you're shooting photographs or movies, as follows:

>> **Live View photography:** Your only option for changing the AF Operation setting is to put the camera in Quick Control mode (press the Q button or tap the Q touchscreen symbol). The left screen in Figure 5-19 offers a look at the Quick Control screen as it appears when the AF Operation setting is active. To change the setting, highlight the AF Operation icon, as shown in the figure, and then rotate the Quick Control dial or Main dial or just tap the setting you want to use.

>> **Movie mode:** By default, the camera uses a special continuous autofocus setting called Movie Servo AF. The camera focuses automatically on the object within the focusing frame — you don't have to press the shutter button halfway to set focus as you do for still photography. To interrupt focus adjustment, tap the Servo AF icon in the lower-left corner of the screen, labeled on the right in Figure 5-19. Tap again to resume continuous autofocusing.

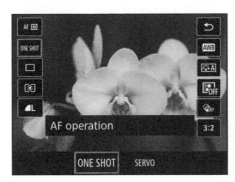 

Tap to pause/restart continuous autofocusing

During shooting, you can tap the screen to reset focus on a different portion of the screen. Your movie footage may be blurred for a second or two during the time the camera adjusts focus.

The downside to Movie Servo AF is that with some lenses, the sounds made by the autofocusing system can be heard on the movie audio track. Do some tests with your lens to find out whether the focusing noise is disruptive; if so, you may want to disable continuous autofocusing altogether. To do so, open Shooting Menu 3 and change the Movie Servo AF setting to Disable. You then set focus by pressing the shutter button halfway; focus remains locked even if you release the button. When you record the movie using P, Tv, Av, or M exposure modes, you also have the option of using the AF ON button to set focus. And in any exposure mode, you can tap the screen to set focus on that area. If needed, reset focus by pressing the shutter button again, keeping in mind the same problems that arise when you reset focus when using Movie Servo AF.

There is one other wrinkle related to continuous autofocusing that you need to consider. If you choose, you can turn on a still-photography version of Movie Servo AF. That is, you can instruct the camera to initiate continuous autofocusing immediately after you select Servo as the AF Operation method. The idea is to give the camera a focusing head start so that it can focus nearly instantaneously when you press the shutter button halfway or press the AF ON button. I know this sounds like a good thing, and it may be exactly what you need in situations where you're unsure of where in the frame a moving subject is going to be at the moment you want to take the picture. But there's a really big downside: Because the lens and the rest of the autofocusing system are working nonstop, the camera's battery is going to drain much more quickly than if you turn the feature off. If you set the Drive mode to burst shooting (the camera captures a series of frames as long as you hold down the shutter button), you also reduce the number of frames you can capture per minute. Because of those issues, the feature is turned off by default. If you want to try it out, visit Shooting Menu 5 and change the Continuous AF setting to Enable. (The menu option appears only when the camera is in Live View mode.)

Don't confuse the Continuous AF setting with the Servo AF setting just discussed. Servo AF tells the camera to wait until you press the shutter button halfway (or press the AF ON button) to begin autofocusing. Continuous autofocusing still happens — just not until you tell the camera to get to work on that task.

TIP

WHY FACE- AND EYE-DETECTION AUTOFOCUS ISN'T A SURE THING

In the Face+Tracking autofocus mode, the camera searches for faces in the frame. If it finds one, it displays a focus frame over the face. In a group shot, the camera chooses one face to use as the focus point; you can move the focus frame over a different face by pressing the right or left edge of the Quick Control dial (or top and bottom, if you want to move the frame vertically). You also can simply tap the face.

When the conditions are *just right* in terms of lighting, composition, and phase of the moon, the face-detection technology works fairly well. However, it has a number of "issues":

- People must be facing the camera to be detected. The feature is based on the camera recognizing the pattern created by the eyes, nose, and mouth. So if you're shooting the subject in profile, don't expect face detection to work.

- The camera may mistakenly focus on an object that has a similar shape, color, and contrast to a face.

- Face detection sometimes gets tripped up if the face isn't just the right size with respect to the background, is tilted at an angle, is too bright or dark, or is partly obscured.

- Autofocusing isn't possible when a subject is very close to the edge of the frame. The camera alerts you to this issue by displaying a gray frame instead of a white one over your subject. You can always temporarily reframe to put the subject within the acceptable autofocus area, press and hold the shutter button halfway to lock focus, and then reframe to your desired composition.

If the camera has trouble finding your subject's face, the fix is easy: Just tap the touchscreen to position the focus frame yourself. Alternatively, you can set the AF Method to 1-Point AF and move the focus frame over the face. If possible, position the frame over the eye closest to the lens; that will ensure the best portrait results, at least as far as focusing goes.

Manual focusing in Live View and Movie modes

Manual focusing is the easiest of the Live View focusing options — and in most cases, it's faster, too. The first part of the chapter provides information on manual focusing basics, but also be aware of these points specific to Live View and Movie mode:

WARNING

>> **If Servo AF is engaged, exit Live View or Movie mode before changing the lens switch to the MF (manual focus) position.** Moving the switch while continuous autofocusing is engaged can damage your equipment.

>> **The Live View and Movie displays don't offer any indication that manual focusing is in force.** The screens continue to show the current AF Method and AF Operation symbols, along with the respective autofocus frames.

TIP

>> **You can magnify the display to verify focus.** Most people who shy away from manual focusing do so because they don't trust their eyes to judge focus. But thanks to a feature that enables you to magnify the Live View preview, you can feel more confident in your manual focusing skills. See the next section for details.

FOCUS PEAKING: HIGHLIGHTING THE SHARPEST "EDGES"

In digital imaging lingo, the word "edge" refers to a border between a dark and light area. For reasons we don't need to explore here, it's easier for a camera to focus when contrast exists between your subject and its surroundings — imagine a white teacup set on a blue tablecloth. Focus peaking helps you find those edges by outlining them in color on the monitor.

Focus peaking is available in all exposure modes except Scene Intelligent Auto, but only during Live View shooting. To enable the option, open Shooting Menu 5 and select MF Peaking Settings. On the next screen, change the Peaking option to choose On. You're then offered two other settings: Level and Color. Level determines the amount of contrast that has to occur before an outline is placed along an edge; the default is High, but you can change the setting to Low. (Experiment to see which setting does the best job on your subject.) The second option, Color, enables you to change the default outline color from red to yellow or blue. Choose the color that makes the outlines easiest to see in your scene.

Zooming in for a focus check

Here's a cool focusing feature not available during viewfinder photography: You can magnify the Live View or Movie display to ensure that focus is accurate. This trick works during manual focusing or when you autofocus using any AF Method but Face+Tracking.

After setting focus, follow these steps to magnify the display:

1. **Position the focus frame over the area you want to inspect.**

   For example, in Figure 5-20, the frame appears over the center of the rose. (The frame appearance depends on which AF Method you use; for this example, I used Zone AF.) To position the frame, just tap the screen where you want to place it or press the edges of the Quick Control dial.

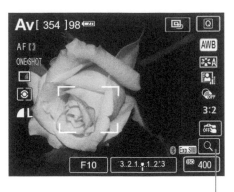

Tap to magnify display

2. **Press the AF Point Selection button or tap the magnifying glass on the screen, highlighted in Figure 5-20.**

   You then see a magnified view of the area inside the focus frame, as shown in Figure 5-21. In the lower-right corner of the screen, you also see a navigation box that contains a white thumbnail. That box represents the entire image; the thumbnail represents the portion of the scene that you're currently viewing. Atop the navigation box, the number displayed represents the magnification level — 5x, in the figure.

3. **Press the AF Point Selection button or tap the magnifying glass symbol again to increase the magnification level.**

   You can display a magnification level up to 10x.

Magnification level

Move focus area to center

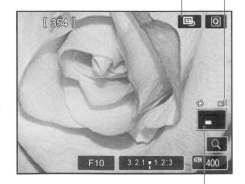

Area being displayed

FIGURE 5-21:
The magnification level and a box indicating the area of the frame you're inspecting appear in the zoomed view.

4. **To scroll the display, just drag your finger across the screen as you would when viewing pictures on a smartphone.**

   You also can press the edges of the Quick Control dial to view a different part of the scene.

5. **To exit the magnified view, press the shutter button halfway.**

   Or just keep tapping the Magnifying Glass icon or pressing the AF Point Selection button until you return to the original view. (One tap or press takes you to 5x view; a second, to 10x view; and a third, back to the original, unmagnified screen.)

Be sure to exit magnified view before you actually take the picture. Otherwise, exposure may be off. However, if you *do* take the picture in magnified view, the entire frame is captured — not just the area currently displayed on the monitor.

CORRECTING LENS DISTORTION AND DIFFRACTION

Some lenses can cause slight distortion or result in *diffraction,* a phenomenon that causes a loss of sharpness at certain aperture settings. In P, Tv, Av, and M exposure modes, you may be able to deal with these issues by choosing Lens Aberration Correction from Shooting Menu 1. If the text at the top of the next screen shows your lens model, the camera has the information it needs to apply the corrections.

By default, Distortion Correction is disabled. That's because in order for this feature to work, the camera has to capture a slightly narrower image than it normally does. Some other downsides are a small change in the angle of view of your photo and a slight reduction in apparent image resolution. If you think you want to use this feature, do some test shots with and without it enabled so that you fully understand what it does to your pictures. And here's a quick warning: In the Group Portrait SCN mode, Distortion Correction is applied automatically. So be sure to frame those group portraits a little loosely to make sure that no one important gets cropped out of the image as a result of the correction.

To get to the diffraction correction, choose Digital Lens Optimizer, found just below the Distortion Correction option on the menu screen. This setting is enabled by default, which tells you that Canon believes that any downsides are minor compared to the benefits. In addition to correcting diffraction, this feature can also reduce other lens-related issues, such as *chromatic aberration,* which is a color-related defect.

If you turn off Digital Lens Optimizer, you can enable and disable the chromatic aberration filter and diffraction correction filters independently.

Manipulating Depth of Field

Getting familiar with the concept of depth of field is one of the biggest steps you can take to becoming a better photographer. Chapter 3 introduces you to depth of field, but here's a quick recap:

>> *Depth of field* refers to the distance over which objects in a photograph appear acceptably sharp.

>> With a shallow depth of field, the subject is sharp, but objects in front of and behind it appear blurry. The farther an object is from the subject, the blurrier it looks.

>> With a large depth of field, the zone of sharp focus extends to include objects at a greater distance from your subject.

Which arrangement works best depends on your creative vision and your subject. In portraits, for example, a classic technique is to use a shallow depth of field, as in the example shown in Figure 5-22. But for landscapes, you might choose to use a large depth of field, as shown in Figure 5-23. Because the historical marker, lighthouse, and cottage are all sharp, they have equal visual weight in the scene.

Shallow Depth of Field

Large depth of field

FIGURE 5-22:
A shallow depth of field blurs the background and draws added attention to the subject.

FIGURE 5-23:
A large depth of field keeps both near and far subjects in sharp focus.

Again, though, which part of the scene appears blurry when you use a shallow depth of field depends on the spot at which you establish focus. Consider the lighthouse scene: Suppose you opted for a short depth of field and set focus on the lighthouse. In that case, both the historical marker in the foreground and the cottage in the background might be outside the zone of sharp focus.

REMEMBER

So how do you manipulate depth of field? You have three points of control:

>> **Aperture setting (f-stop):** The aperture is one of three main exposure settings, all explained fully in Chapter 4. Depth of field increases as you stop down the aperture (by choosing a higher f-stop number). For shallow depth of field, open the aperture (by choosing a lower f-stop number).

Figure 5-24 offers an example. Notice that the tractor in the background is in much sharper focus in the first shot, taken at f/20, than in the second image, shot at f/2.8.

>> **Lens focal length:** *Focal length,* which is measured in millimeters, determines what the lens "sees." As you increase focal length, the angle of view narrows, objects appear larger in the frame, and — the important point in this discussion — depth of field decreases. Additionally, the spatial relationship of objects changes as you adjust focal length.

For example, Figure 5-25 compares the same scene shot at focal lengths of 138mm and 255mm. The aperture was set to f/22 for both examples.

f/20, 93mm   f/2.8, 93mm

FIGURE 5-24:
Lowering the
f-stop value
decreases depth
of field.

138mm, f/22 255mm, f/22

FIGURE 5-25:
Using a longer
focal length also
reduces depth of
field.

Whether you have any focal-length flexibility depends on your lens. If you have a zoom lens, you can adjust the focal length by zooming in or out. If your lens offers only a single focal length — a prime lens in photo-speak — scratch this means of manipulating depth of field (unless you want to change to a different prime lens, of course).

>> **Camera-to-subject distance:** When you move the lens closer to your subject, depth of field decreases. This statement assumes that you don't zoom in or out to reframe the picture, thereby changing the focal length. If you do, depth of field is affected by both the camera position and focal length.

REMEMBER

Together, these three factors determine the maximum and minimum depth of field that you can achieve, as follows:

>> **To produce the shallowest depth of field:** Open the aperture as wide as possible (select the lowest f-stop number), zoom in to the maximum focal length of your lens, and move as close as possible to your subject.

>> **To produce maximum depth of field:** Stop down the aperture to the highest possible f-stop setting, zoom out to the shortest focal length your lens offers, and move farther from your subject.

Here are a few additional tips and tricks related to depth of field:

>> **Aperture-priority autoexposure mode (Av) enables you to easily control depth of field while enjoying exposure assistance from the camera.** In this mode, you rotate the Main dial to set the f-stop, and the camera selects the appropriate shutter speed to produce a good exposure. The range of available aperture settings depends on your lens.

If you're not up to Av mode, experiment with the Background Blur setting available when you shoot in Scene Intelligent Auto mode. You access it through the Creative Assist option. Just don't expect miracles: For reasons I explain in Chapter 3, the Background Blur feature doesn't always deliver as much or as little blurring as you'd like. Some SCN modes also offer the Background Blur option.

>> **For greater background blurring, move the subject farther from the background.** The extent to which background focus shifts as you adjust depth of field also is affected by the distance between the subject and the background.

TIP

>> **Use the Depth-of-field Preview button to see the effect of the aperture setting on depth of field.** When you look through your viewfinder and press the shutter button halfway, you see only a partial indication of the depth of field that your current camera settings will produce. You can see theeffectoffocallengthandthecamera-to-subject distance, but because the aperture doesn't actually stop down to your selected f-stop until you take the picture, the viewfinder doesn't show you how that setting will affect depth of field.

By using the Depth-of-Field Preview button on your camera, however, you can do just that when you shoot in the advanced exposure modes. Almost hidden away on the front of your camera, the button is labeled in Figure 5-26. (I took the lens off the camera to give you a better view of the button.)

Depth-of-field Preview button

FIGURE 5-26:
Press this button to see how the aperture setting will affect depth of field.

To use this feature, press and hold the shutter button halfway and simultaneously press and hold the Depth-of-Field Preview button with a finger on your other hand. Depending on the selected f-stop, the scene in the viewfinder may get darker. In Live View mode, the same thing happens in the monitor preview. Either way, this effect doesn't mean that your picture will be darker; it's just a function of how the preview works.

Note that the preview doesn't engage in P, Tv, or Av mode if the aperture and shutter speed aren't adequate to expose the image properly. You have to solve the exposure issue before you can use the preview.

IN THIS CHAPTER

» Exploring white balance and its effect on color

» Creating a custom White Balance setting

» Fine-tuning all White Balance settings

» Bracketing white balance

» Experimenting with Picture Styles

» Setting the color space (sRGB or Adobe RGB)

Chapter **6**

Mastering Color Controls

Compared with certain camera settings — resolution, aperture, shutter speed, and so on — your camera's color options are fairly simple to figure out. Most color problems can be easily fixed by adjusting one setting, White Balance. And getting a grip on color requires learning only a couple of new terms, an unusual state of affairs for an endeavor that often seems more like university-level science than art.

Some of the settings screens you use to adjust color options, on the other hand, are more than a little confusing, often presenting symbols or letters that don't offer much of a clue as to their meaning. This chapter helps you make sense of things so that you can more easily control color.

Before you start exploring this chapter, though, note this rule of the color road: You can adjust the settings discussed in this chapter only in a Creative Zone exposure mode (P, Tv, Av, or M). Also, settings discussed in this chapter apply to both still photography and movie recording, with one exception: The Color Space option is out of your control in Movie mode.

Understanding White Balance

Every light source emits a particular color cast. The old-fashioned fluorescent lights found in most public restrooms, for example, put out a bluish-green light, which is why our reflections in the mirrors in those restrooms look so sickly. And if you think that your beloved looks especially attractive by candlelight, you aren't imagining things: Candlelight casts a yellow-red glow that's flattering to the skin.

TECHNICAL STUFF

Science-y types measure the color of light, or *color temperature,* on the *Kelvin scale.* You can see an illustration of the Kelvin scale in Figure 6-1.

When photographers talk about "warm light" and "cool light," though, they aren't referring to the position on the Kelvin scale — or at least not in the way we usually think of temperatures, with a higher number meaning hotter. Instead, the terms describe the visual appearance of the light. Warm light, produced by candles and incandescent lights, falls in the red-yellow spectrum you see at the bottom of the Kelvin scale; cool light, in the blue-green spectrum, appears at the top of the scale.

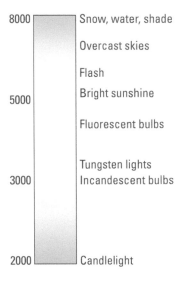

FIGURE 6-1:
Each light source emits a specific color.

At any rate, most of us don't notice these fluctuating colors of light because our eyes automatically compensate for them. Except in extreme lighting conditions, a white tablecloth appears white to us no matter whether we view it by candlelight, fluorescent light, or regular house lights. Similarly, a digital camera compensates for different colors of light through a feature known as white balancing. Simply put, white balancing neutralizes light so that whites are always white, which in turn ensures that other colors are rendered accurately. If the camera senses warm light, it shifts colors slightly to the cool side of the color spectrum; in cool light, the camera shifts colors in the opposite direction.

Your camera's Auto White Balance (AWB) setting tackles this process well in most situations. In some lighting conditions, though, it doesn't quite do the trick. Problems most often occur when your subject is lit by a variety of light sources. For example, Figure 6-2 features an alabaster-colored figurine set against a black velvet background. The scene was lit by both tungsten photo lights and strong daylight coming through a nearby window. In Automatic White Balance mode, the original image, shown on the left in the figure, has a golden color cast. Switching to the Tungsten Light option rendered colors correctly, as shown on the right.

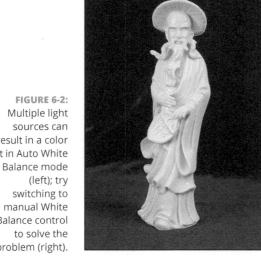

FIGURE 6-2: Multiple light sources can result in a color cast in Auto White Balance mode (left); try switching to manual White Balance control to solve the problem (right).

The next several sections explain how to make a basic white-balance adjustment and discuss some advanced White Balance options. Again, remember that these options are available only for the P, Tv, Av, and M exposure modes.

TIP

If you're not ready to step up to the Creative Zone modes, you can make limited color adjustments in Scene Intelligent Auto mode through the Creative Assist options. Additionally, the Food and Candlelight SCN modes enable you to make colors warmer or cooler. For help, visit Chapter 3.

Changing the White Balance setting

A symbol representing the current White Balance setting appears in the Quick Control and Live View displays, in the areas labeled in Figure 6-3. (If your Live View screen doesn't show the symbol, press the Info button to cycle through the Live View display variations until you see the one shown in the figure.)

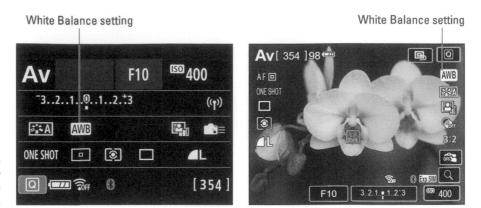

White Balance setting   White Balance setting

FIGURE 6-3:
AWB stands for
Auto White
Balance.

Figure 6-4 shows the icons used to represent the various White Balance settings. Don't worry about memorizing the symbols or the Kelvin temperature associated with each, though; as you scroll through the options when selecting a setting, the camera displays that data for each option. A few settings do demand a bit of further explanation, however:

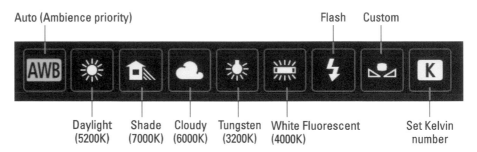

Auto (Ambience priority)   Flash   Custom

FIGURE 6-4:
You can choose
from prefab
White Balance
settings, create a
Custom setting,
or select a
specific Kelvin
temperature.

Daylight   Shade   Cloudy   Tungsten   White Fluorescent   Set Kelvin
(5200K)   (7000K)   (6000K)   (3200K)   (4000K)   number

>> **You can choose from two AWB (Auto White Balance) options, Ambience Priority and White Priority.** Your choice is relevant only when you shoot in tungsten lighting (or a light source that has a similar color temperature, such as incandescent household bulbs). With the Ambience Priority setting, the camera doesn't completely remove the warm cast created by tungsten lighting. For portraits and certain other subjects, that little hint of warmth is lovely. But if you want your whites to be white, switch to White Priority. (I provide the how-tos in a bit.) When White Priority is in force, a *W* appears to the right of the AWB symbol. If you don't see the W, Ambience Priority is active.

When you use flash, the camera uses Ambience Priority even when White Priority is selected, however. Flash light has a cool color cast, and if the camera added to that light the cooling used to neutralize warm light in White Priority mode, subjects could appear blue — literally.

>> **Choose Custom to create a White Balance setting precisely tuned to the current lighting conditions.** This setting is useful when you're dealing with mixed light sources, such as when shooting a dinner party where guests are illuminated by candle light on the table and incandescent lighting from an overhead chandelier. The next section shows you how to take advantage of this feature.

>> **Use the K setting to tune white balance to a single Kelvin temperature.** This option comes in handy for photographers who are using lights that have a specific Kelvin rating. Just be sure that those lights are the only thing illuminating your subject; otherwise, going the Custom route typically works better.

You can change the White Balance setting in the following ways:

>> **Press the top edge of the Quick Control dial, where the WB label appears (viewfinder shooting only).** Figure 6-5 shows you where to press. You then see the White Balance selection screen that's shown on the monitor in the figure. Rotate the Quick Control dial to scroll through the White Balance settings. To lock in your choice and exit the settings screen, tap the option you want to use. Or highlight it and then tap the Set symbol or press the Set button.

FIGURE 6-5:
Press WB on the Quick Control dial to display the White Balance settings screen.

While the settings screen is displayed, you may need to take a few intermediate steps depending on the White Balance option you select, as follows:

- *To switch from the Ambience Priority AWB to White Priority AWB, select the AWB option and then press the Info button or tap the Info label on the screen.* You then see the screen shown on the left in Figure 6-6. Tap the AWB W setting or rotate the Quick Control or Main dial to highlight that option, as shown on the right in the figure. Tap Set or press the Set button to exit the screen.

FIGURE 6-6:
After selecting
AWB on the main
White Balance
selection screen,
tap the Info
button to access
these screens,
where you can
choose between
Ambience Priority
and White Priority
Auto.

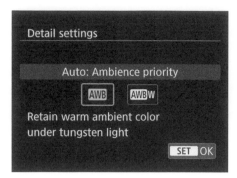
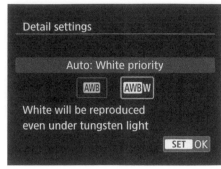

- *If you select K as the White Balance setting, the options shown in Figure 6-7 appear.* The current Kelvin temperature appears in the area labeled in the figure. Raise or lower the number by rotating the Main dial (notice the half-wheel icon that's supposed to represent that dial, also labeled in the figure). Tapping the arrows on either side of the current value also adjusts the number. Tap Set or press the Set button to lock in your decision and exit the screen.

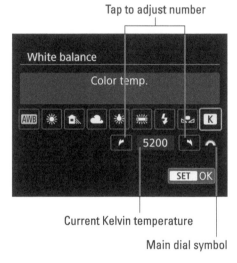

FIGURE 6-7:
After selecting the K symbol, rotate the Main dial to set the Kelvin value.

>> **Use the Quick Control feature.** This method of changing the White Balance setting works in Live View and Movie mode as well as for viewfinder photography. Press the Q button or tap the Q touchscreen symbol to shift to Quick Control mode and then highlight the White Balance icon. (Refer to Figure 6-3 for help finding the icon.) After you highlight the icon, the currently selected option appears at the bottom of the screen; rotate the Main dial or Quick Control dial to cycle through the remaining options.

When the AWB option is highlighted, as shown on the left in Figure 6-8, press the Set button to display the screen where you can shift between the two AWB priority settings. This is different from the way you do things if you use the technique in the preceding bullet point, where pressing Info brings up the screens. In Quick Control mode, pressing or tapping Info accesses controls for fine-tuning white balance and setting up white balance bracketing, features

I cover a little later in this chapter. This same advice applies when the K option is highlighted; again, press or tap Set to get to the screen where you specify the Kelvin temperature you want to use.

TIP

The Live View and Movie Quick Control screens provide a White Balance adjustment benefit that you don't enjoy during viewfinder photography: As you change the White Balance setting, the monitor updates to show you the effect on the subject colors, as shown in Figure 6-8. This feature makes it easy to experiment with different settings to see which one renders colors best. For example, in the left screen in the figure, the AWB option is enabled; in the right screen, the Tungsten light option is selected.

Tap to toggle AWB priority setting

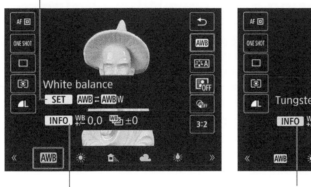

FIGURE 6-8: In Live View mode, the preview updates to show how the current White Balance setting affects colors.

Tap to fine-tune or bracket white balance

>> Select the White Balance option from Shooting Menu 3. Figure 6-9 gives you a look at the menu option. After you select White Balance from the menu, you see the same screen shown on the monitor in Figure 6-5.

REMEMBER

Don't see Shooting Menu 3? Check the Mode dial. Remember, you can adjust White Balance only when the camera is set to the P, Tv, M, or Av exposure mode; if any other mode is selected, you get only two Shooting menus.

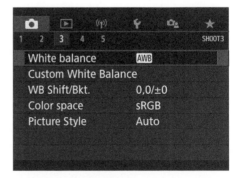

FIGURE 6-9: You also can adjust the White Balance setting from Shooting Menu 3.

A few final tips before I move on to advanced White Balance features:

>> **Your selected White Balance setting remains in force for the P, Tv, Av, and M exposure modes until you change the setting.** To avoid accidentally using an incorrect setting later, get in the habit of resetting the option to the automatic setting (AWB) after you finish shooting whatever scene caused you to choose a different setting.

>> **When shooting in mixed light, choose the White Balance setting based on the most prominent light source.** If none of the prefab settings produce accurate colors, give up on them and try the customized White Balance options outlined next three sections.

Creating a custom White Balance setting

Through the Custom White Balance option, you can create a white balance setting that's precisely tuned to the color of the light hitting your subject, whether that light comes from one or many sources. To use this technique, you need a piece of card stock that's either neutral gray or absolute white — not eggshell white, sand white, or any other close-but-not-perfect white. You can buy reference cards made for this purpose in many camera stores.

After positioning the reference card in the lighting you plan to use for your subject, follow these steps to create the custom setting:

1. **With the camera in still photography mode (i.e., not Movie mode), set the Mode dial to P, Tv, Av, or M.**

   You can't use this feature in any of the other exposure modes. In M exposure mode, ensure that the exposure is correct before taking the reference photo. If the image is greatly under- or overexposed, the resulting white balance will be affected.

TIP

   Although you can't create a custom setting in Movie mode, you can select one that you create in still photography mode. Just choose the Custom option as your White Balance setting. (Refer to Figure 6-4 for a look at the symbol that represents the Custom setting.)

2. **Take a picture of the reference card.**

   Frame the shot so that the reference card fills the viewfinder or, if you're using Live View, the monitor. For best results, focus manually. The autofocus system usually has a hard time focusing on a blank field of color, and depending on your autofocus settings, the shutter won't release until focus is achieved. That's not a problem when you use manual focusing.

3. **Display Shooting Menu 3 and choose Custom White Balance, as shown on the left in Figure 6-10.**

   You then see the screen shown on the right in the figure. The image you just captured should appear in the display, along with a brief message telling you the camera will only display that image and others that were shot in a mode compatible with custom white balancing. If your picture doesn't appear on the screen, rotate the Quick Control dial or press its right or left edges to scroll through your images until you find the reference photo. (Your screen may show more data than what you see in Figure 6-10 if you're using a different playback display mode. Press the Info button to cycle through the various playback displays.)

   Again, notice the Custom White Balance symbol appearing in red in the top-left corner of the screen and inside the Set label at the bottom of the screen.

REMEMBER

Custom White Balance symbol

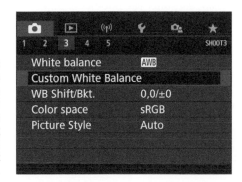
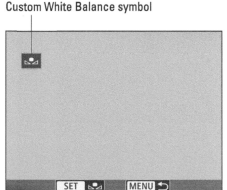

FIGURE 6-10: Choose this option from Shooting Menu 3 to create a White Balance setting precisely tailored to the current lighting.

4. **Tap the Set icon (or press the Set button) to select the displayed image as the basis for your custom white balance reference.**

   You're asked to confirm that you want to use the image to create the custom white balance.

5. **Tap OK or highlight it and press the Set button.**

   A message tells you that the custom setting is stored.

6. **Tap OK (or highlight it and press Set) to finish.**

Your custom setting remains stored until the next time you replace it by working your way through these steps again. Any time you want to base white balancing on this custom setting, just look for the Custom symbol in the White Balance selection screens.

Fine-tuning color with White Balance Shift

In addition to creating a custom White Balance setting, you can use White Balance Shift to recalibrate the White Balance system so that no matter which White Balance setting you choose, colors are shifted toward a particular part of the color spectrum. (In the instruction manual, this feature is named White Balance Correction, but goes by the Shift moniker on camera screens and menus.)

As with other White Balance features, this one is available only in P, Tv, Av, and M exposure modes. However, you can set up White Balance Shift in Movie mode as well as during still photography. After setting the Mode dial to P, Tv, Av, or M, follow these steps:

1. Display the White Balance Shift screen.

You can get to the screen in two ways:

- *Use the Quick Control feature.* During viewfinder photography, the White Balance Shift option appears after you put the camera in Quick Control mode, as shown on the left in Figure 6-11. Tap the option or highlight it and press Set to display the screen shown on the right.

White Balance Shift/Bracketing setting

Tap triangles to move adjustment marker

Shift marker

Shift amount

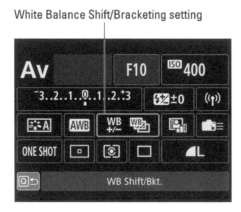

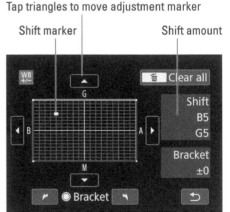

FIGURE 6-11:
After putting the camera in Quick Control mode, select the White Balance Shift/ Bracketing option (left) to display the adjustment screen (right).

In Live View or Movie mode, the Quick Control screen displays an Info label when the White Balance option is active, as shown on the left in Figure 6-12. Tap that label or press the Info button to get to the adjustment screen shown on the right.

White Balance Shift/Bracket setting

Shift amount

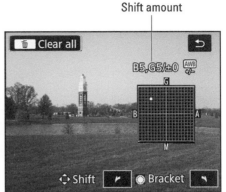

FIGURE 6-12:
In Live View or Movie mode, tap the Info icon (left) or press the Info button to access the adjustment screen (right).

- *Open Shooting Menu 3 and select White Balance Shift/Bkt, as shown in Figure 6-13.* The camera displays the same adjustment screen shown on the right in Figure 6-11.

Both versions of the adjustment screen contain a grid that's oriented around two color pairs: green and magenta (represented by the G and M labels) and blue and amber (represented by B and A).

2. **Move the shift marker (the white square) in the grid to set the amount and direction of the adjustment.**

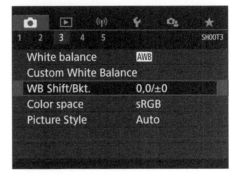

FIGURE 6-13:
You can also get to the White Balance Shift settings through Shooting Menu 3.

When using the adjustment screen shown in Figure 6-11, move the marker by tapping the grid, tapping the directional arrows around the perimeter of the grid, or pressing the left/right/top/bottom edges of the Quick Control dial. In Live View or Movie mode, tap the grid or press the edges of the Quick Control dial to move the marker. (The symbol that appears to the left of the word *Shift* at the bottom of Figure 6-12 reminds you that you can press the top/bottom/left/right edges of the dial to move the marker.) The round symbol, to the left of the word *Bracket,* indicates that you rotate the dial to set up White Balance bracketing, discussed in the next section.

As you move the white marker in the grid, the Shift area of the display shows the amount of color bias you've selected. For example, in Figure 6-11 and 6-12, I shifted colors five levels toward blue and five levels toward green.

If you're familiar with traditional lens filters, you may know that the density of a filter, which determines the degree of color correction it provides, is measured in *mireds* (pronounced "my-reds"). The White Balance grid is designed around this system: Moving the marker one level is the equivalent of adding a filter with a density of 5 mireds.

3. **Press the Set button to apply the change and return to the initial menu or Quick Control screen.**

   You also can tap the exit arrow (lower-right corner of the viewfinder or menu version of the adjustment screen; upper-right corner of the Live View and Movie screens).

4. **Press the shutter button halfway and release it to exit the menu or Quick Control display.**

   As a reminder that White Balance Shift is in force, the symbol labeled on the left in Figure 6-14 appears in the Quick Control display. A +/– sign appears under the White Balance symbol on the Live View and Movie screens, as shown on the right.

White Balance Shift enabled

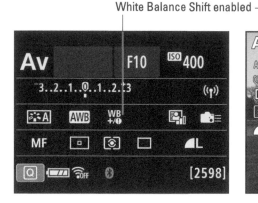

FIGURE 6-14:
These symbols remind you that White Balance Shift is being applied.

By default, you also see an exclamation point in the viewfinder, at the left end of the data display. However, the exclamation point also appears if you set the Picture Style option to Monochrome (as covered later in this chapter), and when you set the Hi ISO Speed Noise Reduction feature to the Multi Shot setting (as explained in Chapter 4). You can specify which of these features results in the alert through Custom Function 11. Access the Custom Functions through Setup Menu 5.

To see the exact White Balance Shift values, open Shooting Menu 3 and check the first pair of numbers. (The values after the slash indicate the White Balance Bracketing setting, explained in the next section.) For example, in Figure 6-15, the menu screen indicates a shift of five steps toward blue and five steps toward green.

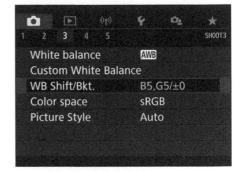

FIGURE 6-15:
You can view the current amount of White Balance Shift on Shooting Menu 3.

WARNING

5. **To cancel White Balance Shift, repeat Steps 1 and 2 and then set the marker back to the center of the grid.**

Be sure that both values in the Shift area of the display are set to 0.

TIP

For a fast way to move the marker to the center of the grid, press the Erase button (lower-right corner of the back of the camera) or tap its onscreen symbol. However, doing so also cancels White Balance Bracketing, explained later in this chapter.

ELIMINATING COLOR FRINGING (CHROMATIC ABERRATION)

Pictures taken with some lenses may reveal *chromatic aberration*, a defect that creates weird color halos along the edges of objects. This phenomenon is also known as *color fringing*.

Your camera has a filter designed to help address this issue. Called the Chromatic Aberration filter, it's normally applied by default along with some other lens-defect filters via the Digital Lens Optimizer feature, which you can find by choosing Lens Aberration Correction from Shooting Menu 1. Digital Lens Optimizer, however, applies some corrections that you may prefer to leave turned off because they can cause certain side effects, such as added image noise.

To apply the chromatic aberration filter only, set the Mode dial to P, Tv, Av, or M and open Shooting Menu 1. Choose Lens Aberration Correction and then check the text at the top of the next screen. If your lens is listed, it's compatible with the corrective filters. Disable Digital Lens Optimizer, and Chromatic Aberration appears as a separate option on the menu.

See the Chapter 5 sidebar that discusses lens distortion and defraction for more information about the Digital Lens Optimizer feature and its related filters.

Bracketing White Balance

Chapter 4 introduces you to Automatic Exposure Bracketing, which makes it easy to *bracket exposures* — capture the same scene at three different exposure settings. Similarly, the camera offers White Balance Bracketing, which accomplishes the same thing but varying white balance instead of exposure between frames.

Before you explore the steps involved in bracketing white balance, here are some preliminary points to understand:

>> **You can take advantage of White Balance Bracketing only in the P, Tv, Av, and M exposure modes.** Also, the feature isn't available for movie recording.

>> **White Balance Bracketing is based on the same color grid you use to set up White Balance Shift.** In fact, you adjust both settings on the same screen. If you want, you can enable both white-balance shift and bracketing.

>> **You can bracket white balance along one axis of the color grid only.** That is, you can shift colors along either the blue/amber axis or the green/magenta axis as you shoot your series of three frames. You're limited to a maximum shift of three steps between shots.

REMEMBER

>> **You take just one picture to create a bracketed series.** The camera records one shot when you press the shutter button, rendering the image according to the current White Balance setting. From that frame, the camera creates two copies, adjusting the colors of each copy according to the bracketed color shift you set up.

Because the camera needs time to process the second and third images, your shot-to-shot frame rate may slow when you enable White Balance Bracketing.

Figure 6-16 offers an example of the kind of results you can expect from White Balance Bracketing. For this series, frames were bracketed along the blue/amber axis, using the maximum amount of color shift between the neutral, blue, and amber frames. As you can see, the difference is subtle, although your mileage may vary depending on the subject of the photo.

To enable White Balance Bracketing, follow these steps:

1. **Set the Mode dial to P, Tv, Av, or M.**

2. **Display the setup grid shown in Figure 6-17 by using Quick Control mode or by selecting WB/Shift Bkt. from Shooting Menu 3.**

   The steps in the earlier section "Fine-tuning color with White Balance Shift" provide specifics; refer to Figures 6-11 and 6-12 for a visual reminder of how the Quick Control screens appear during viewfinder shooting and Live View photography, respectively. In Live View mode, tap the Info label or press the Info button to get to the color grid.

+3 Blue bias   Neutral   +3 Amber bias

FIGURE 6-16:
With White Balance Bracketing, the camera automatically creates three frames that vary in color.

Bracketing indicators   Type and amount of adjustment between frames

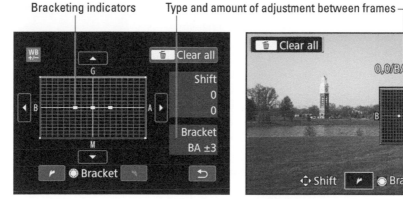

FIGURE 6-17:
To establish bracketing settings, rotate the Main dial or tap the arrows to the left and right of the Bracket label.

3. **Rotate the Quick Control dial to set the amount and direction of the bracketing shift.**

Rotate the dial to the right to apply bracketing along the blue/amber axis; rotate left to bracket along the green/magenta axis.

As you rotate the dial, three markers appear on the grid, indicating the amount of shift that will be applied. The text above the grid also shows the bracketing type and amount. For example, in Figure 6-17, the bracketing is set to plus and minus three levels on the blue/amber axis.

TIP

You also can adjust the settings by tapping the arrows on either side of the word *Bracket,* at the bottom of the screen.

4. **In Quick Control mode, exit the bracketing setup screen by tapping the exit arrow or pressing the Set button.**

You return to the initial Quick Control screen, which remains active so you can adjust other settings if needed. To exit to shooting mode, just press the Q button or tap the Q symbol on the screen.

5. **If you established your bracketing settings via Shooting Menu 3, press the Set button or tap Set to return to shooting mode.**

Verify the bracketing value by checking the White Balance Shift/Bkt. setting on Shooting Menu 3; the value after the slash shows the bracketing setting. The two values to the left of the slash indicate the White Balance Shift direction and amount.

The Quick Control display contains a White Balance Bracketing symbol, as shown in Figure 6-18, when bracketing is turned on. In the Live View display, the White Balance setting symbol appears smaller than usual and blinks to indicate that bracketing is enabled. Neither display shows you the specifics of the bracketing setting; you have to check Shooting Menu 3 for that detail.

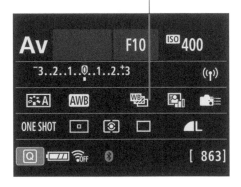

Appears when White Balance bracketing enabled

FIGURE 6-18:
The Quick Control screen displays this alert when White Balance Bracketing is turned on.

6. **Take the picture.**

Remember, you shoot just one frame to create all three bracketed images. After you take the first picture, give the camera a few seconds to create the color-adjusted copies.

WARNING

White Balance bracketing remains in effect until you turn off the camera. You can also cancel bracketing by revisiting the adjustment screen (refer to Figure 6-17) and resetting the Bracketing value to 0. You can do this quickly by tapping the Clear All symbol or pressing the Erase button on the back of the camera.

Taking a Quick Look at Picture Styles

Picture Styles give you an additional way to tweak image colors. But the Picture Style setting also affects color saturation, contrast, and image sharpening.

TECHNICAL STUFF

Sharpening is a software process that adjusts contrast in a way that creates the illusion of slightly sharper focus — emphasis on the word *slightly*. Sharpening cannot remedy poor focus, but instead produces a subtle improvement to this aspect of your pictures.

The camera offers the following Picture Styles, which are indicated in the displays by the initials shown in the list:

>> **Auto (A):** Analyzes the scene and determines which Picture Style is the most appropriate. (This setting is the default.)

>> **Standard (S):** Produces the image characteristics that Canon considers as suitable for the majority of subjects.

>> **Portrait (P):** Reduces sharpening slightly to keep skin texture soft.

>> **Landscape (L):** Emphasizes greens and blues and amps up color saturation and sharpness.

>> **Fine Detail (FD):** Offers extra sharpening and slightly more intense colors.

>> **Neutral (N):** Reduces saturation and contrast slightly compared to how the camera renders images at the Standard setting.

>> **Faithful:** Renders colors as closely as possible to how the human eye perceives them.

>> **Monochrome:** Produces black-and-white photos.

TIP

When you select this setting and set the Quality option to Raw, cRaw, or a Raw+Large/Fine combination, the camera displays your JPEG image on the monitor in black and white during playback. But during the Raw conversion process, you can go with your black-and-white version or view and save a full-color version. Even better, if you shoot only in Raw, you can process and save the image once as a grayscale photo and again as a color image.

If you *don't* capture the image in the Raw or cRaw format, you can't access the original image colors later. In other words, you're stuck with *only* a black-and-white image. For this reason, shooting in the Monochrome Picture style in JPEG only isn't a great idea.

>> **User Def. (1, 2, and 3):** You can create and store three of your own Picture Styles. More on that possibility a little later.

The extent to which Picture Styles affect your image depends on the subject, the exposure settings you choose, and the lighting conditions. Figure 6-19 shows the Auto version of an image; Figure 6-20 shows the variations produced by the other full-color Picture Styles.

Auto Picture Style

You have control over the Picture Style setting only in the P, Tv, Av, M, and Movie modes. In the Quick Control screen and Live View displays, the symbol labeled in Figure 6-21 represents the current setting. (In Movie mode, the symbol appears in the same spot as in Live View still-photography mode.)

To change the Picture Style setting, use these methods:

FIGURE 6-19:
Here's how the Auto Picture Style rendered the example image.

>> **Quick Control method:** After shifting to Quick Control mode, highlight the Picture Style icon and then rotate the Main dial or Quick Control dial to cycle through the available styles. To see all styles on a single screen, press Set or tap the Picture Style icon. On that second screen, highlight the style you want to use and press Set to finish up. Or just give the setting a quick tap on the touchscreen.

Figure 6-22 shows the Quick Control screens as they appear during viewfinder photography. In Live View and Movie mode, the screens vary in appearance, but the process of selecting and adjusting the setting is the same.

>> **Shooting Menu 3:** Select Picture Style from the menu to display a variation of the selection screen shown on the right in Figure 6-22.

>> **Bottom edge of the Quick Control dial (viewfinder shooting only):** When you're not in Live View or Movie mode, you have an even faster option for getting to the Picture Style setting: Just press the bottom edge of the Quick Control dial — where you see the symbol that decorates the Picture Style setting in the displays. Figure 6-23 offers a look.

Standard   Portrait   Landscape

Fine Detail   Neutral   Faithful

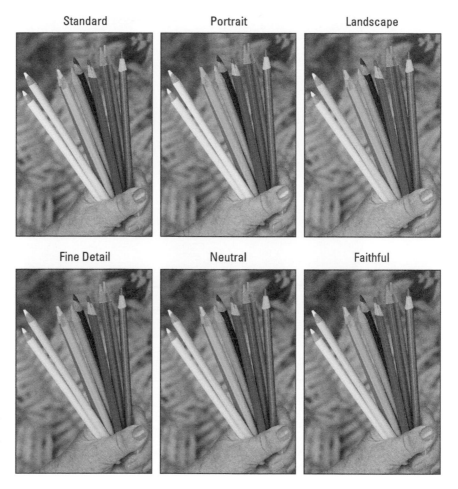

FIGURE 6-20:
And here are the variations produced by the six other full-color Picture Styles.

Picture Style setting   Picture Style setting

FIGURE 6-21:
This symbol represents the Picture Style.

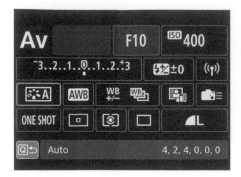

FIGURE 6-22:
You can select a Picture Style via the Quick Control screen.

FIGURE 6-23:
During viewfinder photography, pressing the bottom of the Quick Control dial takes you directly to the Picture Control settings screen.

Press to display Picture Style setting screen

Now for the question on everyone's mind: What the heck is the deal with all the crazy numbers and symbols that appear in the Picture Control settings screens? Well, in their very Canon-like cryptic style, the symbols represent specific picture characteristics, such as sharpness, color saturation, and contrast. The number values indicate the strength at which those characteristics are applied to the picture when the camera processes the image data. But the different characteristics are based on different number ranges, so those values aren't a big help unless you spend time researching and understanding them.

TIP

So why does Canon go to the trouble of including these details? Because you can modify a Picture Style by adjusting the values for the various picture characteristics. Unless you're tickled pink by the prospect of experimenting with Picture Styles, however, stick with the default setting (Auto) and ignore the fine-tuning options. Why add one more setting to the list of options you have to remember, especially when the impact of changing it is minimal?

Second, if you want to play with the characteristics that the Picture Style options affect, you're better off shooting in the Raw format (or its sibling, cRaw) and making those adjustments on a picture-by-picture basis in your Raw converter. (See Chapter 10 for help processing Raw files.) For these reasons, this book presents just this brief introduction to Picture Styles, making room for functions that make a bigger difference to your photographic success. For details on Picture Style features not covered here, consult the camera manual.

Changing the Color Space

By default, your camera captures JPEG images in the *sRGB color space,* which refers to an industry-standard spectrum of colors. (The *s* is for *standard,* and the *RGB* is for *red, green, blue,* which are the primary colors in the digital color world.) Because sRGB leaves out some colors that *can* be reproduced in print and onscreen, at least by some devices, your camera also offers a second color space, Adobe RGB, which includes a larger spectrum of colors. However, some colors in the Adobe RGB spectrum *can't* be reproduced in print; the printer substitutes the closest color if necessary.

If you plan to print and share your photos without making any adjustments in your photo editor, stick with sRGB; most printers and web browsers are designed around that color space. Also realize that while all photo-editing programs support sRGB, some do not support Adobe RGB.

REMEMBER

You can't use Adobe RGB when recording movies or when shooting in any exposure mode except P, Tv, Av, or M. Change the setting via the Color Space option on Shooting Menu 3, shown in Figure 6-24. The filenames of pictures captured in the Adobe RGB color space start with an underscore, as in _MG_0627.jpg. Pictures captured in the sRGB color space start with the letter *I,* as in IMG_0627.jpg.

FIGURE 6-24:
For most photographers, the sRGB color space is the best choice.

Chapter **7**

Putting It All Together

E arlier chapters break down critical picture-taking features, explaining controls that affect exposure, picture quality, focus, color, and more. This chapter pulls all that information together to help you set up your camera for specific types of photography. Keep in mind, though, that there's no one "right way" to shoot a portrait, landscape, or whatever. So feel free to wander off on your own, tweaking this exposure setting or adjusting that focus control, to discover your own creative vision — experimentation is part of the fun of photography!

Recapping Basic Picture Settings

For some camera options, such as exposure mode, aperture, and shutter speed, the best settings depend on your subject, lighting conditions, and creative goals. But for certain basic options, the same settings work well for almost every scenario. Table 7-1 offers recommendations for these settings and lists the chapters where you can find more information about each option.

TABLE 7-1 **All-Purpose Picture-Taking Settings**

Option	Recommended Setting	See This Chapter
Image Quality	Large/Fine (JPEG), Raw, or cRaw (CR3)	2
Drive mode	Action photos, Continuous Low or High; all others, Single	2
ISO	100	4
Metering mode	Evaluative	4
Exposure Compensation (P, Tv, and Av modes only)	Set as needed; raise value for brighter exposure, lower for darker exposure	4
AF Operation mode	Moving subjects, AI Servo; stationary subjects, One Shot	5
AF Area Selection mode	Moving subjects, Auto Selection; stationary subjects, Single Point	5
White Balance	Auto (AWB), Ambient Priority	6
Auto Lighting Optimizer	Standard for P, Tv, and Av modes; Disable for M mode	4
Picture Style	Auto	6

Figure 7-1 shows the information display, where you can see the current status of many of these settings. (You may need to press the shutter button halfway or press the DISP button to view the screen.) Don't forget that by pressing the Q button or tapping the Q touchscreen symbol, you activate Quick Control mode, which enables you to adjust settings right from the screen. Chapter 1 explains the process.

REMEMBER

One key point: The instructions in this chapter assume that you're using one of the advanced exposure modes: P, Tv, Av, or M. Other modes prevent you from accessing settings that can be critical for capturing certain subjects, especially in difficult lighting. Also, this chapter discusses viewfinder photography. However, most things work the same way during Live View photography, with the exception of focusing options, which are quite different.

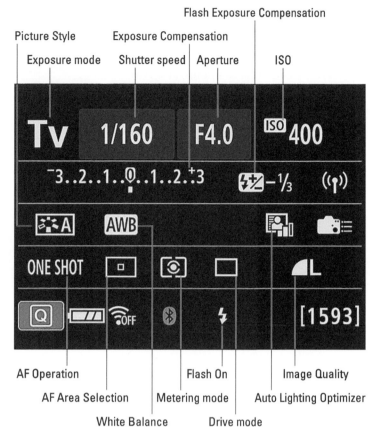

Flash Exposure Compensation

Picture Style Exposure Compensation

Exposure mode Shutter speed Aperture ISO

Tv 1/160 F4.0 ISO 400

⁻3..2..1..0..1..2.⁺3 ⚡±−⅓ ((ᵗ))

AF Operation

AF Area Selection

White Balance

Flash On

Metering mode

Drive mode

Image Quality

Auto Lighting Optimizer

FIGURE 7-1:
The information
display shows the
most critical
picture settings.

Shooting Still Portraits

By *still portrait,* I mean that your subject isn't moving. For subjects who aren't keen on sitting still, use the techniques given for action photography instead.

The classic portraiture approach is to keep the subject sharply focused while throwing the background into soft focus, as shown in Figure 7-2. A blurred background emphasizes the subject and diminishes the impact of any distracting background objects.

The following steps show you how to achieve this look:

1. **Set the Mode dial to Av and rotate the Main dial to select the lowest f-stop value possible.**

   A low f-stop setting opens the aperture, which not only allows more light to enter the camera but also shortens *depth of field*, or the distance over which focus appears acceptably sharp. So dialing in a low f-stop value is the first step in softening your portrait background.

   WARNING

   For a group portrait, you typically need a higher f-stop than for a single portrait. At a very low f-stop, depth of field may not be large enough to keep everyone in the sharp-focus zone. Take test shots and inspect the results to find the right f-stop setting.

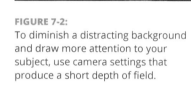

   FIGURE 7-2:
   To diminish a distracting background and draw more attention to your subject, use camera settings that produce a short depth of field.

   Also remember that when you use aperture-priority autoexposure mode (Av), the camera selects the shutter speed that will properly expose the image at your chosen f-stop. But you still need to pay attention to shutter speed to make sure that it's not so slow that any movement of the subject or camera will blur the image.

2. **Check the lens focal length.**

   A focal length of 85–120mm is ideal for a classic head-and-shoulders portrait. Avoid using a short focal length (wide angle lens) for portraits. It can cause features to appear distorted — sort of like how people look when you view them through a security peephole in a door. On the flip side, a very long focal length can flatten and widen a face.

   Keep in mind that focal lengths are stated in terms of 35mm equivalency. The 18–55mm kit lens produces an equivalent focal length of 29–88mm, so it's fine for portrait work as long as you zoom to its longest focal length. Chapter 1 explains this issue.

3. **To further soften the background, get closer to your subject and put more distance between subject and background.**

   A good rule is to put your subject at least an arm's distance from the background.

4. **Check composition.**

   Two quick pointers on this topic:

   - *Consider the background.* Scan the entire frame, looking for distracting background objects. If necessary and possible, reposition the subject against a more flattering backdrop.

   - *Frame the subject loosely to allow for later cropping to a variety of frame sizes.* Your camera produces images that have an aspect ratio of 3:2. That means your portrait perfectly fits a 4-x-6 print size but will require cropping to print at any other proportion, such as 5 x 7 or 8 x 10.

5. **For indoor portraits, shoot flash-free if possible.**

   Shooting by available light rather than flash produces softer illumination and avoids the problem of red-eye. During daytime hours, pose your subject near a large window to get results similar to what you see in Figure 7-3.

   On the T8i, keeping the flash closed disables the flash. If flash is unavoidable, see the tips at the end of these steps to get better results.

6. **For outdoor portraits in daylight, using flash may help.**

   Even in daylight, a flash can add a beneficial pop of light to subjects' faces, as illustrated in Figure 7-4. A flash is especially important when the background is brighter than the subject; when the subject is wearing a hat; or when the sun is directly overhead, creating harsh shadows under the eyes, nose, and chin. To use flash in Av mode, raise the built-in flash. Then open Shooting Menu 1, choose Flash Control, and set the Flash Firing option to Fire.

Courtesy of Mandy Holmes

FIGURE 7-3:
For soft, even lighting, forego flash and instead expose your subject using daylight coming through a nearby window.

WARNING

One caveat about using flash outdoors: The fastest shutter speed you can use with the built-in flash is 1/200 second, and in extremely bright conditions, that speed may be too slow to avoid overexposing the image even if you use the lowest ISO (light sensitivity) setting. If necessary, move your subject into the shade.

No Flash   With Flash

FIGURE 7-4:
To better illuminate faces in outdoor portraits, use flash.

If you use an external flash, you may be able to select a faster shutter speed than 1/200 second; see your flash manual for details. Your other option is to stop down the aperture (use a higher f-stop setting), but that brings more of the background into sharp focus.

7. **Press and hold the shutter button halfway to engage exposure metering and, if using autofocusing, to establish focus.**

REMEMBER

Setting the AF Operation mode to One-Shot and the AF Area Selection mode to Single Point works best for portrait autofocusing. After selecting a focus point, position that point over one of your subject's eyes (ideally, the eye closest to the camera) and then press and hold the shutter button halfway to lock focus. (If you shoot in Live View mode, you also can try the Eye Detection autofocus feature; see Chapter 5 for details.)

8. **Press the shutter button the rest of the way to capture the image.**

When flash is unavoidable, try these tricks for best results:

» **Pay attention to white balance if your subject is lit by flash and ambient light.** When you mix light sources, photo colors may appear slightly warmer or cooler (more blue) than neutral. A warming effect typically looks nice in portraits, giving the skin a subtle glow. If you aren't happy with the result, see Chapter 6 to find out how to fine-tune white balance. Don't forget that your camera offers two Auto settings, one that holds onto a slight warm cast when you shoot in incandescent light (Ambient Priority mode) and one that eliminates that color cast (White Priority mode).

- » **Indoors, turn on as many room lights as possible.** With more ambient light, you reduce the flash power needed to expose the picture. Adding light also causes the pupils to constrict, further reducing the chances of red-eye. (Pay heed to the preceding white-balance warning, however.) As an added benefit, the smaller pupil allows more of the iris to be visible, so you see more eye color in the portrait.

- » **In dim lighting, try enabling Red-Eye Reduction.** Warn your subject to expect both a light coming from the Red-Eye Reduction Lamp, which constricts pupils, and the actual flash. See Chapter 2 for details about this flash option.

- » **For nighttime pictures, try switching to Tv exposure mode and using a slow shutter speed.** The longer exposure time enables the camera to soak up more ambient light, producing a brighter background and reducing the flash power needed to light the subject. Just remember that the slower the shutter speed, the greater the possibility subject movement or camera shake will blur the image. So use a tripod and ask your subject to remain as still as possible.

- » **For professional results, use an external flash with a rotating flash head.** Then aim the flash head up so that the flash light bounces off the ceiling and falls softly down on the subject. (This is called *bounced light.*) An external flash isn't cheap, but the results make the purchase worthwhile if you shoot lots of portraits. Compare the portraits in Figure 7-5 for an illustration. In the first example, the built-in flash resulted in strong shadowing behind the subject and harsh, concentrated light. Bounced lighting produced the better result on the right.

  Make sure that the surface you use to bounce the light is white; otherwise the flash's light will pick up the color of the surface and influence the color of your subject.

- » **Invest in a flash diffuser to further soften the light.** A *diffuser* is simply a piece of translucent plastic or fabric that you place over the flash to soften and spread the light — much like sheer curtains diffuse window light. Diffusers come in lots of different designs, including small, fold-flat models that fit over the built-in flash.

- » **To reduce shadowing from the flash, move your subject farther from the background.** Moving the subject away from the wall helped eliminate the background shadow in the second example in Figure 7-5. The increased distance also softened the focus of the wall a bit (because of the short depth of field resulting from the f-stop and focal length). You may also wish to light the background separately.

Direct flash   Bounced flash

FIGURE 7-5:
To eliminate
harsh lighting and
strong shadows
(left), use bounce
flash and move
the subject
farther from the
background
(right).

TIP

If you can't move the subject farther from the background, try going the other direction: If the person's head is smack against the background, any shadow will be smaller and less noticeable.

Capturing Action

A fast shutter speed is the key to capturing a blur-free shot of any moving subject, whether it's a spinning Ferris wheel, a butterfly flitting from flower to flower, or in the case of Figures 7-6 and 7-7, a hockey-playing teen.

In Figure 7-6, a shutter speed of 1/125 second was too slow to catch the subject without blur. A shutter speed of 1/1000 second froze the action cleanly, as shown in Figure 7-7. (The backgrounds are blurry in both shots because the images were taken using a lens with a long focal length, which decreases depth of field. Also, in the first image, the skater is farther from the background, blurring the background more than in the second image.)

FIGURE 7-6:
A too-slow
shutter speed
(1/125 second)
causes the skater
to appear blurry.

FIGURE 7-7:
Raising the
shutter speed to
1/1000 second
freezes the
action.

Along with the basic capture settings outlined earlier (refer to Table 7-1), try the techniques in the following steps to photograph a subject in motion:

1. **Set the Mode dial to Tv (shutter-priority autoexposure).**

   In this mode, you control shutter speed, and the camera chooses the aperture setting that will produce a good exposure at the current ISO setting.

2. Rotate the Main dial to select the shutter speed.

The shutter speed you need depends on how fast your subject is moving, so you have to experiment. Another factor that affects your ability to stop action is the *direction* of subject motion. A car moving toward you can be stopped with a lower shutter speed than one moving across your field of view, for example. Generally speaking, 1/500 second should be plenty for all but the fastest subjects — speeding hockey players, race cars, or boats, for example. For slower subjects, you can often drop the shutter speed to 1/250 or even lower. (Again, take test shots to make sure that your shutter speed freezes the subject.)

Remember that when you increase shutter speed in Tv exposure mode, the camera opens the aperture to maintain the same exposure. At low f-stop numbers, depth of field becomes shorter, so you have to be more careful to keep your subject within the sharp-focus zone as you compose and focus the shot, especially if the subject is moving toward or away from your camera.

TIP

You also can take an entirely different approach to capturing action: Instead of choosing a fast shutter speed, select a speed slow enough to blur the moving objects, which can create a heightened sense of motion and, in scenes that feature very colorful subjects, cool abstract images such as the carnival ride images in Figure 7-8. For the left image, the shutter speed was 1/30 second; for the right version, 1/5 second. In both cases, I used a tripod, but because nearly everything in the frame was moving, the entirety of both photos is blurry — the 1/5 second version is simply more blurry because of the slower shutter.

FIGURE 7-8:
Using a shutter speed slow enough to blur moving objects can be a fun creative choice, too.

For an alternate effect, try *panning* (moving the camera horizontally or vertically) parallel to the movement. The subject you track during the pan will remain relatively sharp, even with a slower shutter speed. (Lots of practice and experimentation are required to get it right.)

If the aperture value blinks after you set the shutter speed, the camera can't select an f-stop that will properly expose the photo at that shutter speed and the current ISO setting.

3. **Raise the ISO setting to produce a brighter exposure, if needed.**

In dim lighting, you may not be able to create a good exposure at your chosen shutter speed without taking this step. Raising the ISO increases the possibility of noise, but a noisy shot is better than a blurry shot. You can access this setting quickly by pressing the ISO button on top of the camera.

If Auto ISO is in force, ISO may go up automatically when you increase shutter speed. Auto ISO can be a big help when you're shooting fast-paced action; just be sure to limit the camera to choosing an ISO setting that doesn't produce an objectionable level of noise. Chapter 4 provides details on Auto ISO.

Why not just add flash to throw some extra light on the scene? That solution has a number of drawbacks. First, the flash needs time to recycle between shots, which slows down your shooting pace. Second, the fastest possible shutter speed when you enable the built-in flash is 1/200 second, which may not be fast enough to capture a quickly moving subject without blur. (You can use a faster shutter speed with certain Canon external flash units, however.) And finally, the built-in flash has a limited range, so unless your subject is pretty close to the camera, you're just wasting battery power with flash, anyway.

4. **For rapid-fire shooting, set the Drive mode to one of the Continuous options.**

The camera then shoots a burst of images as long as the shutter button is pressed. In High-speed Continuous mode, the camera can capture as many as seven frames per second; in Low-speed Continuous mode, three frames per second. You can access the Drive mode setting quickly by pressing the left edge of the Quick Control dial (it's marked with a few of the Drive mode symbols).

5. **If autofocusing, set the AF Operation mode to AI Servo (continuous autofocus) and the AF Area Selection mode to Automatic Selection.**

When you use these autofocus settings, the camera initially sets focus on the center focus point. So frame your subject under that point, press and hold the shutter button halfway (or press and hold the AF ON button) to set the initial focusing distance, and then reframe as necessary to keep the subject within the area covered by the focus points. As long as you keep the shutter button or AF ON button pressed, the camera continues to adjust focus up to the time you take the shot. Chapter 5 details these autofocus options.

6. **Compose the subject to allow for movement across the frame.**

Don't zoom in so far that your subject might zip out of the frame before you take the shot — frame a little wider than usual. You can always crop the photo later to a tighter composition. (Many examples in this book were cropped to eliminate distracting elements.)

One other key to shooting sports, wildlife, or any moving subject: Before you even put your eye to the viewfinder, spend time studying your subject so that you get an idea of when it will move, where it will move, and how it will move. The more you can anticipate the action, the better your chances of capturing it.

Capturing Scenic Vistas

Providing specific camera settings for landscape photography is tricky because there's no best approach to capturing a stretch of countryside, a city skyline, or another vast subject. Depth of field is an example: One person's idea of a super cityscape might be to keep all buildings in the scene sharply focused. Another photographer might prefer that a foreground building appears sharply focused while the other structures are less so, thus drawing the eye to that first building.

That said, here are a few tips to help you photograph a landscape the way *you* see it:

>> **Shoot in aperture-priority autoexposure mode (Av) so that you can control depth of field.** If you want extreme depth of field so that both near and distant objects are sharply focused, select a high f-stop value. Keep in mind that f-stop is just one factor that determines depth of field, though: To extend depth of field, use a wide angle lens (short focal length) and increase the distance between the camera and your subject.

WARNING

The downside to using a high f-stop to achieve greater depth of field is that you need a slower shutter speed to produce a good exposure. If the shutter speed is slower than you can comfortably handhold, use a tripod to avoid picture-blurring camera shake. No tripod? Turn on Image Stabilization, if your lens offers it. (Chapter 1 details that lens feature.) You also can increase the ISO setting to increase light sensitivity, which in turn allows a faster shutter speed, but that option brings the chance of increased image noise. See Chapter 4 for details.

>> **In large landscapes, include a foreground subject to provide a sense of scale.** The bench in Figure 7-9 serves this purpose. Because viewers are familiar with the approximate size of a typical wooden bench, they can get a better idea of the size of the vast mountain landscape beyond.

Courtesy of Kristen Holmes Reyes

>> **For dramatic waterfall and fountain shots, consider using a slow shutter to create that "misty" look.** The slow shutter blurs the water, giving it a soft, romantic appearance, as shown in Figure 7-10. Shutter speed for this shot was 1/15 second. Again, use a tripod to ensure that camera shake doesn't blur the rest of the scene.

TIP

In bright light, using a slow shutter speed may overexpose the image even if you stop the aperture all the way down and select the camera's lowest ISO setting. As a solution, consider investing in a *neutral-density filter* for your lens. This type of filter works something like sunglasses for your camera: It simply reduces the amount of light that passes through the lens, without affecting image colors, so that you can use a slower shutter than would otherwise be possible.

FIGURE 7-10:
For misty water movement, use a slow shutter speed (and tripod).

>> **At sunrise or sunset, base exposure on the sky.** The foreground will be dark, but you can usually brighten it in a photo editor, if needed. If you base exposure on the foreground, on the other hand, the sky will become so bright that all the color will be washed out — a problem you usually can't easily fix after the fact.

You can also invest in a graduated neutral-density filter, which is a filter that's dark on top and clear on the bottom. You orient the filter so that the dark half falls over the sky and the clear side over the dimly lit portion of the scene. This setup enables you to better expose the foreground without blowing out the sky colors.

Enabling Highlight Tone Priority can also improve your results, so take some test shots using that option, too. Chapter 4 offers more information.

>> **For cool nighttime city pics, experiment with a slow shutter.** Assuming that cars or other vehicles are moving through the scene, the result is neon trails of light, like those you see in Figure 7-11. Shutter speed for this image was 10 seconds. The longer your shutter speed, the blurrier the motion trails.

TIP

Rather than change the shutter speed manually between each shot, try *Bulb* mode. Available in M (manual) exposure mode, access this option by lowering the shutter speed until you see Bulb displayed. Bulb mode records an image for as long as you hold down the shutter button. So just take a series of images, holding down the button for different lengths of time for each shot. And in Bulb mode, you can exceed the camera's normal slow-shutter limit of 30 seconds.

FIGURE 7-11:
A slow shutter also creates neon light trails in city-street scenes.

>> **For more dramatic lighting, wait for the "golden hours" or "blue hours."** *Golden hours* is the term photographers use for early morning and late afternoon, when the light cast by the sun gives everything a soft, warmed glow. By contrast, the *blue hours,* just after sunset and before sunrise, infuse the scene with a cool, bluish light.

>> **In tricky light, bracket shots.** *Bracketing* simply means to take the same picture at several different exposures to increase the odds that at least one

captures the scene the way you envision. Bracketing is especially a good idea in difficult lighting situations such as sunrise and sunset. Your camera offers automatic exposure bracketing (AEB). See Chapter 4 to find out how to take advantage of this feature.

Also experiment with the Auto Lighting Optimizer and Highlight Tone Priority options; capture some images with the features enabled and then take the same shots with the features turned off. (See Chapter 4 for help.) Remember, though, that you can't use both these tonality-enhancing features concurrently; turning on Highlight Tone Priority disables Auto Lighting Optimization.

Capturing Dynamic Close-Ups

For great close-up shots, start with the basic capture settings outlined earlier in Table 7-1. Then try the following additional settings and techniques:

>> **Check your owner's manual to find out the minimum close-focusing distance of your lens.** How "up close and personal" you can be to your subject depends on your lens, not on the camera body.

>> **Take control of depth of field by setting the camera mode to Av (aperture-priority autoexposure) mode.** Whether you want a shallow, medium, or extreme depth of field depends on the point of your photo. For the scene shown in Figure 7-12, for example, setting the aperture to f/5.6 blurred the background, helping the subjects stand out from the similarly colored background. But if you want the viewer to clearly see all details throughout the frame — for example, if you're shooting a product shot for your company's sales catalog — go the other direction, stopping down the aperture as far as possible.

FIGURE 7-12:
Using a shallow depth-of-field helped the subjects stand apart from the similarly colored background.

>> **Remember that zooming in and getting close to your subject both decrease depth of field.** Back to that product shot: If you need depth of field beyond what you can achieve with the aperture setting, back away, zoom out, or both. (You can always crop your image to eliminate excess background.)

- >> **When shooting flowers and other nature scenes outdoors, pay attention to shutter speed.** Even a slight breeze may cause your subject to move, causing blurring at slow shutter speeds.

- >> **Experiment with adding flash for better outdoor lighting.** As with portraits, a bit of flash can improve close-ups when the sun is your primary light source. You may need to reduce the flash output slightly, via the camera's Flash Exposure Compensation control. Remember that turning on the built-in flash limits the maximum shutter speed to 1/200 second, however, and that mixing sunlight with flash light may affect image colors. Chapter 2 helps you deal with all these issues.

- >> **When shooting indoors, try not to use flash as your primary light source.** Because you're shooting at close range, the light from your flash may be too harsh even at a low Flash Exposure Compensation setting. If flash is inevitable, turn on as many room lights as possible to reduce the flash power that's needed.

- >> **To get really close to your subject, invest in a macro lens or a set of diopters.** A macro lens enables you to focus at a very short distance so that you can capture even the tiniest of critters or, if you're not into nature, details of an object. I used a 90mm macro lens to snap an image of the ladybug in Figure 7-13 just before she got annoyed and flew away home. Notice how shallow the depth of field is: The extreme background blurring is due to the long focal length of the lens and the short distance between the lens and the subject. I used an f-stop of f/10, which may seem high when you're going for a shallow depth of field. But because the focal length and subject distance already combined for a very shallow depth of field, I needed that higher f-stop to keep the entire subject in the focus zone.

FIGURE 7-13:
A macro lens enables you to focus close enough to fill the frame with even the tiniest subjects.

Unfortunately, a good macro lens isn't cheap; prices range from a few hundred to a couple thousand dollars. If you enjoy capturing the tiny details in life, though, it's worth the investment. For a less-expensive way to go, you can spend about $40 for a set of *diopters,* which are like reading glasses that you screw onto your lens. Diopters come in several strengths — +1, +2, +4, and so on — with a higher number indicating a greater magnifying power. With most sets, you can stack one diopter on top of another for increased power. The downside of a diopter is that it typically produces images that are very soft around the edges, a problem that doesn't occur with a good macro lens.

Chapter **8**

Shooting and Viewing Movies

I n addition to being a stellar still-photography camera, your T8i/850D can record high-definition (HD) digital movies. This chapter gets you started on your cinematic path by providing step-by-step instructions for recording movies the easy way — that is, using Scene Intelligent Auto exposure mode, autofocusing, and auto just-about-everything else. After that, you can find details on how to adjust recording settings such as movie frame size and audio-recording volume.

Some camera settings — such as those that affect autofocusing, exposure, and color — work the same way for movie-recording as they do for still photography. Rather than covering those options in detail again here, this chapter concentrates on movie-specific features. See Chapters 4–6 if you need more information about exposure, focus, and color options, respectively.

For help with two specialty video functions, Video Snapshot and Time-Lapse Movies, see Chapter 12. That chapter also shows you how to apply special effects during recording and how to trim frames from the beginning and end of a movie.

Recording Movies Using Default Settings

Recording a movie using the camera's default settings is a cinch. The following steps show you how:

1. **To use an external microphone, plug the mic into the jack on the side of the camera, labeled in Figure 8-1.**

   Otherwise, sound is recorded via the internal microphone, which collects audio signals via two holes on the built-in flash cover, shown in Figure 8-2. Be careful not to cover up the microphone holes with your finger, and remember that anything you say during the recording likely will be picked up by the internal mic. Also, don't confuse the camera's speaker, labeled in the figure, with the microphone openings. When you play back your movie, the sound will come wafting out of the speaker.

Attach external microphone here

FIGURE 8-1:
You can attach an external microphone here.

Speaker   Built-in microphone

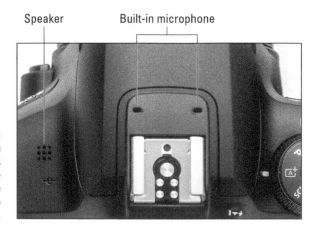

FIGURE 8-2:
The built-in microphone is located on the flash cover; the speaker, just to the left.

2. **Set the On/Off/Movie switch to the Movie mode position, as shown in Figure 8-3.**

The Movie mode icon looks like a movie camera (although in the figure, it looks like the switch is pointing to the DISP button). At any rate, as soon as you move the switch to that position, the viewfinder shuts off, and the live preview appears on the monitor. By default, you see limited data onscreen, as shown on the left in Figure 8-4. Press the Info button to cycle through the available Movie displays, each of which presents a different assortment of data.

WARNING

An important note here: See the item labeled "Available recording time on memory card" in Figure 8-4? Although most people assume this value indicates that you can record a video that's as long as that number indicates — 1 hour and 42 minutes, in the figure — that's not the case. Each video clip can be only 29 minutes and 59 seconds in length. When you reach the maximum clip length, recording stops automatically. You can start a new recording right away, though, and record as many clips as will fit into the available time shown on the screen.

Scene Intelligent Auto

Movie-recording symbol

FIGURE 8-3:
Set the On/Off switch to Movie mode and set the Mode dial to Scene Intelligent Auto.

Available recording time on memory card

Elapsed recording time

Recording in progress

FIGURE 8-4:
Tap the red dot to start and stop recording.

Tap to pause/restart autofocusing

Tap to start recording

Tap to stop recording

3. **Set the Mode dial to Scene Intelligent Auto, as shown in Figure 8-3.**

    In this mode, the camera handles all critical recording settings for you.

4. **Frame your initial shot and set focus.**

    By default, the camera uses continuous autofocusing (Movie Servo AF) and the Face+Tracking AF Method setting. Chapter 5 has details, but here's the short story: If the camera detects a face, it automatically focuses on that face; otherwise, it looks for a focusing target elsewhere in the frame, usually selecting the largest object closest to the camera.

    In Movie mode, continuous focusing begins automatically when you use the default autofocusing settings. The Servo AF symbol near the bottom-left corner of the screen indicates this autofocusing setup. Tap that symbol, labeled in Figure 8-4, to pause autofocusing; tap again to resume it. You also can pause and restart continuous autofocus by pressing the shutter button halfway or by pressing the AF ON button. Press to pause; lift your finger off the button to restart autofocusing.

    If your subject doesn't come into focus automatically, try tapping it on the touchscreen. A white box appears to mark the spot you tapped, and the camera tries to focus on that area.

5. **To start recording, press the Live View button or tap the red record symbol, labeled in the left screen in Figure 8-4.**

    You see a screen like the one shown on the right in Figure 8-4. The red dot and letters REC in the upper-right corner indicate that recording is in progress. The movie timer also immediately changes to show the elapsed recording time, again labeled on the right screen in Figure 8-4. Notice that the red dot you can tap to start recording (left screen in Figure 8-4) changes to a red square (see the right screen in the figure).

6. **To stop recording, press the Live View button or tap the red square, highlighted on the right in Figure 8-4.**

When you record a movie at these default settings, you get a full HD (high definition) video with sound recorded. The maximum length of a video is 29 minutes and 59 seconds. All movies are recorded in the MP4 video format, which means that they should play on just about any computer or mobile device. Skip to the end of this chapter to find out how to play your videos on your camera.

That's all there is to recording a video using the camera's default settings. But of course, you didn't buy this book so that you could remain locked into the camera's default behaviors. So the next several pages explain all your recording options, which range from fairly simple to fairly not.

As is the case with still photography, how many recording settings you can adjust depends on which exposure mode is dialed in when you flip the On/Off switch to the Movie position. You get the most control in the Creative Zone modes (P, Tv, Av, and M). But even in Scene Intelligent Auto and other Basic Zone modes, you get access to the settings labeled in Figure 8-5. If these symbols don't appear on your screen, press the Info button to cycle from the simplified display features in Figure 8-4 to the more detailed ones shown in 8-5. Upcoming sections explain all the options labeled in Figure 8-5, with one exception: Video Snapshot. Chapter 11 explains how to use this specialty video feature.

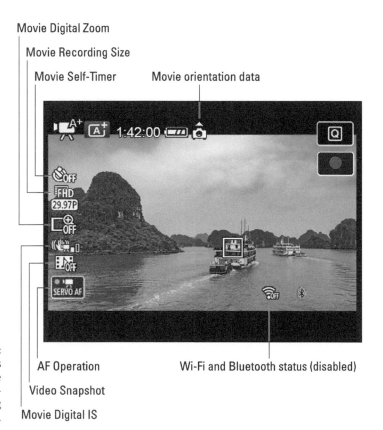

Movie Digital Zoom

Movie Recording Size

Movie Self-Timer   Movie orientation data

AF Operation   Wi-Fi and Bluetooth status (disabled)

Video Snapshot

Movie Digital IS

FIGURE 8-5: These symbols represent the major movie-recording options.

TIP

In Figures 8-4 and 8-5, I set the exposure mode to Scene Intelligent Auto. Notice that in the upper-left corner of the display, you see two icons that represent Automatic shooting. The left symbol, with the movie camera and the A+, represents the movie version of the Scene Intelligent Auto icon. To the right of that symbol, you may see a symbol like the one in the figures, which show the same markings as the Scene Intelligent Auto icon on the Mode dial. Why the two Auto mode symbols? Well, as it does during Live View still photography, the camera employs *automatic scene selection* when the Mode dial is set to Scene Intelligent Auto. After analyzing the scene in front of the lens, the camera makes its best guess as to what type of subject you're shooting, and then it chooses settings that it thinks will best capture that subject. If you see the symbol shown in the figure, the camera's using standard, all-around generic settings. But if the camera detects faces, for example, the symbol may change to a portrait icon, and the recording settings will be adjusted accordingly. Unless you want to shift to an exposure mode other than Scene Intelligent Auto, you're stuck with whatever scene type the camera chooses, so don't worry about it. I just wanted you to know what those two symbols in the upper-left corner of the screen mean. If you choose a Creative Zone mode, you see only a movie-camera symbol. You have to check the Mode dial if you forget what exposure mode you're using.

Setting the Broadcast Standard (NTSC or PAL)

Your very first movie-setup step should be to open Setup Menu 3 and check the Video System option, shown in Figure 8-6. This setting tells the camera which of two television standards to use when recording your movie: NTSC or PAL. Your camera was set at the factory to the standard used by the country in which it was meant for sale. The United States, Canada, and Japan are among countries that use NTSC. Australia and many European countries adhere to the PAL standard.

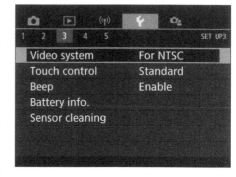

FIGURE 8-6:
Set the Video System option to the television broadcast standard used by the country in which the movie will be shown.

The selected Video System option determines the frame-rate options you're given when you set the movie recording size, as outlined in the next section. More importantly, you can't play an NTSC movie on a TV or other device that uses the PAL standard, and vice versa.

Understanding the Movie Recording Size Setting

Next up in your video prep is to choose the Movie Recording Size setting, which is without a doubt the most confusing recording option but, unfortunately, critical to understand. This setting determines important aspects of how your movie is created, including the frame size, number of frames captured per second, and the amount of compression applied to the final video file. Together, those options affect the look of the video as well as the maximum length of the video clip you can record.

You can take two routes to the setting. If you prefer menus, choose Movie Recording Size from Shooting Menu 1, as shown on the left in Figure 8-7, which brings up the settings screen shown on the right. The text box near the top of the screen offers details about the chosen setting. (In the figure, the default option is selected.)

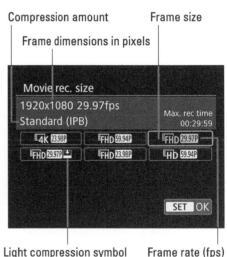

FIGURE 8-7:
Select Movie
Recording Size
from Shooting
Menu 1 (left) to
display the
settings screen
shown on the
right.

You also can select the Movie Recording Size setting by using the Quick Control method. While the movie screen is displayed, press Q or tap the Q button to shift to Quick Control mode. Then highlight the Movie Recording Size symbol, as shown on the left in Figure 8-8. The initial text label lets you know that you've chosen the right icon. At the bottom of the screen, you see symbols representing each of the six available Movie Recording Size settings. To select a different setting, rotate the Quick Control dial or Main dial, moving the orange selection box over the option you want to use. The text box then changes to provide details about the currently selected option, as shown on the right in the figure.

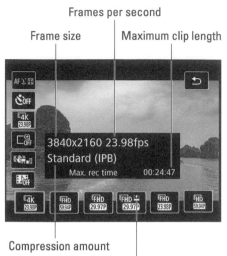

Frames per second

Frame size   Maximum clip length

3840x2160 23.98fps
Standard (IPB)
Max. rec time   00:24:47

Compression amount

Light compression symbol

FIGURE 8-8:
You also can use
Quick Control
mode to change
the Movie
Recording Size
setting.

The trick, of course, is figuring out what the heck all the stuff you see on the settings screens means so that you can choose the option that best serves your needs.
The following list offers some help; refer to the labeled pieces of data in the right
screens in Figures 8-7 and 8-8 to see where to find each piece of information.

>> **Frame size (4K, FHD, or HD):** Like still photos, digital movies are made out of
pixels, and the total pixel count — or resolution — determines the size of each
movie frame. In the video world, a resolution of 1920 x 1080 pixels is considered *Full HD* (*High Definition,* as in HDTV). A resolution of 1280 x 720 is *Standard
HD* and produces slightly lesser quality than Full HD when both are displayed
at the same size. For an even larger frame size, your camera offers 4K
recording, which produces frame sizes of 3840 x 2160. Regardless of the
frame size, the aspect ratio of all movies is 16:9.

TIP

What's the right call? Well, first off, just because 4K gives you the largest frame
size, it doesn't mean that it's the best choice for your recordings. Remember,
as with still photos, every pixel adds to the size of the file, so you can fit fewer
minutes of 4K video on your memory card than you can if you shoot at the
lower resolutions. Shooting in 4K also limits you to the lowest frames per
second setting (about 24 fps). The next bullet point explains how that option
affects the look of your videos

That said, I can think of a few reasons when 4K would be beneficial. You might
choose 4K for videos you create for display on a huge screen that has 4K
display capabilities — something you're presenting at an industry conference,
for example. Second, if you want to pull a single frame from a recording to
print or display as a photograph, having a frame size of 3840 x 2160 enables
you to create a larger image than frames shot at the lower resolutions. The

camera even offers a tool for grabbing a single frame during movie playback; the last section of this chapter offers details. If you want to pull a frame from a video shot at another resolution, you have to do it in a movie-editing program.

» **Frame rate (frames per second):** This value determines how many frames are used to create 1 second of footage — thus, *fps,* or *frames per second.* When the camera is set to the NTSC Video System, you can choose from three frame rates: 23.98, 29.97, and 59.94. (In the everyday world, most people round those values up to 24, 30, and 60 fps, but the camera screens use the exact values, so I stick with them here.) For PAL, you're limited to a choice of two frame rates, 25 and 50 fps.

It's hard to explain in words the difference that frame rate makes to the look of your video, but to give you some reference, 29.97 fps is the NTSC standard for television-quality video, and 25 is the PAL broadcast standard. A frame rate of 23.98 fps, available for NTSC recording, is the motion picture standard and delivers a slightly softer appearance. Recordings at 50 (PAL) and 59.94 (NTSC) appear very sharp and detailed.

For fast-moving subjects, a higher frame rate usually transfers to a smoother playback. Additionally, a high frame rate is good for maintaining video quality if you edit your video to create slow-motion effects. And if you want to "grab" a still frame from a video to use as a photograph, as just discussed, the highest frame rate gives you more frames from which to choose.

» **Compression (IPB Standard or Light):** To keep the size of movie files reasonable, the camera applies *IPB file compression.* With this form of video compression, the camera looks for stretches of video that contain multiple frames that are the same. In that way, it can reuse the data from a single frame instead of storing the same data over and over for each frame. Don't worry about what IPB means — really, it will tangle your brain cells. Just know that you can choose from two compression levels, Standard and Light. Despite what the names may lead you to think, the Standard setting applies less compression than Light, so Light files are smaller. Only one Movie Recording Setting size offers this compression setting: FHD at 29.97 fps. I labeled the symbol that represents the Light compression setting in the right screens in Figures 8-7 and 8-8.

» **P:** The letter *P* at the end of each setting stands for *progressive video,* which refers to the way that the individual frames of a video are recorded. (The other option, *interlaced video,* is an older technology that isn't available on your camera.) If you are a video expert, you may need to remember that the T8i/850D records only progressive video because it can be important if you want to edit footage taken with this camera with interlaced video you already have. Also, if you're at a gathering of video enthusiasts and someone asks about your camera's capabilities, you can say, "Oh, I'm a progressive person, all the way." Other than that, you can ignore the *P* and concentrate on the other details presented in the choices of Movie Recording Size settings.

Again, the combination of frame size, frame rate, and compression level determine the movie file size and image quality. Lots of pixels, a high frame rate, and the Standard compression setting result in the largest files; the FHD/29.97 fps/Light setting produces the smallest files. As for quality, the goal is to choose the setting that produces the quality you need at the smallest possible file size. To figure out that answer, do some test recordings and play them on the device that you plan to use to screen the movie. That will give you a better idea about which setting is right for your project.

It's also important to know that the camera imposes some restrictions on the size and length of the video files you can create, and that information may also affect your decision. Here's the deal:

>> **The maximum file size for a single video clip is 4GB.** Obviously, you reach that limit faster when you record a movie using a large frame size, high frame rate, or Standard compression than when you reduce the frame size or frame rate or set the compression option to Light.

At the default setting (Full HD, 29.97 fps, and Standard compression), you hit 4GB at about 17 and a half minutes. But if you up the frame rate to 59.94 fps, you can fit only about 8 and a half minutes in that same 4GB.

>> **Your memory card determines what happens when you continue recording beyond the 4GB limit.** Although the maximum file size for a single clip is 4GB, you can continue recording after you reach that limit, as long as your memory card has room for more frames. But whether you wind up with a series of individual 4GB clips or a single file that includes all the clips combined into one movie depends on your memory card.

To figure out how things will work with your card, check the card label to see whether it bears the initials SD, SDHC, or SDXC. An SD card tops out at 4GB of storage space; an SDHC card contains up to 32GB of space; an SDXC card, more than 32GB.

Obviously, recording stops automatically at 4GB on an SD card (before that, if the card has a lower capacity). But there's more to the memory card story than mere capacity. When you format the card using the Format Card option (Setup Menu 1), the camera performs the formatting differently for SDHC cards than it does for an SDXC card. That formatting determines what the camera does when you keep recording past the 4GB file limit.

With an SDHC card, the camera creates a new movie file each time you reach the 4GB limit. You can keep recording as many 4GB movies as card space allows, but they exist as separate files, which means you have to play each clip one at a time. ("Okay, this movie is the first half of Johnny's awesome violin performance . . . now here's the second half . . . and here's the final clip, where he gets a standing ovation from the entire third grade.")

TIP

With an SDXC card, the camera still creates a new file for each 4GB movie clip, but the files are collected into a single movie file so that you enjoy seamless playback.

Long story short (too late, you say?): If you do a lot of movie shooting, invest in SDXC cards and format them in the camera before use. Also choose cards that have the fastest data read-write rates you can afford, especially if you plan to shoot 4K video. (Chapter 1 provides help with choosing video cards.)

» **For all Movie Recording Size settings, the maximum length of a single movie clip is 29.59 minutes.** Recording stops automatically if you reach the time limit; if you want to keep recording, just start a new clip by pressing the Movie Record button.

Selecting Audio Options

As discussed in the first section of this chapter, you can record audio by attaching an external microphone to the camera or using the built-in microphone. (Figures 8-1 and 8-2 help you locate the jack for an external mic and the holes that lead to the built-in microphone.) Either way, options on Shooting Menu 1 enable you to control sound recording.

In Scene Intelligent Auto and other Basic Zone modes, you have limited control over the audio portion of your movie: You can choose to record sound or disable audio recording. Make your preferences known through the Sound Recording option on Shooting Menu 1, as shown in Figure 8-9.

When you set the camera to P, Tv, Av, or M exposure mode, you get a larger set of audio recording options. To explore them, choose Sound Recording from Shooting Menu 1, as shown on the left in Figure 8-10, to display the screen shown on the right.

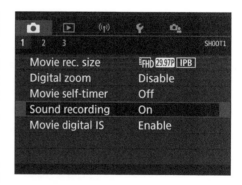

FIGURE 8-9:
In Scene Intelligent Auto and other Basic Zone exposure modes, your only control over audio is to enable or disable sound recording.

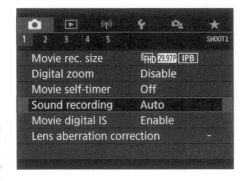 

FIGURE 8-10:
In P, Tv, Av, and M
exposure modes,
you have a few
more audio
options.

Audio meter

If you're new to sound recording, allow me a few sentences to explain the audio meter at the bottom of the right screen in Figure 8-10. An audio meter provides guidance about the sound level being picked up by the microphone. Stereo audio contains two channels, left and right, so you see a volume meter for each channel. Note that although the built-in mic is a stereo mic, you can't control the channels individually, so both meters always reflect the same data when you record using that microphone.

TECHNICAL
STUFF

Audio levels are measured in decibels (dB). Levels on the volume meter range from –40 (very, very soft) to 0 (as loud as can be measured digitally). The goal is to set the audio level so that sound peaks consistently in the –12 range. The indicators on the meter — the notches that run horizontally across the L and R bars of the meter — turn yellow in this range, as shown in the figure. The extra space beyond that level, called *headroom,* gives you both a good signal and a comfortable margin of error. But if the sound is too loud, the volume indicators peak at 0, with the last notch on the meter turning red, warning you that the audio may be distorted.

With Audio Meters 101 out of the way (was that the easiest class ever, or what?), here's the rest of what you need to know about the three options on the Sound Recording settings screen (right screen in Figure 8-10):

>> **Sound Rec.:** You get three choices:

- *Auto:* At the default setting, Auto, the camera adjusts sound volume automatically. You may want to open the menu screen and take a look at the audio meter before you begin recording to make sure that the sound levels aren't too high or too low at the Auto setting.

- *Disable:* Choose Disable to record a video without sound. When this setting is in force, a microphone and the word *Off* appear at the top of the Live View screen, as shown in the left screen in Figure 8-11.

- *Manual:* Select Manual if you want to set the audio recording levels yourself and also to gain access to the additional settings described next. When you opt for this setting, a minimalist version of an audio meter appears in the lower-left corner of the Live View screen, as shown on the right in Figure 8-11.

Audio recording disabled · · · · · · · Audio meter (for Manual audio recording)

>> **Rec. Level:** This option — the one bordered by the red selection box on the left in Figure 8-12 — enables you to adjust the audio level after you switch to manual volume control. The volume scale to the right of the option name shows the current setting; to make an adjustment, tap the option name or highlight it and press Set. You see the screen shown on the right in Figure 8-12. To change the volume level, tap the triangles at the end of the scale or rotate the Quick Control dial. As you do, a white marker appears atop the scale to indicate the new level; the blue marker, the original level. Tap Set or press the Set button to return to the Sound Recording menu screen.

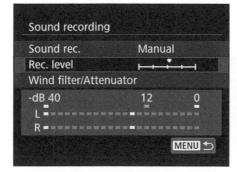 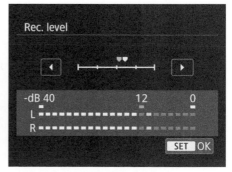

>> **Wind Filter/Attenuator:** Regardless of whether you select Auto or Manual as your Sound Recording method, you also can enable or disable the following two features. Choose Wind Filter/Attenuator from the main Sound Recording screen (left screen in Figure 8-12) to access the features. They work as follows:

- *Wind Filter:* Ever seen a newscaster out in the field, carrying a microphone that looks like it's covered with a big piece of foam? That foam thing is a wind filter. It's designed to lessen the sounds the wind makes when it hits the microphone. You can enable a digital version of the same thing via the Wind Filter option. By default, the Wind Filter is set to Auto, and the camera decides whether to apply it and at what strength.

  Essentially, the filter works by reducing the volume of noises that are similar to those made by wind. The problem is that some noises *not* made by wind can also be muffled when the filter is enabled. So when you're indoors or shooting on a still day, keep this option set to Disable. Also note that when you use an external microphone, the Wind Filter feature has no effect.

- *Attenuator:* This feature is designed to eliminate distortion that can occur with sudden loud noises. Experiment with enabling this feature if you're shooting in a location where this audio issue is possible.

WARNING

The internal microphone may pick up sounds made by the camera's autofocusing system, especially if you use an older lens. (Newer Canon lenses offer quieter autofocusing operation.) The best solution is to use an external microphone or lock in autofocusing before you start recording.

Using Movie Digital Zoom

Movie digital zoom enables you to capture a movie using a smaller area of the image sensor than normal. The recorded frames are then enlarged so that you wind up with whatever frame size is called for by your chosen Movie Recording Size setting. The result is a movie that gives you a smaller angle of view, as if you zoomed to a longer focal length to record the scene — or, to put it another way, as if you shot the movie using the whole sensor and then cropped away the perimeter of each frame.

TIP

You need to understand two important aspects of this feature. First, because the camera is enlarging the frame, filling in pixels to create the original frame size you requested when you set the Movie Recording Size, the video quality will be reduced. Second, and perhaps more difficult to deal with on a practical level, the camera can only "zoom" to the center of the frame. You can't choose which area of the frame you want to enlarge and record. So compose your initial shots with your subject in the center of the frame.

With those caveats out of the way, the following steps show you how to access the feature via the Quick Control method:

1. **Set the Mode dial to any exposure mode except SCN or Creative Filters.**

2. **Set the Movie Recording Size to one of the following options:**

   - FHD, 29.97P fps, Standard compression
   - FHD, 29.97P fps, Light compression
   - FHD, 23.98P fps, Standard compression

   When any other setting is selected, Movie Digital Zoom is disabled. Adjust the Movie Recording Size setting via the Quick Control screen or Shooting Menu 1.

3. **Choose Movie Digital Zoom from the Quick Control screen, as shown on the left in Figure 8-13.**

Digital IS (Image Stabilization)

Movie Digital Zoom   1-Point AF Method

FIGURE 8-13: Enable Movie Digital Zoom via the Quick Control screen.

4. **Select the 3-10x setting.**

   The scene is immediately enlarged in the frame, as shown on the right in Figure 8-13.

5. **Return to shooting mode by tapping the exit arrow (upper-right corner of the screen) or by pressing the shutter button halfway and releasing it.**

   The live preview now appears something like what you see on the left in Figure 8-14. The screen shows how the display appears in Scene Intelligent Auto mode, using the detailed display mode. (Press the Info button as needed to get to that display.)

Initially, the zoom level is set at x3.0 magnification, with that value appearing in the area labeled in the left screen in Figure 8-14.

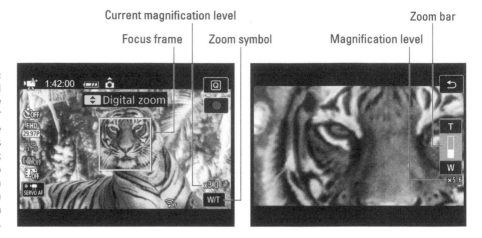

Current magnification level

Focus frame   Zoom symbol

Zoom bar

Magnification level

FIGURE 8-14:
From the initial zoomed view (left), tap the W/T icon or press the up/down edges of the Quick Control dial to display a screen where you can adjust the zoom level (right).

REMEMBER

When you enable Movie Digital Zoom, the camera restricts you to using 1-Point AF mode, and you see that square focus frame on the screen. Again, the focus frame is glued to the center of the screen, and that's where the camera will look for focusing information. If necessary, you can reframe your scene, but you can't reposition the focus frame.

For a few moments, the "Digital zoom" label appears at the top of the screen, with the up and down arrows indicating that in order to change the magnification level, you press the top and bottom edges of the Quick Control dial. Then the label disappears pretty quickly, but don't worry — Step 6 shows you the other way to magnify the view so you can just forget about the label if you missed it.

6. **To change the zoom level, press the up/down edges of the Quick Control dial or tap the W/T symbol, labeled "Zoom symbol" in Figure 8-14.**

(W/T for *wide/telephoto,* as in wide angle/telephoto lens.) Whether you tap the symbol or press the up/down edges of the Quick Control dial, you see the adjustment screen shown on the right in the figure. Keep pressing up or down on the edge of the Quick Control dial to adjust the zoom level. You also can tap the top of the zoom bar to increase the zoom level and tap the bottom to decrease the level. The number at the bottom indicates the current magnification level (x5.6 in the figure).

7. **Return to shooting mode by tapping the exit arrow or pressing the shutter button halfway and releasing it.**

8. **Ensure that focus is set.**

   If Movie Servo AF is in force (as it is by default), the area under the focus frame should already be in focus. When you turn off Movie Servo AF, press the shutter button halfway to set focus. You can then lift your finger off the shutter button.

9. **Press the Live View button to start and stop recording.**

10. **To cancel Movie Digital Zoom, press Q to reactivate the Quick Control settings screen and change the setting at the bottom of the screen to Off.**

You can also enable and disable Movie Digital Zoom via Shooting Menu 1. After you exit the menu, everything works as just described in the preceding steps and figures.

REMEMBER

Although Movie Digital Zoom is a fun tool, keep these limitations in mind:

» **You can't take advantage of Movie Digital IS (Image Stabilization).** I talk more about this feature, which is designed to compensate for camera shake when you handhold the camera, later in the chapter. For now, any time you don't use the feature, put the camera on a tripod to prevent camera shake.

» **The maximum ISO speed when using digital zoom is ISO 6400.** In very dim lighting, that may not be adequate to produce a good exposure.

» **Autofocusing may be slower than usual.** The slowdown occurs because the camera has to use a different type of autofocusing than when digital zoom is turned off.

Recording Vertical Movies

If your goal is a movie that you can share on Instagram or other social media sites that require videos that have a vertical orientation, you're probably aware that one of the features most hyped in T8i/850D marketing materials is that the camera has the ability to record such videos.

Here's how you take advantage of this option:

1. **With the camera in Movie mode, open Setup Menu 1 and set Add Movie Rotate Info to Enable, as shown in Figure 8-15.**

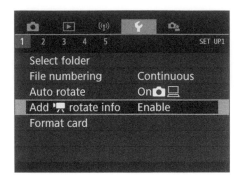

   When you enable this option, the camera embeds in the movie file hidden data (metadata) the camera orientation you used when recording. Movie players that can read that data then have the information they need to properly display the video. If you change the setting to Disable, all movies are played in horizontal orientation regardless of how the camera was oriented when you made the recording.

   FIGURE 8-15:
   Enabling this option is key to recording videos that can be played in vertical orientation on a smartphone.

2. **After exiting the menu and returning to the live movie preview, look for the symbol labeled "Movie orientation" in Figure 8-16.**

   If your screen is devoid of data, press the Info button until it appears.

   Look closely at the symbol, and you can see a tiny triangle on top of the camera graphic. That triangle indicates "up," as in, this edge of the frame will be the top of your video. As you rotate the camera, the symbol rotates, with the arrow indicating the orientation of your movie. For example, before taking the screenshot shown on the right in Figure 8-16, I rotated the camera 90 degrees counterclockwise from its usual horizontal orientation so that the right side of the camera was up. The orientation symbol reflects that position.

3. **Rotate the camera to the desired orientation and record your video.**

When you play the movie on your camera, it will always play in horizontal orientation on the monitor. But if you rotate the camera to the same orientation you used when shooting, you can view the movie as it will appear when you post it on Instagram or whatever other destination you have in mind.

Two tips to wrap up this discussion:

>> **Find out whether the site where you want to post your video has size limitations.** Then choose the Movie Recording Size setting that gets you closest to that file size. You may still need to use a movie-editing program to compress the original file to meet the guidelines or, in some cases, to convert the file to a video format that the online site requires. Again, the camera produces movies in the MP4 format.

Movie orientation symbol

FIGURE 8-16:
The triangle on top of the camera symbol indicates the orientation that will be logged with the video recording.

>> **You can change the orientation of an existing movie.** Just go to Playback Menu 1 and choose Select Change Movie Rotate Info. Scroll to the movie you want to alter by pressing the left or right edge of the Quick Control dial or by swiping the screen like you do when viewing photos on your phone or tablet. When you reach the movie, press the Set button or tap the Set icon on the screen. Each press or tap rotates the movie 90 degrees (a text label pops up to explain which side will be "up" when you play the movie on a phone or other device). When you exit the menu, the orientation data for the movie file will be updated to reflect the change you just made.

Reviewing Other Movie Options

Depending on your exposure mode, you can access some or all of the additional recording features labeled in Figure 8-17. The next sections detail these options along with a few others that you control via the menu system. If you want to access all the options shown in the figure, you must set the Mode dial to P, Tv, Av, or M. Also, if your display doesn't contain all the data shown in the figure, press the Info button to cycle through the various Movie display styles until you get to the detailed version.

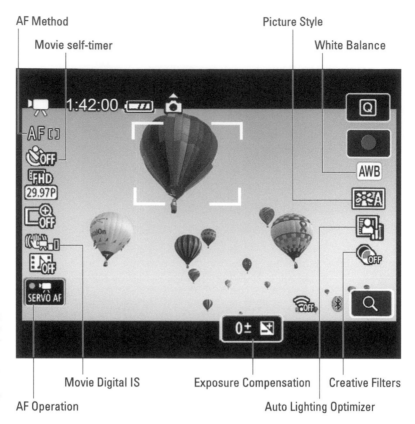

AF Method

Movie self-timer

Picture Style

White Balance

FIGURE 8-17:
You may have
control over
these additional
options,
depending on
your exposure
mode.

AF Operation

Movie Digital IS

Exposure Compensation

Auto Lighting Optimizer

Creative Filters

Autofocusing options

REMEMBER

In Movie mode, autofocusing behavior depends on the same two settings that affect Live View still-photography autofocusing: AF Method and AF Operation, which Chapter 5 details. Things are only slightly different for movie recording:

>> **AF Method:** You get the same settings as for Live View photography: Face+Tracking AF (with or without eye-detection); Spot AF; 1-Point AF; and Zone AF. If you turn on Movie Digital Zoom, however, the camera insists on using 1-Point AF. You can read about Movie Digital Zoom earlier in the chapter.

>> **AF Operation:** For this one, you get only two choices: You can enable or disable continuous autofocusing, called Movie Servo AF. Tap the icon labeled "AF Operation" in Figure 8-17 to toggle that feature on or off. (The symbol in the figure shows Movie Servo AF enabled.) If you turn off continuous autofocusing, press the shutter button halfway to set focus. You can then lift your finger off the shutter button, and focus will remain set at the current focusing distance.

When Movie Servo AF is enabled, pressing the shutter button halfway interrupts continuous autofocusing and resets the focus point. Continuous focusing resumes when you lift your finger off the button.

For help understanding and adjusting both settings, see the Live View autofocusing section of Chapter 5.

Movie Digital IS

Some lenses, including the 18–55mm kit lens featured in this book, offer *image stabilization,* which helps reduce blurring caused by camera shake (minor movement of the camera during the exposure). When you shoot movies, you can turn on an additional level of shake compensation, called Movie Digital IS. You can take advantage of this feature in an exposure mode except SCN and Creative Filters.

An icon representing the current Movie Digital IS setting appears in the detailed movie display, as shown in Figure 8-17. By default, the feature is disabled. Turn it on via the Quick Control method or Shooting Menu 1.

Choose the Enable setting for the least amount of anti-shake correction; select Enhanced for a stronger effect. If your lens has its own stabilization system, be sure to enable it as well — otherwise, Movie Digital IS won't work. On the kit lens, move the Stabilizer switch to the On position.

TIP

The neat thing about this feature is that it works even with lenses that don't offer their own stabilization systems. However, because this stabilization is digital in nature, it does present one complication: Your subject is magnified slightly at the Enable setting and slightly more at the Enhanced setting. To put it another way, the normal angle of view is reduced when you enable the feature. Thankfully, the monitor accurately displays the subject area that will be recorded.

A few other pointers about Movie Digital IS:

>> **Movie quality may be lower.** Specifically, your movie may appear grainier than normal. In some cases, your subject may briefly go out of focus as the digital stabilization does its thing.

>> **Your lens makes a difference.** Not all lenses can deal with Movie Digital IS. The Canon website has information on compatible lenses; just do a search on the term "Canon Movie Digital IS" to find the details. If your lens isn't listed, turn the feature off.

Lens focal length also has an impact. Movie Digital IS works best with wide angle lenses (short focal length), and it doesn't work at all with lenses that have a focal length exceeding 800mm.

>> **Turn the feature off when using a tripod.** Otherwise, the system may actually increase blurring by trying to compensate for camera movement that isn't occurring.

Playing with exposure and color

In the Basic Zone modes, you don't have any control over these aspects of your movie. The one exception is SCN mode, which offers an HDR option that captures a larger spectrum of darks to lights than can normally be recorded. (See the side-bar "What's an HDR Movie?" for more information.)

Set the Mode dial to P, Tv, Av, or M, and you gain a bit more control, as follows:

>> **M mode gives you full control over exposure, just as for still photography.** However, determining the correct shutter speed involves slightly different considerations than for still photography. This option is best left to experts and involves more details than can fit in this book, so see the camera instruction manual for the full story.

>> **You can control ISO only in the M exposure mode, but you can limit the maximum ISO the camera selects in P, Tv, and Av modes.** In M mode, set the ISO value by pressing the ISO button, tapping the ISO symbol on the touchscreen, or through the ISO Speed Settings option on Shooting Menu 3.

In P, Tv, and Av modes, you're locked into using Auto ISO. But again, you can limit the maximum ISO the camera can choose. Choose ISO Speed Settings from Shooting Menu 3, as shown on the left in Figure 8-18, and then choose Max for Auto on the next screen, shown on the right in the figure.

FIGURE 8-18:
The camera forces you to use Auto ISO in the P, Tv, and Av exposure modes, but you can limit the maximum ISO value that it can select.

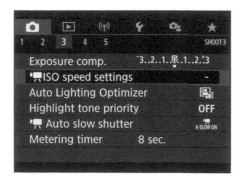

>> **In P, Tv, and Av modes, you can adjust exposure via Exposure Compensation.** The symbol labeled in Figure 8-17 (look near the bottom of the screen) indicates how much compensation is applied — none, in the figure. To adjust the setting, tap the Exposure Compensation symbol on the screen or choose the option from Shooting Menu 3. (Refer to the first menu item shown on the first screen in Figure 8-18.) A higher EV value produces a brighter recording; a lower value reduces brightness.

When the camera is in Movie mode, the Exposure Compensation setting screen doesn't offer the Automatic Exposure Bracketing (AEB) options that you see on the menu screen during still photography. Exposure bracketing isn't possible during movie recording.

>> **In P, Tv, and Av exposure modes, you can press the AE Lock button to interrupt continuous exposure adjustment.** When you shoot in these exposure modes, the camera adjusts exposure during the recording as needed. If you prefer to use the same settings throughout the recording — or to lock in the current settings during the recording — you can use AE (autoexposure) Lock. Just press the AE Lock button. A little asterisk appears in the lower left of the screen to remind you that the exposure settings are locked.

To cancel AE Lock during recording, press the AF Point Selection button. When recording is stopped, AE Lock is cancelled automatically after 8 seconds by default. This shutoff timing is determined by the Metering Timer option, which is the last item on Shooting Menu 3. (Refer to the left screen in Figure 8-18.)

>> **You also can adjust exposure through the Auto Lighting Optimizer setting, whose icon is labeled in Figure 8-17.** The Highlight Tone Priority option is also available, although its status doesn't appear on the monitor display. Enable or disable these options via Shooting Menu 3, that now-famous screen shown on the left in Figure 8-18. You can also set Auto Lighting Optimizer via the Quick Control screen.

Chapter 4 details these options, so head there if you're not sure which one might best address your exposure issue. As with still photography, you can enable only one at a time.

>> **Experiment with Auto Slow Shutter option found on Shooting Menu 3.** If you choose a Movie Recording Size option that produces a frame rate of 59.94 fps (NTSC) or 50 fps (PAL), you have access to this menu option. By default, its enabled and causes the camera to automatically use a slow shutter speed when you record a movie in dim lighting. To be specific, the shutter speed is 1/30 second if the Video Mode is set to NTSC and 1/25 second if that option is set to PAL. See the earlier section "Setting the Broadcast Standard (NTSC or PAL)" if that last sentence made no sense.

The result of using a slower shutter speed is a brighter movie than you would get at a faster shutter speed. But if you're recording in dim lighting, I suggest you record a couple of short test movies, shooting one with the feature on and one with it turned off. Then compare the results to see whether the slow shutter actually produces a better video. With a slow shutter, objects that move through the frame may appear to be trailed by ghostly images of themselves. Your footage may appear smoother and, if you're not using a tripod, suffer from less evidence of camera shake if you turn off Auto Slow Shutter. Of course, that footage will be darker.

» **The White Balance and Picture Style options work the same way as they do for still photography.** Figure 8-17 shows you where to find the icons that represent the current settings. You can adjust both through the Quick Control screen or Shooting Menu 4. On the menu, you also can create a custom White Balance setting or apply White Balance Shift (choose WB Correction). See Chapter 6 for help with these and other color features.

WHAT'S AN HDR MOVIE?

Setting the Mode dial to SCN and putting the camera in Movie mode automatically selects a special recording mode: HDR Movie. HDR stands for *high dynamic range,* which refers to a spectrum of brightness values that is larger than what your camera can normally capture in a single frame. When shooting a high-contrast subject (one with both bright highlights and deep shadows), give this feature a whirl, which is designed to retain more detail in the brightest areas of the scene.

Understand, though, that your other recording options are limited when creating an HDR movie. You can turn audio recording on or off and adjust autofocusing settings, but that's about it. You can't even change the Movie Recording Size; it's locked in at Full HD (FHD), 29.97 fps, and Standard IPB compression for NTSC video mode and FHD, 25 fps, Standard IPB compression for PAL. And you can't use Movie Digital Zoom or Movie Digital IS (image stabilization).

To produce the greater brightness range of an HDR movie, the camera exposes frames at multiple settings and then merges them to create the final movie file. Because of that processing, you may notice a loss of movie quality, with some portions appearing distorted or noisy (grainy). Camera shake also may become more noticeable, so for best results, use a tripod.

Checking out a few final features

To wrap up movie-recording coverage, the following list offers a look at few miscellaneous settings not already covered:

>> **Movie Self-Timer:** Just as when shooting still photos, you can tell the camera to wait either 2 or 10 seconds after you press the record button to actually start recording. The delay gives you time to get into the shot. By default, the delay is off; see the icon representing that setting in Figure 8-17. To choose the 2- or 10-second delay, press Q to enter Quick Control screen and highlight the Self-Timer icon, as shown on the left in Figure 8-19. Make your selection and then tap the exit arrow to return to the Quick Control screen. You also can set the self-timer delay from Shooting Menu 1, shown on the right in the figure. To disable the delay, set the option to Off.

FIGURE 8-19:
You can delay the start of recording by 2 or 10 seconds with the Movie Self-Timer option.

>> **Metering Timer:** By default, exposure information such as f-stop and shutter speed disappears from the display after 8 seconds if you don't press any camera buttons. If you want the exposure data to remain visible for a longer period, you can adjust the shutdown time through this option, found on Shooting Menu 3. This option is accessible only in the P, Tv, Av, and M exposure modes.

>> **Shutter Button Function for Movies:** This option, found on Setup Menu 4 and shown in Figure 8-20, enables you to change what happens when you press the shutter button halfway and what happens when you press it all the way.

FIGURE 8-20:
This option lets you specify what exposure and autofocus actions you want the camera to take when you press the shutter button halfway.

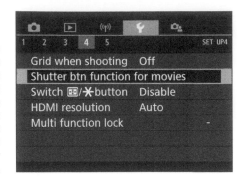

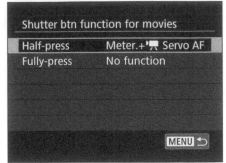

At the default setting, which is the one highlighted in the right screen in the figure, a half-press of the shutter button kickstarts exposure metering and continuous autofocusing (Servo AF); a full press does nothing (because you can't take a still photo in Movie mode). You do have other choices, which you can uncover by selecting the options shown on the right in Figure 8-20. Select Half-press from the menu screen, and you can choose to have a half-press of the shutter button begin metering and focus using the One-Shot AF Method (focus is locked at the time you press the button halfway). Or you can choose to have a half-press of the shutter button button initiate exposure metering only. You then have to start and stop autofocusing by tapping the Servo AF symbol (lower-left corner of the screen) or set focus manually.

If you select Fully-press from the right screen shown in Figure 8-20, you can specify that you want to be able to start and stop movie recording by pressing the shutter button all the way down.

For now, I suggest you leave these settings alone, or many of the instructions given in this chapter and in the camera manual won't work the way you expect.

>> **Grid Display:** You can display three different grid styles on the monitor to help ensure alignment of vertical and horizontal structures when you're framing the scene. Enable the Grid When Shooting option on Setup Menu 4, shown in Figure 8-20.

>> **Lens Aberration Correction:** This option appears on Shooting Menu 1 when the Mode dial is set to P, Tv, Av, or M. It provides access to tools that try to automatically correct image defects that can occur with some lenses. In Movie mode, you can apply only two of the settings that are available for still photography: Peripheral Illumination Correction and Chromatic Aberration Correction. The first one attempts to brighten image corners that appear unnaturally dark, as detailed in Chapter 4. Chromatic Aberration Correction tackles a color defect that you can read about in Chapter 6.

>> **Lens Electronic MF:** Also found on Shooting Menu 1 in the P, Tv, Av, and M modes only, this option enables you to fine-tune autofocusing by using the lens's manual focus ring without officially switching the lens to manual-focusing mode. See Chapter 5 for details.

>> **Remote Control:** This option, found on Shooting Menu 2, applies if you use certain Canon remote control units: Wireless Remote Control BR-E1, which connects to the camera wirelessly via Bluetooth; and Canon RS-60E3, which is a wired remote that plugs into the remote terminal hidden under the frontmost of the two rubber doors on the left side of the camera. Set the Remote Control menu option to Enable if you want to use the remote control to start and stop movie recording. See the camera manual for specifics on how to use the remote units. The appendix of this book has information about setting up your camera's wireless functions.

Playing Movies

 To play a movie, press the Playback button to put the camera in Playback mode. When a movie file is displayed, the touchscreen contains two items, as shown on the left in Figure 8-21: a play button (center of the screen) and a Set symbol.

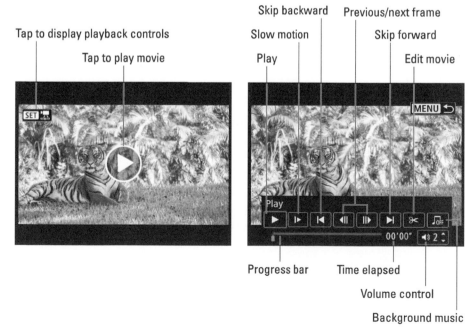

FIGURE 8-21:
Tap the arrow to begin playback or tap Set to display playback controls.

If you see thumbnails instead of a full movie frame, tap the movie thumbnail or press the left/right/top/bottom edges of the Quick Control dial to highlight it. Then tap the thumbnail again or press the Set button to display the file in the full-frame view.

Use these techniques to start, stop, and control playback:

>> **Start playback.** You can start playback two ways:

  • *Tap the play button,* labeled in Figure 8-21. Your movie begins playing, with a progress bar and time-elapsed value provided at the bottom of the screen. (Press the Info button if you don't see the progress bar.)

  • *Press the Set button or tap the Set icon.* Now you see the first frame of your movie plus a slew of playback control icons, as shown on the right in Figure 8-21. To start playback, tap the Play icon or highlight it and then press the Set button.

>> **Adjust volume.** The icon at the far-right end of the bottom of the playback display shows the current volume. (I labeled the icon on the right in Figure 8-21.) Press the top edge of the Quick Control dial to increase volume; press the bottom edge to lower it. You also can tap the volume icon to display a larger volume-adjustment control.

>> **Pause playback.** Tap anywhere on the screen or press the Set button to pause playback and redisplay the movie-control symbols. To resume playback, tap the Play symbol or press Set again.

>> **Play in slow motion.** Tap the slow-motion icon, labeled in Figure 8-21, or select it and press Set. Press the right edge of the Quick Control dial to increase playback speed; press the left edge to decrease it. You also can adjust the speed by dragging your finger along the little scale that appears in the upper-right corner of the monitor during slo-mo playback.

>> **Skip backward/forward 4 seconds.** Select the control labeled "Skip backward" in Figure 8-21 to rewind about 4 seconds worth of footage. Use the control labeled "Skip forward" to move ahead by 4 seconds. Each time you tap or select the control, you go back or forward another 4 seconds.

>> **Go forward/back one frame while paused.** Use the symbols labeled "Previous/next frame" in Figure 8-21. Tap or highlight the symbol representing the direction you want to go. Then press the Set button once. Each time you press the button, you go forward or backward one frame.

>> **Fast forward/fast rewind.** Use the same process just described, but keep holding down the Set button until you reach the frame you want to view.

>> **Enable Background Music.** If you recorded a movie without sound, you can enable the Background Music option to play a sound file. To use this feature, you must install Canon EOS Utility, a program that you can download from the

Canon website. Use that program to copy music files to your camera memory card. The EOS Utility program's user guide, also available for download, offers the details you need to know to copy music files to the card.

>> **Edit the movie.** After you begin playing the movie, the Scissors symbol, labeled "Edit movie" in Figure 8-21, becomes available. Tap the icon or highlight it and press Set to trim frames from the start or end of the movie. Chapter 12 steps you through this process.

>> **Exit playback.** Tap the Menu icon or press the Menu button.

If you recorded the movie in 4K, the strip of playback controls contains one additional icon, which is inserted between the Edit Movie (scissors symbol) and Background Music (music notes) icons. That control is key to selecting a single frame of a 4K movie and saving it as a still photo. The sidebar "Grabbing a frame from a 4K movie" tells all.

GRABBING A FRAME FROM A 4K MOVIE

If you record a movie using the 4K Movie Recording Size setting, you can extract a single frame from the movie and save it as a still image. The resulting file, saved in the JPEG format, has the same dimensions as the movie itself — 3840 x 2160 pixels — giving you a photo with a total resolution of about 8.3 MP and a file size of roughly 3MB.

To extract a frame, play the movie until the frame you want to grab appears. Press the Set button or tap anywhere on the monitor to pause playback. (You may then need to start, stop, and go forward and backward a bit to get to the exact frame you want.) Then look for the Frame Grab symbol in the playback controls shown here. The symbol appears only when you play 4K movies, so it's not in the group shown in Figure 8-21. Tap that symbol or select it, as shown in the figure, and press the Set button. The camera asks whether you want to save the frame as a still image; answer in the affirmative to make it happen.

3

After the Shot

IN THIS CHAPTER

» Exploring picture playback functions

» Magnifying your picture to check details

» Deciphering the picture information displays

» Understanding histograms

Chapter 9
Picture Playback

Without question, one of the best things about digital photography is being able to view pictures right after you shoot them. No more guessing whether you got the shot you want or need to try again; no more wasting money on developing and printing film pictures that stink.

Displaying your pictures is just the start of the things your camera can do in Playback mode, though. You also can see which settings you used to take the picture, view graphics that alert you to exposure problems, and magnify a photo to check details. This chapter introduces you to these playback features and more.

Note: Although some playback features discussed in this chapter work for movies as well as still photos, some functions do not. The sections describing each feature spell out whether it's available for movies. For help with movie-only playback steps, see the end of Chapter 8.

Adjusting Instant Image Review

After you take a picture, it automatically appears on the monitor for 2 seconds. You can adjust the post-capture display time via the Review Duration option on Shooting Menu 1, shown in Figure 9-1. (The figure shows the menu as it appears in P, Tv, Av, and M exposure modes; the Basic Zone version contains fewer options, but the Review Duration setting is always available.)

You can select from the following Image Review options:

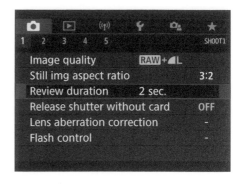

>> **A specific review period:** Pick 2, 4, or 8 seconds.

TIP

>> **Off:** Disables image review. Turning off the monitor saves battery power, so keep this option in mind if the battery is running low. You can still view pictures by pressing the Playback button.

FIGURE 9-1:
Control instant review of photos through this menu option.

>> **Hold:** Displays the current image indefinitely or until the camera automatically shuts off to save power. Camera shutdown timing is controlled through the Auto Power Off option on Setup Menu 2.

Viewing Pictures in Playback Mode

To switch to Playback mode, press the Playback button, labeled in Figure 9-2. Then scroll through picture or movie files one by one by pressing the right or left edges of the Quick Control dial or by swiping your fingertip horizontally across the touchscreen.

Here are a few other playback fundamentals to note:

>> **Press the Info button to change the data display.** You can display your photo as shown in Figure 9-2, or display various shooting data, such as the shutter speed and f-stop you used, along with the image. Press the Info button, highlighted in the figure, to change how much data appears. The upcoming section "Viewing Picture Data" explains how to interpret the data.

>> **If you see multiple thumbnails on the screen, press the Set button to return to single-image view.** See the next section for more information on thumbnails view, officially called Index mode.

>> **You can access several playback features via the Quick Control screen.** However, to get to the screen, you must press the Q button. There's no Q touchscreen symbol to tap as there is when the camera is in shooting mode.

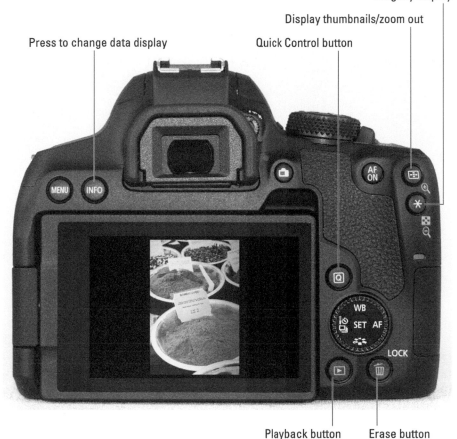

Press to change data display

Magnify display

Display thumbnails/zoom out

Quick Control button

Playback button

Erase button

Figure 9-3 offers a map to the various tools accessible via the Quick Control screen. Details on most features are provided in this chapter and Chapter 10; see the Appendix for help using the Send to Smartphone feature. If a tool's symbol appears dimmed or disappears from your Quick Control screen, the tool isn't compatible with the type of file you're currently viewing.

Chapter 1 explains how to select and adjust options via the Quick Control screen, if you need details on that process.

» **Many of the gestures you use to view photos and movies on a smartphone or tablet also work on your camera.** In addition to swiping a finger across the monitor to scroll through your images and movies, you can pinch outward to magnify an image and pinch in to reduce the magnification. Details on how and where to tap, pinch, or swipe appear later in this chapter, in discussions related to these playback features.

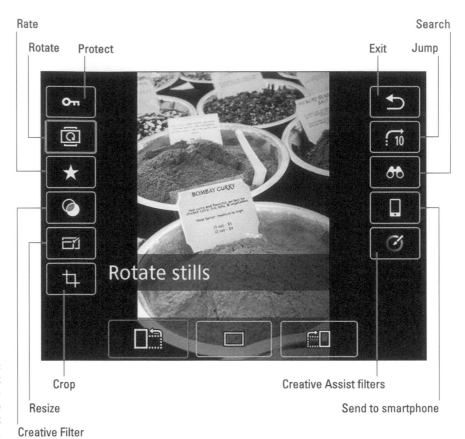

Rate

Rotate   Protect

Search

Exit   Jump

Rotate stills

FIGURE 9-3:
Press the Quick
Control button
for fast access to
these playback
features.

Crop

Resize

Creative Filter

Creative Assist filters

Send to smartphone

>> **You can choose which image or movie appears after you turn off the camera, restart it, and press the Playback button.** When you turn off the camera, it makes note of which photo or movie you most recently viewed. The next time you turn the camera on and enter playback mode, the camera can either display that most-recently viewed file or, instead, show you the picture or movie that you most recently shot. To make the call, open Playback Menu 4 and select View from Last Seen. Choose Enable if you want playback to pick up where you left off the last time you used the camera. Choose Disable if you prefer to view your most recent work.

>> **To exit playback mode and return to shooting, press the Playback button or give the shutter button a quick half-press and release.**

Viewing multiple thumbnails at a time (Index mode)

In Index mode, you can view 4, 9, 36, or 100 thumbnails, each representing a photo or the first frame of a movie. Figure 9-4 shows the 9- and 36-thumbnail views.

Movie file   Selected thumbnail   Scroll bar

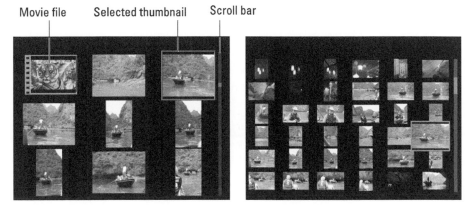

FIGURE 9-4:
Pinch inward or press the Index/Reduce button to switch to display multiple image thumbnails instead of a single picture.

Here's your guide to viewing images and performing other tasks in Index mode:

>> **Shift from single-image view to Index mode:** Use these techniques:

- *Pinch inward on the touchscreen.* In other words, put one finger on one edge of the monitor and your thumb on the opposite edge. Then drag both fingers toward the center of the screen. Each time you pinch, you display more thumbnails.

- *Press the Index/Reduce button.* That's the button shown in the margin here and labeled "Display thumbnails/zoom out" in Figure 9-2. Officially, the button has the lengthy name *AE Lock/FE Lock/Index/Reduce* because it performs all those functions. But for playback purposes, only the Index/Reduce part of the name applies, so that's the name used in sections that discuss playback features.

  Whatever you call the button, your first press puts the camera in Index mode. Each subsequent press displays more thumbnails at a time.

TIP

Note the blue checkerboard and magnifying glass under the button. Blue labels indicate that a button serves a playback function. In this case, the checkerboard indicates the Index function (the little boxes are supposed to represent thumbnails) and the minus sign in the magnifying glass is visual shorthand for "reduce size." Many people refer to this button as the *zoom-out button,* which is perfectly fine, too.

>> **Display fewer thumbnails:** Press the button shown in the margin and labeled "Magnify display" in Figure 9-2. This button also has a blue magnifying glass icon, this time with a plus sign in the center to indicate that pressing it enlarges the size of the displayed thumbnails so that fewer fit on the screen. The button's official name is AF Point Selection/Magnify button, but for the purposes of discussions relating to playback, let's call it the Magnify button, okay?

Whatever you want to call it, press the button once to switch from 100 thumbnails to 36; press again to go from 36 to 9; press once more to switch from 9 thumbnails to 4; and press one last time to switch from 4 thumbnails to single-image view. You also can pinch outward on the touchscreen to reduce the number of thumbnails. In single image view, you use the button to magnify the displayed photo, as discussed in the upcoming section "Zooming in for a closer view."

>> **Distinguish picture files from movie files:** Movie files are decorated with a border like the one that appears on the top-left thumbnail in Figure 9-4. The design is supposed to evoke the sprocket holes in traditional movie film.

>> **Scroll to the next screen of thumbnails.** If a scroll bar appears on the right side of the screen, as shown in Figure 9-4, additional pages of thumbnails are just out of sight. To scroll to the next page, swipe your finger up or down the screen, rotate the Main dial, or press the top or bottom edge of the Quick Control dial.

>> **Select a photo or movie file:** You can perform many file operations, such as deleting images, while in Index mode. But you first have to select the thumbnail of the image or movie file. A highlight box surrounds the currently selected file, as shown in Figure 9-4. To select a different file, tap its thumbnail or rotate the Quick Control dial to move the highlight box over it. You also can press the left/right/top/bottom edges of the dial to position the box.

When the display shows 36 or 100 thumbnails, the currently selected photo is slightly enlarged compared to the rest, as shown in the right screen in Figure 9-4. This makes it a little easier to spot amid all the other thumbnails.

TIP

If you want to select multiple files at a time, check out "Taking Advantage of Image Search," later in this chapter. That option enables you to select all files that meet specific criteria, such as being taken on a particular date.

>> **Return to single-image view:** You can keep pinching outward or pressing the Magnify button until you cycle from thumbnails to single-frame view. But if more than four thumbnails are displayed, it's quicker to just tap a thumbnail or to select the thumbnail and press the Set button. The image or movie then appears all by its lonesome on the monitor.

Jumping through images

If your memory card contains scads of images, here's a trick you'll love: By using the Jump feature, you can leapfrog through images rather than scrolling the display a bazillion times to get to the picture you want to see. To initiate a jump, rotate the Main dial or swipe two fingers from left to right across the screen. Jumping only works when you have a single image or movie displayed on the monitor, though.

You can choose from these options to specify where you want the camera to land when it jumps:

TIP

» **Display Images One by One:** This option, in effect, disables jumping, restricting you to browsing pictures one at a time. What's the point? Well, it enables you to use the Main dial to scroll through files during regular playback — an action that's a bit easier to complete than swiping across the touchscreen or using the Quick Control dial. You're still technically jumping — the function of the Main dial during playback — you're just jumping from one image to the next.

Note that both movie files and still photos are displayed when you use this option.

» **Jump 10 Images:** This setting, which is the default, advances the display ten files at a time. Again, although the name indicates that the setting jumps only through images, movies are included in the ten-file grouping.

» **Jump a specified number of files:** Choose any value between 1 and 100.

» **Display by Date:** If your card contains pictures and movies shot on different dates, you can jump from a picture taken on one date to the first file created on the next date. For example, if you're viewing the third of 30 pictures taken on June 1, you can jump past all others from that day to the first image taken on, say, June 5.

» **Display by Folder:** If you create custom folders on your memory card — an option outlined in Chapter 11 — choose this setting to jump from the current folder to the first photo in a different folder.

» **Display Movies Only:** Does your memory card contain both still photos and movies? If you want to view only the movie files, select this option. Then rotate the Main dial or do the two-finger touchscreen swipe to jump from one movie to the next without seeing any still photos.

» **Display Stills Only:** This one is the opposite of the Movies option: Movie files are hidden, and the camera displays one photo at a time, just like when you use the Display Images One by One option.

>> **Display Protected Images Only:** By using the Protect feature covered in Chapter 10, you can tag your best images in a way that prevents them from being erased by the camera's normal file-deletion tools, also detailed in Chapter 10. Selecting this Jump option limits playback to protected files.

WARNING

A little side note here: The Protect option does *not* safeguard files from being deleted when you format the memory card, an operation discussed in the Chapter 1 section that covers memory cards.

>> **Display by Image Rating:** If you rate photos, another Chapter 10 topic, you can use this Jump method to view all rated photos or only those with a specific rating.

To specify which type of jumping you want to do, use either of these methods:

REMEMBER

>> **Quick Control screen:** In Figure 9-5, the Jump option is set to Number of Images. (The *C* in the icon for this setting presumably stands for *custom.* Or *count.* Or possibly, *Canon,* as in "Why do you make me think about these things, Canon?")

At any rate, when you select the Number of Images setting or the Rating setting, an Info symbol appears, as shown in Figure 9-5. Tap the symbol or press the Info button to display a screen where you can specify the number of images to jump at a time or the rating you want the Jump function to use.

FIGURE 9-5:
You can specify a Jump method by using the Quick Control screen.

>> **Playback Menu 3:** Select the last option on the menu, as shown in Figure 9-6. (The "w/" followed by a notched semi-circle is shorthand for *with the Main dial.*) After you select the menu option, you see the selection screen shown on the right. You see the same options as in the Quick Control screen shown in Figure 9-5, but for this figure, I chose the Display by Image Rating option. As with the Quick Control method, choosing any setting that allows you to customize things — in this case, to specify what rating criteria the image should meet to be displayed when you jump — displays a settings screen. The Display by Image Rating setting screen appears on the right in Figure 9-6. To change the rating level, rotate the Main dial or tap the arrows on either side of the displayed rating symbol (five stars, in the figure). Tap Set or press the Set button to lock in your choice.

Press the Playback button to return to Playback mode.

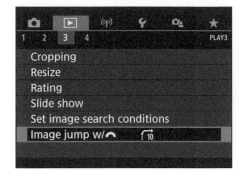

FIGURE 9-6:
You can also select the Jump method via Playback Menu 2.

After selecting a Jump method, take the following steps to jump through your photos during playback:

REMEMBER

1. **Set the camera to display a single photo.**

   If the camera is in Index mode, you can switch to single-photo view by tapping a thumbnail or selecting a thumbnail and pressing the Set button.

2. **Rotate the Main dial or swipe two fingers across the screen.**

   The camera jumps to the next image or movie according to the Jump setting you selected. At any setting but Display Images One by One, a *jump bar* appears for a few seconds at the bottom of the monitor, indicating the current Jump setting.

3. **To exit Jump mode, press the right or left edge of the Quick Control dial or swipe a single finger across the touchscreen.**

Rotating still pictures

When you take a picture, the camera can tag the image file with the camera orientation (that is, whether you held the camera horizontally or vertically). When you view the picture, the camera can read the data and rotate the image so that it appears upright in the monitor, as shown on the left in Figure 9-7, instead of on its side, as shown on the right. The image is also rotated automatically when you view it in the Canon photo software that ships with your camera (as well as in some other programs that can read the rotation data).

TECHNICAL STUFF

Photographers use the term *portrait orientation* to refer to vertically oriented pictures and *landscape orientation* to refer to horizontally oriented pictures. The terms stem from the traditional way that people and places are photographed — portraits, vertically; landscapes, horizontally.

FIGURE 9-7:
Display vertically
oriented pictures
upright (left) or
sideways (right).

By default, the camera tags the photo with the orientation data and rotates the image automatically on both the camera and your computer screen. But you have other choices, as follows:

>> **Disable or adjust automatic rotation:** Open Setup Menu 1 and select Auto Rotate to display the three options shown in Figure 9-8. From top to bottom, the settings are

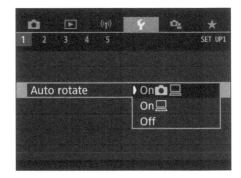

- *On (Camera and Computer):* This option is the default. Images get the orientation tag, and rotation happens both on the computer and camera.

- *On (Computer Only):* The orientation tag is added to the file, but pictures are rotated only on a computer monitor.

FIGURE 9-8:
Go to Setup Menu 1 to disable or adjust automatic image rotation.

- *Off:* New pictures aren't tagged with the orientation data, and existing photos aren't rotated during playback on the camera, even if they're already tagged.

>> **Rotate pictures during playback:** If you stick with the default Auto Rotate setting, you can rotate pictures to a different orientation during playback when needed. You might do so to get a larger view of a picture shot in vertical orientation, for example (refer to Figure 9-7).

You can rotate a picture in two ways:

- *Use the Quick Control screen.* Figure 9-9 shows the Rotate option (second icon from the top, left side of the screen) and its three settings, which appear at the bottom of the screen.

- *Select Rotate Stills from Playback Menu 1, as shown on the left in Figure 9-10.* In single-image view, you then see a screen similar to the one shown on the right in the figure. Tap the Set icon at the bottom of the screen or press the

FIGURE 9-9:
During playback, the fastest way to rotate an image is to use the Quick Control screen.

Set button to rotate the image 90 degrees. Press or tap again to rotate 180 additional degrees; press or tap once more to return to the picture's original orientation (0 degrees of rotation). If you were displaying pictures in Index view before choosing the Rotate Image option, select the image you want to rotate and then tap the Set icon or press the Set button. Tap the Menu symbol or press the Menu button to return to the menu system. Or press the Playback button to return to viewing pictures.

REMEMBER

After you exit the Quick Control or menu screen, the photo remains rotated only if the Setup Menu's Auto Rotate option is set to the default — On (Camera and Computer).

Rotate symbol

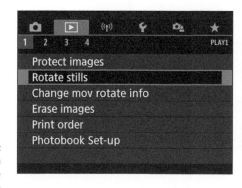

Tap to rotate   Exit to menu

FIGURE 9-10:
You also can choose Rotate Stills from Playback Menu 1.

Also be aware of this bit of weirdness: If the Auto Rotate option is set to one of the other two settings, the images don't appear rotated when you select the Rotate option from the Quick Control screen or Playback Menu 1 option. But the file is tagged with the rotation directions you apply nonetheless. So if you later turn Auto Rotate back on or view the photo in compatible software, the image does appear rotated.

TIP

None of these image-rotation settings affect movies. However, you can tag movie files with camera orientation data so that they will play in vertical orientation when uploaded to social media sites like Instagram. See the section related to recording vertical movies in Chapter 8 for details. When you play movies on the camera, they always play in horizontal orientation, regardless of whether you add the orientation tag. To view your movie in its vertical format, just turn the camera on its side before you press the play button.

Zooming in for a closer view

During playback, you can magnify a photo to inspect details, as shown in Figure 9-11. Zooming works only for photos in single-image view. If the camera is currently displaying thumbnails, shift to single-image view by tapping the thumbnail of the picture you want to inspect (or by selecting it and pressing Set).

Magnified area

FIGURE 9-11:
After displaying your photo in single-image view (left), you can magnify the display to check details (right).

Here's a rundown of how to use the magnification feature for still photos (it's not available for movies):

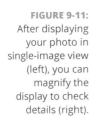

>> **Zoom in:** Use any of the following techniques:

- Press the Magnify button.

- Pinch out from the center of the touchscreen.

- Double-tap the screen with one finger.

Each pinch or press of the Magnify button increases the magnification level; you can enlarge the image up to ten times its normal display size. But a second double-tap on the screen returns the image to its original, unmagnified view.

>> **View another part of the magnified picture:** When the image is magnified, a thumbnail representing the entire image appears in the lower-right corner of the monitor, as shown on the right in Figure 9-11. The solid white box indicates the area of the image that is shown on the monitor. To scroll the display so that you can see a hidden portion of the image, drag your finger on the touchscreen or press the edges of the Quick Control dial in the direction you want to shift the display.

TIP

>> **View more images at the same magnification:** While the display is zoomed, rotate the Main dial to display the same area of the next photo at the same magnification. (The Jump feature, normally triggered by rotating the dial, is disabled while a photo is magnified.) For example, if you shot a group portrait several times, you can easily check each one for shut-eye problems.

>> **Zoom out:** To reduce the magnification level, pinch in toward the center of the touchscreen or press the Index/Reduce button. Each pinch or press decreases the zoom level another step.

>> **Return to full-frame view when zoomed in:** To exit magnified view in one quick step, tap the Menu symbol at the bottom of the screen or press the actual Menu button or Playback button. You also can double-tap the screen to exit magnified view.

Showing focus points during playback

You have the option of seeing the focus point (or points) that the camera used to establish focus during playback, as shown on the left in Figure 9-12. To turn focus–point display on, open Playback Menu 4 and set AF Point Disp to Enable, as shown on the right in the figure.

TIP

This feature is helpful for troubleshooting focus problems. If the focus point is correctly placed over the subject, you can eliminate the position of the focus point as a possible cause of poor focus. You then know that the problem is a result of some other factor: camera shake during the exposure; exceeding the lens' minimum focusing distance (you were too close to the subject); or a shutter speed too slow to capture a moving subject without blur. See Chapter 5 for details on focusing.

Focus point

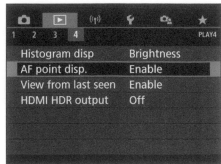

FIGURE 9-12:
You can display the focus point (or points) the camera used to establish focus.

Viewing Picture Data

REMEMBER

During playback, you have a choice of three display modes:

>> **No Information:** This display hides all shooting information, giving you an uncluttered view of your image or movie. All figures up to this point in the chapter show this display mode, with the exception of Figure 9-12, which displays the focus point used to take the picture.

>> **Basic Information:** Okay, so "basic" is a relative term here. This screen, shown on the left in Figure 9-13, does contain basic shooting settings, such as the shutter speed. But in terms of understanding how the camera presents all the Basic Information data, you may need a little assistance. See the next section for help.

>> **Shooting Information:** This display mode presents the smorgasbord of data shown on the right in Figure 9-13. As if the initial screen shown in the figure isn't intimidating enough, you can scroll the display down to uncover several more pages of data. But don't worry, the upcoming section "Shooting Information display mode" helps sort things out.

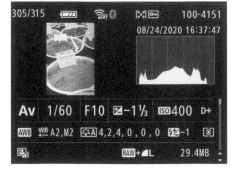

FIGURE 9-13:
Press the Info button to change the amount of data displayed with your photo.

To cycle from one display mode to the next, just press the Info button. However, be aware that the Shooting Information mode isn't available when you're viewing thumbnails (Index mode playback). To return to single-image view, tap the thumbnail or select it and press Set.

REMEMBER

You can choose any display mode for movies, but after you begin playing the movie, most or all of the data shown on the initial display disappears. See the end of Chapter 8 for a map to movie-playback controls.

Basic Information display mode

Figure 9-14 labels the data presented in Basic Information display mode. Note that the figure shows every possible data item that may appear, and the settings don't reflect those I actually used to take the example photo. If you don't see a particular value on your screen, it just means that you didn't take advantage of the associated feature when you took the picture. For example, you see an Exposure Compensation value only if you enabled that tool, which is explained in Chapter 4.

Here's an overview of each bit of data on the screen:

>> **Playback number/total files:** These values (upper-left corner of the screen) show the current file number and the total number of files on the memory card. For example, the numbers in the figure show that you're looking at file 305 out of 315. *Note:* The playback number is *not* the same as the file number that's part of the image or movie filename. It's just an indication of what position the file holds in the total batch of files on the memory card.

>> **Battery status:** Keep an eye on this symbol; grab your battery charger if the bars on the symbol indicate that the battery is running low on juice. You may also want to put off viewing any more photos if you have more shooting to do because the monitor requires a lot of battery power.

>> **Wi-Fi/Bluetooth indicators:** Which of these indicators appears depends on the Wireless Communication settings available through Network Menu 1. The appendix provides more detail about these features and what each symbol means.

>> **Rating:** If you rated the photo, a topic covered in Chapter 10, this symbol shows how many stars you assigned it.

>> **Protected:** The key icon appears if you used the Protect feature to prevent your photo from being erased when you use the normal picture-deleting feature. Find out how to protect photos in the next chapter.

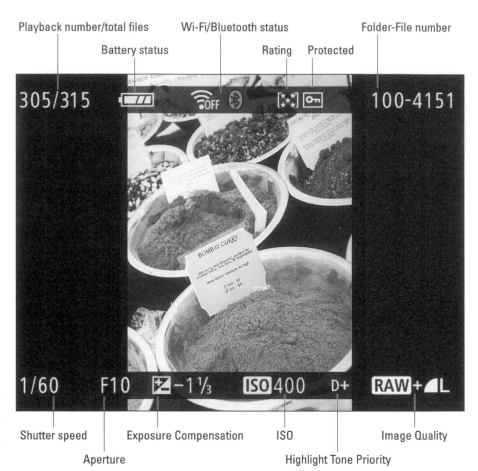

Playback number/total files · Wi-Fi/Bluetooth status · Folder-File number
Battery status · Rating · Protected

305/315 · OFF · [★★] · 100-4151

1/60 · F10 · ±−1⅓ · ISO400 · D+ · RAW+◢L

Shutter speed · Exposure Compensation · ISO · Image Quality
Aperture · Highlight Tone Priority

FIGURE 9-14:
You can view
basic exposure
and file data in
this display
mode.

>> **Folder number and last four digits of file number:** See Chapter 1 for information about how the camera assigns folder and file numbers. And visit Chapter 11 for details on how you can create custom folders.

As for the four-digit number — 4151 in the figure — *this* number is part of the image filename. By default, filenames begin with the characters IMG (for *image*) followed by an underscore and then the four-digit number in the upper-right corner of the playback display. So the image in the figure, for example, has the filename IMG_4151. A three-letter extension indicating the file type follows the number — JPG for JPEG files and CR3 for images shot in the Raw or cRaw format. (Chapter 2 explains formats.)

>> **Exposure settings:** Along the bottom of the playback screen, the Basic Information display includes the shutter speed, f-stop (aperture), and ISO setting, all labeled in Figure 9-14. If you applied Exposure Compensation, the amount of the adjustment is displayed; if you enabled Highlight Tone Priority, a D+ symbol appears. You can read about these exposure features in Chapter 4.

>> **Image Quality:** Again, Chapter 2 explains this setting, which determines the file type and resolution of the picture. In the figure, the symbols indicate that the Raw+JPEG Large/Fine setting was selected. (The *L* stands for *Large;* the smooth arc before it represents the Fine JPEG compression setting.) At this setting, two files are produced, one in the JPEG format and one in the Raw format. But you see just one preview on the camera during playback; you won't see the individual files until you download them to your computer.

Shooting Information display mode

From the Basic Information display, press the Info button to shift to Shooting Information display mode, featured in Figure 9-15. This display provides detailed shooting data plus charts called *histograms,* which are graphics related to image exposure and color. You can get schooled in the art of reading histograms in the next section.

How much data you see depends on the exposure mode you used to take the picture. Figure 9-15 shows the data dump that occurs when you shoot in the advanced exposure modes (P, Tv, Av, and M), which enable you to control all the settings indicated on the playback screen. When you shoot in other exposure modes, you get a less-detailed playback screen.

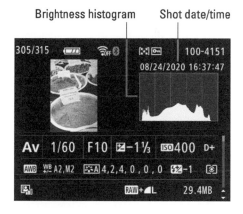

Brightness histogram   Shot date/time

FIGURE 9-15:
The first screen of the Shooting Information display offers this feedback.

I'm going to go out on a limb here and assume that if you're interested in the level of detail provided by the Shooting Information display, you *are* shooting in the advanced exposure modes. So the rest of this section concentrates on the data screens related to shots taken in those modes.

REMEMBER

The first thing to know is that what you see in Figure 9-15 is just the tip of the iceberg. Notice the scroll bar near the lower-right edge of the screen? If you press the top or bottom edges of the Quick Control dial or drag your finger up or down on the touchscreen, the lower half of the display scrolls to reveal several additional pages of information. Well, okay, half pages of information. The top half of the display remains constant when you scroll.

The following list explains what each part of the display reveals. Again, the figures show all possible settings for illustration purposes only. They don't show the settings used to capture the example image, and you're not likely to take a picture that takes advantage of all the features indicated in the figure, either. When you review your photos, values appear only if you enabled a particular feature when shooting; otherwise, that area of the screen is empty.

>> **Top half of the display (appears on all pages):**

- *Basic information*: The top row of the screen contains the same information as the top of the Basic Information display (refer to Figure 9-14).

- *Thumbnail highlight alerts (blinkies):* If you look closely at the thumbnail for images that contain very bright areas, you may notice that those areas blink on and off. Known in the biz as *the blinkies,* those flickering spots indicate pixels that are absolute white. A large area of blinkies may indicate a loss of detail in the brightest portions of the scene, which happens when areas that should include a range of very light to white pixels instead contain only full-on white.

  However, if your subject is exposed properly and the blinkies exist only in the background or some other insignificant area, don't give the issue too much thought. The important thing is whether you're happy with the subject's exposure.

- *Shot date/time*: This information indicates when you took the picture or recorded the movie. If the information isn't accurate, head for Setup Menu 2 and adjust the camera's clock via the Date/Time/Zone setting. (This change affects only new pictures you shoot; your existing photos still bear the old date/time information.)

- *Brightness histogram*: This chart provides another exposure-evaluation tool. If you're new to histograms, upcoming sections explain how to interpret what you see.

>> **Detail pages:** Again, the bottom half of the display is a scrollable list of picture data. Figures 9-16 through 9-18 break up the pages for easier digestion.

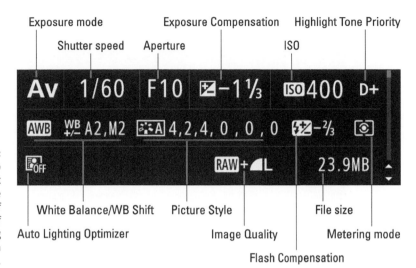

Exposure mode
Shutter speed   Aperture   Exposure Compensation   ISO   Highlight Tone Priority

Av 1/60 F10 ☒–1⅓ ⒤400 D+

AWB WB A2,M2 4,2,4,0,0,0 –⅔ ⊡
+/-

OFF   RAW+ L   23.9MB

White Balance/WB Shift   Picture Style   File size
Auto Lighting Optimizer   Image Quality   Metering mode
Flash Compensation

FIGURE 9-16:
Here's a map to the data that appears on the bottom half of the first screen of the Shooting Information display.

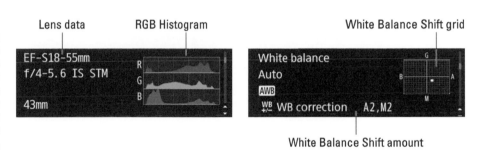

FIGURE 9-17:
The second page has lens details and an RGB histogram (left); the third page concentrates on White Balance settings (right).

Lens data   RGB Histogram   White Balance Shift grid

EF-S18-55mm
f/4-5.6 IS STM
43mm

R
G
B

White balance
Auto
AWB
WB WB correction   A2,M2
+/-

White Balance Shift amount

A bit of information to help you interpret the data shown in the figures:

>> **Exposure settings:** Check out Chapter 4 for help with the exposure-related data that fills the first row of the readout shown in Figure 9-16. The same chapter also covers the metering mode setting, which got shoved down one floor, to the right end of the second row.

>> **White Balance information:** For whatever reason, information about the White Balance setting appears both on the first page of data (see Figure 9-16) and on the third page, shown on the right in Figure 9-17. The only difference is that the second of the two includes a color grid that makes it easier to see how much and what type of White Balance Shift is in force, if any. In both cases, you see a small *W* next to the AWB (Auto White Balance) symbol if you change the AWB Priority setting from the default, Ambience Priority, to White Priority. I stuck with Ambience Priority for my example photo, so you see only AWB.

Chapter 6 explains White Balance as well as other color-related settings.

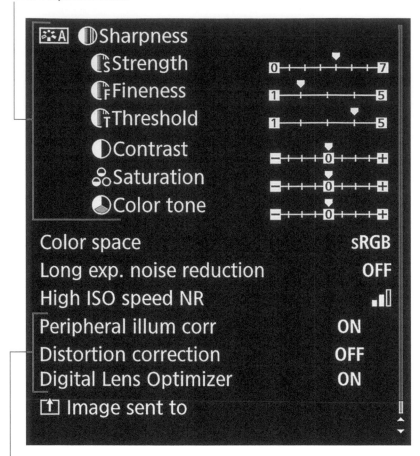

Picture Style information

Color space · sRGB
Long exp. noise reduction · OFF
High ISO speed NR
Peripheral illum corr · ON
Distortion correction · OFF
Digital Lens Optimizer · ON
⬆ Image sent to

Lens correction settings

FIGURE 9-18: Keep scrolling to see these additional settings, which are spread over multiple pages in real life.

» **Flash information:** The Flash Compensation value shown in Figure 9-16 appears only if you adjusted the flash power, as discussed in Chapter 2. Otherwise, a lightning bolt appears to show that you used flash. But wait, there's more: If you set the High ISO Speed NR (Noise Reduction) option to Multi Shot, the flash slot in the display is replaced by an NR symbol. (In my classes, nine out of ten students vote this setup the most ridiculously complex of all the Canon data displays. Student number 10 sleeps through this part of the lecture.)

» **Picture Style data:** This feature, too, gets double billing in the display. The first page (see Figure 9-16) shows you the symbol representing the Picture Style (*A,* for Auto, in the figure) and numbers indicating the strength at which various characteristics applied by the style are added to the image. Scroll to the page shown in Figure 9-18 to get a detailed look at those characteristics. Chapter 6 also covers Picture Styles.

>> **Lens data and focal length:** The left side of the first screen shown in Figure 9-17 provides some specifications about the lens used to take the picture. In the figure, *EF-S* stands for the type of Canon lens, and 18–55mm is the lens focal-length range. On the next row, the values tell you the maximum aperture of the lens at its shortest and longest focal length; you see both values only for zoom lenses. (Otherwise, you see just a single maximum aperture value.) The letters *IS* indicate that the lens offers Image Stabilization; and *STM* stands for Canon's Stepping Motor autofocusing technology. You can read about these lens issues in Chapter 1.

REMEMBER

A more important number to note is the focal length used to take the picture — 43mm, in the figure. As Chapter 5 explains, focal length contributes to depth of field, or the distance over which focus appears acceptably sharp. Don't forget that focal lengths are presented in terms of 35mm equivalents; see Chapter 1 for help understanding that issue.

>> **RGB histogram:** By default, the Brightness histogram remains displayed at the top of the screen at all times and you must scroll to the screen shown on the left in Figure 9-17 to view the RGB histogram. If you prefer things the other way around, open Playback Menu 4 and set the Histogram Disp option to RGB. The next sections explain what you can learn from both types of histograms.

>> **Color Space:** You can record pictures in either of two color spaces, sRGB or Adobe RGB. Stick with the default, sRGB, until you consider the issues involved with making the change to Adobe RGB (which are covered with other color issues in Chapter 6).

>> **Long Exposure Noise Reduction and High ISO Speed NR:** These options, also shown in Figure 9-18, indicate whether the camera applied tools designed to deal with *noise,* a defect that gives your image a grainy look. See Chapter 4 for details.

>> **Lens Correction settings:** The next three lines of information in Figure 9-18 relate to corrections the camera can apply to compensate for specific defects that can occur with some lenses. See Chapter 4 for help with Peripheral Illumination; Chapter 5 for help understanding Distortion Correction and Digital Lens Optimizer feature. Chapter 6 talks about another lens-correction tool, Chromatic Aberration Correction, which is a color-related feature that becomes available only if you turn the Digital Lens Optimizer feature off.

Understanding histograms

In Shooting Information display mode, you can view two types of histograms — a brightness histogram and an RGB histogram. The next sections explain how to understand what each reveals about your image.

Interpreting a brightness histogram

One of the most difficult problems to correct in a photo-editing program is known as *blown highlights* or *clipped highlights*. Both terms mean that the brightest areas of the image are so overexposed that they appear as a blob of solid white, with none of the details you'd see if the area were rendered using a range of brightness values.

In Shooting Information display mode, areas that fall into this category blink in the image thumbnail. The *Brightness histogram*, shown at the top of the Shooting Information display by default, offers another analysis of image exposure. This graph, featured in Figure 9-19, indicates the distribution of shadows, highlights, and *midtones* (areas of medium brightness) in an image. Photographers use the term *tonal range* to describe this aspect of their pictures.

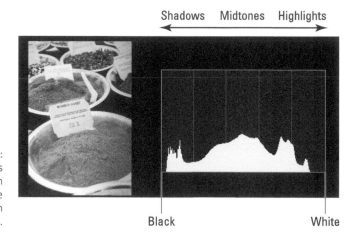

FIGURE 9-19: A Brightness histogram indicates the tonal range of an image.

The horizontal axis of the graph represents the range of 256 possible brightness values, from black (a brightness value of 0) to white (255). And the vertical axis shows you how many pixels fall at a particular brightness value. A spike indicates a heavy concentration of pixels. For example, in Figure 9-19, the histogram for the example image indicates a broad range of brightness values but with very few at the very brightest end of the spectrum.

Keep in mind that there is no "perfect" histogram that you should try to duplicate. Instead, interpret the histogram with respect to the amount of shadows, highlights, and midtones that make up your subject.

TIP

Also, when you're shooting a subject that contains important highlight details, such as the white spoons and silver rims of the spice bowls in the example photo, a histogram that shows a thin population of pixels at the bright end of the scale, as in the figure, is actually a good thing. If you increase exposure to shift more pixels to the right, you can easily lose detail in those highlights, leaving you with a chunk of solid white where there should be a range of varying shades from almost white to white.

Reading an RGB histogram

Along with a Brightness histogram, the Shooting Information display provides an RGB histogram like the one shown in Figure 9-20. You need to scroll the display to get to the page that contains this graphic, shown in its entirety on the left in Figure 9-17.

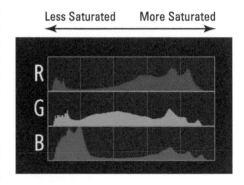

FIGURE 9-20:
The RGB histogram can indicate problems with color saturation.

To make sense of an RGB histogram, you need to know that digital images are known as *RGB images* because they're created from three primary colors of light: red, green, and blue. In the image file, the brightness values for those colors are contained in three separate vats of color data, known as *color channels*. Whereas the Brightness histogram reflects the brightness of all three color channels rolled into one, RGB histograms let you view the values for each individual channel.

When you look at the brightness data for a single channel, though, you glean information about color saturation rather than image brightness. This book doesn't have enough pages to provide a full lesson in RGB color theory, but the short story is that when you mix red, green, and blue light, and each component is at maximum brightness, you create white. Zero brightness in all three channels creates black. If you have maximum red and no blue or green, though, you have fully saturated red. If you mix two channels at maximum brightness, you also create full saturation. For example, maximum red and blue produce fully saturated magenta. And, wherever colors are fully saturated, you can lose picture detail: Imagine a rose petal that should have a range of tones from medium to dark red appearing instead as an expanse of solid, fully saturated red.

The upshot is that if all the pixels for one or two channels are slammed to the right end of the histogram, you may be losing picture detail because of overly saturated colors. If all three channels show a heavy pixel population at the right end of the histograms, you may have blown highlights — again, because the maximum levels of red, green, and blue create white. Either way, you may want to adjust the exposure settings and try again.

A savvy RGB-histogram reader can also spot color balance issues by looking at the pixel values. But frankly, color balance problems are fairly easy to notice just by looking at the image on the camera monitor.

TIP

If you're a fan of RGB histograms, remember that you can swap the standard Brightness histogram that always appears near the top of the Shooting Information playback display with the RGB histogram. Just set the Histogram option on Playback Menu 4 to RGB instead of Brightness.

Taking Advantage of Image Search

TIP

Your camera's Image Search function enables you to quickly find pictures and movies that fall into certain categories, such as all files recorded on a particular date. After you set the search criteria, only files that meet the search conditions appear during playback. You also can use the search function to easily select a group of photos prior to performing certain file operations, such as assigning a rating or including the files in a slide show.

To set the search criteria, open Playback Menu 3 and select Set Image Search Conditions, as shown on the left in Figure 9-21. Or, when the camera is in Playback mode, press the Q button to display the Quick Control screen and then select the binoculars symbol — representing the search function — as shown on the right in the figure. After you select the menu item or the binoculars symbol, press the Set button or, in Quick Control mode, tap the Set icon at the bottom of the screen.

Image Search option

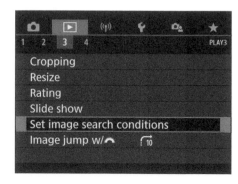

FIGURE 9-21: You can set up a search from Playback Menu 3 (left) or, during playback, from the Quick Control screen (right).

Whichever route you go, you see the setup screen shown in Figure 9-22. Here, you specify what criteria images or movies need to meet to be included in the search results. The following list offers details:

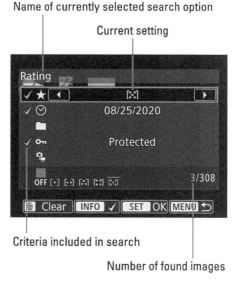

Name of currently selected search option

Current setting

Criteria included in search

Number of found images

» **You get a choice of five search conditions.** The five options work as follows:

- *Rating:* After you assign ratings, a feature explained in Chapter 10, you can tell the camera to search for files that carry a particular rating, all files that carry any rating, or files that have not been rated.

- *Date:* Use this filter to search for all movies or photos taken on a specific day.

- *Folder:* If your memory card contains multiple image folders, choose this option to limit the search to a specific folder. By default, the camera sets up just one folder, named 100Canon.

- *Protected:* Choose this option to narrow the search to files that you protected by using the Protect Images feature, also discussed in Chapter 10.

- *Type of file:* Using this option, you can search for all stills, all movies, or stills that were taken using a specific Image Quality setting, such as Raw. Chapter 2 explains Image Quality settings.

TIP

When you highlight an option, its name appears in the top-left corner of the screen. It's easy to miss amid all the other stuff on the screen. For example, in Figure 9-22, the Rating option is selected and highlighted on the display.

» **To enable a search condition, highlight it and then tap the Info icon or press the Info button.** A checkmark appears next to the search condition, as shown in Figure 9-22. Press or tap Info again to toggle the checkmark off and remove the condition from the search.

» **After selecting a search option, press the left/right edges of the Quick Control dial to cycle through the option settings.** For example, in Figure 9-22, the Rating option is set up to include pictures that have a rating of five stars, were shot on August 25, 2020, and have protected status. (I explain the rating and protect features in the next chapter.) At the bottom of the screen, symbols appear to represent the various settings for the search option you're currently adjusting. In the figure, the Rating setting is active, so options related to that setting appear. The currently selected option is shown in blue — again, five stars, in the figure.

>> **Each time you turn on or change a search filter, the camera indicates how many files meet the current criteria.** Look for this value in the lower-right corner of the display. The number of files that meet the criteria is shown in blue; the total number of files on the card (or in the current image folder) appears in white. So in Figure 9-22, 3 out of 308 files meet the search criteria. (The camera also displays thumbnails of the images that made the cut, but the thumbnails are so faint in the display that they're not much help.)

>> **You can enable as many search filters as you want.** However, in some cases, selecting one condition automatically disables another. Suppose that you select the Protected option and then set the Type of File to Movies only. If you haven't protected any movies, the camera clears the checkmark from the Protected filter.

>> **After setting up the search parameters, press the Set button or tap the Set icon at the bottom of the screen.** You then see a confirmation screen; select OK. If the OK option is dimmed or nothing happens when you press Set, the camera didn't find any files that met all the search criteria.

>> **To view files that meet the search criteria, put the camera in Playback mode.** In the display, a bright yellow frame appears around the perimeter of the monitor screen to tell you that the search function is active. In Index view, one thumbnail is also selected, which is indicated by an orange box, as shown in Figure 9-23. You see the yellow search box around the entire screen even in single-image view, however.

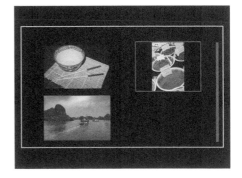

FIGURE 9-23:
The yellow frame reminds you that you're viewing photos turned up by a search; in Index view, the orange box surrounds the selected photo.

>> **Until you cancel the search, certain file operations affect all "found images" — the ones that met your search criteria.** For example, suppose that you ask the camera to find all images with a rating of four or five stars. After the search is completed, you can protect all of them by selecting Protect Images from Playback Menu 1 or by choosing the Protect icon on the Quick Control screen.

Along with protecting files, you can perform the following *batch processes* (that's geek speak for doing something to a group of selected files): rating files, erasing files, adding files to a photobook setup or print order, and including files in a slide show.

When an operation presents a screen asking you which files you want to affect, choose the All Found Images setting.

>> **The search is cancelled when you turn off the camera or it goes to sleep at the time specified by the Auto Power Off setting.** If the Auto Power Off setting (Setup Menu 2) is 4 minutes or less, however, the camera tacks on extra time, giving you 6 minutes before putting the camera to sleep. You may want to extend the Auto Power Off delay to give yourself a little more time to get things done before the search is cancelled.

>> **Several other actions also cancel the search.** Taking a picture or recording a movie cancels the search, as does formatting the memory card or creating an edited copy of a photo.

>> **To manually exit the search, reopen the Search setup box and then tap the Clear icon or press the Erase button.** You can see the icon at the bottom of the screen in Figure 9-22 (look in the lower-left corner).

REMEMBER

You then need to press the Set button or tap the Set icon to officially call off the search. The message "Image search cancelled" appears briefly to let you know that the camera did as you asked.

Chapter **10**

Working with Picture and Movie Files

E very creative pursuit involves its share of cleanup and organizational tasks. Painters have to wash brushes, embroiderers have to separate strands of floss, and woodcrafters have to haul out the wet/dry vac to suck up sawdust. Digital photography is no different: At some point, you have to stop shooting so that you can download and process your files.

This chapter focuses on some of these after-the-shot tasks, such as assigning ratings to your photos and movies and deleting files you no longer want. It also covers the camera's built-in editing tools, which enable you to remove red-eye from portraits, crop your photos, and create JPEG versions of images that you shoot in the Raw or cRaw file format. Following that, you can get help with transferring files to your computer and preparing images for online sharing.

REMEMBER

For information about transferring pictures wirelessly to a computer, smartphone, or tablet, see the appendix.

Deleting Files

When you spot clunkers during your picture and movie review, use the Erase button or the Erase Images function on Playback Menu 1 to get rid of them.

REMEMBER

Be aware, though, that neither option deletes files that you protected by using the feature discussed in the next section. Follow the steps in that section to unprotect files you want to erase.

The following list explains options for erasing a single file, a group of files, or all files:

» **Erase images one at a time:** Display the photo in single-image view or select it in Index (thumbnails) view. Then press the Erase button, labeled in Figure 10-1. The words *Cancel* and *Erase* appear at the bottom of the screen, as shown in the figure. Tap Erase or highlight it and then press Set.

If you captured the image using one of the JPEG+Raw Image Quality options, you see just a single thumbnail. But you're offered the choice of erasing the JPEG file only, the Raw file only, or both files. Again, tap the option you prefer or select it and press Set. If you delete one version of the file, the thumbnail for the other version remains.

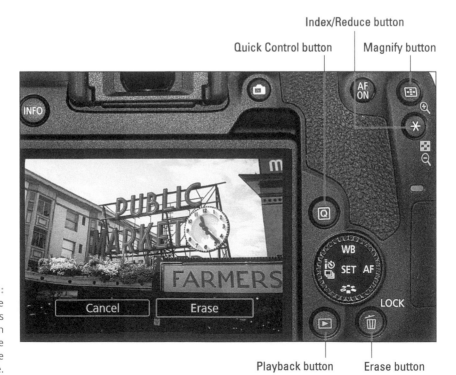

FIGURE 10-1: During picture playback, press the Erase button to delete the displayed image or movie.

>> **Erase all images on memory card:** Open Playback Menu 1 and choose Erase Images, as shown on the left in Figure 10-2. Then choose All Images on Card, as shown on the right. On the confirmation screen that appears, choose OK.

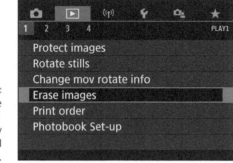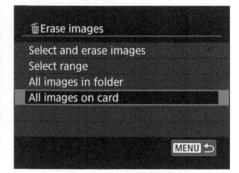

FIGURE 10-2:
Choose these
Playback Menu 1
options to quickly
delete all
unprotected files.

TIP

>> **Erase all images in a selected folder:** If your card contains more than one folder, you can limit the image dump to a specific folder. Instead of selecting All Images on Card from the screen shown on the right in Figure 10-2, choose All Images in Folder. Choose the folder you want to empty and then tap the OK symbol or press the Set button. On the resulting confirmation screen, tap OK or highlight it and press the Set button.

>> **Erase a batch of selected files:** After choosing Erase Images from Playback Menu 1, choose Select and Erase Images, as shown on the left in Figure 10-3. If the camera is set to single-image playback mode, you see the current image in the monitor, as shown on the right in the figure. At the top of the screen, a check box appears. Initially, the box is empty. (If your screen shows more information than you see in the figure, you can press the Info button to change the amount of data displayed. You may need to press the button a couple of times to get to the uncluttered version you see in the figure.)

To the right of the check box is a number showing you how many files are currently tagged for erasure (3, in the figure). To tag the current file, tap the check box, tap the Set icon at the bottom of the screen, or press the Set button. A check mark then appears in the box, and the picture is officially marked for erasure. If you change your mind, use the same techniques to remove the check mark.

To tag more files, use the normal playback techniques to scroll through your pictures, adding the check mark to all the files you want to trash.

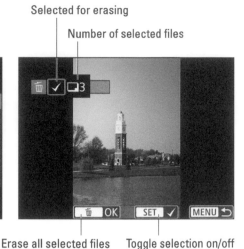

Selected for erasing

Number of selected files

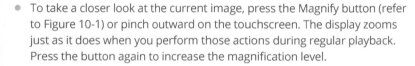

Erase all selected files   Toggle selection on/off

FIGURE 10-3:
Tag a file as ready
for the trash by
tapping the Set
symbol or
pressing the Set
button.

A couple of tips on using this option:

- To take a closer look at the current image, press the Magnify button (refer to Figure 10-1) or pinch outward on the touchscreen. The display zooms just as it does when you perform those actions during regular playback. Press the button again to increase the magnification level.

    To reduce the level of magnification, press the Index/Reduce button (refer to Figure 10-1). Press as many times as needed to return to the unmagnified view. You also can press the Menu button or tap the Menu symbol to exit magnified view.

- If you don't need to inspect each image closely, you can display up to three thumbnails per screen. From the initial screen shown on the right in Figure 10-3, press the Index/Reduce button to shift to the three-thumbnail display. Use the same methods to tag images for erasure and to scroll through files as you do when viewing them one at a time. To return to full-frame view, press the Magnify button or pinch outward on the touchscreen.

When you finish selecting images, press the Erase button or tap the Erase symbol on the touchscreen (refer to the right screen in Figure 10-3). You see a confirmation screen asking whether you really want to get rid of the selected images; if you're ready to take the leap, choose OK.

>> **Select a range of files:** Here's an even faster way to select a group of consecutive files: After selecting Erase Images from Playback Menu 1, choose Select Range to display the screen shown on the left in Figure 10-4. Then move the blue box over the first image you want to delete (tap the thumbnail

or rotate the Quick Control or Main dial to move the box). Next, tap Set First Img, labeled on the left in Figure 10-4, or just press the Set button. The symbol changes to read Set Last Img.

Number of selected files   Last image in range

Selected image   First image in range

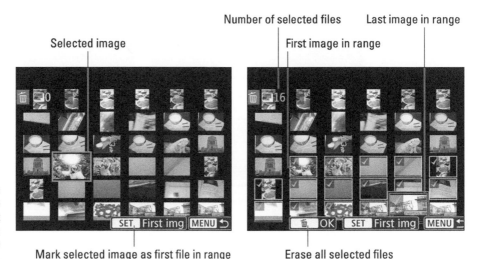

FIGURE 10-4:
Use Select Range to quickly select and delete a consecutive series of files.

Mark selected image as first file in range   Erase all selected files

Next, move the blue box over the last file in the group and tap Set Last Img or press the Set button. The camera immediately selects the first and last files and all files in between, as shown on the right in the figure. The number of files selected appears in the upper-left corner of the screen, as shown on the right in Figure 10-4. If you're satisfied that all the files you want to delete are selected, tap the trash can symbol in the lower-left corner of the screen or press the Erase button. A confirmation screen appears; choose OK.

>> **Erase files found by the Image Search function:** By using the Image Search function explained near the end of Chapter 9, you can tell the camera to locate all files that meet certain parameters — date shot, type of file, assigned rating, and so on. Immediately after completing the search, choose Erase Images from Playback Menu 1, as shown on the left in Figure 10-5. The selection screen shown on the right in the figure then offers an option called All Found Images. Select that option to delete just the files turned up by the search. ***Important:*** If you don't choose the Erase Images option as soon as you finish your image search, the All Found Images option becomes unavailable.

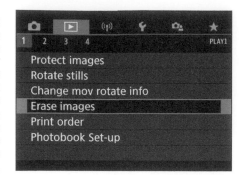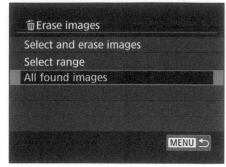

FIGURE 10-5:
If you choose
Erase Images
immediately after
you use the
Image Search
function, the
camera offers an
All Found Images
option that erase
files that met the
search criteria.

Protecting Photos and Movies

You can protect pictures and movies from accidental erasure by giving them protected status. After you take this step, the camera doesn't allow you to delete the
file from your memory card by using the erase options outlined in the preceding
section. (The only way to wipe a protected file off a memory card is to use the
Format Card command, found on Setup Menu 1.)

Additionally, when you download protected files to your computer, they show up
as *read-only* files, which means that you can't overwrite the originals. The easiest
fix is to save the original under a new name. It's also the safest option because you
can edit the copy while your original remains intact.

When you're ready to protect a file or group of files, use these techniques:

>> **Quick Control screen:** Put the camera in Playback mode, display the photo in
single-image view, and press the Q button to display the Quick Control screen.
Select the Protect Images symbol, as shown on the left in Figure 10-6, and
then choose Enable. A key symbol appears at the top of the frame, indicating
the file is now locked (protected). To remove the protected status,
choose Disable.

To protect a batch of images, tap the Info symbol (see the left screen in
Figure 10-6) or press the Info button. The screen shown on the right in the
figure appears, enabling you to select a range of files, protect all files on the
memory card, or remove protection from all locked files. See the preceding
section for help selecting a range of files.

Protect Images option   Protected symbol

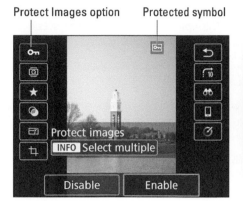

FIGURE 10-6:
During playback,
use the Quick
Control screen to
protect the
current file.

>> **Playback Menu 1:** The Protect Images option on Playback Menu 1, shown on
the left in Figure 10-7, provides the options shown on the right in the figure,
which work as follows:

● *Select Images:* Choose this option to protect specific photos or movies.
Select a thumbnail and then tap the Set icon or press the Set button to lock
the file. A key appears to indicate the locked status. To remove protection,
tap the Set icon or press Set to make the key disappear. Scroll the display
in the usual playback fashion to reach the next file you want to protect and
then lather, rinse, and repeat.

● *Select Range:* Use techniques outlined in the preceding section to select a
range of sequential images.

● *All Images in Folder:* If your memory card contains multiple folders, choose
this option to select all images in a specific folder.

● *Unprotect All Images in Folder:* Use this option to unlock all protected images
in the folder you select.

FIGURE 10-7:
You can access a
few additional
options for
selecting files to
protect if you
choose Protect
Images from
Playback Menu 1.

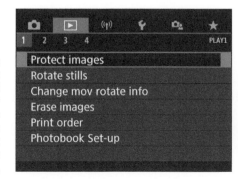

- *All Images on Card:* This option does just what it says: Locks all images on the card.

- *Unprotect All Images on Card:* Select this option to unlock all pictures and movies on the card.

REMEMBER

Whichever option you choose, the last step is to tap the Menu symbol or press the Menu button to exit the protection screens.

Again, things work differently if you tackle image-protection chores immediately after using the Image Search function discussed in Chapter 9. Instead of the Quick Control options shown on the right in Figure 10-6, your options are Select Range, All Found Images, or Unprotect All Found Images. Go through Playback Menu 1, and you get Select Images, Select Range, All Found Images, and Unprotect All Found. Select Range and Select Images enable you to lock specific files turned up by the search function; the last two protect or unprotect all those files.

Rating Photos and Movies

TIP

Using your camera's Rating feature, you can assign a rating to a picture or movie file: five stars for your best work, one star for those you really dislike, and so on.

What's the point, you ask? Well, rating pictures has several benefits. First, when you create a slide show, as outlined in Chapter 11, you can tell the camera to display only photos or movies that have a certain rating. Using the Image Search function, introduced in Chapter 9, you can enjoy the same ratings-based filtering to limit the files that are displayed during regular playback and are thus available for such playback functions as protecting and deleting.

Some photo programs, including Canon Digital Photo Professional 4, covered later in this chapter, can read the ratings as well. So after you download files to your computer, you can sort files by rating, making it easier to cull your photo and movie collection and gather your best work for printing and sharing.

You can assign a rating as follows:

>> **Quick Control screen:** Put the camera in playback mode and then press the Q button to display the playback version of the Quick Control screen. Select the Rating option, as shown on the left in Figure 10-8, and then select the rating you want to use from the bottom of the screen.

Tap to assign same rating to multiple files

Rating option   Current rating

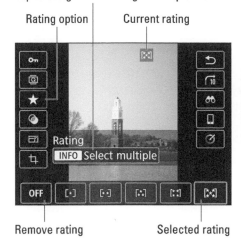

FIGURE 10-8:
You can rate
photos via the
Quick Control
screen.

Remove rating   Selected rating

To assign the same rating to a batch of files, first choose the number of stars you want to award. Then press the Info button or tap the Info symbol on the screen. You then see the options shown on the right in the figure. You have the choice of selecting a range of continuous pictures (the process works the same way as outlined in the first section of the chapter) or applying the rating to all files on the card.

>> **Playback Menu 2:** After choosing Rating, as shown on the left in Figure 10-9, select one of the four options shown on the right. These all work the same as for the Erase Images option, explained at the start of the chapter, except that you're assigning a particular rating instead of tagging pictures for erasing.

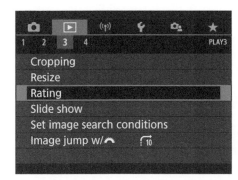

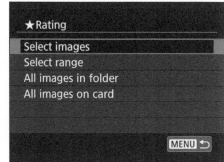

FIGURE 10-9:
The Rating
feature on
Playback Menu 2
offers a few more
options for
selecting the
photos to rate.

The one thing that may trip you up is the Select Images option, which initially shows the screen on the left in Figure 10-10. The symbols seem to indicate that you press the top or bottom edge of the Quick Control dial to change the rating, but that doesn't produce any results. Instead, tap the Set icon or press the Set button to get to the screen shown on the right in the figure. Now you can set the rating by tapping the up/down symbols at the bottom of the screen or pressing the up or down edge of the Quick Control dial.

Number of files with this rating

Selected rating

FIGURE 10-10:
After choosing Select Images, tap Set (left), tap the up or down arrows (right) to change the rating, and then tap Menu.

Tap to raise/lower rating

Notice that at the top of both screens in Figure 10-10, a value appears to the right of each rating. The number indicates how many files on the memory card have been assigned that rating. For example, the right screen of Figure 10-10 shows a four-star rating being assigned. The number 1 next to the four-star icon shows that the image is the first to be awarded that grade level. Six other pictures on the card have a five-star rating; no pictures have been assigned any of the other ratings.

After you set the rating, tap the Menu symbol or press the Menu button.

Whether you rate photos from the Quick Control screen or Playback Menu 2, your choices for selecting files to rate change if you just used the Image Search tool, explained in Chapter 9. The All Images in Folder and All Images on Card options disappear, and you instead get the option to rate found images — again, that's the term for images that met the criteria of your search.

Fixing Red-Eye

If a portrait you shot using flash suffers from red-eye, the camera may — *may* — be able to correct the problem. I add the qualification because the camera must be able to detect red-eye in your photos, and it's not always successful.

To give the red-eye removal filter a whirl, open Playback Menu 2 and select Red-eye Correction, as shown on the left in Figure 10-11. Scroll to the image that has the problem and then put the tool to work by tapping the Set icon at the bottom of the screen or by pressing the Set button. A "camera busy" message appears as the filter looks for eyeballs covered with red pixels. If the tool can't find any red eyes, it lets you know. But if it's successful, the repair is done, and a white frame appears around the person's face, as shown in Figure 10-12.

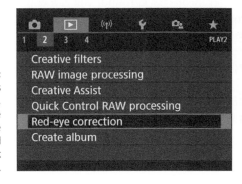

FIGURE 10-11: If flash portraits exhibit red eye, try using the Red-Eye Correction tool on Playback Menu 2.

To magnify the display so that you can check the results, press the Magnify button (magnifying glass with the plus sign in it) or use the touchscreen zoom gesture: Pinch outward from the center of the screen. (The magnifying glass symbol in the upper-right corner is there only to remind you of the magnification possibility; you can't tap it to zoom in on the photo.) After you magnify the image, use the same techniques outlined in Chapter 9 to increase or decrease the zoom level and scroll the display. Tap the menu icon or press the Menu button to return to the initial results screen. To save the retouched image as a new file, tap OK or press the Set button.

FIGURE 10-12: The white box indicates where the repair was made; choose OK to save the corrected image as a new file.

Notice that in the example image, the filter was able to repair the boy's eyes, but it didn't know what to do with the flash reflection in his pup's eyes. That's because red-eye correction filters only understand how to hunt down and replace red pixels. For animal eyes, which turn yellow, white, or green as a result of the flash reflection, you'll need a photo editor. (You can find apps and specialty tools that repair animal eyes or you can simply use your editor's paintbrush to paint in the correct eye colors.)

See Chapter 2 to investigate ways to avoid red-eye when using flash.

Cropping Photos

When a picture includes extraneous background, you can eliminate the excess by using the in-camera crop tool. The feature saves your cropped photo as a new file, leaving the original intact.

A few points to consider before you try out it out:

>> **Cropping is off-limits for Raw files.** Only JPEG photo files can be cropped. See Chapter 2 for help understanding Raw and JPEG.

>> **You can't apply the crop tool to an already cropped copy.** You can, however, start with the original and create a second cropped copy using different crop settings.

>> **You can't perform certain other file operations on a cropped image.** You can't use the Resize option, which eliminates pixels throughout the image to reduce file size. Nor can you apply a Creative Filter to a cropped photo. In other words, make cropping your last editing step, at least when you use the camera's crop tool.

>> **Some file information is stripped from the cropped copy.** Any focus-point information stored with the original file doesn't carry over to the cropped copy, so you can't display the focus point during playback. (Chapter 9 explains that option.) If you take advantage of the Dust Delete Data function, which provides a map for Canon Digital Photo Professional 4 to use when trying to remove sensor dust from an image, that data isn't included in the cropped file, either. See Chapter 12 for help with this dust-buster feature.

As with the other file operations discussed so far, you can get to the crop tool in two ways:

>> **Quick Control screen:** After putting the camera in Playback mode, display the picture you want to crop, press the Q button to display the Quick Control screen, and highlight the Crop symbol, as shown on the left in Figure 10-13. Tap the Crop Image option at the bottom of the screen or press the Set button to get to the cropping tools, detailed momentarily.

>> **Playback Menu 3:** Choose Cropping, as shown on the right in Figure 10-13. On the next screen, which shows a single image, use the standard methods to scroll to the photo you want to crop. Then tap the Set symbol at the bottom of the screen or press the Set button.

 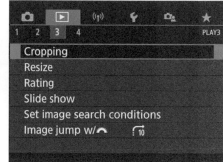

FIGURE 10-13: You can get to the cropping tool through the Quick Control screen (left) or Playback Menu 2 (right).

Either way, your photo appears in a window that contains the controls labeled in Figure 10-14. If you took the photo in landscape orientation, the screen displays the photo normally. If you took the photo holding the camera vertically, the photo isn't rotated and instead appears sideways, as shown in the figure. (This issue isn't affected by the auto rotation options discussed in Chapter 9.)

Your next step is to adjust the crop frame, which is the green box overlaying the image, so that it contains the area of the photo you want to retain. Here's how:

>> **Set the aspect ratio and frame orientation (vertical or horizontal):** Rotate the Quick Control dial to choose the symbol labeled "Change aspect ratio/ orientation" in Figure 10-14. Then press Set. You can choose an aspect ratio of 3:2, 16:9, 4:3, or 1:1, and you can set the frame to a landscape or portrait orientation. Each press of the Set button produces a new combination of aspect ratio and orientation, so just keep pressing until you get the framing you want.

Preview image   Change aspect ratio/orientation

Correct tilt   Save cropped image   Exit

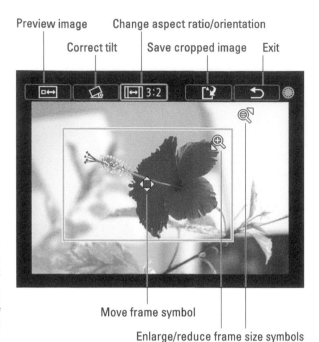

FIGURE 10-14:
Use these
controls to set
the size, angle,
orientation, and
aspect ratio of
the cropped
photo.

Move frame symbol

Enlarge/reduce frame size symbols

>> **Reposition the crop frame:** Move the frame by pressing the edges of the Quick Control dial (up, down, left, right). Or just use your fingertip to drag the frame into place. The symbol I labeled "Movie frame symbol" in Figure 10-14 is (I guess) supposed to remind you that you can press the edges of the Quick Control dial to move the frame. Tapping the symbol doesn't do anything.

>> **Change the size of the frame:** To shrink the frame, press the Index/Reduce button or, pinch inward on the touchscreen. Remember that the smaller the frame, the more original image pixels you're trimming away; the remaining pixel count will determine how large you can print the cropped photo. See Chapter 2 to understand more about how the pixel count, or resolution, affects your print possibilities.

To enlarge the frame, press the Magnify button or pinch outward on the touchscreen.

>> **Correct a tilting horizon line:** This part of the Crop feature really should have its own menu slot because it does more than just trim off excess background: It rotates the image within the crop frame, which enables you to straighten a tilting horizon line. Figure 10-15 offers an illustration.

TIP

To get started, rotate the Quick Control dial to select the second symbol from the left, I labeled "Correct tilt" in Figure 10-14. Then press Set. You also can just tap the symbol. Either way, the screen changes to display an alignment grip over your photo, as shown on the left in Figure 10-15.

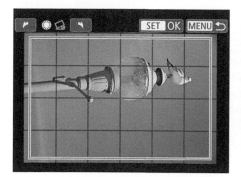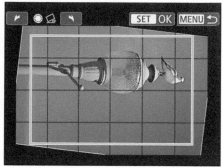

Use the Quick Control dial to rotate the image by one-tenth of a degree; tap the arrow symbols in the upper-left corner of the screen to rotate the image in half-degree increments. You can adjust the angle up to 10 degrees in either direction. The preview updates to show you the rotated image.

Because the correction rotates part of your image off the invisible "canvas" on which it rests, you wind up with empty, black areas around the edges of the scene, as shown on the right in the figure. The camera automatically resizes the crop frame to exclude those areas. (After finishing the rotation, you can further adjust the frame size, position, and aspect ratio if necessary.)

To finalize the rotation, tap the Set icon or press the Set button. You're returned to the initial crop screen (Figure 10-14).

>> **Preview the cropped image:** Rotate the Quick Control dial to select the far-left symbol at the top of the screen, labeled "Preview Image" in Figure 10-14. Or just tap the symbol. Either way, the crop frame disappears so that you can see the boundaries of your image if you use the current crop settings.

>> **Create the cropped copy:** Tap the Save icon, labeled in Figure 10-14, or highlight it and press Set. The camera asks permission to save the cropped photo as a new file; answer in the affirmative to go forward. When the new file is created, the camera displays the filename and then redisplays the original photo.

>> **Exit without cropping:** Tap the exit arrow in the upper-right corner of the screen or use the Quick Control dial to highlight the symbol and then press Set.

In Playback mode, the symbols labeled in Figure 10-16 appear with the cropped image if you set the display to include either basic or detailed information. (Press the Info button to change the display.) The first symbol is a general "this image is an edited copy of an original" notation; the second symbol represents the crop function. That symbol looks like the mechanical crop tools used for trimming photos in a traditional darkroom. (Remember those? Yah, getting kind of vague in my memory, too.)

Edited symbol

Crop symbol

FIGURE 10-16:
You see these symbols during playback when you display a cropped photo.

Processing Raw Images in the Camera

Chapter 2 introduces you to the Raw file format, which enables you to capture images as raw data. The T8i/850D offers two Raw options: Regular Raw and cRaw, for *compact Raw.* The latter format produces a smaller file size than the standard Raw format. From the purposes of this discussion, I use the term Raw generically to refer to both formats.

Photographers who shoot in the Raw format do so because it gives them control over how the raw data captured by the camera is turned into a photograph. They can make their own decisions about picture characteristics such as color saturation, color tone (warm or cool), sharpness, and so on. When you shoot in the JPEG format, the other option on your camera, those factors are baked into the file. Although you can modify them in a photo editor, your options are more limited because you're not starting with raw — uncooked — data.

The downside of Raw is that you can't do much of anything with Raw photos until you *process* them — which just means to convert them to a standard file format, such as JPEG. During the Raw conversion process, you specify all the aforementioned picture qualities and more.

If you already own a program that offers a good Raw converter, such as Adobe Photoshop or Adobe Lightroom, you can use that program to do your Raw processing. You also can do your Raw processing and other editing in Canon's free program, Digital Photo Professional 4, which you can download for free from the Canon website and preview near the end of this chapter.

For times when you don't have the option of doing your Raw processing on a computer, the camera offers a built-in Raw conversion tool that creates a JPEG copy of your original Raw image. As a rule, I do my raw processing on the computer, not just because my photo software offers a higher level of editing tools but also because being able to see my image on a large monitor makes it easier to make critical decisions than when I have to rely on the small (by comparison) camera monitor. In addition, when highest image quality is important, JPEG isn't the best option for saving your converted files. TIFF, a longtime standard in the print publishing world, is better because it doesn't compress your images using the destructive compression formula applied by JPEG.

That said, having the option to convert a Raw file into a JPEG file on the spot is handy, especially if you need to share an image on social media or get a photo printed at a retail lab — neither of which you can do with a Raw file — and you don't have access to a computer.

Understanding the basic approach

The way Canon presents the Raw conversion options is a little confusing, but once you understand what's what, actually processing your files isn't hard. To get the lay of the land, take a look at Playback Menu 2, shown in Figure 10-17, and focus on the following three settings, all highlighted in the figure.

Raw processing choices

FIGURE 10-17:
The first two highlighted settings provide different ways to process Raw files; the third determines which of the two appears on the Quick Control screen.

>> **Raw Image Processing:** This option gives you the most advanced level of control of how your processed image appears. Don't worry; "advanced" doesn't mean complicated in this case. I step you through using this method of Raw processing in the next section.

>> **Creative Assist:** When you select this option, you're limited to the same simple image-adjustment tools available when you use Creative Assist in Scene Intelligent Auto mode, covered in Chapter 3. Actually, you get one less adjustment: Background Blur isn't available. In addition, you can't specify the Image Quality (resolution and quality) of your processed JPEG file as you can when you go Raw Image Processing route; Creative Assist saves every image using the Large/Fine setting.

» **Quick Control Raw Processing:** Okay, this is what I mean by "the way Canon presents the Raw conversion options is a little confusing." What does this menu option offer? Another way to process Raw images? Nope. This setting simply controls which of the two processing options is accessible via the the playback Quick Control screen. By default, the Quick Control screen offers the Creative Assist option; the left image in Figure 10-18 shows you where to look. If you prefer that the Quick Control screen offer the more advanced conversion option, open Playback Menu 2, choose Quick Control Raw Processing, and change the setting to Raw Image Processing. The right side of Figure 10-18 shows you the Quick Control icon representing Raw Image Processing. Note that you can always use either method by choosing it from the menu — you just can have only one or the other on the Quick Control screen. (In case you haven't figured it out, I vote for making the change to Raw Image Processing.)

Creative Assist Raw processing | Raw Image Processing icon

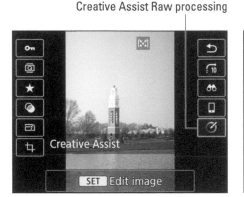

FIGURE 10-18: By default, the Creative Assist Raw processing option appears on the Quick Control screen (left), but you can change it to display the more advanced processing option (right).

The next two sections provide details on using both Raw processing tools. But you need to know a few preliminary factoids:

» **Whichever Raw processing tool you use, your original Raw image is left intact.** The JPEG copy is added as a separate file to the memory card. Because your Raw file is never harmed or deleted, you can create as many processed JPEG versions as you like. You might create a full-color version, for example, and a second, monochrome version.

» **If you shot the image with the Still Image Aspect Ratio set to anything other than 3:2, the processed JPEG version will use that selected aspect ratio.** When you display the Raw file, you see the entire 3:2 frame, but with lines indicating the frame area resulting from the aspect ratio you originally chose. As soon as you choose one of the Raw processing options, only the area inside those frame lines remains visible, and that's all that will appear in your converted JPEG file. If you decide you want to retain more of the original Raw file, do the conversion in Canon Digital Photo Professional 4 instead. In that program, you can choose any aspect ratio when converting the file. (After you open the image, display the editing panel marked with a crop tool; the aspect ratio option is housed on that panel.)

Back to in-camera processing: The next two sections explain how to use each of the in-camera Raw processing tools. I spend more time on the more advanced option because it's the one I recommend you use.

Using the Raw Image Processing tool

As just explained, this option provides the most control over the look of your converted Raw images. Here's how to access it:

>> **After setting the Quick Control Raw Processing option on Playback Menu 2 to RAW Image processing, put the camera in playback mode and press Q.** When the Quick Control screen appears, highlight the Raw Processing setting and then choose the third option at the bottom of the screen, which is named Customize RAW processing, as shown on the right in Figure 10-18. Press the Set button or tap the Set icon to move forward.

>> **Open Playback Menu 2 and choose RAW Image Processing.** On the next screen, choose Select Images. A playback screen appears, as shown on the left in Figure 10-19. Scroll to the image you want to process and press Set to place a checkmark in the box labeled "Selected for processing" in the figure. Then press the Q button or tap the OK symbol at the bottom of the screen. Don't press Set, which is probably your inclination — that toggles the selection box on and off.

After you press the Q button or tap OK, you're presented with a screen that looks like the one on the right in the figure, with three options: Use Shot Settings, Customize Raw Processing, and Cancel. Choose Door Number 2.

After you choose Customize Raw Processing, you see the screen shown in Figure 10-20, which is full of icons representing the image-adjustment options. I labeled these icons as well as a few other controls in the figure.

Use the Quick Control dial to highlight an adjustment — the name of the selected option appears at the top of the screen — and then press Set to display controls for tweaking that picture characteristic. Tap the return arrow in the upper-right corner of the screen to return to the main processing screen.

Selected for processing

Select to access all processing controls

FIGURE 10-19:
Press Set to select the image (left), press the Q button, and then choose Customize Raw Processing (right).

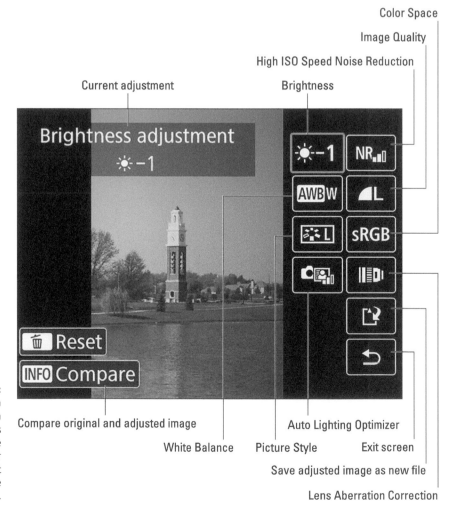

Color Space

Image Quality

High ISO Speed Noise Reduction

Brightness

Current adjustment

FIGURE 10-20:
Select an adjustment icon and then press Set to access the controls for tweaking that picture characteristic.

Compare original and adjusted image

White Balance

Picture Style

Auto Lighting Optimizer

Save adjusted image as new file

Exit screen

Lens Aberration Correction

Here's a quick guide to the adjustments you can make, with information on which earlier chapters in the book can provide more insight:

>> **Brightness:** Adjusts exposure of the entire image. Unfortunately, there's no way to brighten just the darkest parts or tone down the too-bright areas. Visit Chapter 4 for a look at exposure tools you can use to prevent exposure miscues on your next shot.

>> **White Balance:** Use this option to manipulate colors — again, all colors are affected. Chapter 6 explains white balance.

>> **Picture Style:** Also covered in Chapter 6, this feature affects color, saturation, sharpness, and contrast.

>> **Auto Lighting Optimizer:** This tool is designed to improve high-contrast images. You can read more about it in the section of Chapter 4 that deals with exposure correction tools.

>> **High ISO Speed NR (Noise Reduction):** Designed to soften the grainy appearance caused by image noise, this feature is detailed in Chapter 4.

>> **Image Quality:** Be sure to check the status of this option before you wrap up your file conversion. It's the option that sets the resolution (pixel count) and quality of your JPEG files. See Chapter 2 for help understanding this setting.

>> **Color Space:** Leave this one set to sRGB unless you have good reason to change to Adobe RGB — like, an art director insists on it or you're a pro at high-end color management. Be sure to read the information in Chapter 6 to understand why shifting to Adobe RGB can cause problems when you print or share your photo.

>> **Lens Aberration Correction:** Through this option, you can access five different tools designed to deal with defects created by some lenses. The fab five are Peripheral Illumination Correction (Chapter 4), Distortion Correction (Chapter 5), Digital Lens Optimizer (Chapter 5), Chromatic Aberration Correction (Chapter 6), and Diffraction Correction (Chapter 5).

As you work your way through the settings, use these tricks to decide if you've made things better or worse than they looked at the original shot settings:

>> **Compare the original with the adjusted image:** At any time, you can press the Info button or tap Info on the screen to display a before and after view of your photo. First, the camera displays the After image, as shown on the left in Figure 10-21. On the right side of the screen, symbols that appear orange indicate picture options you adjusted. To toggle to the Before view, rotate the Quick Control dial. This screen carries the label "Shot settings," as shown on the right in the figure. Tap Menu or press the Menu button to exit the comparison screen and return to the Raw processing screen.

Lens Aberration Corrections

FIGURE 10-21:
Tap Info or press
the Info button
and then rotate
the Quick Control
dial to toggle
between the
adjusted photo
(left) and the
original (right).

Look closely at the individual adjustment icons in Figure 10-21, and you'll see some symbols not visible on the original adjustment screen. These symbols represent the five different changes you can make by using the Lens Aberration Correction option (labeled in Figure 10-20). I highlighted them on the left side of Figure 10-21.

>> **Magnify your view:** For certain adjustments, zooming in on your image can help you decide how much or how little of an effect to apply. You can only magnify the view from the initial adjustment screen, however, so you have to set an adjustment level, return to that main screen, and then zoom in to see the results.

To magnify the display, press the Magnify button. While the display is zoomed, press the edges of the Quick Control dial to scroll the display so that you can look at other areas of the image.

You can cancel out of zoom view by pressing the Menu button or the Index/Reduce button.

>> **Reset everything to square one.** If you really mess up and want to try again using different adjustments, don't take the time to exit the Raw conversion tool and start over. Just press the Erase button or tap the Reset icon in the lower-left corner of the main conversion screen. (Refer to Figure 10-20.)

After making your way through all the Raw processing options, select the option labeled "Save adjusted image as new file" in Figure 10-20. On the confirmation screen that appears, choose OK. You're then asked whether you want to view the original image or the processed JPEG. To make your selection, tap it or highlight it and press the Set button. When you do view the processed image, it sports a symbol to let you know that it has been edited — the same symbol that appears when you apply any of the other editing tools discussed in this chapter. Figure 10-22 offers a reminder of how the symbol looks. To the right of that symbol, you see the symbol representing the JPEG Image Quality you selected when saving the file (Large/Fine, S2, and so on). Chapter 2 explains all the JPEG settings and shows you the symbol that represents each. In Figure 10-22, the symbol represents Large/Fine (choose that option to ensure the highest possible quality and resolution for your converted file).

If you've been stepping through these instructions with your camera in hand, you probably noticed that I skipped a couple of options along the way:

Edited symbol

Large/Fine Image Quality symbol

FIGURE 10-22:
These symbols indicate that you converted the file to a JPEG with the Large/Fine Image Quality setting.

>> **Select a Range of Images:** If you choose Raw Image Processing from Playback Menu 2 instead of selecting it from the Quick Control screen, the menu page where you choose Select Images has a second option that enables you to select a range of images for batch processing — that is, you can adjust and convert multiple photos at a time. If you have a series of images that all need the exact same adjustments, feel free to use the select range option (see the first part of this chapter if you need help selecting a range of thumbnails). But more often than not, each image will need slightly different processing.

>> **Use Shot Settings:** Whether you choose Raw Image Processing from the menu or from the Quick Control screen, you are given the option to simply convert the Raw file to a JPEG file without making any adjustments. The option is called Use Shot Settings. It may come in handy if you just need to ship a JPEG off to someone and the picture looks pretty good as is. It's the middle icon at the bottom of the Quick Control screen (refer to the right screen in Figure 10-18) and the top option on the right menu screen in Figure 10-19.

Processing Raw images using Creative Assist

I don't want to spend much page space on this Raw-conversion option because the level of control it gives you over image colors, exposure, and other characteristics is minimal. But because Canon has set this as the default Quick Control Raw processing tool, I want to at least provide a quick once-over.

When you press the Q button to display the Quick Control screen in playback mode, the Creative Assist symbol appears in full color only if you're viewing a Raw file. (Again, this assumes that you haven't yet swapped out Creative Assist with the Raw Image Processing tool, as discussed in the section "Understanding the basic approach," earlier in this chapter.) Otherwise, the icon is dimmed because you can't use it to alter JPEG images.

After selecting the icon, as shown on the left in Figure 10-23, tap Set or press the Set button. On the next screen, shown on the right in the figure, you see a strip of icons along the bottom of the screen. Choosing the first icon enables you to access various preset effects; the other icons represent tools that apply individual changes to color, brightness, and so on. These are the same effects you can apply when shooting in the Scene Intelligent Auto mode, covered in Chapter 2. Only one option is missing: Background Blur. The Background Blur effect relies on the f-stop setting you use when shooting the photo, so you can't manipulate that result after the fact.

Creative Assist raw processing

Tap to save converted image

FIGURE 10-23:
The Creative Assist raw-processing tool offers most of the same simple adjustments you can choose when shooting in Scene Intelligent Auto mode.

After highlighting an effect icon, as shown on the right in Figure 10-23, press the Set button to display a screen where you can select the strength of the effect or, in the case of the Monochrome option, decide whether you want a black-and-white monochrome image or one that has a tint, such as sepia. Play with the settings until you're satisfied with the result and then press Set to exit the settings screen and redisplay the strip of icons.

After you make your first adjustment, a Reset option appears on the screen; you can tap that symbol or press the Index/Reduce button to reset all options to their default settings. (The Reset option doesn't appear in Figure 10-23 because no adjustments have been made yet; see Figure 10-1 if you need help locating it.)

DOWNLOADING THE FREE CANON SOFTWARE

Your camera purchase entitles you to free copies of a couple of Canon photo programs, which you can download from the Canon website. Point your browser to www.usa. canon.com if you live in the United States; to access the global version of the site, visit www.canon.com.

The most helpful tool is Canon Digital Photo Professional 4, which is a full-featured image browser and editor. You can also use it to process Raw images, an option that provides you with a much greater degree of control over the process and enables you to save in a non-destructive file format, such as TIFF, instead of JPEG, which can lower image quality.

Some of the other free offerings include:

- **Canon EOS Utility:** This software enables you to transfer pictures from the camera to your computer via a USB cable or through a Wi-Fi connection. When the camera is connected to the computer, you can also operate the camera remotely through the software. Keep in mind that you also can use your smartphone or tablet for that purpose (although the software is more full-featured in the camera options you can control). Digital Photo Professional 4 also offers remote camera operation if you connect via a USB cable. (Professionals refer to operating your camera from the computer as *tethered shooting.*)

- **EOS Lens Registration Tool:** for adding lens data used by the camera's various lens-correction filters, such as Lens Aberration Correction. (You don't need to take this step unless the camera says it doesn't have any such data for your lens.)

Both of these programs require that your camera be connected to the computer. Digital Photo Professional 4 is a standalone program that works with or without input from the camera.

Canon also makes available Canon Camera Connect, an app that enables you to connect your camera to an Android or iOS smart device to view photos, upload images to the web, and use your device as a wireless remote control. Check the appendix of this book for information about the app and other wireless features.

 To convert and save your file, press the Magnify button or tap the Save symbol, located in the upper-right corner of the screen and labeled in Figure 10-23. This symbol appears from the moment you first display the screen in case all you want to do is create a JPEG copy of your Raw file without making any of the Creative Assist adjustments. After you choose Save, you're asked for the go-ahead to save the processed image as a new file; choose OK to move forward. The camera displays the filename of the converted image and tells you that it's going to redisplay the original next. Tap OK or press Set.

TIP All images that you convert using the Creative Assist option are saved using the Large/Fine Image Quality setting. If you need to reduce the file size, see the last section of this chapter for an in-camera tool that can do that for you.

Sending Pictures to the Computer

When you're ready to download photos and movies to your computer, you have a couple of options:

>> **Connect the camera to your computer via a USB cable or Wi-Fi.** For a USB connection, you need to buy the necessary cable: Canon Interface Cable IFC-600PCU (about $12 from the Canon website).

>> **Use a memory-card reader.** A memory-card reader is a device that enables your computer to access the files on your card. Many computers have card readers built in, but you can also buy USB-enabled card readers for about $20. The only requirement is that the reader be compatible with the type of cards you use in your camera (SD, SDHC, or SDXC). Figure 10-24 shows a card reader that can handle different types of cards so that you also can use it to transfer data from devices that don't use SD cards (such as some game consoles).

FIGURE 10-24: The most convenient way to transfer picture and movie files to a computer is to use a card reader.

Because my job is to guide you in the best direction, I recommend that you ignore the camera-to-computer options, which just aren't as efficient or trouble-free as using a card reader. When you connect the camera via USB cable — which used to ship with the camera but doesn't any more — or via Wi-Fi, you run down the camera battery because the camera has to be turned on the whole time. And if the battery dies during the transfer, your image and movie files can be corrupted. Transferring via a card reader, on the other hand, is fast, simple, and requires no camera battery power.

That said, I recognize that you may at times need to transfer files when you don't have a card reader close at hand, so the appendix explains how to get that done over Wi-Fi. You use the same software, EOS Utility, for Wi-Fi transfers and USB connections, so you can easily adapt the steps in the appendix to USB transfer if you opt to go that route.

But let's return to the easiest and fastest way to transfer files, shall we? The following steps show you how to view and transfer photo and movie files from a card reader. You can use this method with any photo software or even with the Mac Finder or Windows File Explorer, but I'll show you how it works using Canon Digital Photo Professional 4 so that you can get a look at that program and decide whether you're interested in downloading it. I think it's worth your time, unless you're already married to another option, such as Adobe Lightroom. It *is* free, after all. Also, some other photo editors may not be able to work with Raw files from your camera, especially if you use the new cRaw format.

Back to the job at hand, here's the download process:

1. **Open Digital Photo Professional 4, shown in Figure 10-25.**

   Your program window may not look exactly like the one you see in the figure; you can customize the window by using options on the View and Window menu. If you don't see the folder list, open the View menu, select Open/Close Pane, and then select Left. To change the thumbnails display, choose one of the Thumbnails options from the View menu.

2. **Look for the memory card name in the folder list.**

   The memory card shows up as a drive in the folder list, bearing the name EOS_Digital, as shown in the figure. To get to the files it holds, open the DCIM folder (Digital Camera Images) and then open the image folder, named 100Canon by default. Thumbnails of the images in the folder then appear in the main window, as shown in the figure.

FIGURE 10-25:
You can use
Canon Digital
Photo Profes-
sional 4 to drag
and drop files
from your
memory card to a
folder on your
computer.

Memory card   Image folder

3. **Select the files you want to copy.**

To choose a single file, just click its thumbnail. To select multiple files, click one
and then hold down the Ctrl key (Windows) or the Cmd key (Mac) as you click
each subsequent file. To select all files on the card, press Ctrl+A on Windows or
Cmd+A on a Mac.

4. **Use your mouse to drag the selected files to the folder where you want to**
store them on your computer.

In Figure 10-25, the red arrow illustrates this process; the destination folder in
this example is the Pictures folder. Note that you won't see a red arrow on your
screen, but you should see a tiny thumbnail graphic along with a plus sign near
your cursor as you drag the files. The plus sign indicates that you're copying
files to the computer, not moving them from the card. This is the safe way to
go because if anything goes awry during the process, your originals remain
intact on the memory card.

5. **After all files have been copied, choose the USB-device eject command on**
your computer.

Once upon a time, you could just remove your memory card from the reader
when you finished downloading. Now, computers want to know that's about to
happen so that they can, um, I don't know, look for another way to mess up
your life? At any rate, on a Windows 10 machine, there's usually a pop-up
symbol representing USB devices at the far-right edge of the taskbar (that strip

of icons at the bottom of the screen). The one you want has the name Safely Remove Hardware Devices and Eject Media. On a Mac, one method is to right-click on the desktop icon that represents the memory card and then choose Eject from the pop-up menu. (The specifics for this step vary depending on which version of your computer's operating system is in use, so please consult the computer's Help system or use the Google Machine to verify the exact procedure.)

After taking the step to digitally eject the card, you can safely remove the card return it to the camera.

Two more bits of business about image (and movie) downloading:

>> Don't like the drag-and-drop method of copying files? After you make your selections in Step 3, click the Save button at the top of the Digital Photo Professional 4 window. You're presented with a window where you can specify where you want to copy the photos. You also can convert Raw files and resize images from inside the Save window.

>> Before erasing files from the card, first verify that your pictures made it to the computer. If the card doesn't contain any data that you need to keep, format the card using the command on the camera's Setup Menu 1. Formatting erases all files, even those you've protected, and makes sure your card is properly prepared for your next round of shooting. When you don't want to wipe the entire card, use the Erase tools covered at the beginning of the chapter instead.

TIP

>> After clicking on a thumbnail in Digital Photo Professional 4, you can display the image *metadata,* or hidden data that stores the settings you used to take the picture. Open the View menu and then choose Info to display the metadata. Many photo programs enable you to view metadata, but not all can display all the Canon-specific settings. Figure 10-26 gives you a glimpse of a sample metadata screen. Chapter 9 shows you how to view a limited set of metadata during playback.

FIGURE 10-26: You can learn a lot about what went wrong or right with a picture by studying its *metadata* (a text file containing the settings you used to shoot it).

Preparing Pictures for Online Sharing

Have you ever received an email message containing a photo so large that you can't view the whole thing on your monitor without scrolling the email window? This annoyance occurs because monitors can display only a limited number of pixels. The exact number depends on the screen resolution setting, but suffice it to say that most of today's digital cameras produce photos with pixel counts in excess of what the monitor can handle.

Thankfully, the newest email programs incorporate features that automatically shrink the photo display to a viewable size. But that doesn't change the fact that a large photo file means longer downloading times and, if recipients hold onto the picture, a big storage hit on their hard drives.

Sending a high-resolution photo *is* the thing to do if you want the recipient to be able to generate a good print. But for simple onscreen viewing, a good practice is to limit the image size to about 1,000 pixels on the longest side. That ensures that people who use an email program that doesn't offer the latest photo-viewing tools can see the entire picture without scrolling the viewer window.

REMEMBER

Because you need lots of pixels if you want to produce decent prints — and adding pixels after the fact lowers image quality — always shoot your originals at a resolution appropriate for print. You can then create a low-res copy of the picture for email sharing or for other online uses, such as posting to Facebook. (Posting only low-res photos to Facebook and online photo-sharing sites also helps dissuade would-be photo thieves looking for free images for use in their company's brochures and other print materials.)

In addition to resizing high-resolution images, also check their file types; if the photos are in the Raw or cRaw format, you need to create a JPEG copy for online use. Web browsers and email programs can't display Raw or cRaw files.

By using your camera's Raw Image Processing tool, covered earlier in this chapter, you can convert a Raw file to a JPEG and shrink its resolution in one step. Just choose S2 as the Image Quality option when you do the conversion. For JPEG images, you can create an S2-sized copy of your original by using the Resize tool. Like other post-capture tools, this one is available through the playback version of the Quick Control screen, shown on the left in Figure 10-27, or Playback Menu 2.

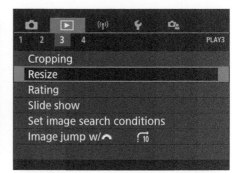

FIGURE 10-27: You can create low-resolution copies of JPEG images using the camera's Resize tool.

Whichever way you go, you're presented only with size options that result in a smaller file than the original. After you choose a setting, tap the Set icon or press the Set button. On the confirmation screen that appears, choose OK. During playback, you can distinguish the resized copy by looking in the lower-right corner of the screen. For the copy, you see the symbol labeled "Edited file" in Figure 10-28, while the neighboring value displays the Image Quality of the copy (S2, in the figure).

Keep in mind that even at the S2 setting, you're creating a pretty large file in terms on online use — a resolution of 2400 x 1600 pixels, with a file size of about 1.8MB. if you have a smartphone or tablet compatible with the Canon app covered in the appendix, you may want to use the app to resize JPEG photos and send them online. The app enables you to create lower-resolution copies than the in-camera Resize tool.

Edited file symbol

Image Quality setting

FIGURE 10-28: These marks indicate an edited photo and the Image Quality setting.

The Part of Tens

IN THIS PART . . .

Customize your camera by changing the functions of some buttons.

Create a personalized menu containing your favorite options.

Tag your files with copyright information.

Use Creative Filters for fun special effects.

Create slide shows, record video snapshots, and trim frames from the beginning and end of a movie.

Connect your camera to an HDTV for big-screen playback.

Chapter **11**

Ten More Customization Options

E arlier chapters discuss major ways to customize your camera, such as chang-ing the data displayed during picture playback and adjusting autofocusing performance. This chapter details ten customization options that aren't as critical but may come in handy on occasion. Because I'm am ordered by the High Council on Dummies Books to keep Part of Tens chapters short, I'm limited in most cases to giving you just a quick introduction to these features. Should you want more details, download the electronic copy of the camera instruction manual from the Canon support site.

Giving the Set Button an Extra Job

Normally, the main role of the Set button is to select items from the camera menus and Quick Control screens. When you shoot in the P, Tv, Av, and M exposure modes, though, you can use the button to perform one of several additional tasks.

To take advantage of this feature, display Setup Menu 5 and choose Custom Functions. Next, scroll to Custom Function 13, Custom Controls, as shown on the right in Figure 11-1.

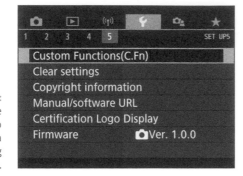
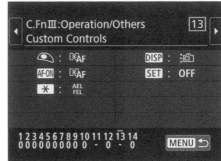

FIGURE 11-1: You can configure the Set button to perform an extra function during shooting.

Through this screen, you can customize five buttons, and I discuss buttons other than the Set button later in the chapter. For now, focus on the Set button. To move forward with assigning it a new function, press the button or tap any of the button icons in the middle of the screen. You then access the button-assignment command module, shown on the left in Figure 11-2. Tap the Set icon or move the yellow frame over it, as shown in the figure, and then press the Set button. Now you see the screen shown on the right in the figure. The icons displayed represent the tasks you can assign to the Set button. For me, the most useful function is highlighted in the figure. If you select this option, you can adjust the Exposure Compensation amount when shooting by holding down the Set button and rotating the Main dial. (Exposure Compensation is a great exposure-adjustment tool you can explore in Chapter 4.) Notice the label at the top of the screen in the figure — it explains what function the icon enables the Set button to accomplish.

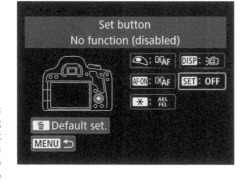
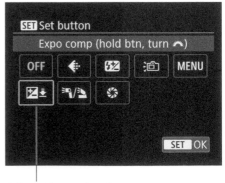

FIGURE 11-2: After choosing Set (left), select which function you want to assign to the button (right).

Selected button function

To finish, tap OK or press the Set button. Then press Menu or tap the Menu icon a couple of times to return to Setup Menu 5. Press the Menu button again to return to shooting. To reset the button to its original role, revisit the right screen in Figure 11-2 and change the setting back to Off.

TIP

When you reconfigure most buttons on the camera, they cease to perform as indicated elsewhere in this book (and in the camera instruction manual). For the Set button, however, that's not true. It can actually do dual duty. After you assign it a function, it still does its normal job of selecting the currently highlighted menu item and Quick Control option.

Customizing Four Other Buttons

Follow the same menu path shown in Figure 11-1, and you can customize four buttons in addition to the Set button: The shutter button, the AF-ON button, the AE Lock/FE Lock button, and the DISP button.

When you get to the screen where you select the button you want to customize, there's a graphic that highlights the location of the button currently selected for customization. In Figure 11-3, for example, I selected the shutter button (and no, I don't understand how that symbol in any way looks like the shutter button, which is why it's good you get both the location graphic and a label that identifies the selected button). The label also indicates the current function of the button.

FIGURE 11-3:
After you highlight an icon, the graphic tells you where the button is located on the camera.

The process of setting a new function for a button is the same as just described for the Set button. There are different functions available for different buttons, and as you highlight each option, the camera indicates what the button will do if you assign it that function.

If you customize buttons, you can return to the screen shown on the right in Figure 11-1 for a reminder of which task you assigned to each button. To restore all the buttons to their default assignments, visit the screen shown on the left in Figure 11-2 and tap the Default Set. symbol or press the Erase button. (To get to the screen, open Setup Menu 5, choose Custom Functions, choose Custom

Function 13, and press the Set button.) *Note:* Your custom button assignments are *not* reset when you choose the Clear All Custom Func. option, which you select by opening Setup Menu 5 and choosing Clear Settings. You have to dig into the customization screen shown on the left in Figure 11-2 to restore the button defaults.

Disabling the AF-Assist Beam

In dim lighting, your camera may emit an AF (autofocus) assist beam from the built-in flash when you press the shutter button halfway — assuming that the flash unit is open, of course. This pulse of light helps the camera "see" its target better, improving autofocus performance.

In situations where the beam may be distracting, you can disable it — but again, only when using the P, Tv, Av, and M exposure modes. Make the change via the AF-assist Beam Firing option on Shooting Menu 5. Along with the basic Enable and Disable settings, you get two options related to using an external flash. Choosing the Enable External Flash Only option permits an external flash to emit the beam but prevents the built-in flash from doing so. The other setting, IR AF Assist Beam Only, allows an external flash that has infrared (IR) AF-assist to use only the IR beam, which is less noticeable than the regular light.

REMEMBER

These and other external flash options work only with certain flash units; your camera manual provides specifics on compatible models.

Creating a Custom Menu

Through the My Menu feature, you can create a custom menu containing up to five tabs, each of which can hold six menu items. The idea is to enable you to group your favorite menu options together in a way that makes more sense to you than the standard menu organization. In Figure 11-4, for example, the first tab contains six shooting options that appear on separate tabs in the normal menu configuration.

Having this kind of control may appeal after you're fully aware of how all your

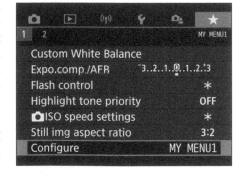

FIGURE 11-4:
The My Menu feature lets you create a custom menu.

camera settings work and which features you use the most. But when you're just beginning, stick with the standard menu structure so that what you see on your camera matches the instructions found in this book and other resources.

Two other issues to note about the My Menu feature: First, you can access it in the P, Tv, Av, and M exposure modes only. In any other exposure mode, your custom menu doesn't appear, which means that you have to learn two menu layouts instead of just one. The other thing required before the My Menu feature appears is that you switch from the default guided menus/displays to the standard versions, which you do via the Display Level menu. (Chapter 1 has information on that process.)

To create a custom menu, display the My Menu tab, which is marked with a white star on a green background. At first, the only option available is Configure. Select that option to display options that enable you to add items to the first tab of your menu, to sort the items you add, to delete individual items, to delete an entire tab, or to give a tab a name.

After you add six items to fill up My Menu 1, the Configure option appears at the bottom of the screen, as shown in Figure 11-4. In fact, it appears on every tab you create so that you can always add tabs, rearrange items, and perform other menu-maintenance tasks.

Adding Custom Folders

Normally, your camera automatically creates folders to store your images. The first folder has the name 100Canon; the second, 101Canon; and so on. Each folder can hold 9,999 photos. However, you can create a new folder before the existing one is full at any time. You might take this organizational step so that you can segregate work photos from personal photos, for example. To create the folder, open Setup Menu 1 and choose Select Folder, as shown on the left in Figure 11-5. On the next screen, choose Create Folder, as shown on the right.

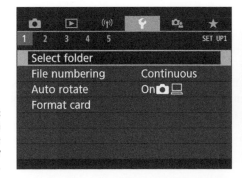
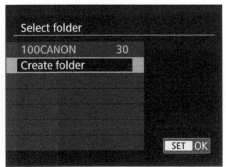

FIGURE 11-5: You can create a new storage folder at any time.

The camera asks for permission to create the folder. To move forward, choose OK and press Set. The folder is automatically assigned the next available folder number and is selected as the active folder — the one that will hold any new photos or movies you shoot. Press the Set button or tap the Set icon to return to Setup Menu 1.

To make a different folder the active folder, choose Select Folder again, choose the folder you want to use, and press or tap Set. When you choose a folder that contains photos or movies, the camera displays thumbnails of the first and last files in the folder on the right side of the screen, along with a total count of all the files in the folder.

If you create custom folders, several playback features enable you to limit operations to a specific folder. For example, you can choose to delete all files from a specific folder. ("Oops, honey, you know that folder you created to hold your 900 pictures of the custom wheel rims on your car? I'm sooooo sorry, but I accidentally deleted it because the memory card was full and I needed to take a bunch of photos of my orchid house for garden club.")

Turning Off the Shooting Settings Screen

When you turn on your camera, the monitor automatically displays the screen that shows shooting settings for normal, through-the-viewfinder photography. If you prefer not to see the display upon startup, set the Mode dial to P, Tv, Av, or M, select Custom Functions from Setup Menu 5, and bring up Custom Function 12, Screen Display When Power On. Change the setting from the default, Display On, to Previous Display Status.

WARNING

The setting name reflects the fact that the camera remembers the current display status when you turn the camera off. Then it returns to that previous status the next time you turn the camera on. So if you don't want the display to appear on startup, press the DISP button to shut off the display before powering down the camera.

Although disabling the automatic display saves battery power, having to remember to turn the display off each time you shut down the camera is a pain. So I stick with the default setting and then press the DISP button to toggle the screen on and off if the battery is running low. Also note that if the camera is set to any of the Basic Zone modes when you turn on the camera, the display appears regardless of the setting you choose for the Custom Function.

Embedding Copyright Notices

If you sell your photography or have other reasons why people need to know that you are the photographer of an image, this customization feature is definitely worth enabling. You can embed a copyright notice into the *metadata* — hidden text data — that's included in every photo or movie you capture. Anyone who views your picture in a program that can display metadata can see your copyright notice. (Chapter 10 explains how to view metadata in Canon Digital Photo Professional 4.)

REMEMBER

You can enter copyright data only when the camera is set to P, Tv, Av, or M exposure mode, but the information you enter is added to all new files you create, regardless of which exposure mode you used to capture them.

Follow these steps to create your copyright notice:

1. **Open Setup Menu 5 and choose Copyright Information, as shown on the left in Figure 11-6.**

   You see the screen shown on the right in Figure 11-6.

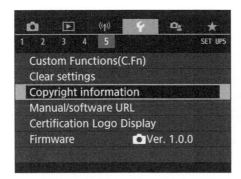

FIGURE 11-6: Enter your name and other copyright information that you want tagged to your images.

2. **Choose Enter Author's Name to display the digital keyboard shown in Figure 11-7.**

3. **Enter your name.**

   The easiest option is to use the touchscreen: Just tap the letters you want to enter; the characters you select appear in the text box above the keyboard. Tap the symbol labeled "Cycle through keyboards" in the figure to shift the keyboard display from letters to numbers and symbols and then to numbers and different symbols.

To move the cursor in the text box (I labeled in cursor in Figure 11-7), tap inside the box or tap the arrows at the end of the text box. To erase the character to the left of the cursor, tap the icon labeled "Delete character" in the figure.

If you prefer button pushing to touchscreen tapping, use the Quick Control dial to highlight a key and then press the Set button. You can rotate the dial to move quickly through the keyboard or press the top/bottom/left/right edges to move character by character.

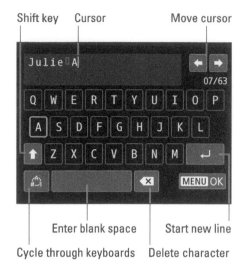

FIGURE 11-7:
Enter the text you want to include in your copyright notice.

4. **When you finish entering your name, tap Menu or press the Menu button. Then choose OK and press Set.**

   The camera redisplays the Copyright Information screen (right screen in Figure 11-6).

5. **Choose Enter Copyright Details to return to the keyboard and add any additional data you think necessary.**

   You might want to add the year or your email address, for example. (You don't need to enter the word *Copyright* — it's added automatically.)

6. **Tap the Menu icon or press the Menu button to exit the text entry screen.**

7. **On the confirmation screen, choose OK.**

   You're again returned to the Copyright Information screen. If you want to check your work, choose Display Copyright Info (it becomes available after you enter copyright text).

8. **Tap Menu or press the Menu button again to return to Setup Menu 5.**

9. **Press the Menu button one more time to exit the menu system.**

Disable copyright tagging by returning to Setup Menu 5, choosing Copyright Information, and then selecting Delete Copyright Information from the next screen that appears. (The option is unavailable, as in Figure 11-6, until you add copyright data.)

Adding Cleaning Instructions to Images

If small spots appear consistently on your images — and you know that dirt on your lens isn't the cause — your sensor may need cleaning. The Dust Delete Data feature, designed for use with Canon Digital Photo Professional 4, provides a stop-gap measure until you can take the camera to a service shop for sensor cleaning.

You start by recording a data file that maps the location of the dust spots on the sensor. To do this, you need a white piece of paper and a lens that offers a focal length of 50mm or longer. Put the camera in the P, Tv, Av, or M exposure mode, set the lens to manual focusing, and then set the focus distance at infinity. (If you're holding the camera in the horizontal position, turn the lens focusing ring counter-clockwise until it stops.) Next, open Shooting Menu 4, choose Dust Delete Data, and then select OK.

Position the paper 8 to 12 inches from the camera, make sure that the paper fills the viewfinder, and then press the shutter button all the way. No picture is taken; the camera just records the Dust Delete Data in its internal memory. When you see the message "Data obtained," choose OK. The current date appears on the initial Dust Delete Data screen.

After you create your Dust Delete Data file, the camera attaches the data to every image you shoot. To clean a photo in Digital Photo Professional 4, select the image thumbnail, open the Adjustment menu, and then click Apply Dust Delete Data. The program's instruction manual, available for download from the Canon website, offers additional details.

Stopping a Retractable Lens from Closing

If your lens is one that retracts — collapses from front to back to create a smaller footprint when you're not using the camera — you can decide whether you want the lens to retract automatically every time you turn the camera off. That's the default setting, and it makes sense unless you're in a situation where you're powering the camera on and off every few minutes, as you might do when preserving every ounce of battery power is critical. In that scenario, having to wait for the lens to retract and then reopen every time you power the camera down and back up again is annoying and, with some lenses, a little noisy. To prevent the auto retracting, open Setup Menu 5, choose Custom Functions, and navigate to Custom Function 14, Retract Lens on Power Off. Then change the setting from Enable to Disable.

A couple of fine points related to this issue: Even when you leave the setting at Enable, the lens doesn't retract when the you reach the delay time selected for the Auto Power Off setting on Setup Menu 2. (That's the setting that automatically puts the camera to sleep after a period of inactivity.) Also, never try to detach the lens when it's not retracted. If you set the Retract Lens on Power Off setting to Disable, check the lens manual to find out how to retract the lens. (Most retractable lenses have their own switch to perform this function.)

Swapping the AF Point Selection and AE Lock Button Functions

See the two buttons highlighted in Figure 11-8? Normally, the top one is used to choose an autofocus point during shooting and to magnify photos during playback. The other button — often referred to as the asterisk button, for obvious reasons — has two functions during shooting and two during playback. During shooting, you press the button to lock the current autoexposure settings, preventing any further adjustment to those settings before you take the picture. (Chapter 5 has details on this feature, called AE Lock.) When you're using flash, you use the asterisk button for FE Lock (flash exposure lock), which sets a custom flash power based on the object at the center of the frame (Chapter 2 details that one). When viewing your images, the button changes the playback from single-image view to thumbnails view and, when an image is magnified, reduces the magnification level. The official name of this button is the AE Lock/FE Lock/Reduce/Index button.

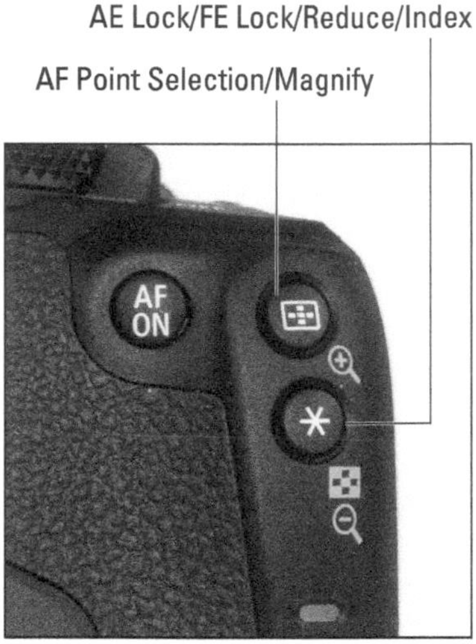

FIGURE 11-8:
You can swap the functions of these two buttons, but I advise against it.

Through the Setup Menu 4 option selected in Figure 11-9, you can swap the functions of these two buttons. What's the benefit, you ask? Well, if you use the AE Lock and FE Lock features a lot, it's easier to locate the top button and press it with your thumb than it is to find and press the lower button, which is the one that does the job by default.

Although I like that Canon provides this option, I also wish they supplied little stickers to cover the buttons with the markings that reflect their new functions after you make this change. I know it would take me some time to remember that I had changed them, but then again, it takes me some time to remember my address these days. Maybe if you're handy with nail polish or model-car paint, you could do your own relabeling? At any rate, if you swap the button functions, remember that you did so when you read instructions I give in earlier chapters related to the two buttons. Otherwise, things aren't going to work the way the instructions indicate they should. Ditto for instructions you may read in the camera's instruction manual.

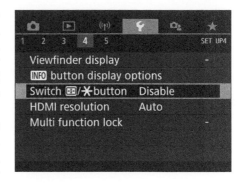

FIGURE 11-9:
You can swap the functions of these two buttons through this Setup Menu 4 option.

As an alternative, consider assigning the AE Lock and FE Lock functions to the AF ON button, if you don't use that button for its intended purpose often. (By default, pressing the button does the same thing as a half-press of the shutter button: initiating autoexposure and autofocus.) See the section "Customizing Four Other Buttons," earlier in this chapter, for the how-tos. I think that this option is the better one if you find the position of the asterisk button inconvenient — the AF ON button is within easy reach of your thumb, and the other two buttons then are left to do the jobs they were originally assigned. The good news is that you have two ways to make using AE Lock and FE Lock more convenient; pick the one that makes the most sense to you.

IN THIS CHAPTER

» Shooting time-lapse movies and video snapshots

» Capturing long exposures using mirror lockup

» Investigating printing features and special-effects filters

» Doing some minor movie editing

» Setting up slide shows

» Viewing photos and movies on a TV

Chapter **12**

Ten Features to Explore on a Rainy Day

Consider this chapter the literary equivalent of the end of one of those late-night infomercial offers — the part where the host exclaims, "But wait! There's more!" Options covered here aren't the sort of features that drive people to choose one camera over another, and they may come in handy only for certain users, on certain occasions. Still, they're included at no extra charge with your camera, so check 'em out when you have a spare moment. Who knows; you may discover just the solution you need for one of your photography problems.

Because Part of Tens chapters are meant to offer bite-sized nuggets of information, this chapter doesn't provide full-length explanations of every feature. For more details, consult the camera manual, which you can download from the Canon website.

Shooting a Time-Lapse Movie

After you put the camera in Movie mode, you can access the *time-lapse movie* feature, which records single frames at periodic intervals and then stitches the frames into a movie. The idea is to wind up with a movie that shows a subject changing or moving at a much faster rate than it actually did. Think of a night-blooming flower that appears to open and then close in a few seconds, when in real life, the process occurs over hours. Or you might train the camera lens on the night sky to create a video that makes it appear that it took but minutes for the stars and moon to make their dusk-til-dawn journey across the heavens.

To use this feature, take these steps:

1. **Set the mode dial to Scene Intelligent Auto, P, Tv, Av, or M.**

   Scene Intelligent Auto is the easiest to use if you're not schooled in choosing exposure settings for movies.

2. **Put the camera into Movie mode by moving the on/off switch all the way forward, to the position marked by the movie camera symbol.**

3. **Open Shooting Menu 2 and choose Time-Lapse Movie.**

4. **On the next screen, select Time-Lapse to get to the initial movie setup screen.**

   You can choose from three preset recording options, Scene 1, 2, or 3. As you select each one, the menu displays the type of subject the preset is designed to record. For more control, though, pass these by and move on to Step 5.

5. **Scroll down through the setup options and choose Custom.**

   Now you can control all the settings discussed in Step 6.

6. **On the next screen, choose the time-lapse recording options.**

   Make your way through the following settings:

   - **Interval/Shots:** The Interval option sets the delay between shots; the second option determines how many frames are captured. You can set the interval delay as high as 60 minutes; for the number of shots, you can enter a value as high as 3600. As you change the values, refer to the numbers at the bottom of the screen. On the left, the number next to the movie-camera symbol tells you how long it will take the camera to record all the frames. On the right side of the screen, the number next to the playback symbol indicates the length of the resulting movie.

- **Movie Recording Size:** You get two frame size choices: 4K (3840 x 2160 pixels) or FHD (1920 x 1080 pixels). Either way, the frame rate is 29.97 fps. (Chapter 8 explains these settings and the impact on the look of your movie and the size of the movie file.) Movies are recorded in the MP4 format and use a type of compression called ALL-I. (Yeah, that's different than the compression used for regular movie recording, but don't worry about it; you can't change it anyway.)

- **Auto Exposure:** Choose Fixed First Frame to record all frames using the exposure settings the camera selects for the first frames. Choose Each Frame if you want the camera to reset exposure before each shot. The second option will work best if the lighting on your subject will change over the course of the shot recording and you want the subject to appear well lit throughout. But if your goal is to show *how* the light changes, such as when doing a time-lapse recording of a sunrise or sunset, then set this option to Fixed First Frame.

- **Screen Auto Off:** At the default setting, Disable, the live preview remains on during the first 30 minutes of shooting and then turns off. To save battery power, consider changing the setting to Enable, which turns the monitor off about 10 seconds after the first frame is recorded. Either way, you can press the Info button to turn the monitor on or off during shooting.

- **Beep as Image Taken:** When set to Enable, which is the default, the camera beeps after each frame is captured, which is a good way to annoy everyone within earshot. Change the setting to Disable to silence the beep.

7. **Exit the setup screen by pressing the menu button or tapping Menu on the screen.**

8. **Press the Menu button to exit the menu system.**

9. **Frame your shot and press the shutter button halfway to initiate autofocusing and exposure metering.**

   Make sure that focus is accurate — the camera won't adjust focus between frames.

10. **To begin capturing frames, press the Live View button.**

    Recording stops automatically after all frames are captured. The camera than creates the movie. See the end of Chapter 8 for movie-playback tips.

Enabling Mirror Lockup

One component in the optical system of a dSLR camera is a mirror that moves when you press the shutter button. The vibration caused by the mirror movement can result in image blur when you use a very slow shutter speed, shoot with a long telephoto lens, or take extreme close-ups. To eliminate this possibility, your camera offers *mirror lockup,* which delays the shutter release a little longer than normal so that the picture isn't recorded until after the mirror movement is completed. Of course, you should also mount the camera on a tripod so that camera shake caused by handholding the camera doesn't create blur.

You can take advantage of mirror-lockup shooting only in P, Tv, Av, or M exposure mode. Enable it through Custom Function 10, shown in Figure 12-1.

REMEMBER

Mirror-lockup shooting requires a special picture-taking process: First, set focus by pressing the shutter button halfway or by pressing the AF ON button (if autofocusing) or by rotating the lens focus ring (if focusing manually). Then press the shutter button all the way down to lock up the mirror. Release the button and press it all the way down again to take the picture.

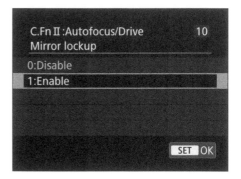

FIGURE 12-1:
Mirror lockup eliminates the chance that mirror movement blurs the photo.

Note that the camera will always capture a single frame even if the Drive mode is set to one of the continuous (burst mode) or continuous self-timer settings. You can, however, delay the shutter release by using the 2-second and 10-second Self-Timer modes. Also, be sure to completely select all shooting settings before locking up the mirror, as menus and other shooting functions are disabled after you do so. Return the Mirror Lockup feature to Disable when you're done using it.

Exploring a Few Obscure Printing Options

Your camera offers a feature called *DPOF (dee-poff),* which stands for Digital Print Order Format. If your printer also supports this technology, you can select and print pictures stored on your memory card without having to first download the images to your computer. Choose Print Order from Playback Menu 1, as shown in

Figure 12-2, to select the images you want to print and to specify how many copies you want. You can also choose to output an index print, which contains thumbnails of all selected images. The only rule is that you're limited to printing photos shot in the JPEG format; no Raw or cRaw files allowed.

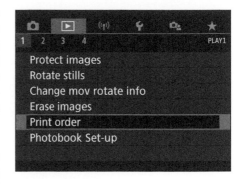

After setting up the print job, you can get the images to the printer in two ways. If your printer has an SD card slot, you just take the memory card out of the camera and put it in that card slot. The printer checks your "print order" and outputs the requested prints. If your printer doesn't have a

FIGURE 12-2:
If your printer has an SD card reader, use this feature to select images for printing; when you put the card in the printer, it outputs your "order."

card slot but has a USB port for connecting external devices, you can instead connect the camera directly to the printer. The USB cable you need is Canon part IFC-600PCU, which is about $12.

A couple of other print-related features that may be of interest:

>> **Wireless printing through PictBridge:** Printers that offer wireless capabilities and a second print technology called PictBridge give you another way to print without having to download photos to your computer: You just send images from the camera to the printer via Wi-Fi. See the appendix to find out how to start using your camera's wireless functions.

>> **Photobook Set-up (Playback Menu 1):** If you enjoy creating and printing photobooks through sites such as Shutterfly or Blurb, this menu option is designed to make it easy for you to separate the images you want to put in a book from the rest of the files on your memory card. After you choose the menu option, you can tag individual files just as you do when selecting them for deleting, protecting, and rating, as discussed in Chapter 9.

Sounds good, right? But it's the after-selection process that leads me to think that you're probably not going to find this feature too useful. First, the end result of all that file selecting is that when you download the images to your computer, the tagged files are put in a folder separate from other photos you may be downloading. Second, and more problematic, is that this feature only works when you connect the camera to your computer via a USB cable (the same one previously mentioned) and use the Canon EOS Utility software to download the photos.

TIP

All in all, that seems like a lot of work just to organize your best photos into separate folders. My alternative suggestion: Use the rating feature discussed in Chapter 9 to assign a particular star rating to photos you want to put in a book. After you download the photos (see Chapter 10 for my recommended method), you can view your photos in Canon Digital Photo Professional 4, sort them according to rating, and then move those photos into a new folder you set up to hold your photobook pictures. Of course, you can do the same thing with any software you prefer. If you use a non-Canon program, check to verify that it can "see" your in-camera ratings before you go to the trouble of adding them. If not, you usually can rate and sort photos in the software program after downloading.

Adding Special Effects to Photos

During playback, you can add special effects to your photos by using the Creative Filters feature. The camera creates a copy of your image and applies the filter to the copy; your original remains intact. Figure 12-3 offers a look at three filter effects along with the original photo.

You can choose from these effects:

>> **Grainy B/W:** Creates a noisy (grainy) black-and-white photo.

>> **Soft Focus:** Blurs the photo to make it look soft and dreamy.

>> **Fish-Eye:** Distorts the picture to produce the look of photos taken with a fish-eye lens.

>> **Art Bold:** Produces a vivid, high-contrast oil-painting effect.

>> **Water Painting:** Softens colors and focus to mimic the look of a watercolor painting.

>> **Toy Camera:** Creates an image with dark corners — called a *vignette* effect. Vignetting is caused by poor-quality lenses, like those found in toy cameras — thus the effect name. You can also add a warm (yellowish) or cool (blue) tint when you apply the filter.

>> **Miniature:** Blurs all but a very small area of the photo to create a result that looks something like one of those miniature dioramas you see in museums. This effect works best on pictures taken from a high angle, like the one featured in Figure 12-3.

Original

Fish-Eye

Toy Camera

Miniature Effect

FIGURE 12-3:
Here's a look at
how three
Creative Filters
affected a city
scene.

 The easiest way to apply the filters is to put the camera in Playback mode, display the photo you want to alter, and then press the Q button to bring up the Quick Control screen. Select the Creative Filters option, as shown on the left in Figure 12-4, to display symbols representing the available filters at the bottom of the screen. Select a filter and press the Set button (or tap the Set icon) to display a preview of your picture along with options for adjusting the effect, as shown on the right in the figure. For most of the filters, you can increase or decrease the strength of the filter by pressing the right and left edges of the Quick Control dial or by tapping directly on the Effect scale.

FIGURE 12-4:
During playback,
apply Creative
Filters through
the Quick Control
screen.

For the Miniature effect, a narrow focus box appears. Your goal is to move the box over the area of the photo that you want to keep in sharp focus. Press the top/bottom/left/right edges of the Quick Control dial to move the box and change its orientation. You also can rotate the Main dial or Quick Control dial to reposition the box.

If you like the effect you see in the preview, press Set to save the altered image as a new file. Or, to cancel out of the operation and check out a different filter, press the Menu button or tap the Menu symbol. You're taken back to the initial filter-selection screen (left screen in Figure 12-4).

You also can get to the special effects by choosing Creative Filters from Playback Menu 1. Scroll to the picture you want to doctor and press Set. From there, everything works as just described.

Note that you can't apply Creative Filters effects to images that you have already edited, such as a cropped version of an original photo. Also, if you shot the original using the dual format option — JPEG plus Raw or cRaw — the filter is applied to the Raw version, with the resulting image saved as a new JPEG file.

Adding Effects During Shooting

Set the Mode dial to Creative Filters, as shown in Figure 12-5, to apply effects as you record pictures or movies. (This is the only way to create a movie with effects.) In this case, you don't wind up with an unfiltered original and a special-effects version; you get only the special-effects image or movie.

Some effects offered during playback are available during shooting; you also get a few effects not provided during playback. The available effects vary depending on whether you're shooting stills or movies.

To explore your options, press the Q button to put the camera in Quick Control mode and then choose the Creative Filters symbol, labeled on the left in Figure 12-6. (The figure shows the viewfinder-shooting version of the Quick Control screen; Live View shooting is up momentarily.) Tap the symbol or press Set to display the screen shown on the right in the figure. The left side of the screen has a scrolling list of effects; as you land on each one, you see a bit of information and a sample image created with the effect. Press Set or tap the icon of the effect you want to use.

FIGURE 12-5:
Choose this exposure mode to add special effects to photos or movies as you shoot.

FIGURE 12-6:
Select Choose Filter from the Quick Control screen (left) to display a screen where you can select the effect you want to use (right).

Creative Filters setting   Effect strength   Scrolling list of effects

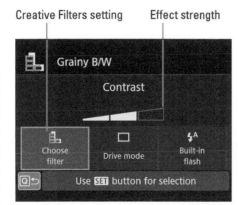

For some effects, the Quick Control screen offers a control that enables you to adjust the impact of the filter. For example, the adjustment option for the Grainy Black and White filter is labeled on the left in Figure 12-6. To access that setting, press up or down on the edge of the Quick Control dial. Rotating the dial or pressing left or right adjusts the filter amount.

Put the camera in Live View mode (press the Live View button or set the On/Off switch to the movie position) to see exactly how the filter will work with your subject. An icon representing the current filter appears in the upper-left corner of the screen; to explore other filters, shift to the Creative Filters version of the Quick Control screen, shown in Figure 12-7. (Press the Q button or tap the Q icon on the screen to enter Quick Control mode.) For effects that offer strength settings or other adjustments, you can apply them through the Quick Control screen as well; select the icon just below the filter icon. I labeled this control "Effect strength" in the figure. The adjustment icons appear only if the filter offers that type of control.

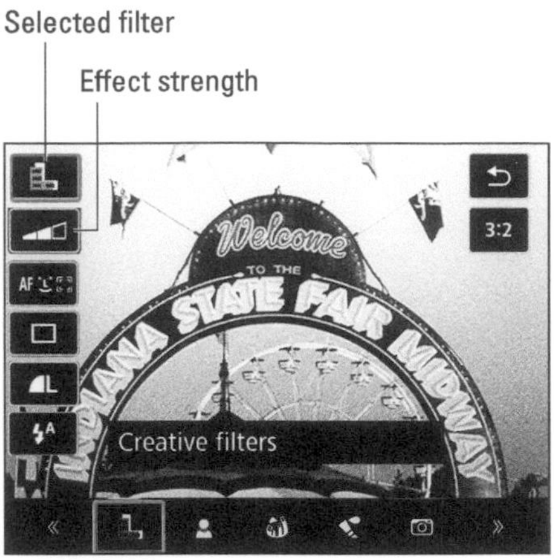

Selected filter

Effect strength

FIGURE 12-7:
In Live View mode, you can preview the effect of a filter before deciding to use it for your next shot or movie.

A few other quick pointers:

>> For still photos, all images that you capture using the Creative Filters shooting mode are stored in the JPEG format, even if the Image Quality option is set to Raw.

>> During Live View and Movie shooting, you can also access creative effects when the Mode dial is set to P, Tv, Av, or M. Just display the Quick Control screen and look for the Creative Filters symbol on the right side of the screen. The symbol looks like the one that marks the Creative Filters setting on the Mode dial. If the symbol is dimmed, another setting is interfering; for example, you can't apply a filter when the Multi-Shot Noise Reduction option is enabled.

Creating Video Snapshots

The Video Snapshot feature captures short video clips that are stitched into a single recording, called a *video album.* You can set the clip length to 8, 6, or 4 seconds long. (All clips in an album must be the same length.)

When might recording a series of seconds-long clips come in handy? One scenario might be that you're a tennis teacher, and you want to record each serve made by your star student during a match. If you use the Video Snapshot feature, the two of you can easily study just those brief interludes without having to bother with fast-forwarding during a longer recording.

That's the best example I can come up with, but lots of Canon users must like this feature because the symbol that tells you whether Video Snapshot recording is on or off has a permanent home on the information display when the camera is in Movie mode. I labeled the symbol on the left screen in Figure 12-8. (If you don't see any data onscreen, press the Info button to change the display style.)

Video Snapshot setting   Turn feature off   Snapshot length (in seconds)

To create a video snapshot, press Q to enter Quick Control mode and select the Video Snapshot icon, as shown on the right in Figure 12-8. Then set the clip length by choosing one of the icons at the bottom of the screen. Press Q or tap the exit arrow (top-right corner of the screen) to return to shooting mode.

Begin recording as you do any movie: Just press the Live View button. A blue progress bar appears to let you know how many seconds of recording time remain. When the time is up, you're offered three options: create a new album to store the clip; play the clip; or delete the clip. After you make your choice, you can record your second clip. When you create clip number two, you get a new post-recording option: You can add the clip to the first album or create a new album for it.

You can control a few additional Video Snapshot settings through Shooting Menu 2. If the Video Snapshot item is set to disable, change it to Enable. Then choose that option again to display the available customization options. You *can't* change the Movie Recording Size setting; video snapshots are always recorded using a setting of FHD (1920 x 1080 pixels), 29.97 frames per second, and Standard IPB compression.

You can't record normal movies when the Video Snapshot feature is enabled, so when you're done creating clips and albums, turn it off via the menu or through the Quick Control screen.

Trimming Movies

Your camera's movie-edit feature makes it possible to remove unwanted material from the beginning or end of a movie. Here's how to trim frames from the start of a movie:

1. **Set the camera to Playback mode and display the movie file.**

2. **Tap the Set symbol in the upper-left corner of the screen or press the Set button to display the controls shown on the left in Figure 12-9.**

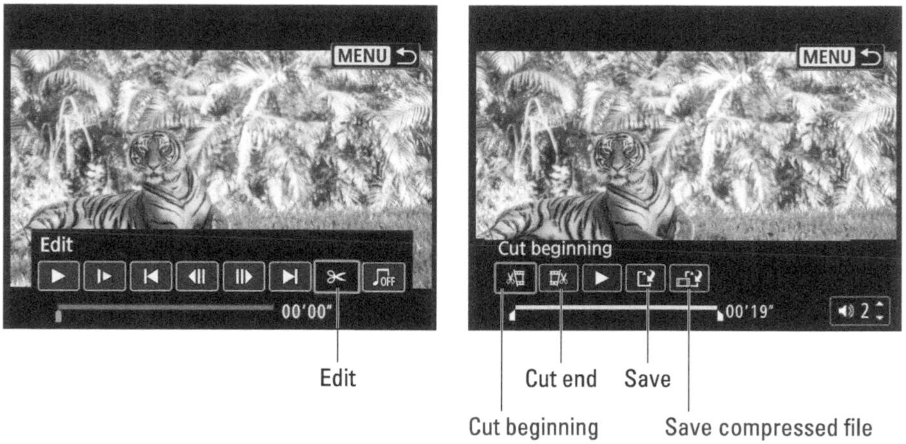

FIGURE 12-9:
From the playback screen, select the scissors icon to get to the movie-editing functions.

Edit

Cut end   Save

Cut beginning   Save compressed file

3. **Select the scissors symbol, labeled "Edit" in the figure, and press Set.**

4. **On the next screen, choose the first icon, labeled "Cut beginning" on the screen shown on the right in Figure 12-9.**

   If you've got the right control, the text label "Cut beginning" appears briefly above the strip of control icons, as shown in the figure.

5. **Press the right and left edges of the Quick Control dial to advance or rewind one frame at a time.**

   To fast-forward, hold down the right edge of the dial.

The bar under the controls represents the entire movie. As you advance the playback, the orange marker moves to the right to show you the position of the current frame. The other marker indicates the end point of the movie.

6. **When you reach the first frame you want to keep, press the Set button.**

7. **Save the edited movie.**

   You have a few choices here. If you choose the Save icon (refer to Figure 12-9), the camera asks if you want to save the movie as a new file, overwrite the existing file, or cancel the edit altogether. To reduce the size of the edited movie file, choose the icon labeled "Save compressed file." The compression option isn't available if you recorded the movie using the one Movie Recording Size setting that already compresses the file (FHD, 29.97fps, Light IPB).

8. **When the confirmation screen appears, choose OK.**

   You're returned to the movie playback screen.

To trim the end of a movie, follow the same process, but choose the Cut End icon (labeled in Figure 12-9) instead of the Cut Beginning icon. Now the orange marker indicates the last frame that will appear in the edited movie.

TIP

If you shot the movie using the 4K Movie Recording Size setting, you see an additional icon on the control strip shown on the left in Figure 12-9, just to the right of the scissors symbol. That icon enables you to extract a single frame from a movie and save it as a photo. See the end of Chapter 8 for details. (You don't see the 4K frame-grab symbol in Figure 12-9 because I didn't shoot the movie in 4K.)

Setting Up for Smooth HDTV Playback

When you connect your camera to an HDTV to play your photos, movies, or a slide show, an option tucked away on Setup Menu 4 may affect how quickly the camera can transition from one file to the next. Called HDMI Resolution, it's set by default to Auto, as shown on the left in Figure 12-10. In this mode, the camera talks to the HDMI display to find out what resolution to use when handing off each file. That discussion can slow playback because it takes place before each file is displayed.

For smoothest playback, change the setting from Auto to 1080p, as shown on the right in the figure. This resolution is known as Full High Definition and results in images and movies that look just fine onscreen. The only reason not to use it is if you recorded movies in 4K and you have a device capable of outputting 4K video. Just remember that downside of potential playback lag time that can occur after one movie ends and the next movie or still photo appears.

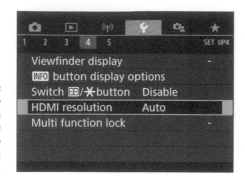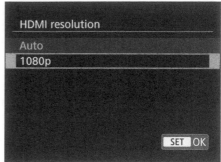

FIGURE 12-10:
For lag-free
display on an
HDTV or other HD
device, change
this setting from
Auto to 1080p.

Presenting a Slide Show

The Slide Show feature automatically displays photos and movies one by one, with each picture appearing for a period of time that you specify. (Movies always play in their entirety.) You can view the show on the camera monitor or connect your camera to an HDTV, as explained next, to display your work on a larger screen.

REMEMBER

Your first step in setting up a slide show is to consider whether you want all photos and movies to be included. If not, head to Chapter 10 and read the section related to the Image Search feature. Through that option, you can limit playback to files that meet certain criteria, such as the date they were created or a rating that you assigned. If you don't set up a search, all files on the memory card are displayed during the show.

Immediately after taking that step — again, necessary only if you don't want all files on the memory card to appear in the slide show — open Playback Menu 3 and choose Slide Show, as shown on the left in Figure 12-11. You then see a screen resembling the one shown on the right in the figure. The thumbnail shows the first image or movie that will appear; you also see the total number of files that are included. Choose Set Up to specify how long you want each photo to appear and whether you want the show to repeat automatically after it ends. You also can choose to add one of five transition effects and add background music. The background music thing is a bit complex, though: You have to use Canon EOS Utility software to download music to the memory card. The EOS Utility program instruction manual provides details. (You can download the program and manual from the Canon website.)

Also note the warning displayed at the bottom of the screen. It refers to the HDMI Resolution option discussed in the preceding section. Again, to avoid potential lag time, change that setting (Setup Menu 4) from Auto to 1080p.

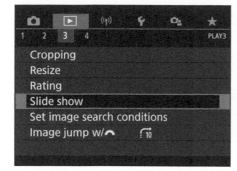

FIGURE 12-11:
Head to Playback
Menu 3 to create
a slide show.

After selecting playback options, tap Menu or press the Menu button to return to the screen shown on the right in Figure 12-11. Choose Start to begin playing the show. You can then control playback as follows:

>> **Pause playback.** Press the Set button or, if you're viewing the show on the camera, tap anywhere on the touchscreen. (Touchscreen functions are disabled when the camera is connected to a TV.) While the show is paused, you can press right or left on the Quick Control dial to view the next or previous photo. Press Set again or tap the Set icon to continue playback from the current slide.

>> **Change the information display style.** Press the Info button.

>> **Adjust sound volume.** Press the top edge of the Quick Control dial for higher volume; press the bottom edge for lower volume. If you're viewing the show on a TV, though, you must control volume on the TV. The camera volume control won't work. Additionally, the camera doesn't offer a feature known as CEC, which enables some TV remote-control units to adjust the camera volume. Yes, that's right, you're going to have to get up and press the volume button on your TV if the sound is too loud or soft. Of course, it never hurts to try your remote control anyway (you know you're going to do it, and there's always the chance that some digital angel gave your remote special powers that gave it volume-control power).

>> **Exit the slide show.** Press the Menu button to return to the menu display. To instead return to normal picture playback, press the Playback button. Remember that any search you set up before the show is still in force. See Chapter 9 to find out how to cancel the search so that you can once again access all files on the memory card.

Viewing Photos and Movies on a TV

Your camera is equipped with a feature that allows you to play your pictures, movies, and slide shows on an HDTV screen. However, you need to purchase an HDMI cable to connect the camera and television; the Canon part number is HTC-100.

REMEMBER

Before connecting the two devices, check out these camera menu settings:

>> **Video System, Setup Menu 3:** Choose the video standard used in the region in which you're screening your work. In the United States, NTSC is the standard; in many European countries, PAL is required. (The correct setting should have been set at the factory, but if you purchased your camera in another country, you may need to change the setting.)

>> **HDMI Resolution, Setup Menu 4:** Check out the earlier section "Setting Up for Smooth HDTV Playback" to decide whether you want to change this option from Auto 1080p. (My advice is yes, unless you're planning on playing a movie recorded in 4K on a 4K-enabled TV.)

>> **HDMI HDR Output, Playback Menu 4:** Enable this option, and you can view photos show in the Raw or cRaw format in high definition on your TV. You may experience some lag time if you shift from playback mode to the menu system and back.

>> **HDMI Info Display, Shooting Menu 4, available only when the camera is in Movie mode:** By default, the data that normally appears when you play a movie on your camera also shows up on the TV screen. But you have two other options: To hide data from movies you recorded in 4K, choose Clean 4K output. To hide data from movies recorded in Full HD, choose Clean FHD Output. Be aware that you can't perform some camera functions while anything other than With Info is in force, including recording new movies, taking pictures, or using wireless functions.

In addition to decluttering the screen when you play your movies, this option is useful for people who use their cameras to live-stream video on the internet, which you can do if you connect your camera to a video-capture card on your computer. Having all the data appearing on the screen would distract from your presentation.

After making your decisions on these settings, turn the camera off. Connect the smaller end of the HDMI cable to the HDMI port, shown in Figure 12-12, and connect the other end to the HDMI terminal on your TV. Turn your camera on to send the video signal to the TV. (Consult the TV instruction manual to find out whether you need to select a specific channel or input source to view the camera's output.)

A few playback pointers to wrap up this chapter:

HDMI out port

FIGURE 12-12:
Plug the small end of the HDMI cable into this port.

TIP

» **Using the touchscreen:** When you plug your camera into a TV, the camera monitor goes dark, but some touchscreen operations still work. It's a little weird because you have to use the TV screen as a visual reference, but you can scroll the display from one picture to the next or, in Index mode, from one page of thumbnails to the next. In single-image view, you also can pinch in and out to change the image magnification.

» **Controlling playback using camera buttons:** You also can control playback by using the same camera buttons you normally do to view pictures and movies on the camera monitor. (See Chapter 9 for details.) The only aspect you can't control through the camera is sound volume; if you're playing movies or a slide show with background music, adjust the volume on the TV set.

Appendix

Exploring Wireless Connections

Your camera enables you to connect wirelessly to a computer, smartphone, or tablet. After you make the wireless link, you can download files to your computer or smart device, use your computer or smart device to control your camera remotely, and perform other functions. Before you can enjoy these features, however, you need to do the following:

>> **Install Canon EOS Utility software on your computer.** This free program serves as the concierge for wireless communication with a computer. The next section explains what you can do with the software.

As I write this, Canon has not posted EOS Utility on the support pages for the T8i/850D, which is where you normally find software provided to Canon camera owners. In fact, none of the Canon software, including Digital Photo Professional 4, introduced in Chapter 10, has been put on the support site. By the time you read this, that may have changed. If not, go to the support page for the T7i/800D and download the software from there. Canon assures me that the software for that camera will work for the T8i/850D as well. Be sure to download the most recent version of each program; when they update a program, they don't delete the previous version.

>> **Install the Canon Camera Connect app on your smartphone or tablet.** This app, available for Android and iOS devices, is needed to connect your camera to a smartphone or tablet. Go to Google Play for the Android app; head to the App Store for the Apple iOS version. Check the app's system requirements to make sure your device can run the app.

Unfortunately, there isn't room in this book to provide detailed information on the wireless functions because things work differently depending on your computer or smart device, the security your wireless network employs, and so on. If you need more help after scanning this appendix, download the electronic version of the camera instruction manual, also available at the Canon website. The manual has extensive coverage of all the menus, options, and features associated with the camera's wireless capabilities. You can also download a copy of the instruction manual for Canon EOS Utility, if you need help using that program. Unfortunately, there is no separate manual for the Canon Camera Connect app, but the camera manual offers lots of troubleshooting tips to help you work out connection kinks, which are the source of the problems most people experience.

REMEMBER

Before I dive into the wireless features in more detail, I want to alert you to one service that you can access after you get your pictures on your computer or while the camera is connected to your smart device. Canon operates a photo-storage and sharing site, reachable at www.image.canon.com, which is free to Canon camera owners. Free is good, but I have a couple of concerns to share: First, after 30 days, your images are automatically deleted unless you move them into a longer-term storage bank, which offers 10GB of digital shelf space. More worrisome, a glitch in the site recently caused the digital destruction of all photos that were stored there. Check it out, by all means, to see if anything about the service interests you, but be aware of the limitations. If you do find it useful, you may want to download the service's own app to simplify the job of sending photos to the site. You'll find links to the app at the aforementioned web address, along with other details about using the service. (The user reviews are helpful, too, in determining whether the app and service fit your needs.)

Reviewing the Camera's Network Menus

All of the camera's wireless functions are controlled through settings found on Network Menus 1 and 2, shown side by side in Figure A-1. Here's a quick preview of what each menu option does:

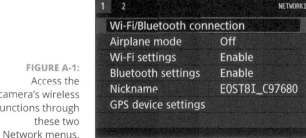

FIGURE A-1: Access the camera's wireless functions through these two Network menus.

» **Wi-Fi/Bluetooth Connection:** Choose this option to begin the process of connecting your camera to your computer or smartphone or tablet. You also can connect to a wireless printer, the Canon Wireless Remote Control BR-E1, and to Canon's cloud storage site, just discussed. In this appendix, I concentrate on connections to a computer and smart devices.

» **Airplane Mode:** By default, the camera's wireless systems are turned on all the time. That's fine when you're using a wireless connection a lot, but the wireless systems also consume a lot of battery power. So my recommendation is to set Airplane Mode to On until you really need the wireless features. (This is the same feature you find on your phone and tablet — the one you're asked to use when your airplane is about to take to the skies.) When you're ready to use Wi-Fi or Bluetooth connections, change the Airplane Mode setting to Off.

» **Wi-Fi Settings**: Through this option, you can enable and disable only Wi-Fi transmission from the camera and specify options related to Wi-Fi connections. To access this menu option, you must turn Airplane Mode off.

Selecting Wi-Fi Settings also provides access to the following important options:

- **Password:** One of the ways you can connect to a computer or smart device is by using the camera as an *access point* — which is just a way of saying that the camera serves as its own network. You then connect through that network instead of whatever network your computer or smart device is currently using.

  By default, the camera displays a password that you have to enter on the computer as the last step in connecting the computer to the camera's network. You can disable this option, but it's a really bad idea because it enables people with all sorts of ill intent to scan their computer's list of available networks, connect to your camera, and help themselves to all the juicy stuff on your memory card. I'm pretty sure this is a plotline in an upcoming Avengers movie. Compromising photos of the Hulk is my guess.

- **Auto Send Images to Computer:** Yeah, here's another one to leave at its default setting, Disable. If you enable the option, you can set things up so that after you connect the camera with your computer, the camera automatically initiates image transfer anytime your camera comes within range of that computer. Better to control when the transfer occurs yourself. Remember, wireless transmission eats battery power, and you may need that power to finish the day's shooting.

- **Send to Smartphone After Shot:** This option also enables you to set up automatic image transfer, but this time to your smart device. Unless you want *all* your photos to go to your phone — even the ones where Uncle Tim blinked *again* in the family photo — leave the setting at its default, Disable.

>> **Bluetooth Settings:** Use this option to turn Bluetooth transmission on and off separately of Wi-Fi when you don't want to disable both by turning Airplane Mode on. You also can see information about any device the camera is currently connected to via Bluetooth and view the camera's Bluetooth address (a series of numbers that identify your camera to other devices).

>> **Nickname:** By default, your camera shows up on other devices with a name that begins with EOST8I_ followed by some specific identifying numbers, as shown on the left menu screen in Figure A-1. If you want to give your camera another name, choose Nickname and create the name using the keyboard on the screen that appears. (See Chapter 12 if you need help using the camera's keyboard.)

If you're a solo T8i (or 850D) user, you probably don't need to go to the trouble of giving your camera a new name unless you really like the idea. But if you're working with other shooters using the same camera model, all of whom have their cameras' wireless features enabled, things can get messy. All the cameras are going to show up as possible connection points, and it's hard to distinguish one camera from another when you're looking at a random string of numbers.

>> **GPS Device Settings:** Through the magic of GPS, you can embed geographical location data into a photo file. You can send the data to the camera either from a smartphone that offers geotagging or through the Canon GPS receiver GP-E2, which attaches to the flash hot shoe. Use the GPS Device Settings menu option to specify which device you'll use to send the GPS data to the camera. Or choose Disable to turn the feature off. For the smartphone option, you must enable Bluetooth and connect the camera to the phone via the Canon Camera Connect app *before* you take the picture.

>> **Clear Wireless Settings:** As its name implies, this option resets all the other networking options to their defaults. If you encounter a "glitch" — meaning, you've spent hours trying to figure out why you can't get your camera to communicate with your computer or smart device after having previously being successful — sometimes choosing the Clear Network Settings option can resolve things. (You'll have to enter any network passwords again, which is a pain, but that's life in the digital age.)

TIP

Icons representing the status of the Airplane Mode, Wi-Fi, and Bluetooth settings appear on the Quick Control screen as well as the Live View display. But the symbols are, um, "a little less than intuitive." The following notes may help:

>> When you enable Airplane Mode, you see the symbols labeled on the left in Figure A-2. The plane indicates Airplane Mode; okay, that one's easy enough. The other symbol represents the Wi-Fi setting. When it's dimmed, as in the figure, the option is disabled. The word *Off* can appear even when Wi-Fi *is*

enabled, though. In this case, *Off* means that Wi-Fi isn't currently in use. The dimmed symbol is what tells you that the menu option is set to Disable.

>> When Airplane Mode is off and Wi-Fi and Bluetooth are enabled but not in use, the symbols shown on the right in Figure A-2 appear. The word *Off* with the Wi-Fi symbol and the dimmed Bluetooth symbol are what tell you that the services aren't doing anything at the moment.

>> If Bluetooth is disabled via the Bluetooth Settings menu option, you don't see that symbol at all.

>> When Wi-Fi and Bluetooth are in use, the word *Off* disappears from the Wi-Fi symbol and the Bluetooth symbol turns white. You also see a third symbol indicating the strength of the Wi-Fi symbol.

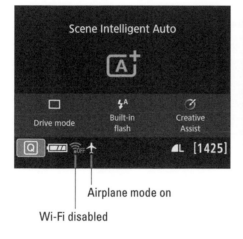
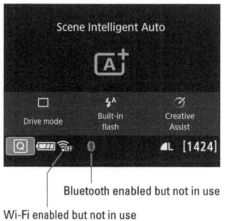

FIGURE A-2:
These symbols indicate Wi-Fi and Bluetooth status.

Airplane mode on

Wi-Fi disabled

Bluetooth enabled but not in use

Wi-Fi enabled but not in use

Got that? If not, simply open Network Menu 1 to verify the state of these settings. I present this trivia here just so that when you see the symbols on your monitor, you'll know that they have something to do with the camera's wireless functions.

Connecting to a Computer via Wi-Fi

After installing the EOS Utility Software on your computer and browsing through the wireless rules of the road just laid out, you're ready to connect the camera to a computer.

You can go about this step in two ways. The first is to connect the camera to the same network that the computer is using. The second is to allow the camera to act as an *access point*, which is like a private network that you can use to connect two devices.

The following steps explain how to connect to the network used by your computer. Information about using the access point approach appears after the steps.

1. **Display Network Menu 1 and set Airplane Mode to Off.**

2. **Set Wi-Fi Settings to Enable.**

3. **Choose Wi-Fi/Bluetooth Connection, as shown on the left in Figure A-3.**

   You see the screen shown on the right in the figure. The five icons represent the devices you can access wirelessly: a smartphone (or tablet), Wi-Fi–enabled computer; Wi-Fi–enabled printer, the image.canon website, and the Canon wireless remote control BR-E1.

4. **Tap the computer icon or highlight it and press Set.**

   You see the screen shown on the left in Figure A-4.

5. **Choose Add a Device to Connect To.**

   The screen shown on the right in Figure A-4 appears. The information in the gray bar — labeled SSID — relates to the camera's access point. Ignore that for now.

6. **Choose Switch Network in the lower-right corner of the screen.**

   You then see a list of wireless networks that your camera detected, as shown on the left in Figure A-5. A lock symbol next to the network name means that you need to enter a password, so go dig up the scrap of paper that holds that information if you see a lock next to your network.

FIGURE A-4:
Select Add a Device to Connect To (left) and then choose Switch Network (right).

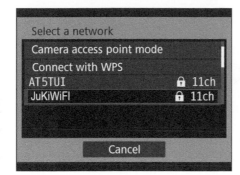

FIGURE A-5:
Choose your wireless network and, if required, enter the network password.

7. **Select your network and then enter the network password on the keyboard, shown on the right in Figure A-5.**

This keyboard is the same one detailed in the Chapter 12 section about adding copyright information; check out that information if you can't figure out how to enter your password. (Tapping the characters on the touchscreen is the easiest method.) Press the Menu button or tap the Menu icon after you put in all the necessary characters.

8. **On the next screen, choose Auto Setting and then choose OK.**

Now you see a screen requesting permission to start pairing devices. *Pairing* is computer speak for linking two devices wirelessly.

9. **Choose OK to start pairing the devices.**

The camera displays a screen saying that pairing is in progress and asking you to start the Canon EOS Utility program on your computer.

10. **On your computer, start the EOS Utility software.**

When the program window appears, click Pairing over Wi-Fi/Lan. A new, small window appears, showing any wireless devices the program detected. It may take a while, but sooner or later, your T8i/850D should appear in the list.

11. In the device list, click your camera and then click Connect.

Your camera displays a screen naming the computer it found (PC Dell, for example).

12. On the camera, choose OK to give the camera permission to connect to the computer.

The camera then displays the screen shown in Figure A-6. Ignore it until you're ready to disconnect from the computer. From this point forward, everything is handled by the EOS Utility software, covered a little later in this appendix.

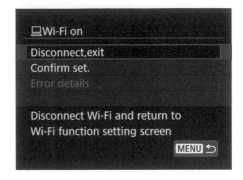

FIGURE A-6:
This screen appears after the wireless connection is established.

Now for details on using the camera as an access point (again, that means that you link your computer to the camera's own private network). Follow the preceding steps until you see the screen shown on the right in Figure A-4. Then, on your computer, find the setting that enables you to choose a wireless network. The list of available networks should include the name shown in the SSID portion of the camera screen. Select that network and enter the password shown on the camera screen. Then follow the prompts on the camera until you're asked to launch EOS Utility on your computer. From there, take Steps 11 through 13 as just described.

A few final tips on connecting to a computer via Wi-Fi:

TIP

>> **Connection via WPS (Wi-Fi Protected Setup):** If your wireless router offers WPS, you may be able to skip the tedious step of entering a password. When you get to Step 8, choose Connect with WPS from the screen shown on the left in Figure A-5. Place the camera near the router and then press the router's WPS button. The router should send out a signal and look for the camera's wireless transmission. See your router instruction manual to find out if this is a possibility for you. If the WPS connection is successful, just follow the prompts on the camera screen until you get to the screen shown in Figure A-6.

>> **Breaking the connection:** To end the connection between your camera and computer, choose Disconnect from the camera screen shown in Figure A-6. Then press the Menu button or tap the Menu icon. To exit the menus and return to shooting or viewing pictures, press the shutter button halfway and release it.

>> **Reconnecting:** To reconnect, open Network Menu 1, choose Wi-Fi/Bluetooth Connection, and select the computer icon. This time, you should see a screen that shows the name of your computer and any other devices you've connected to the camera. Choose your computer and then wait for the camera to

make the connection. Depending on the program preferences you establish for the EOS Utility software, the program either launches automatically or the camera prompts you to start the software. You'll know the connection is active when you see the screen shown in Figure A-6 again.

Reviewing EOS Utility functions

After your camera and computer are connected, the EOS Utility components responsible for the link disappear and you see the program window shown in Figure A-7. From this initial screen, you can select options that enable you to do the following:

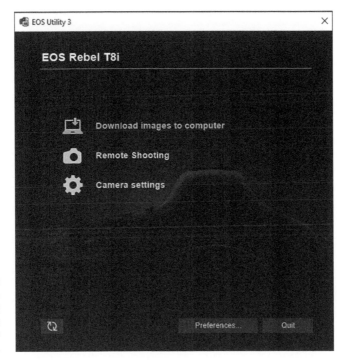

FIGURE A-7:
Choose the function you want to use from the main EOS Utility window.

>> **Download photos and movies to your computer:** After selecting the download option from the screen shown in Figure A-7, you see another screen giving you the choice to transfer everything on the card or to select files to transfer. Choose Select and Download to display the screen shown in Figure A-8, where you can view thumbnails of your files. To select a file for transfer, place a check mark in the box that appears in the lower-left corner its thumbnail. If you rated or protected photos, an option I cover in Chapter 10,

symbols appear with those files, as labeled in the figure. You can also use the tools labeled "Selection filters" in the figure to automatically select files shot on a certain date or that meet other criteria.

After choosing files, click the Download button, which is almost hidden away at the bottom of the thumbnails pane (look in the lower-left corner). You're asked to specify where you want the program to put the files (drive, folder, and so on). Click OK to begin the download.

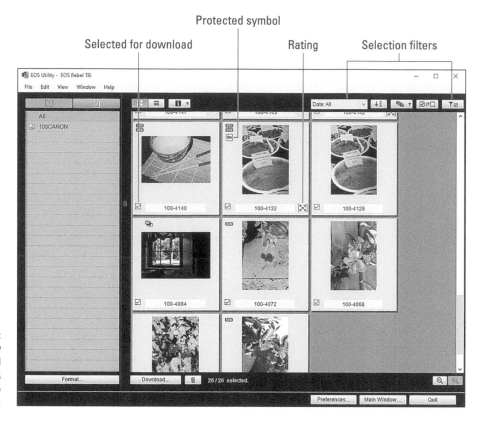

Protected symbol

Selected for download   Rating   Selection filters

FIGURE A-8:
You can preview your files and select the ones you want to download.

>> **Control your camera from your computer:** From the main EOS Utility window (Figure A-7), choose Remote Shooting to display the window shown in Figure A-9. From this window, you can adjust some camera settings, trigger the shutter release, display the captured image on your computer monitor, and even set up automatic image download. If you put the camera in Live View mode, you can see the live preview on your computer display, as I did when capturing the screen shown in Figure A-9.

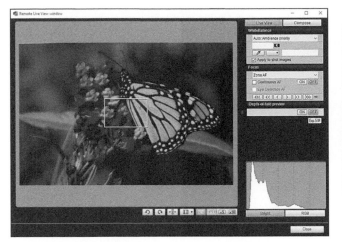

FIGURE A-9:
EOS Utility also offers a tool for *tethered shooting* — that is, controlling your camera from your computer.

TIP

If you like using this function, called *tethered shooting* in the biz (because your camera is tethered to the computer), you may want to buy an extra camera battery or two to account for the extra battery strain caused the the Wi-Fi connection. You might also consider purchasing the AC adapter for the camera. (You need DC Coupler DR-E18 and AC Adapter AC-E6N, which will set you back about $140.) Remember, too, that you can also tether the camera to your computer with a real, wired tether: the USB cable Canon sells as an accessory for the camera (IFC-600PCU, about $12).

>> **Transfer firmware updates, lens registration data, background music files, and other data to your camera.** Choose the Camera Settings option (refer to Figure A-7) to access these options.

For more information about using these and other EOS Utility features, consult the program's instruction manual, available for download from the Canon website.

Connecting to a Smartphone or Tablet

Before you can connect your camera to a smartphone or tablet — hereby known collectively as a *smart device* — you first need to download and install the Canon Camera Connect app on your device. Again, it's available for Android devices at Google Play and for iOS devices at the App Store.

When you install the app, it asks you for permission to access the photos app on the phone, to use Bluetooth, and to send you notifications about what I can only pre-sume is important stuff. Say yes to the first two requests and use your own judgment about the third. (You can adjust these options by opening up your smart device's settings page and opening the Canon Camera Connect settings page found there.)

You also have to agree to the app's terms of service; you can't use the app without saying yes to that one.

For the easiest connection, Canon recommends using Bluetooth rather than Wi-Fi, although you'll need Wi-Fi to use some of the app's functions. (Don't worry, the app will assist you when that time comes.) Here are the steps to take:

1. **On the camera, open Network Menu 1, disable Airplane Mode, and enable Wi-Fi and Bluetooth.**

2. **On the same menu, choose Wi-Fi/Bluetooth.**

   You see the screen with the device icons that shows up when you connect to a computer. (Refer to the right side of Figure A-3.)

3. **Select the phone icon and then choose Add a Device to Connect To.**

4. **On the next screen, choose Do Not Display.**

   You see a screen offering you the choice of connecting via Bluetooth or Wi-Fi.

5. **Choose Pair Via Bluetooth and press the Set button.**

   The camera warns you that once a connection is established, it remains on (eating battery power) even if you turn off the camera. When you want to stop the transmission, you need to go back to Network Menu 1 and turn on Airplane Mode.

6. **Tap OK or press Set to begin the connection process.**

7. **Start the Canon Camera Connect app on your phone.**

   If the camera sniffed out your phone, you see a message on the phone listing your camera's name — by default, EOST8I_ followed by six additional characters.

8. **On your smart device, tap the name of your camera.**

9. **Give the go-ahead for pairing on both your phone and the camera.**

   If all the planets are in alignment, both devices report that they've connected, and the app home screen now offers all the features you see on the left in Figure A-10.

The features I find most useful enable you to do the following:

>> **Use your smart device as a wireless remote control.** Choose Remote Live View Shooting to display the screen shown on the right in Figure A-10. This screen contains the tools available for using your phone or tablet to autofocus and trigger the camera's shutter button. The best way to use this feature is to put your camera on a tripod, frame the shot, select the shot settings, and then

connect the camera to your device. That way, you're not wasting extra battery power needed to maintain the wireless connection while you compose the shot and play with other camera settings. You also can use this function to start and stop movie recording, by the way.

FIGURE A-10: From the app's home screen (left), choose Remote Live View Shooting to use your smart device as a wireless camera controller.

>> **View photos without transferring them from the memory card.** Especially on a tablet, this feature enables you to get a larger view of your images than provided by the camera monitor. Choose the Images on Camera option on the app's home screen to display your photos, as shown on the left in Figure A-11. Tap a thumbnail to display it at a larger size and view some of the camera settings you used to take the picture, as shown on the right in the figure.

>> **Transfer selected files from the camera to the device.** After you display images, you can select the ones you want to transfer. The original files stay on the memory card; the camera sends copies to your device. You can choose to transfer full-resolution copies or opt for low-resolution versions that are more suitable for online sharing and take up less storage space on your device.

TIP

After transferring photos, you can upload them from your device to Facebook, Instagram, or other social media sites. You also can send them via email or just enjoy showing them off when you don't have your camera with you.

FIGURE A-11:
Choose Images
on Camera to see
thumbnails of
images on your
camera (left); tap
a thumbnail to
display it at a
larger size (right).

Some features require a Wi-Fi connection; if you choose one of those functions, the app assists you in switching over from Bluetooth. Unfortunately, what it does not offer is a built-in instruction manual for using the rest of its features, as some apps do. However, you should be able to figure things out if you just tap the various onscreen symbols. You may also want to visit the Canon website and just enter the term *Canon Camera Connect* in the search box. The camera's own instruction manual does a pretty good job of explaining the device-connection options, too.

One final tip: I find that cameras often connect seamlessly with smart devices the *first* time I go through the steps. But often, getting things to work the *next* time is iffy, even if I haven't changed anything on the device or the camera. If this happens to you, don't waste a lot of time trying to figure out what happened. Instead, go into your device's settings screen, and look for your camera in the list of previously connected devices (both Wi-Fi and Bluetooth). When you find your camera, select it and then choose the "forget this device" option (it may be worded differently depending on your phone or tablet). Then try connecting again. Sometimes, just dumping the old connection out of the device's memory is enough to kick the gremlins out of the system. If that doesn't work, go to the camera, open Network Menu 2 and reset all the camera's network settings as well. Now you're really back to square one, and my guess is that the connection will work the way it's supposed to again. Unfortunately, resetting the camera's settings will wipe out any passwords you've entered; you may want to write them down first so that you can re-enter them when necessary.

Index

Numerics

A

About the Author

Julie Adair King is the author of many books about digital photography and imaging, including the best-selling *Digital Photography For Dummies.* Her most recent titles include a series of *For Dummies* guides to popular digital SLR cameras, including the *Canon T7i/800D* and *Canon T7/200D.* Other works include *Digital Photography Before & After Makeovers, Digital Photo Projects For Dummies,* and *Shoot Like a Pro!: Digital Photography Techniques.* A native of Ohio and graduate of Purdue University, she resides in West Palm Beach, Florida.

Author's Acknowledgments

I am deeply grateful for the chance to work with a wonderful publishing team, which includes Kim Darosett, Steve Hayes, and Mary Corder, to name just a few. I am also indebted to technical editor Theano Nikitas, without whose insights and expertise this book would not have been the same.

Publisher's Acknowledgments

Executive Editor: Steven Hayes

Project Editor: Kim Darosett

Technical Editor: Theano Nikitas

Cover Image: Images courtesy of Julie Adair King

Leverage the power

Dummies is the global leader in the reference category and one of the most trusted and highly regarded brands in the world. No longer just focused on books, customers now have access to the dummies content they need in the format they want. Together we'll craft a solution that engages your customers, stands out from the competition, and helps you meet your goals.

Advertising & Sponsorships

Connect with an engaged audience on a powerful multimedia site, and position your message alongside expert how-to content. Dummies.com is a one-stop shop for free, online information and know-how curated by a team of experts.

- Targeted ads
- Video
- Email Marketing
- Microsites
- Sweepstakes sponsorship

20 MILLION PAGE VIEWS EVERY SINGLE MONTH

15 MILLION UNIQUE VISITORS PER MONTH

43% OF ALL VISITORS ACCESS THE SITE VIA THEIR MOBILE DEVICES

700,000 NEWSLETTER SUBSCRIPTIONS TO THE INBOXES OF

300,000 UNIQUE INDIVIDUALS EVERY WEEK

# of dummies

Custom Publishing

Reach a global audience in any language by creating a solution that will differentiate you from competitors, amplify your message, and encourage customers to make a buying decision.

- Apps
- Books
- eBooks
- Video
- Audio
- Webinars

Brand Licensing & Content

Leverage the strength of the world's most popular reference brand to reach new audiences and channels of distribution.

For more information, visit dummies.com/biz

PERSONAL ENRICHMENT

9781119187790
USA $26.00
CAN $31.99
UK £19.99

9781119179030
USA $21.99
CAN $25.99
UK £16.99

9781119293354
USA $24.99
CAN $29.99
UK £17.99

9781119293347
USA $22.99
CAN $27.99
UK £16.99

9781119310068
USA $22.99
CAN $27.99
UK £16.99

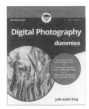
9781119235606
USA $24.99
CAN $29.99
UK £17.99

9781119251163
USA $24.99
CAN $29.99
UK £17.99

9781119235491
USA $26.99
CAN $31.99
UK £19.99

9781119279952
USA $24.99
CAN $29.99
UK £17.99

9781119283133
USA $24.99
CAN $29.99
UK £17.99

9781119287117
USA $24.99
CAN $29.99
UK £16.99

9781119130246
USA $22.99
CAN $27.99
UK £16.99

PROFESSIONAL DEVELOPMENT

9781119311041
USA $24.99
CAN $29.99
UK £17.99

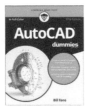
9781119255796
USA $39.99
CAN $47.99
UK £27.99

9781119293439
USA $26.99
CAN $31.99
UK £19.99

9781119281467
USA $26.99
CAN $31.99
UK £19.99

9781119280651
USA $29.99
CAN $35.99
UK £21.99

9781119251132
USA $24.99
CAN $29.99
UK £17.99

9781119310563
USA $34.00
CAN $41.99
UK £24.99

9781119181705
USA $29.99
CAN $35.99
UK £21.99

9781119263593
USA $26.99
CAN $31.99
UK £19.99

9781119257769
USA $29.99
CAN $35.99
UK £21.99

9781119293477
USA $26.99
CAN $31.99
UK £19.99

9781119265313
USA $24.99
CAN $29.99
UK £17.99

9781119239314
USA $29.99
CAN $35.99
UK £21.99

9781119293323
USA $29.99
CAN $35.99
UK £21.99

dummies.com

dummies®
A Wiley Brand